The
Electrified
Tightrope

The
Electrified
Tightrope

by Michael Eigen, Ph.D.
edited by Adam Phillips

JASON ARONSON INC.
Northvale, New Jersey
London

Production Editor: Judith D. Cohen

This book was set in 10 point Baskerville by Lind Graphics of Upper Saddle River, New Jersey, and printed and bound by Haddon Craftsmen of Scranton, Pennsylvania.

10 9 8 7 6 5 4 3 2 1

Library of Congress Cataloging-in-Publication Data

Eigen, Michael
    The electrified tightrope / by Michael Eigen : edited by Adam Phillips.
        p.   cm.
    Collection of essays by Michael Eigen, some reprinted from various sources.
    Includes bibliographical references and index.
    ISBN 0-87668-294-8 (hard cover)
    1. Psychoanalysis. I. Phillips, Adam. II. Title.
    [DNLM: 1. Emotions—essays. 2. Professional-Patient Relations—essays. 3. Psychoanalytic Theory—essays. 4. Psychoanalytic Therapy—methods—essays.   WM 460.6 E347e]
    RC509.E325 1993
    616.89′ 17—dc20
    DNLM/DLC
    for Library of Congress   92-49190

Manufactured in the United States of America. Jason Aronson Inc. offers books and cassettes. For information and catalog write to Jason Aronson Inc., 230 Livingston Street, Northvale, New Jersey 07647.

To Henry Elkin

In memoriam

Ceaseless battle, victory ever in view
What is a life of faith?

Promised lands slip

on hidden sweetness

God's face in the center

of the fall.

— Michael Eigen

Contents

Acknowledgments

I want to thank Adam Phillips for selecting and assembling the papers included in this book. When he interviewed me for a BBC program, he encouraged me to put together a book of my papers, and when I hesitated, he did it himself. This means a lot to me, since this book represents 20 years of writing and 30 years of work. I hope readers find his introduction as thought provoking as I do.

I am grateful to Jason Aronson who responded immediately and wholeheartedly when he received this collection. It is a good feeling to have a publisher who believes in the work he publishes. I wish to thank Carol McKenna for her thoroughness in all aspects of production, and am grateful for Judy Cohen's responsive remarks in the margins of her editing work, which made me feel the book was in human hands throughout the mechanical aspects of its processing.

Since this is a collection of my work, I have the last word. I have included introductory notes for the chapters and an extended Afterword. In the Afterword I write about my life and my leading concerns. In addition to describing some of my current preoccupations, I take the liberty to include informal observations about the mental health field and problems practitioners face. I take advantage of this freedom to say things that are on my mind. Actually, there can be no last word. I am hopeful my words enter a stream of dialogue that quickens our sense of what it means to be a person.

Introduction
by Adam Phillips

How can he remember well his ignorance — which his growth requires — who has so often to use his knowledge?

Walden, Thoreau

"It is difficult to overestimate," Michael Eigen (1986) wrote in his first book *The Psychotic Core,* "the role omniscience plays in deadening one's capacity to experience. If one knows what is going to happen ahead of time, one does not have to experience it" (p. 320). It is the capacity to experience, for the therapist and the patient both, how it can be sustained, and the diverse and subtle ways it can be sabotaged that is the absorbing preoccupation of Michael Eigen's remarkable psychoanalytic essays. The idea of knowing something ahead of time suggests, in the briefest of ironies, that we can cheat Time in our flight from the immediacy, the intensity of emotional experience. What would it mean to suspend one's wish for prediction which, like all defenses, is a preemptive strike against the future? And what is it that might make a person "deaden" his capacity to experience and live as though emotional life needed to be gotten rid of? The essays included in this book return — that is, go back and reshape, often ingeniously — the connection between these two questions. They urge us, that is to say, in the words of the Jewish proverb, to make time for time.

The fantasy of omniscience is a denial of the unconscious. But the critique of omniscience, oddly enough, poses problems for psychoanalysis. And it is these problems, I think, that has drawn Eigen to the work of Winnicott, Lacan, and Bion, each of whom realizes, from quite different perspectives, the way psychoanalysis ironizes fantasies of competence. The authority with which psychoanalysts can write about the unconscious has itself become a dismaying irony (it is worth remembering Freud's point, for example, that we can only know about the repressions that break down). If there is an unconscious, what is the analyst doing when he thinks he knows what he is doing? Each analysis improvises — within mostly unconscious theoretical constraints — descriptions and redescriptions of a particular person's life. So how can the analyst begin his work apparently knowing what a person is, when that is precisely what is in question each time an analysis begins?

Eigen's writing is consistently alert to these dilemmas, the inspiring puzzles with which psychoanalysis began. The visionary pragmatism of Eigen's version of psychoanalysis — veering as he sometimes does in the more recent papers toward that most radical and perplexing possibility, a nonessentialist psychoanalysis — connects him, I think, with the very early analysts Ferenczi and Rank, Federn and Reich, in whose writing one senses the romance of psychoanalysis as it began to produce unanticipated connections and unprecedented sentences. In his writing one finds the same exhilarated skepticism, or, as he has put it (1986) with his own rough subtlety and wit, "My style presupposes a taste for subjectivity" (p. 31). "I believe the liberties taken have their own sort of rigor" (p. 36). Taking liberties, of course, entails a knowledge of constraint.

So if in reading these unusual papers one needs to keep one ear on those early inspired analysts, one needs to keep another ear out, in the covert drama of these papers, for that curious combination of institutionalized professionalism and theoretical melee that is American psychoanalysis. Eigen's work emerges historically, that is to say, between the proliferation of fringe therapies and an increasingly militant psychoanalytic orthodoxy. One finds references in these essays to Burroughs and Castaneda as well as to Hartmann and Mahler. But his interest in the quality of emotional experience, in "aliveness," draws him, often with revisionary relish, to the work of the British analysts Winnicott, Milner, and Bion, and less predictably to the French analyst Lacan. Indeed, one of the distinctive pleasures of these essays is the quality of Eigen's collaborative commentary on these theorists and their most influential precursors, Freud and Klein. "Influence," Eigen wrote in *The Psychotic Core* (1986), "is so important a part of learning and menace" (p. 329). Though uniquely suited to the task, psychoanalysis has yet to produce a theory of admiration that does not involve submission (or that most furtive form of submission called gratitude) — a theory that would include a nonsadomasochistic description of relationships to theoretical precursors, and in particular to the idea of genius. Eigen's use of the psychoanalytic tradition in these papers — exemplary for its celebrations — is a glimpse of what such a theory might look like in practice. And, of course, like all psychoanalysts, his relationship with other theorists, as demonstrated in his writing, mirrors something of his clinical relationship with patients. The many striking clinical vignettes in these essays are distinctive for their unembarrassedly generous identifications with his patients — an obvious pleasure in their (and his) resources that is always braced by the mutual ambivalence that is integral to the analytic encounter. It is, in fact, toward the mutuality of the analytic encounter — that charged and mystifying area that was also of interest to the early analysts — that Eigen is always drawn in his writing.

Because Eigen likes to speak the language of reciprocity (his essays on breathing and the significance of the face are particularly suggestive), he is a fierce and revealing critic, explicitly of Margaret Mahler's influential developmental theory, and more implicitly of the ego-psychology that inaugurated psychoanalysis in America. In short, he is less interested in the restructuring of the personality, and more preoccupied by the terrors (and pleasures) of aliveness; less interested in the prescribed normative life story and psychic structure, and more concerned about what he has called a person's unofficial development. "It is always an open question," he has written, "as to just what meaning or use individuals may make of their developmental possibilities" (*The Psychotic Core* 1986, p. 5). The aim of analysis is to reopen the question.

For the new reader of Eigen's work three things, perhaps, will be immediately noticeable. First, and quite unsurprising to British analysts reared on object relations, there is Eigen's absolute commitment to the mutual constitution of subject and object in early development. "In essence," he writes in one essay, "one's sense of self and other function as figure and ground for one another, each a condition of the other's possibility" (this volume, p. 72). And this entails the impossibility of conceiving of absolute separateness because one is always separate *from*; differentiation always implies an object. "A basic ambiguity," he writes, "—a simultaneity of areas of distinctness and union—represents an essential structure of human subjectivity" (this volume, p. 57). Without a world of people there is no such thing as a person.

There is an unusual eloquence in the way Eigen figures and formulates the matter of reciprocity that sometimes seems against the grain of the language. But this is the second item on my list that represents Eigen's most distinctive contribution. As a consequence of his belief in what he calls *activation of repressed body life* he is committed to working out, in psychoanalytic language where possible, the developmental necessity of intense, or rather excessive, emotional experience, Body-based Emotional Experience. "Desire and idealization are sisters," he writes with necessary but not too much provocation. However, when he redescribes Winnicott's concept of the True Self in the first essay here as "exuding a sense of power . . . it is occultly transcendent and inherently megalomanic" (this volume, p. 8), we are in the presence, for once, of something else.

If, for Freud, desire was always in excess of the object's capacity to satisfy it, for Eigen our profoundest emotional life is in excess of our capacity to make sense of it. "We scare ourselves," he writes in one essay, "with the imagining we produce but cannot adequately process. Our mental creations are often ahead of our ability to assimilate them in meaningful and useful ways" (this volume, p. 234). It is not so much sexuality, Eigen implies, but intensity and the passions, that now constitute the category that has always been *the* object of psychoanalysis, the unacceptable. It is in his writing on excess—excess as plenitude and as emptiness—that Eigen offers something new to psychoanalysis. My third point is of a piece with this, and has to do with Eigen's unusual vocabulary—unusual, that is, in a psychoanalytic context.

Official languages can make innovation look brash; indeed, that might be part of their function. As one reads through these papers, Eigen's distinctive voice begins to emerge out of what is, to begin with, a thicket of metapsychological jargon. This, of course, is not a rare psychoanalytic story; one has only to think of the theorists he most admires—Winnicott, Bion, Lacan, Milner— whose remarkable later papers are quite different from their early professional respectability. But quite early on in Eigen's writing we hear a seemingly anachronistic vocabulary of intensity—genius, inspiration, evil, the Devil, joy, ecstasy—that links psychoanalysis explicitly with the language of Romanticism rather than the scientisms of what is loosely called the Enlightenment. It is an enlivening experience, unique in contemporary psychoanalysis, to find the language of William Blake played off against the language of analytic theory without its seeming arch or modish.

For those of us who do not want the sadomasochistic fantasy of truth in scientific psychoanalysis—truth, that is, as something to which we are obliged to submit—Eigen offers us one of what must be many alternatives. It is a compelling body of work and will, I hope, like all new and unusual things, split the reader, and the readers.

Introductory Notes

1973–1975: POSITIVE ASPECTS OF PATHOLOGICAL TENDENCIES

The first three chapters in this collection emphasize positive contributions to growth of self made by seemingly pathological or disruptive movements within the therapy situation. They cover tendencies Karen Horney described as "away," "against," and "towards." Material for these papers was initially presented at case conference meetings at New Hope Guild, a psychoanalytic psychiatric clinic in Brooklyn, New York.

"Abstinence and the Schizoid Ego" (1973a) charts a period of severe and frightening withdrawal in an impulsive, alcoholic man. I was reading Guntrip at the time and understood the need for dangerous yet potentially restorative regression in some cases. However, I did not find a simple passive seeking of the womb. A hidden, all-seeing mental ego went along with the passive plunge. The regressive tendency was bipolar: passive-helpless *and* active-megalomanic. The schizoid ego described by Guntrip had a complex and not a simple unidimensional structure. Work with schizoid aspects of self is important for what now are called borderline and narcissistic problems.

"The Recoil on Having Another Person" (1973b) touches upon the importance of time experience in the constitution of self, a theme that recurs in my papers. The patient, an art dealer, was too impatient for analysis but was receptive to focusing on images that spontaneously arose. We were able to link an approach–avoidance pattern to temporal meanings of the Other. I was deeply struck by how latent time experience molded and depended upon the structure of the therapy situation. The unique distance–closeness balance of the therapy situation kept approach open, enabling the patient to taste the gap of nonpossession, the lack that always enables one to come a little closer.

"Psychopathy and Individuation" (1975a) focuses on self-affirmative elements in acting out tendencies. In these instances action is on the side of life. What appears as amoral or delinquent behavior may be attempts at narcissistic repair or attempts to constitute an alive and viable self.

1977: UNWANTED PATIENTS

"Working with 'Unwanted' Patients" (1977a) was presented at the New York Center for Psychoanalytic Training (1976) and the Institute for Psychoanalytic Training and Research (1976) and summarizes ten years of clinical work with difficult patients. Most of these patients exhibited what might loosely be called masochistic lifestyles, but what was at stake was severe narcissistic injury. Two of my main concerns were: (1) the therapeutic use that could be made of a range of negative states in the therapist (irritation, discomfort, revulsion, rage, hate, pain of various sorts, impatience, deadness, impotence, frustration, panic, horror, etc.), and (2) the positive use of ideal states experienced by patient or therapist. I tried to evoke a sense of how intricately therapist's and patient's hate and ideal feelings contribute to mutual growth.

In the 1960s I took body process classes given by Stanley Keleman and Anneliese Widman that linked up with the importance Marion Milner (1987) placed "on becoming aware of one's body, even one's big toe, from the inside" (p. 259). These classes supplemented my personal analysis and opened ways of experiencing I otherwise might not have reached.

My body work confirmed but went beyond psychoanalytic theory's emphasis on appetite as a central organizer of body experiencing. The ego may get closer to its sense of being in and out of body by using breathing as a model for psychological functions. "Breathing and Identity" (1977b) delineates self-states associated with breathing in contrast with appetite. I also discuss connections between breathing and time experience and bring out how different worlds of experiencing contribute to growth of self.

1979–1982: THE FACE, IDEAL IMAGES, FAITH, PARADOX

Work with patients in deep regression heightened my appreciation of how central the human face is in the development of self. I brought my findings together in summary fashion in two talks in 1977, one for the Psychotherapy Division of the American Psychological Association (Orlando, Florida), the other for the National Psychological Association for Psychoanalysis (New York). These were expanded and published in a series of papers, beginning with "The Significance of the Face" (1980a). Patients who I wrote about in that paper were focused on more intensively in further studies, including "Instinctual Fantasy and Ideal Images" (1980b), and "Creativity, Instinctual Fantasy, and Ideal Images" (1982).

The nucleus of these studies was the profoundly regenerative effect "beatific" experiences of the face could have. As it turned out, the face was a privileged avenue of ideal experiencing in general. By ideal experiencing I mean something like perfect moments of the sort one wishes could go on forever, a taste of heaven that not merely comforts but uplifts and inspires.

However, ideal experiencing can be perfectly hellish as well as heavenly. The ideal sense or *ideal imago* has a certain free-floating quality. It can be attached to a shoe, feces, good or evil impulses, causes, nations, individuals, art, religion, and so on. It can be in the service of death as well as life; the striving for perfect nullity is as ideal as the wish for perfect fullness.

Neither Freud's life nor death instincts can explain ideal experiencing, since they exploit it. Eros cannot claim to be the exclusive source of ideal experience, since without the latter there would be no such thing as enchantment. One can as easily say that it is the capacity for ideal experiencing that makes eros what it is, rather than, or as well as, the reverse. The papers that follow wrestle with clinical issues related to the body ego's use of ideal states and the latter's theoretical status.

"Ideal Images, Creativity, and the Freudian Drama" (1979) was written on request for *The Psychocultural Review,* and so I was encouraged to focus on broader issues of theory and culture. It was written after my first "face" paper, although published earlier, and shared basic concerns of my "face" papers during this period. I explore uses Freud made of ideal experience in the structure of his theory and in his body imagery. I use Freud my own way to bring out what I consider to be basic structures of self and end with a discussion of the mother–infant ideal. Object relations writers smuggle ideal imagery into their discussion, as Freud did with drives and body ego, without properly crediting the capacity to create ideal states as such. This is a problem that plagues starting points of psychoanalytic theories and while I cannot solve it, dwelling with its difficulties has led to fruitful portrayals of growth processes.

"Soft and Hard Qualities" (1980c) was written while I was Director of Training at the Institute for Expressive Analysis and soon after I headed a training program on Psychoanalysis and Creativity at the New York Center for Psychoanalytic Training. It extended my focus on moment-to-moment self-feelings, adding to my work on breathing, time-experience, the face, and ideal moments in self-experiencing. Our sensitivity to soft and hard qualities runs through many dimensions and adds resonance to the atmosphere of our lives. In this paper I link soft and hard qualities to attitudes and intersubjective states.

After reading this paper, a colleague referred me to Frances Tustin's work on soft and hard objects, which I greatly value. Her focus on the defensive use of hard objects has led me to make the additional observation that either hard or soft objects can be used to express deficits and arrests or add to growth of self, depending on their function in a given context.

"The Area of Faith in Winnicott, Lacan, and Bion" (1981a) amplifies a basic attitude that runs through earlier papers. I often emphasized positive aspects of pathological tendencies, while able to see negative aspects of apparently healthy ones. I suspect many analysts share something of this double attitude. My underlying attitude was faith in the goodness of life, echoing God's appraisal of his work in *Bereishis (Genesis)*. This is not an attitude that everyone shares, or that I always share with myself. Every moment is filled with myriad plus and minus aspects. In some instances the plus seems faint indeed.

I gravitated to Winnicott, Bion, and Lacan because their writings were such intensely alive affirmations of the human spirit in adversity. None of these authors underestimated what we are up against. Winnicott's concern with feeling unreal, Bion's with psychic deadness, Lacan's with self-deception — yet all demonstrated a passionate striving for Truth beyond reach; all were excited by evolution of self.

It seemed to me that Winnicott's "use of object" paper marked a genuine leap in his work, and all that he had written must be reevaluated in terms of it. After reading my "faith" paper, Clare Winnicott wrote to tell me that her husband had felt the same way. She recounted the afternoon he finished the "use of object" paper, his excitement that he had come closer to the mark. He felt a kind of climax, a turning point. When she read my paper she felt pleased that his sense of his own growth was recognized. I believe Winnicott's "use of object" and "transitional experiencing" add something to the meaning of faith.

Bion explicitly became concerned with faith as essential to the psychoanalytic attitude and in the constitution and evolution of self. This apparently is not a popular conception among psychoanalysts. As fine a reader of Bion as Andre Green (1986) entirely omits reference to the importance of faith in Bion's work. Yet Bion's "F in O" becomes central as his major works unfold.

Bion, Winnicott, and Lacan are among the most creative psychoanalytic writers, at the edge of psychoanalytic experiencing, imagining, thinking. They give full voice to the horrors of existence, the macabre twists of the human psyche, yet what I call "the area of faith" comes through. Bringing these workers together in ways that enhance, rather than reduce their contributions, enables us to enhance our own vision of what makes psychoanalysis possible.

"Guntrip's Analysis with Winnicott" (1981b) is a practical application of considerations in the "area of faith" (1981a) paper. It affirms the primacy of faith as setting the tone for growth processes and grew out of my love for Guntrip's (1975) account of his experience with Fairbairn and Winnicott. I was aware of defects in Guntrip's portrayal and picture of himself, but felt that Glatzer and Evans' (1977) harsh attempt to unmask his self-deceptions lacked breadth and wisdom. They tended to throw out the baby with the bathwater.

Alternate visions of the self — the very nature and quality of selfhood — were at stake. The difference was between a therapy that narrowly focused on unconscious hate (the unanalyzed negative transference) and one that placed hate in a broader context so that all currents of self can have a say. In my paper on "unwanted patients" (1977a) the negative transference–countertransference was critically important, but the sense of goodness was not reduced to it. The mutual affirmation inherent in Guntrip's and Winnicott's relationship was more important than unanalyzed hate (although Winnicott also tried to find Guntrip's hate so that it, too, could contribute to growth).

Winnicott's gropings grew out of a primacy of faith, and it is this underlying attitude and quality of being that Guntrip resonated to. Winnicott's thinking and percipience cohered with his basic sense of self in a way that Guntrip found relevant. For Winnicott, destructiveness was important as a potential carrier of true self feelings, but the area of faith made destructiveness creative.

"Breaking the Frame: Stopping the World" (1981c) was written for a special issue of *Modern Psychoanalysis* honoring Marie Coleman Nelson. I studied with Mrs. Nelson in 1974–1975, when I took advanced courses at the Center for Modern Psychoanalysis, which specialized in work with negative narcissistic transferences and correlative induced feelings in the therapist. Mrs. Nelson is best known for *paradigmatic therapy,* various clinical techniques in which the therapist models aspects of toxic introjects. I learned from Mrs. Nelson but was never a follower. Perhaps what I most valued was her underlying interest in ambiguities and complexities of psychocultural life. Paradigmatic techniques are easily trivialized when divorced from their broader underpinning.

I used Mrs. Nelson's paper on Castaneda's Don Juan to highlight her (and my) concern with shifting attitudinal frameworks. Don Juan's remark that "the worst thing one can do is confront human beings bluntly" (Castaneda, quoted in Nelson 1976, p. 351) reminded me of Winnicott's feeling that direct confrontation is a mark of pathology. Mrs. Nelson's work is often playful, a spirit of play that can be very different from Winnicott's, but characterized by a pleasure in paradoxical experiencing. I also linked her interest in multiple realities with aspects of Bion's work and tried to situate Don Juan's therapeutic trickery in a broader clinical and cultural context.

1983: I-YET-NOT-I AND THE SENSE OF CREATIVENESS

1983a: "Dual Union or Undifferentiation?"

I read *A Life of One's Own* by Marion Milner (under the pseudonym of Joanna Field) in 1958 and have followed her work since. I taught the Appendix to *On Not Being Able to Paint* in my seminars for many years. It is a condensed treasure of psychoanalytic musings on creativity. Writing on Milner's work grew naturally out of my seminars and I first published a review of *On Not Being Able to Paint* in 1975, which I mailed to Mrs. Milner before it was published. We met in London in 1975 and have corresponded since.

My "dual union" paper built on a question I raised in my review. It seemed to me that Milner oscillated between two different ways of describing the early self and the sense of psychic creativeness. She used an "I-yet-not-I" language which seemed rich in ambiguity, tension, and suggestiveness. On the other hand she uncritically lumped this moment together with the language of "undifferentiation," which seemed to lead nowhere.

I was sensitive to this shift of language because of the widespread influence (in the United States) of Mahler's "undifferentiation" language to describe the early self. The nuclear healing experience in deep regression seemed better expressed by Milner's "I-yet-not-I" feeling. This may seem like hairsplitting, but it is a hairsbreadth that makes a difference in the quality and direction of self-experiencing and development.

My position is that areas of distinction–union characterize the self wherever or whenever we tap into it. As soon as there is the beginning of self, there is distinction–union, with variable shifts of emphasis. Awareness of the multiple dimensionality running through the self at all developmental levels gives one a firmer and more wholesome foundation for work with regression. We can never expect pure "autism," "undifferentiation," "omnipotence," or a monadic world of drives to be the whole story, no matter where we look.

The nuclear regenerative moment described in my "face" papers was characterized by an uplifting, wondrous mix-up of self–other qualities. The subject felt upheld rather than destroyed by permeability. Yet one cannot say there was no self and other in the bliss. For it was precisely the swim of self–other feelings that felt so wonderfully restorative.

Nor does one lose the contribution of self–other aspects of experiencing in malignant regressions, where destruction of self–other is imminent. If destruction of self and other were total and final, the issue would be closed and no more would be at stake. Even as one vanishes into the void one faces a black hole or blank Other.

Because Milner's work—so rich with self—was important to me I found it helpful to distill what it contributed to my sense of self. I called the primary "I-yet-not-I" structure "dual union" but was unhappy with this locution (too close to Mahler's "dual unity" and so misleading). In my book, *The Psychotic Core,* I renamed it the distinction–union structure, but we are in a domain where words are very difficult.

I extended my critique of the starting point of the self to other analytic writers, especially Mahler, Winnicott, Klein, Kohut, and a number of contemporary workers who share my interests (see my chapters on the face, ideal images, and faith, as well as the present chapter, and my books, *The Psychotic Core* and *Coming Through the Whirlwind*).

Marion Milner (1987) described her reaction to my paper and included some of my letters in her book, *The Suppressed Madness of Sane Men.* She was puzzled by the distinction I made between the paradoxical I-yet-not-I moment and undifferentiation, since she blended them as a matter of course. Apparently my paper was disturbing but also led to further revisualization. As her "Afterthoughts" developed she wrote of the I-yet-not-I area as the paradoxical experience at the heart of her work.

Our correspondence has continued and I would like to include two recent interchanges. In one letter I called attention to the fact that Winnicott did not use the term *undifferentiation* — it was foreign to his sensibility. He instinctively used terms that would not collapse the richness and ambiguity of paradoxical experiencing.

Marion Milner wrote back the following (January 6, 1989): "I have been looking up my collected-papers book to see where I got the term 'undifferentiated' from. It seems to be from M. Little and M. Khan (page 238). I think I took it over a bit uncritically and was on better ground in 1956 with my Job paper." In a more recent letter (February 17, 1992) she wrote: "Have just been re-reading Anton Ehrenzweig's 1955 paper on my *Experiment in Leisure,* which he called 'The Creative Surrender.' I think it's from him that I got the word 'undifferentiated' — which I don't need now."

Perhaps as we keep working with realms of experiencing hinted at by terms such as *primary process, soft boundaries, primordial Self and Other, permeability, symmetrical unconscious, O, alpha function, contact barrier,* and *pulsations through the slit* — ways of expressing and exploring these constitutive and sustaining areas will emerge that lead to a more friendly evolution of our very beings.

"The Structure of Freud's Theory of Creativity" (1983b) was an offshoot of courses I was giving on psychoanalysis and creativity at the Institute for Expressive Analysis. At times the contrast between Freud's and Winnicott's views on creativity seemed enormous. Freud adopted the viewpoint of the traditional European intellectual vis-à-vis the uneducated masses. His emphasis was on intellectual and artistic creativity, cultural acts based on discipline, and sublimation of instinctual life. For Winnicott the baby's lifting a hand (like the Zen master's raising a finger or the child-god's blessing) could mediate the sense of creativeness. Creativity is democratic, part of ordinary aliveness, but, like democracy, subject to tendencies and circumstances that thwart it (Winnicott 1950).

Freud and Winnicott placed creativity at the center of their lives. Sometimes they meant the same thing, sometimes not. It was, after all, Freud who popularized the idea that a baby's movements are connected with creativity. He developed the analogical space in which links between body and meaning run rampant. Winnicott spent most of his career describing how this space *feels* and charting aspects of the milieu in which such a space is born. Winnicott's transitional experiencing and use of object are ways of describing transformations of the sense of creative aliveness, the area of faith and freedom.

Winnicott reworked Freud with his own touch, in his own key. Winnicott would not be Winnicott without the Freudian threads that run through his work. One cannot read Winnicott without reference to his reading of Freud. Yet the Freudian baby and the Winnicottian baby are not identical. This doubleness points to the fact that no human baby is one baby. We do not know what to do with this multiplicity, but we are not free to evade it. We are at a point where we ought not simply choose between perspectives like Freud's and Winnicott's. It is more pertinent and pressing to pursue a dialogue or dialectic between (as well as within) viewpoints. What affective thought forms will be born in the process remains to be seen.

1984: "DEMONIZED ASPECTS OF THE SELF"

"Demonized Aspects of the Self" (1984) was written for a book Marie Coleman Nelson was editing on evil. During the course of our interchanges, Mrs. Nelson asked me to join her as co-editor. I solicited several manuscripts and acted as traffic hub while Mrs. Nelson lived in Africa. This essay was written in 1980–1981, between the ideal image/faith and Milner papers. It gave me a chance to explore the persistence of devil images in analytic work and see what they revealed about processes and structures of self.

Devil images persist not only in clinical work but in informal theoretical discussion as well. Freud and Fairbairn referred to psychoanalysis as a kind of demonology. Freud tended to associate the devil with instinctual drives and Fairbairn with ego deformations. Bion added superego devils and in his studies of psychotic attitudes undertook the most detailed portrayal of the devil's psychodynamics since William Blake—a task he took over from Melanie Klein, although the grounds were long prepared through his earlier love of Milton.

My clinical work led to a portrayal of two main devils or networks of devils: an explosive–fusional body ego and a mocking-controlling covertly transcendent mental ego. I take this to be the governing demonic structure of our time. I implicitly pointed to this bipolar system in my early paper on the schizoid ego (1983a) and elaborated it in my books. It runs through my clinical accounts. In the present paper I connect it with aspects of cultural life and language (especially anal signifiers and the snake), and to a variety of concerns in the psychoanalytic literature (from Tausk's "influencing machine" to current views on the baby self).

1985A: "BETWEEN CATASTROPHE AND FAITH"

I attended Bion's New York seminar in 1977 (Bion, 1980), met with him twice, and have been leading a biweekly seminar on his work for more than a decade. This paper grew out of my seminar.

I became immersed in Bion's writings because of his deep interest in psychotic processes and the central role faith played as his work unfolded. He had the courage to see the madness in himself, others, the world at large. Perhaps he could not look away from it. In the course of his work he stripped away everything that could be stripped away, until all that was left was the raw interplay between catastrophe and faith.

Like Winnicott, he rewrote Freud's life and death drives, although his major writings do not mention drives. He writes about affects, attitudes, capacities (especially the ability to tolerate or not tolerate experiencing), states of being. He did not flinch from exploring what needs to be explored in our age: psychic deadness, meaninglessness, explosiveness. No easy answers emerge from his work — only further explorations, more experiencing, and speaking from experiencing. At the same time, he did not hesitate to give voice to depths of mystical awareness. He initiates the most detailed investigation and use of faith undertaken by a psychoanalyst and discusses significant relationships between faith, knowing, learning, and madness.

I have been reading Winnicott for nearly thirty years and Bion half that time and do not find that I am anywhere near exhausting either. What a welcome contrast to many books and articles in the mental health field! Here the human imagination — psychoanalytic imagination — is alive and well. The horrific is endlessly faced. There are no facile exits. Yet psychic life persists, evolves, survives its annihilation, its extinction. Out of nowhere the fire that never goes out flares up, often at the point where no flame seemed to be possible.

1985–1989: OMNIPOTENCE, MINDLESSNESS-SELFLESSNESS, OMNISCIENCE

The last papers in this collection explore three aspects of madness: omnipotence, mindlessness, and omniscience. All of these states can play a positive role in growth of self and creative work, but they can easily run amok, with grave consequences.

"Omnipotence" (1985b) grew out of the Human Services Workshops, a series of seminars sponsored by the Sisters of Charity. It traces dialectics of power-–powerlessness through more and less wholesome twists and turns. A God image that can take many forms exists in the psyche. We are capable of inflating–deflating ourselves with it. In many papers I emphasize the positive use of ideal states, rather than reduce them to hostile-sexual undercurrents. They often make intrinsic contributions to a growing sense of self, although they may also blur reality and work against growth. The present paper develops a series of clinical images that show how complex the interplay between positive and negative uses of a capacity can be.

"Mindlessness-Selflessness: A Common Madness" (1986b) was written on the request of Dr. Jerome Travers for a journal and book series called, *The Psychotherapy Patient*. The theme for this particular volume was the selfless patient, and I focused on mindless aspects of selflessness. There are many ways to lose or be unable to grow a mind.

Sexual and aggressive impulses feed our sense of self and make us feel alive but also are used to escape the tensions and aliveness they contribute to. We may lose as well as find ourselves through sexual and aggressive actions. We can blank ourselves out via sex and aggression in positive and negative ways.

We can blank ourselves out in more purely mental ways, such as the "dismantling of attention" Meltzer (1975) describes in autistic states. More generally, intellect can be used to escape body and body to escape intellect. Any capacity can be used mindfully or mindlessly, including the wish to be oneself.

Going blank can be a defense against unconscious conflict but as likely signals an inability to let experiencing build. One may blank or bliss out under pressure of an experience one fails to tolerate. For example, blankness can put brakes on panic, while bliss can stupefy horror. One can fill in blanks that ought to be there by precocious use of meaning-making activity, or one can overuse areas of blankout to prevent growth of meaning. This is similar to being busy when one ought to be still or being still when one ought to be busy. Too much or too little misses the moment (although more chances to get it right or better usually are on the way).

Freud's pleasure principle and death wish join in the case of some individuals who do not know they are in a black hole. In the present paper, the patient I call Lenny substitutes well-being for a psyche that is not there. His life of hallucinated satisfaction never leaves the null dimension; fullness blanks out existence at the same time it makes the latter tolerable. One might say Lenny is glued to the hallucinated breast twice over or once or twice removed; he has become a blank breast blankly filled in the place where absence cannot even be hallucinated, but fullness *is* emptiness.

In contrast, Leila's torment spirals toward blank mindlessness, but there is experienced velocity, mental movement, whirling. She knows she must come through the whirlwind and that this is her life's task, an aborted destiny. Because she knows she has a destiny, Leila's mindlessness is excruciatingly painful.

What would happen if Leila and Lenny changed places for a moment? It is easier to think of changing brains than changing psyches, especially psyches that reach vanishing points in contrasting ways, one via the route of pain, one via well-being. At the point of exchange Leila would be slowing down, Lenny would be speeding up. Would they learn from each other or merely complete the exchange, so that Leila's deceleration and Lenny's acceleration would never end, switching tracks to oblivion?

Lenny and Leila have problems with psychic speed. They reach standstills by slowing down or speeding up. Together they show how difficult it can be to find optimal speeds for the timing of meaning and the seminal rhythm of blankness and meaning.

"Omniscience" (1989) was requested by Dr. M. Gerard Fromm for a book on the clinical use of Winnicott's work. Portions of the clinical material appeared in my book, *The Psychotic Core*, but were reworked for the present chapter with Winnicott in mind.

My work with psychotic dimensions of psychic life brought home the importance of distinguishing between omnipotence and omniscience, a distinction usually glossed over in psychoanalytic writings. These two facets of narcissism may help or harm development. When things go wrong, omniscience can be more lethal than omnipotence, and to miss the difference can be disastrous. In *The Psychotic Core* (1986a) and "On Demonized Aspects of the Self"

(1984) I applied this distinction to Tausk's *influencing machine,* the psychology of weaponry, and a variety of symbols and situations.

When Dr. Fromm asked me for a chapter for his book, I thought it would be helpful to see what role omniscience plays in Winnicott's thought. Winnicott does not mention omniscience, but unknowing plays a critical role in his work. He instinctively resists the pull of "the omniscient therapist" and places not being a know-it-all at the heart of paradox and openness.

The groundwork for my discussion of omniscience was laid in my earlier work, which emphasized the basic multidimensionality of psychic life (distinction–union of self–other and mental self–body self). It links up, for example, with my discussion of Federn and the ego's multiple roots (1983a), the ideal image papers, my analyses of psychoanalytic starting points, and many informal clinical writings. Omnipotence can be related to vicissitudes of body self and omniscience to mental self, with every variety of mixture and conflict.

REFERENCES

Bion, W. R. (1980). *Bion in New York and Sao Paulo.* Perthshire, Scotland: Clunie Press.

Castaneda, C. (1973). *Journey to Ixtlan: The Lessons of Don Juan.* New York: Simon and Schuster.

Eigen, M. (1973a). Abstinence and the schizoid ego. *International Journal of Psycho-Analysis* 54:493–497.

———— (1973b). The recoil on having another person. *Review of Existential Psychology and Psychiatry* 12:52–55.

———— (1975a). Psychopathy and individuation. *Psychotherapy: Theory, Research & Practice* 12:286–294.

———— (1975b). Book review: *On Not Being Able to Paint* by Marion Milner. *Psychoanalytic Review* 62:312–315.

———— (1977a). On working with "unwanted" patients. *International Journal of Psycho-Analysis* 58:109–121.

———— (1977b). A note on breathing and identity. *Journal of Humanistic Psychology* 17:35–39.

———— (1979). Ideal images, creativity and the Freudian drama. *Psychocultural Review* 3:287–298.

———— (1980a). On the significance of the face. *Psychoanalytic Review* 67:426–444.

———— (1980b). Instinctual fantasy and ideal images. *Contemporary Psychoanalysis* 16:119–137.

———— (1980c). On soft and hard qualities. *American Journal of Psychoanalysis* 40:267–271.

———— (1981a). The area of faith in Winnicott, Lacan and Bion. *International Journal of Psycho-Analysis* 62:413–433.

———— (1981b). Guntrip's, analysis with Winnicott. *Contemporary Psychoanalysis* 17:103–117.

———— (1981c). Breaking the frame: stopping the world. *Modern Psychoanalysis* 6:89–100.

_____ (1982). Creativity, ideal images and instinctual fantasy. *Psychoanalytic Review* 69:317–339.

_____ (1983a). Dual union or undifferentiation? A critique of Marion Milner's view of the sense of psychic creativeness. *International Review of Psycho-Analysis* 10:415–428.

_____ (1983b). A note on the structure of Freud's theory of creativity. *Psychoanalytic Review* 70:41–45.

_____ (1984). On demonized aspects of the self. In *Evil: Self and Culture,* ed. M. C. Nelson and M. Eigen, pp. 91–123. New York: Human Sciences Press.

_____ (1985a). Toward Bion's starting point: between catastrophe and faith. *International Journal of Psycho-Analysis* 66:321–330.

_____ (1985b). Aspects of omnipotence. *Psychoanalytic Review* 72:149–160.

_____ (1986a). *The Psychotic Core.* Northvale, N.J.: Jason Aronson.

_____ (1986b). Aspects of mindlessness-selflessness: a common madness. *The Psychotherapy Patient* 2:75–81.

_____ (1989). Aspects of omniscience. In *The Facilitating Environment: Clinical Applications of Winnicott's Theory,* ed. M. G. Fromm and B. L. Smith, pp. 604–628. Madison, CT: International Universities Press.

_____ (1992). *Coming Through the Whirlwind.* Wilmette, IL: Chiron Publications.

Fromm, M. G., and Smith, B. L., eds. (1989). *The Facilitating Environment.* Madison, CT: International Universities Press.

Glatzer, H. T., & Evans, W. N. (1977). On Guntrip's analysis with Fairbairn and Winnicott. *International Journal of Psychoanalytic Psychotherapy* 6:81–98.

Guntrip, H. (1975). My experience of analysis with Winnicott and Fairbairn. *International Review of Psycho-Analysis* 2:145–156.

Meltzer, D., Bremner, J., Hoxter, S., et al. (1975). *Explorations in Autism.* Perthshire Scotland: Clunie Press.

Milner, M. (1987). *The Suppressed Madness of Sane Men.* London: Tavistock.

Nelson, M. C. (1976). Paths of power: psychoanalysis and sorcery. *Psychoanalytic Review* 63:333–360.

Winnicott, D. W. (1950). Some thoughts on the meaning of the word "democracy." In *Home Is Where We Start From,* pp. 239–259. New York: Norton, 1986.

1

Abstinence and the Schizoid Ego

Since the dawn of self-awareness some form of asceticism has been used, virtually universally, as a consciousness-raising technique. It appears to have functioned both to heighten awareness for its own sake and as one of the perennial revolutionary media to offset the toxic side-effects of civilization. It is thus not surprising to find radical psychoanalysis, a consciousness revolution of critical importance, an advocate of abstinence as a catalyst for the work of self-transformation. Freud's very theory of personal development portrays an ego capable of increasing itself through its resistance to the collective in nature and culture. The movement toward psychic mastery is achieved by means of mental acts which are grounded on critical renunciations for their power. For Freud the life and growth of consciousness are necessarily ascetic or depend upon an ascetic element. An ascetic therapeutic methodology would appear to flow naturally from his vision of man. Beyond the specifics of the abstinence rule, the analytic situation itself is conceived as a paradigm of the ascetic moment: the patient's need or desire is destined to collide with the analyst's sustained attentiveness, a thwarting which, ultimately, results in the increase of the patient's own capacity for self-awareness.

With the continued development of analytic therapy, the rule of abstinence as a specific therapeutic technique has been disregarded for both theoretical and practical reasons. Therapy is, generally, no longer compressed into intense, short durations. The rise and prevalence of once- or twice-weekly psychotherapy has been required by the fairly broad demand for analytic healing by persons who could or would not afford the time and money investment of many visits per week. With such minimal person-to-person contacts over a long period of time, it seemed impracticable and inadvisable for patients to abstain from sexual relations, important decisions, and other forms of normal acting out. Furthermore, the focus of therapy itself increasingly turned to severe ego pathologies, where, it might appear, the frustration and disorganization consequent upon following the abstinence rule would be too debilitating. In fact, many therapists

1

tended to become more dynamically active-responsive to help offset the already severe presenting disorganization of such patients. It now appears, further, that physical contact is a visibly growing part of the overall therapeutic milieu and cannot be excluded by definition. Finally, the ideology of the age has shifted, at least in certain subcultures, from self-discipline and mastery to spontaneity and impulse, where discipline is perhaps reserved for getting one's way.

It thus seemed surprising when an increasing number of patients in the past few years spontaneously undertook periods of profound abstinence for the sake of their personal development. This group was not confined to any one diagnostic category but included narcissistic, psychotic, borderline, neurotic, and other personality problems. It was as though a reaction to the overstimulating pleasure orientation had begun to set in. Talk in the sessions about inferiority feelings and succeeding with other people markedly decreased. The practical-social milieu was viewed increasingly as lacking in crucial respects and discounted as a place one could want to take root in. Neither people nor things seemed any longer to offer the promise, pleasure, or satisfaction similar patients just some years before compulsively sought with a chronic sense of inadequacy. One wondered how much this trend reflected a massive giving-up of hope in the external world, a broadening-deepening of values as a result of the self-discovery ethic, or advances in analytic ability to penetrate a deeper life of the ego.

The process took place blindly and was often frightening. Most generally, patients felt they were being drawn down out of the world as though by a magnet toward a sense of self they knew they had at bottom. As one person described his experience,

> There was a sliver there, black and radioactive, compressed and dense . . . the very bottom. . . . It was what was unbreakable in me . . . the uncrackable kernel . . . everything else by comparison was confusion and noise . . . only that survived everything . . .

Often a state of seemingly endless, painful emptiness preceded the clear experiencing of this I-kernel. The touching of "rock-bottom," further, was typically followed by a spontaneous recoil or reversal, a turnabout in which the patient felt himself being drawn back out toward the world, although a variably transfigured world.

Such processes have increasingly become a central focus in therapeutic work and appear to be accessible to more careful description than has been possible before. In this paper a representative case will be described in detail. An outline of the most typical aspects of this phenomenon will then be presented, followed by two brief case presentations showing further variations. The final section provides a theoretical discussion of the phenomenon.

> Carl was a hostile, impulsive man in his late 20s who refused to "give in" or compromise his creative vision of art and life. He was a writer and actor who could not get along with his colleagues because they "sold out" or did not ask as much

from their craft as he. Similarly, he could not establish lasting relationships with people in general, especially women. He believed he was able to see through women's ploys and their attempts to gain the upper hand; he could not allow himself to humor them as he saw others do. Carl struggled and met with some success in his field, largely on his own terms. His triumphs, however, were barely able to offset his sense of isolation, so he inwardly felt defeated where he apparently succeeded.

There came a point in therapy where he allowed his disgust with the world ("a great whoredom") free rein and he decided to withdraw. Earlier he typically had withdrawn and fought his withdrawal in alternating periods. He was aware of his withdrawn self both in the sense of the fearful, burnt child and as defiant isolation. Basically, he had alternately fought and withdrawn from a blind, domineering mother and a crude, bullying, indifferent father. In the end he felt crushed by and hated them both. He had found some comfort in friends and an aunt and uncle, enough to give rise to the thought that there might be some promise in the world outside his home. But when he went out on his own he found he perpetuated the same sadomasochistic struggles he had known before.

For some time he struggled with his tendencies to withdraw and fight. Both gave him a life-feeling yet undermined him. He alternately rode with each of these currents and rebelled against them in attempts at mastery, self-defense, and freedom. He clearly saw the struggling infant in himself but could not find an attitude that was genuinely helpful. Understanding, resolve, and temper, as he was able to attain them, were ineffectual. Trying and giving up were alike exhausting.

When Carl made the critical withdrawal under discussion, he resolved to follow the "fed-up" feeling as far as it could take him. It was a resolve which began with a sense of giving in, but of giving in all the way. What began as giving in turned into determination: the compulsion, experientially, turned into a sense of active choice. Carl felt as if he were turning the tables on the world. As he put it, it felt like "a mixture of showing the world my ass and sticking out my tongue . . ."

However, he could not get along with himself any better than he could with the world. He found within what he hated without, and in certain respects more intensely. Earlier, each time he had retreated into himself he had been forced back out by his own ambivalence toward himself and by the fear of the isolation he had hoped would succor him: "I feel like a boomerang . . . whichever way I throw myself—out or in . . ."

When his oscillation reached a peak so that he had to make a choice, he opted for himself: "At least I am always with me . . . that's some place to start even if I've nowhere to go . . ." Once the choice was made he had to struggle with fears of letting go everything outside himself. He steeled himself with the thought that when it came down to it the world seemed more unsatisfactory to him than he did. He was also conscious of an inner pull. He felt himself attracted to something deep within himself and thought it would be cowardly not to follow it. After he broke through his initial fears he experienced exhilaration. He put his solitary time to good use, studying whatever he wished, especially psychology. He explored himself incessantly.

His pleasure in his powers, however, was relatively short-lived. It turned into panic fear, in particular a dread of falling apart. He pictured himself, for example, as a disintegrating body lost in space. He felt being lost in space referred to his social isolation, his fear of going so far out he would have no means of getting back. An unnatural gap would always be between himself and other people. He related his disintegrating body to his sexual abstinence. He was afraid it would do him actual bodily harm. He was aware of the symbolic significance of this delusion, but nevertheless sought reassurance that he would come through physically intact. Normally such intense fear would have been enough to have driven him back to the world, only to continue to repeat the boomerang process he was used to. This time he insisted he wished to let himself disintegrate if I could guarantee that it was purely mental. When I assured him it was psychic, he gave himself to the experience more fully and set off into it with "no intention to return." For, although reassured that he was not physically disintegrating, he felt certain he would die.

However, when he actively allowed or tried to bring about the disintegration he had feared when he was passive, he found it would not easily happen. That he could not actively achieve what he passively feared was a discovery which helped lay the foundation for increasing courage to face whatever he himself might bring forth.

After this period of reprieve his fear of disintegration was replaced by an intense sense of emptiness, which he described as "the depression beneath depressions." The emptiness was like a cloudy medium through which he caught sight of "a hidden I which was drawing me to it . . ." More completely: "The emptiness is like a cloud . . . a vague cloud . . . I can almost see through it . . . sometimes I think I see something on the other side . . . a mirror perhaps . . . a mirror I can see through . . . but something is staring at me from it . . . I am already there . . . I am there looking at me here . . . it's me but more me . . . an *I* I feel I've always had . . . that I've always been moving toward . . . it's been directing me to it from behind somehow . . . like a transmitter . . ." Carl aimed at this I and moved into the emptiness. As he entered the emptiness it grew more intense, more alive with itself, still, like the eye of a storm. Though soundless, it gave the illusion of being loud. "It feels like it's about to give birth . . ." When the loudness reached its peak, the space became clear instead of cloudy.

"It won't move . . . it stands in one place . . . like a light-tower or a bright, dense stone . . . black space endlessly around it . . . I want to touch and break it because it won't give an inch . . . but I'll break before it will . . . as though I'm breakable and it's not . . . I want to unite with it and make it the part of me it is . . . it's more me than me . . . the I-ness of my I . . ."

After this experience Carl had a series of dreams significantly different from his past dream or waking life. First he dreamt of beautiful nature scenes, rich with a sense of peace and freedom. Usually he was alone in them. He then began to dream about several good women figures. In one dream, too, a man who reminded him of his father sat at a kitchen table taking a kindly interest in him. He felt that this man was not his father as he was but as he should have been. These dreams were in marked contrast to his previous chronic persecutory, destructive, and conflictual dreams. They amounted to the first unambivalent experiences he was conscious of having. He conceived a desire to get a taste of such experiences in actual living. The world "out there" now appeared multi-leveled. Carl perceived the negative as clearly as before. However, much of what he formerly had recoiled from now appeared as distortions, a distorted crust and not the core of reality. Where before he felt it would have been cowardly not to follow his impulse toward isolation, he now felt it cowardly not to in some way try to embody his sense of the way he saw things *really* were or could be. He felt it a task to attempt to develop and integrate his mystical positive and mundane negative levels of perception of the world.

The pattern described in Carl's case was, in general, typical: (1) disillusionment with the outer world and the possibility of a truly meaningful life in it; (2) a drawing of libido inward toward a barely sensed ego experience; (3) intense panic-dread of disintegration; (4) intense sense of emptiness, in which it is discovered that the emptiness is alive and full; (5) sighting and uniting with an ego structure which is experienced as the underlying indestructible sense of self—a compressed, dense, magnetic I-kernel, a seeming final contracting point of the I; (6) a perception of some intrinsic merit in the world, usually a beatific experience, however momentary, and the reversal of libido flow, so that a two-way current of outflow and inflow can occur. It is as though the discovery and exploration of the safety zone of the I—an inviolable I within a hidden enclosure—makes possible the generosity which allows the other to become genuinely attractive. A deeper constancy of his own I has been disclosed to the patient, so that he is more able to grant this deeper sense of I to others.

Each case, of course, has its own variations. Two further cases will briefly be presented to give a fuller sense of the clinical possibilities. Their differences rather than similarities with regard to the above example will be concentrated on in order to avoid repetition.

Ben, like Carl, had been raised in a mother-dominated home. However, he had been treated more warmly by his mother, who also periodically became detached and indifferent. He was the only son among four daughters. His father favored two of the girls and took his sadism out on Ben, for whom he set too high goals, beat, and called a girl. Ben saw me for therapy in his early 30s. He had been an alcoholic since his late teens. During that time he had been an AA member without effect. He had been through several therapies which had attempted, in some form, to ward off his wish and underlying pull toward isolation.

Ben's life was characterized by attempts to get out of the hole he was in, followed by recurrent falls, then the climb again. People functioned in his life as coaches and a rooting audience always to be disappointed, and then encourage him again, as he alternated good and bad boy roles. He led an impulsive life, including frequent physical fights and destructive involvements with women. He was periodically impotent.

When his wish for isolation surfaced in our work together, it became clear he had always felt a strong urge to withdraw and be alone. His being a loner in real life symbolized that wish. He had always wanted to try to be alone but had never dared it. He stated that he felt cowardly because he had never followed that urge. Instead he had tried to sidestep it by making excuses or making believe it was not there. He was afraid he was too weak and others in his life had shared that fear. Yet he had the strong sense that unless he followed that urge at least once in his life he would never be able to find himself, he would keep missing something that was crucial.

His fear of withdrawing was that he would become unnatural, that in cutting himself off from others he would turn into a freak. But he felt like a freak when he was with others because of the ways in which he distorted himself in relation to them. In particular, he felt that he was a clown in groups and a "pussy" with women. He wanted to "become his own man." As he withdrew from sexual contact, including chronic masturbation, he felt flooded with streams of feeling and energy. He became frightened he would accost women shoppers in the store he worked in. He went through the fears of disintegration and emptiness with a stubborn persistence. The sense of I he was attracted to seemed a steel sliver of will, cut off from others, a sheer strand of will where others could not touch him or throw him off-center, where he could rest at one with himself. His task shifted from staying "dry" to staying in contact with this I. This state of isolated determination persisted almost seven months in its most severe form. After a growing number of "feeling together alone" experiences, Ben reported seeing others' faces as extraordinarily beautiful. When he left for work one Monday morning after a weekend alone, people seemed full and radiant to him. He had not experienced people that way before. His social contacts began to increase and he made genuine use of AA. He has since entered a technical school to better his work opportunities ("My mind became unclogged"). Relations with women were markedly more gratifying, beset with problems that appeared challenging rather than overwhelming. He eventually left individual therapy with me and has since been able to rely on AA group therapy work. In this case the heightened sense of self and the turn toward the other occurred on an apparently more embodied level than with Carl. Still it was characterized by a movement away from all sense of bodily invasion until a hard-core reliable sense of the isolated I became explicit.

A final example is Linda's case, where the turning toward the other involved one specific person, rather than dreams or a global experience of others and the world. After college Linda's attempts to live an active life were unsatisfying. She could not find work she wanted and eventually withdrew from her job to do little else than stay at home and watch TV. She felt deeply over many of the shows, often moved to tears. People from work sought her out but in the end she stopped answering their calls and would not open the door. She virtually stopped dating and appeared to vegetate. One of her few regular activities involved watching the animals at the zoo. She occasionally helped take care of disturbed children. While she vegetated, Linda did not feel inert, but had a sense of deeply confined aliveness, an aliveness that could not go anywhere.

Linda's period of abstinence was not complete. Occasionally she had sexual relations with a man she was not involved with and suffered guilt feelings afterward. This marked a significant change from her earlier promiscuity without apparent guilt. Their meetings became infrequent. After a long period of relative isolation, Linda spontaneously began to experience deep trust for a man who had been a platonic friend for several years. While they were sitting together after an evening at the cinema, his face seemed to come alive for her and take on a glow. The experience was contagious, reciprocal, and the relationship since has deepened into marriage.

Two further aspects of the therapeutic process described here must be mentioned but will not be taken up in detail, since it is the nature of a particular I-experience which is the focus of the present paper. First, the patient is aware in some basic sense that the process he is undergoing takes place within — and is made possible through — the context of his relationship to the therapist. He is not altogether isolated or cut off. For example, Carl said that he felt as if he were being lowered or lowering himself by a rope into a well, where at the bottom of the blackness he saw himself. The rope was held on the surface of the earth by his relationship with me. Without this he could not have gained the courage to let go everything else successfully. He knew he had someone to hold on to even in the depths of the most negative transference. It was crucial that he had the feeling I valued him even because of — not in spite of — his hatred.

Another important part of the therapeutic process not focused on here involved the patient's changing sense of body feelings. A dialectic between the activation of the detached ego sense and an activation of repressed body-life eventually must go hand-in-hand in order to prevent a one-sided development. Again, however, it is the therapy relationship itself that will permit the integration of split-off body-impulses into central ego structures.

It seems clear we are dealing with a schizoid phenomenon. Guntrip (1969) has already pointed out that the attempt to conceptualize narcissism in terms of the simple ego-superego-id framework is now too global. Descriptions somewhat parallel to those presented above may be found in Winnicott (1965). He speaks of a true, silent, inviolable self, beyond all usual communication with the outside world. This silent self appears safe in a hidden enclosure, out of reach of all impingement. Winnicott described it a grave sin to attempt to invade this sacred core of selfhood, by psychotherapy or otherwise. This, however, implies it can be invaded. The present finding is that it cannot, at least not under the circumstances I have studied it. It is in fact experienced by the subject as "that in me which is safe from all harm." It appears one can always drive or move this sacred zone of safety further back — capable of indefinite contraction — as conditions require. Whether or not there is some final breaking point I have not been able to determine. So far, however, including the psychotic patients I have worked with, subjects report an ultimate zone of safe retreat, some uncracked I-kernel. In this process patients may be surprised to find that apparent breaking points of the I do not turn out to be final breaking points.

However, to call this unbroken — unbreakable? — kernel of self the "true self," with Winnicott, may be an overstatement. For, as Guntrip rightly points out, this would make the true self isolated, a congealed split-off core of what is left after the bombardment is over. Guntrip's account, however, misses the essence of the phenomena described above. In Guntrip's scheme such phenomena must be viewed as expressions of the regressed aspect of the libidinal ego, the most hidden and withdrawn part of the personality, driven out of contact by fear. But the regressed ego, as Guntrip describes it, is wholly passive. It seeks the womb.

The ego structure described here, on the other hand, is intensely alive and active in its compressed density. It is experienced in an aura of power—it exudes a sense of power. The respite here is not passivity in the womb, not a sleep, but an active seeing stillness, compact and electrifying. It does not appear that Guntrip's scheme has a term that aptly describes this ego realm.

This ego structure appears to be a part of what Elkin (1972, pp. 413, 414) has called the "schizoid ego," an aspect of the self which "retreats to a hidden, detached existence" to preserve a sense of psychic freedom or safety at the time the (maternal) superego is formed. It is an area of the I which, in effect, has withstood embodiment to avoid being collectivized. It cannot, therefore, be called the true self, because it remains an unintegrated ego fragment outside embodied existence. It cannot, however, be described as passive, for it is occultly transcendent and inherently megalomanic. The sense of alienation may involve: (1) self-falsification in order to fit in with others; (2) identification with or feeling at the mercy of split-off body-impulses; or (3) self-isolation in order to preserve oneself from others. This last involves a hidden, detached ego estranged from the central ego structures.

In the cases reported here actual isolation and abstinence tended to bring the schizoid ego out into the open as a preliminary step toward its integration with the central or communal ego. Working through the repression of the schizoid ego—previously acted out blindly as life-rejecting tendencies—made possible a powerful I-experience which, in turn, appeared to be a condition for reexperiencing the body and others more openly. This followed, it would seem, because contact with the schizoid ego involved contact with an aspect of the self that had gone beyond fear. Once this contact was established, venturing into the fear-ridden domain of the body and social life became safer.

REFERENCES

Elkin, H. (1972). On selfhood and the development of ego structures in infancy. *Psychoanalytic Review* 59:389–416.

Guntrip, H. (1969). *Schizoid Phenomena, Object Relations and the Self*. New York: International Universities Press.

Winnicott, D. W. (1965). *The Maturational Processes and the Facilitating Environment*. New York: International Universities Press.

2

Psychopathy and
Individuation

Many authors following Nietzsche have pointed to a psychopathic vital streak in human life by means of which an individual may break out of collective social existence. In this vision mere goodness is experienced as a stumbling block in the way of the complete man. To paraphrase Tillich, a man is no bigger than the amount of the diabolic in himself he can assimilate. For both Freud and Jung this meant, ideally, an intrapsychic event in which the ego extends its effective horizons and goes beyond itself by meeting and transforming psychic constellations previously alien to it, for example, representatives of the id or shadow. Man need not act psychopathically in order to recognize and assimilate what is valuable in his psychopathy, at least not higher man.

But few are simply higher men. During a recent session a rather staid middle-class housewife remarked that she occasionally indulged in shoplifting to appease her need for insecurity. The moment's uncertainty and danger added intensity to and uplifted her experience of reality in the way a forbidden love affair might have, too. How many patients have not, at a certain point in therapy, disclosed psychopathic ideals and began experiments in realizing them in the attempt to reclaim what had been left out of their development?

If one seriously believes it is part of the task of an adequate psychotherapy to help meet and integrate dissociated psychopathic tendencies, one faces the dilemma of having to tolerate or at times even evoke the patient's psychopathy with the full awareness that he may be likely, at least for periods or in part, to identify with and act on these impulses. Thus one finds therapists becoming prematurely critical or moralistic, sometimes out of fear, sometimes with a realistic pre-vision of what they are warding off. Other therapists attempt to cultivate what might be described as a "rational psychopathy," the taken-for-granted psychopathy of everyday life which appears to serve normal self-interest.

With the rise and prevalence of psychologies emphasizing interpersonal realities, psychopathic outbursts have been increasingly viewed in terms of the social aims or gains one hopes to derive from them. Asocial acts are interpreted in terms of their supposed social meanings, for example, the responses they try to elicit from others. The essentially nonpsychopathic patient in the midst of a psychopathic episode, confronted by socially oriented interpretations of his experience, often becomes mystified and, finally, hypnotized out of the exhilarating sense of power he had begun to feel. What for him had constituted a momentary sense of exaltation in his self-experience is passed over in favor of emphasizing his underlying dependency and need to get something from others, that is, his weakness. It seems to me a serious therapeutic error, or at least an oversimplification, to hastily attribute the sense of power derived from various forms of psychopathic violence simply to frustration or a feeling of impotence. In face of such a tactic no wonder the patient soon becomes deflated and succumbs to a psychology of need.

Two recent instances vividly illustrate this error because in them the therapist failed in his attempt to impose his values and attitudes on the patient, thereby exposing their limitations. In a therapy group composed of therapists and their patients, one of the patients began to assert himself rather aggressively toward one of the women and suffered a painful rebuff. His young woman therapist interpreted his failure as the result of his egoistic insensitivity and encouraged him to approach the woman in a more vulnerable, contactful manner. His therapist admittedly felt right about the anger his narcissism evoked in her and wanted him to realize, through her own experience, what he was doing to make women reject him. She wished to use her own instinctive repulsion to his behavior as a tool to help him out of his pattern of failure. Apparently she was not able, did not wish, or did not think it necessary to become the mirror his narcissism required.

For a moment he looked wounded, almost puppyish, and admitted his fear of showing weakness. He sounded bewildered and vague. However, before the session ended his primal outrage rose up toward the woman he wanted and once more was rejected. His therapist expressed accepting warmth for his compulsive setback, although signs of irritation and reproach escaped her. Finally she revealed her reaction to her patient in the hope that her openness would be helpful. At this point the patient became defiant and refused to give in. He said that the cost was too high, he would have to give up more than he wished. The group expressed sympathy for his defensiveness, a gesture which angered him more. He expressed the wishful fantasy that the woman he wanted should react with pleasure or at least tolerate his wish to possess and kill her. He pictured the Virgin taming the Unicorn with a glance and wanted, in the same way, the woman to like him while all his ugliness came out until he reached the point where he could feel happy or weep. He wanted the group to side with his feeling of strength, not his fear of weakness. If they first did what he wanted he could allow his weakness to surface without in any way feeling that he had compromised himself. In the end, he tended to see the group members as castrated beings and himself a lone fighter against the inevitable. Viewing the others he could not imagine castration could be humanizing, although he expressed a groping feeling that it might be. When he left the session feeling misunderstood, some of the participants said he must be psychotic and almost everyone gave expressions of sympathy to his rejected therapist.

In another instance a talented, schizoid young woman told her therapist she was looking for the Holy Grail. He tried to suggest that what she really wanted was contact with people. She then felt he was cold and lacked vision and, in a few more sessions, terminated therapy. Eventually she found a therapist who understood people looking for the Holy Grail.

To what extent did the above therapists fail to influence their patients because of a lack of expertise, the severity of the patient's pathology, or the insistence of the patient's life drive? What would have been the nature of the cure had therapy succeeded? In practice is it principally a matter of personal disposition how far one will go in accepting a patient's psychopathic tendencies? I remember once spontaneously flaring up at an impulsive young man who revealed he was defrauding the post office in order to pay for his sessions. I told him that unless he found an honest way to see me I would terminate treatment. This young man was also on welfare and receiving disability insurance, yet I had not previously objected to these little sins although he was physically able. The young man felt I reacted so strongly because I identified with him and was afraid of my identification.

From the patient's viewpoint in the above instances the therapists tended to cut short what the patients experienced as tentative and necessary steps in a profound process of ego repair or formation. The patients felt they rightly fought against a tendency in the therapists to prematurely socialize and short-circuit asocial tendencies and the raw vitality they embodied. They were not yet ready to give up or suppress these tendencies which they identified with and felt to be basically life affirming.

It seems essential that dissociated psychopathic as well as schizoid tendencies receive integration by central or communal ego structures in the course of authentic personal growth (Eigen 1973, Elkin 1972). It is desirable that they undergo transformation within the context of the therapy relationship itself so that destructive acting out is minimized. In optimal work the skilled therapist seems automatically to sense how much of the patient's psychopathy to release and when, so that the emphasis is placed less on controls or cleverness than on the progressive assimilation of the ever new. However, it is not always possible to work through such urges without acting out. How one reacts to inevitable acting out must depend on its meaning or on what level of development the patient has attained. Where acting out is part of a more general process of self-awakening one helps the patient more by viewing his actions in light of their broader context than by playing the ego splitting game, however subtly, of too simply siding with one side of the self against the other. It is both crude and subtly oppressive to try to undercut the patient's pathology without helping to bring to light and assimilate the capacities and tendencies that the pathology embodies. To accomplish the latter requires a sensitivity to the rhythm and sensed aims of fresh stirrings in the patient whatever forms they may take and, among other things, the patience and persistence to outwait or outflank their more pathological expressions. Such "waiting," however, is not dead or inert but intensely alive and accurate in its shifting sense of where the patient is moving. Accurate seeing and valuing of the patient's urge to affirm himself in his actions is a prerequisite for freeing the active tendencies[1] tied up in his psychopathic attempts at self-expression. The interpenetrating aliveness and evolving meaning of the therapy situation itself helps ensure that the patient does not get stuck in endless patterns of faulty repetition.

In the present paper three cases will be described in which acting out of psychopathic tendencies by essentially nonpsychopathic persons seemed to be unavoidable and have a positive function in the person's development as a whole. In these instances the therapist's presence acted as an integrative medium which helped sustain the patient's attempts to form himself throughout his various upheavals and changes of direction. In each case the psychopathic phase came as a release, an outburst or building up which eventually peaked and subsided. It often had its grimly frightening aspects but it also carried a vaguely sensed purpose or curative aim. It grew and receded with its own natural rhythm or sense of time which included or in some way took into account the therapist's own pace or rhythm. It invited an apprehensive trust like a sacred thread, while, at the same time, displaying every reason why fear or indignation should win out. However, waiting on its own necessity paid therapeutic dividends in the sense of a fuller organic unfolding than might have been possible with a more overtly realistic social or ethical standpoint.

In the course of this paper a number of issues concerning the theory and therapy of psychopathic tendencies are raised but not adequately discussed. For example, what determines whether, how much, or when a patient's psychopathy can, should, or need be acted out rather than given a verbal form of expression such as fantasy. However, the aim of this paper is not theoretical or systematic but to informally evoke a sense of instances in which the patient's psychopathy was able to play a positive role in his overall development, an outcome greatly aided by the therapist's ability to recognize and provide an atmosphere for the distillation and release of the healthy tendency struggled toward by the patient's pathology.

I began working with Tom, then 8 years old, when I was a teacher in a class for disturbed children. He stayed with me when I became a therapist and we worked together until he was 16, at which time he and his family left New York. When I

---

[1]The active side of psychopathic self-affirmation rather than psychopathy as a defense against passive tendencies is the psychological level focused on in the present paper.

first met Tom he reminded me of David in *David and Lisa,* except that Tom was far more primitive, more like a feral child with the life gone out. One of my better teachers was fond of saying to practicum groups, "Schizophrenic children don't have flat affect, only their therapists do."

Most often Tom was quiet and still. Sometimes he rocked with his hand patting his chest rhythmically; sometimes he watched with eyes like alert guns. Sometimes he was all weird and vague. If someone touched him he would scream or close his eyes and hold his body like a tightly sealed embryo. He knew how to talk but rarely did. From time to time his more verbal screams clearly told us that he feared actual loss of body parts when someone reached for him. He literally feared breaking apart. He had twice been hospitalized after "falling out" of his low floor apartment window and often hurt himself in accidents.

In time Tom took to staying in the coat closet. He would climb up on the hat shelf and have us close the door. There in the darkness he sat for hours each day, making whining and howling sounds like a crying dog or wolf. I could do little except be mildly friendly and tell him it felt like he was in mourning, filled with misery and grief. I felt his knowing we were there, watching us out of the corners of his eyes, even though a vacuum existed between us.

Eventually Tom spent more time out of his closet, sporadically doing things in isolation, watching us, painting, touching his body. He began to walk among or rather around us, to look at our work, and see what we were doing. He sometimes looked as if he wanted to take part but did not know how.

One day he spontaneously, abruptly started going to gym when the older children went. He rarely went to gym with his own class. He apparently wanted to be with the older, tougher kids. Some staff opposed this but Tom's life drive won out. Although all of us were at least a little afraid, he was allowed to do as he wished.

He tried to plant himself in the middle of the activity as the big boys played. Sometimes he was jostled and bruised but, overall, the older boys somehow must have divined what was happening and unconsciously protected him. Tom was never really hurt. What was surprising, too, was that the big boys did not make fun of him. There was simply no question of his being able to keep up and play with them. He mostly had to stand and watch.

When Tom did begin to join his own class in gym he became a bully. He had to have his way. Before the year was up he had become quarrelsome and a compulsive fighter. He was caught stealing in stores repeatedly. By the end of the next year the court had twice put him on probation for a number of delinquent acts. At the same time he began to read, write, and do arithmetic.

At one point he took me to an automobile graveyard where, in secrecy and utter silence, he often smashed car windows and hurled rocks against their bodies to his heart's content. When I was with him I encouraged him to vocalize and he screamed sounds and words along with his actions while in fantasy he cursed and destroyed his enemies. His letting go of his voice and actions began to visibly thaw out chronic muscular contractions in his face, neck, and back. I saw him as a mean Don Quixote, an image he seemed to relish. Some of his stunts were more than usually hair-raising, like throwing bottles down an elevator shaft. His academic interests, however, continued to mount and his body became more pliable and loose. He had dreams of falling and we speculated on the meanings of descent. We made up endless stories about up and down. He no longer got caught when he stole things and his tendency to get into accidents faded away. When he sought self-comfort he often allowed one of us to hold him.

Tom was literate and ready to try a normal class by the age of 13. After 13 he began to appear more thoughtful and pleasant. His stealing subsided and virtually ceased. The major channel for his psychopathy appeared to be a winning manner with girls. At last reports he completed high school, held several jobs, and decided to take technical training for TV repair work. Although he might not be symptom free, he apparently had outgrown his early withdrawal and subsequent delinquency. A natural peaking of his withdrawal and then of his delinquency seemed to occur. Yet without therapy it is unlikely such a "natural" sequence would have been achieved. The chances seem good that he would have remained in a deteriorated position or, at least, stabilized at a lower level of functioning than the one he appears to have attained. He, of course, continued therapy with someone else after he and his family moved away from the city.

Throughout my time with Tom I felt I was part of a most subtle steering process. It was as though I had become "locked in" with his evolving, in some sense one of its eyes. Although I was outside it—had the process failed he would have gone his way and I mine, just as in success—there was consubstantiation of a highly specialized sort. It felt as though his ego lodged in me as I did repair work on it, poking about as needed until the operation or psychic chiropractic was over. I could not rush the process; the fever had to peak in its own way and time. But without an adequate sustaining stimulus, a "good enough" therapist, it is not likely it could have evolved so economically.[2]

Ann entered treatment on the advice of a priest friend. She had tried to become a nun but failed because of strong sexual feelings. Once in New York she became promiscuous. She also did some jazz singing and eventually became part of a drug culture which, through one of her boyfriends, led to some prostitution, stealing, and heavy dealing. Throughout this period she deeply missed her religion and was acutely pained at not being able to take communion. Twice, out of a love of God she could not hold back, she could not help taking communion even though she was not supposed to since she was living in mortal sin.

Ann was raised in a southwest Protestant community in a shacklike house on the outskirts of town. She was, therefore, in a minority group and poor, and felt like an alien. Her father was crippled and her mother earned what livelihood she could until the boys were old enough to contribute money. Ann was raised with five brothers. At home she tended her father whom she found a gentle though bitter man. She really liked most of her brothers and the feeling of aliveness they gave off. In horseplay she tried to be one of them, but they teased her because she was the only girl. She said she enjoyed that too. Later she transferred her feeling of aliveness with them to other men. Sex became a light in her life. At no time during her "illness" did she betray her enjoyment of it. She had found in it a revelation of intense joy and love in the most concretized way possible.

---

[2]The notion of the "good enough" therapist refers to Winnicott's (1958, 1965) descriptions of the "good enough mother."

During therapy Ann revealed a need to let herself fall until she found bottom. She wanted to debase herself to the point where nothing could debase her further. She courted acts and dangers inherently repulsive to her in order to distort herself beyond recognition. She wanted, literally, to feel unrecognizable, a kind of maniacal self-obliteration. Yet each time she performed some new immolation she would feel, "Now I've done it. This time I've really gone *too* far . . . Now I've *really* lost Him . . ." When the experience settled, as it always did, however traumatic the aftermath, He would surface again, bobbing up wherever she thought she had lost Him. For her this was a surprise, perhaps her critical learning. Although she could twist herself beyond self-recognition, He still recognized her; she could alienate herself but not Him. There was nothing she could do so revolting that it would lose His love, no matter what gap she tried to drive between herself and the acceptable.

It began to dawn on her that her downward spiral expressed a drive for self-purification. She felt her "evil thread" would lead her to her zero point by somehow burning herself out. She had become a kind of caricature or distorted mirror of her sick spot with the hidden hope of getting back to the place her sense of inferiority emanated from, where she might start from scratch. At the same time she was testing God to see if He *really* loved her for herself alone. Each time she lost Him and He found her again, she wept and laughed with gratitude and lost Him again, over and over, until the reality struck home. I was reminded of a young woman I once knew who flunked out of college to see if her parents still would accept her. After convincing herself they did, she returned to and finished school.

In the process Ann learned there was no experience her life could bring forth that she could not assimilate. Therapy created a situation in which she could integrate and go beyond her need to experience herself as a sinner. She did not wish to be analyzed in any usual sense. She was psychologically sophisticated and did not want any treatment that sounded psychological to her. Yet she did want a place, a contact where she could be, unravel, and gradually experience herself anew. There is no doubt she would have left a treatment which did not respect her point of departure. She wanted a sense of deeper significance without psychodynamics and in our attempt to find our way into this we both felt involved in a process with intrinsic meaning. For the most part we worked within her religious and everyday language. In her refusal to define God in terms of her doubts and fears she was driven to tests of masochistic-psychopathic self-destruction until, ultimately, God defined Himself through her as that which she really *knew* He was.

Eventually she married, apparently happily, and settled in a large western city. Her need for convent life was satisfied in doing charity work for a sisterhood. Her total time in New York was a little over four years, although it seemed so much longer. She left a year after narrowly escaping a sentence for dealing, which she avoided by a boyfriend's prudently turning state's evidence.

Again, as with Tom, working with her was like nursing a storm. I had the feeling my fingers were on the pulse of the storm and that though I could not control it I had some influence inside it. Something in Ann may have been appeased by our attempts to subtitle the storm's progress, giving it a context beyond itself. In some ways we did not seem to do more than ride it out. Reality put the finishing touches on when she was apprehended. Yet reality cannot completely account for the reversal. It was not a totally blind riding. We each had the feeling that we were doing what we had to do and that when the time came the next thing would happen. Even from the outset there was a vaguely sensed direction toward an end point and even in the downward spin one could sense an ultimate reversal. I would think something in this shared sensing, a sort of seeing through and subtle mutual steering, helped make the difference. The autonomic feeling was akin to "body English," the gesture one makes after a ball is released to help it find target, a rapt and muted cognition not quite like the usual sharing with friends.

Ken was an ambitious and talented but apparently paralyzed man who could not use himself effectively in life. When I met him he had twice failed his doctoral exams and had been hanging on in graduate school almost nine years. I thought it odd he wanted to work with me since I, too, had difficulty with my doctorate (I completed a psychoanalytic psychotherapy program before my doctorate). I cautioned him that his choice of analyst was strange under the circumstance, but we persevered for several years.

It was no secret that I admired his gifts and was often stunned by his perceptions of others and himself. I thought him creative, independent of his grandiosity, and I felt puzzled and pained that he so shortchanged himself in life. I also could identify with his need for honesty and the trouble it often led him into.

As it turned out, his obsession with integrity became a central focus of our time together. Throughout his life he had sided with his integrity and directed his anger against the system. He felt the teachers he met were less advanced and honest than he and that they would reject him if he did not cater to their egos. He systematically suppressed his powers in order to get along with them. The outcome was they found him arrogant and reacted against him. However, he also found himself lacking and inhibited in terms of his ideal visions. He lived in a mental world governed by an intolerant schoolmaster. As sessions progressed his feelings oscillated between whining self-pity and bitter resentment.

As he gave full expression to his hate and self-pity he gradually began to feel victimized by his idealized sense of integrity, as well as by the system. He felt caught between two tyrants, reality and what he most treasured in himself. The academic system did not reward him for what he considered his real work. In his phrase, "It broke the back of the honest man." On the other hand he could not deny that his teachers were right about his arrogance. Several dreams confirmed and deepened his predicament.

In one dream his integrity appeared as a cross he carried. When he climbed up on the cross his most vivid feeling was one of being above others. At some point he began to fly and on the cross below was printed the word, "Megalomania." Soon afterward he had several dreams in which he had to exert himself against obstacles and dangers. In one dream his powers were inadequate and he seemed just about to fail when a fox saved him. With that he understood that in his mental conceit he had placed himself above cunning and that he needed to develop practical shrewdness in order to survive.

As his idealization of integrity, partly a reaction formation, began to crack he held onto and cultivated his emerging identification with the fox. Early childhood events and patterns became relevant. His previous repudiation and repression of the function embodied by the fox had been tied to an overly rapid and acute disillusionment with his father, his early representative of the practical world.

Self-protectively he idealized good aspects of his relationship with his mother which he reworked into a needed substitute for the father by means of a vision of the "good mind." By turning from father to mind Ken ensured his independence. His idealization of mind, moreover, provided a durable form for the emotion which had been most precious early in life, his good feelings with his mother.

Once beginning a dialogue with his fox he managed to cheat his way through graduate school in a comparatively short time. He rationalized his action saying the system was not worth more of a commitment since it punished him for his best efforts. Because his integrity and vision of the Good were quite real, he suffered intense pain and guilt over his actions. However, he refused to give in to this guilt. He held fast and grimly moved with or through it, no matter what the cost. He depersonalized himself to accomplish what he felt he had to, becoming, as he said, "stone cold." The crucifixion he had attempted to escape by turning to the fox had overtaken him through the fox itself.

Nevertheless, whatever his psychopathy cost him, on a human level he felt he had made some unexpected and lasting gains. He had never been so tolerant of people. Apparently self-betrayal helped open him to a more profound understanding of human fault. He found himself experiencing other lives and failings with a new empathy and humor. He gained more distance from himself through having to forgive himself for the hardening of his will. Further, his remaining resolute and sustaining the full impact of his guilt strengthened him. By betraying his ideals while at the same time remaining attached and dedicated to them he was forced to draw on a strength he did not know he had, or rather, which he had only sensed but did not have to use before. Even so, he did not give up hoping. He hoped against hope it would someday work out that he could live at one with his daimon and achieve his creative vision with genuine, not brittle, integrity.

Ken left treatment with me shortly after achieving his doctorate, beginning life anew. He has had several therapists since and we have kept in contact. Some of his early professional work was not free from liberties taken with the material but his creative work since has moved forward and, to my mind at least, has justified his early "sins." With success his need for psychopathic manipulation has subsided into the background or, perhaps, has been transformed into realistic effectiveness. It seems he has acquired something of a simple, straightforward practicality which helps mediate his creative listening.

Whether Ken's extended psychopathic episode could have been avoided is an open question. I do not feel I condoned or condemned his psychopathy as such. I did like and appreciate the release of his energy, the undoing of his inhibition toward life, although I also experienced fright and sorrow over the form it seemed to have to take or pass through. Still, given the limitation of our personalities, it seems clear this phase contributed radically to Ken's development. Ken's therapy catered to the release of his powers, whatever form they took—insurance against his leaving treatment cured but dull. The faith is when goodness comes it will be the richer, the goodness of experience. This path clearly supports Freud's propaedeutic dictum that uncensoring awareness—the cognitive essence of compassion—is a critical condition for the profound unfolding of the patient's experience and for the analyst's comprehension of it.

In each of the cases presented the patient's psychopathy was experienced as a natural, inevitable phase of a total process. It began gradually or explosively, built up to a sustained, fairly long-lasting peak, and with periodic bursts, subsided, its purpose apparently accomplished. A teleological sense was part of the experience. Once accomplished the powers, energies, or functions released took their place as a part of the total personality, some deep-seated dissociation overcome or diminished. Deep aggression was liberated and tested out in the form of outright hostility, trickery and deception, or defiant self-hatred. Since an important tendency previously left out of development now entered into communion with and eventually was balanced by other aspects of the self, it could begin to undergo transformation into the active virtue it pointed to: realistic effectiveness and practical self-assertion. The hold of guilt or idealized goodness was, in some instances, self-consciously defied, broken down by means of systematic or persistent immoral and criminal acts. As past identifications broke down, a more fully human sense of self, linked with the capacity for self-forgiveness, emerged. In certain important respects a morality beyond guilt, based on a sense of existential brotherhood, spontaneously appeared to develop. The main thrust of the patients' immoral and criminal actions seemed to reflect a determined concretizing of the right to be and the ability to do, the "I am" and "I can." Perhaps it was the "I can" which received the greater emphasis (in Ann's case, "I can be what I am").

One person's dream at a turning point in therapy succinctly captures the meaning of this process. The patient, Norma, suffered from a serious mind-body dissociation. She walked about vaguely detached from her body, flying overhead or picturing herself observing others while dead. At night she woke up terrified, feeling her mind leaving her body, certain the instant it fully left she would die. A consultant suspected Norma had a special form of epilepsy, but the neurological examination was negative.

At a point in therapy after having a number of dreams in which she was drugged or induced into drugged states by the devil, she dreamt a crook stole some money from a mental health institution. His girl friend, apparently a drug addict, saw the money and said, "We'll buy really good dope with this, not the cheap kind." The crook laughed at the girl as though suddenly waking up, saying, "You're an addict. I don't need you. You've got to be kidding. I'm not going to marry you."

Through this active criminal impulse, fed by therapy (the mental health institution), Norma began to see through and experience powers beyond her hapless passivity. The deceitful criminal was a kind of transition point or elemental missing link between mind and body. He represented tricky, deceitful mind (or one experienced as such) combined with aggressive action, a primitive surge of the right to be, to do, and to have, the will not to be submerged. This dream came after Norma's "splitting" already had begun to diminish, and since the general time of the dream, now almost a year, no further night splitting has recurred. My own reaction to the coming of the criminal was a sigh of relief. I felt some reassurance that Norma's therapy was likely to succeed. The psychopathic phases in each of the instances described above functioned as transition points in bringing about a closer and better mind-body relationship.

Although the purpose of this paper is not primarily theoretical, some indication can be given concerning the psychological area the phenomena described appear to engage. In the cases presented phases of psychopathic acting out were in the service of repairing chronic narcissistic injury or the sense of injury. Psychopathic activity while the person was involved in therapy helped the damaged or constricted ego to enter and experience embodied or worldly life more thoroughly. Whatever autistic use was made of bodily existence in the process, the patients' worldly horizons were vastly extended. Their ability to be in the world significantly increased in quality and extent.

In an overlapping context Kohut (1971) calls attention to the lying and delinquent acts which may occur in initial or transitional phases in working with the "grandiose self." Such self-expressions may be secondary offshoots on the way toward releasing and consolidating the patient's creativity. Kohut notes that an attitude of "benevolent acceptance" is a prerequisite for the emergence and, ultimately, the adequate analysis and resolution of the need for these actions. He points out the destructive and inhibiting effects a prematurely realistic or moralistic attitude on the part of the analyst can have. Balint's (1968) descriptions of his work with pre-oedipal experience in some respects covers similar ground. He points out the danger of trying to interpret or organize the patient's experience when what is needed is an open mood or atmosphere for it to evolve in. He also notes that creative and restorative actions may be immoral or amoral as well as moral, and require time and knowledgeable flexibility on the part of the therapist.

In work with stifled or overt grandiosity one frequently unearths the secret sense of being a god or godlike with the rights and privileges taken as a matter of course by a special being. The grandiose self, as Kohut points out, often needs mirroring from others in order to augment its sense of coherence. For Winnicott (1958, 1965), in cases where the patient's infantile omnipotence has been pathologically obstructed and inverted, the responsive analyst in some sense allows himself to be created by the patient's omnipotence in order to allow the proper development and outgrowing. Balint (1968) likens the analyst on this level to natural elements such as air or water through which the patient can safely experience the "interpenetrating harmonious mix-up" of self and environment. As the patient changes, the therapist naturally shifts in location on the distance–closeness continuum and in the kinds of responses he offers. In time the patient will develop a genuine wish to see the therapist as a real person and will demand less "preciousness." A flexible back and forth between subject- and object-oriented responses is required throughout treatment. Needless to say, the therapist must carefully monitor his own reactions to avoid: (1) destructive acting out because of his own impatience and indignation; or (2) the unconscious provocation of the patient's acting out in order to allay his, the therapist's, sense of impotence and disorganization.

Among other issues not taken up in detail in the present paper are the questions of patient likeability and therapist responsibility. The patients described in this paper were all basically likeable. Perhaps, therefore, their actions could be ridden out without too much difficulty — if one takes for granted that therapy here takes place on a kind of electrified tightrope. Whatever these people did one wished them well. This seems fairly easy to do with someone blocked who wants to be free. But what if a Hitler comes into the office? Is likeability really significant in all cases? Perhaps every patient is likeable by some therapist somewhere, if not oneself. How far can, should, or must one say yes? What ethical responsibility does the therapist have when he plays host to psychopathic tendencies, especially in the case of failure?

The therapeutic relationship is not society at large but a place to throw off and become free from mass psychology. Whatever the misuses and limitations of our work, it seems to offer the most reliable means of beneficial personality change today, perhaps more reliable than any secular therapy previously known — at least where quality work with individuals is concerned. The quality of any therapeutic outcome is likely to be affected by the nature of the therapist's experiencing and handling of asocial tendencies. It seems particularly important for the therapist to be able to recognize when asocial behavior manifested by the patient is part of a deep-seated regeneration process. To amplify Freud, psychopathic as well as schizoid needs cannot be transformed in absentia or in effigy. The question, at what risks, remains open to new definition in each therapeutic situation.

REFERENCES

Balint, M. (1968). *The Basic Fault: Therapeutic Aspects of Regression.* London: Tavistock.

Eigen, M. (1973). Abstinence and the schizoid ego. *International Journal of Psycho-Analysis* 54:493–498.

Elkin, H. (1972). On selfhood and the development of ego structures in infancy. *Psychoanalytic Review* 59:389–416.

Kohut, H. (1971). *The Analysis of the Self.* New York: International Universities Press.

Winnicott, D. W. (1958). *Collected Papers.* New York: Basic Books.

———— (1965). *Maturational Processes and the Facilitating Environment.* New York: International Universities Press.

3

The Recoil on Having Another Person

In both clinical practice and everyday life one frequently encounters persons who quickly lose interest in others once the other is known, "solved," or "had." It is as though the other is interesting as long as he is far, little known, or perceived as unattainable. Once he is near, known, and in some sense mastered or seen as comfortably human, he tends to become a dead spot in one's interest and passed by as no longer live currency.

An often-present aspect of this experience is a sensed loss of freedom after acquiring inner power over the other or the representation of him. One then breaks relationship in an attempt to reestablish the feeling of freedom which this grasp on the other deadened, contrary to the expectancy that mastery enhances freedom. In fact, feelings of freedom do accompany the initial moments of such moves toward, but unless sustained by some form of manic denial, such a person ends more narrowly encircled in isolation.

R. was an art dealer in his mid-thirties who ran through close friendships with innumerable artists of both sexes, both successful and unsuccessful people. Although he often campaigned energetically to win his chosen targets, when he gained someone's intimacy he lost interest in the person. He came to therapy because he felt he was too mistake-prone in the financial aspect of his business, a tendency he believed kept him from becoming more than moderately successful. That his relationships with others lacked a basic stability (perhaps the pattern of finding-having-dropping was the most stable aspect) did not seem to bother him. He rationalized his labile style as expressive of vigor and a growing interest in all life. There would be time enough to settle down and become dull when he was older. Now was still the time for adventure and exploration.

Therapy of necessity focused on the possible underlying themes which might be related to his business block and R., in part because of his adroitness in mental engineering, became expert at interpreting his need or wish to fail, fear of success, guilt, and self-punitiveness, sense of unworthiness, difficulties with competing and surpassing, and so on. In fact, his tendency to make poor judgments diminished and his business ability improved. Attempts to link his problems in business with his more general style of relationship met with resistance. He would only work piecemeal.

An unexpected situation eventually brought R.'s way of being with others into primary focus. It happened that he conceived an intense desire for social intimacy with two male artists, N. and K., but succeeded only with N. In an absolute sense he did not fail with K.; K. was basically friendly toward R. but did not enter into the kind of intimacy R. was courting. As might be predicted R.'s interest waned for N. and quickened for K. However, it began to haunt him that, so far as he could tell, the qualities of these two men were objectively on a par. Neither was, so far as he could judge, superior to the other. Their basic difference for him was that one said "yes" and one said "no." In fact, he regretted the waning of his feelings for the man who was attainable, for he highly prized N.'s good qualities. R. felt his need to give N. up as a personal loss, as much a loss as not attaining K. This experiential quality of being caught between two losses is what baffled him and turned him back upon himself. That is, the sustained simultaneity of wanting but having to lose both persons, one because he was always just beyond his reach and the other because he was within it, forced him to radically question himself.

R. ran through a number of possible explanations for his behavior and began to link them with his problems in business. He saw himself as afraid of closeness, needing distance, having to prove himself, trying to make the rejecting parent accept him, and the like. He often appeared able to help himself by rehearsing what he called his "slogan about himself." It seemed a form of rigid play. He floated somewhere between name-calling and actually experiencing what he called himself. He related the qualities he described to his past and brought up important memories he had never been able to deal with properly before. However, he was too impatient to await the outcome of a long therapy. The two men he was caught up with were important in his life *now*. In R.'s case patience seemed poor, if inevitable, counsel and would perhaps provoke him to terminate therapy. R.'s desire to "solve" his relationship with these two particular men took on a sense of urgency which his presenting business problems never seemed to have.

R.'s therapy began to involve focusing and meditating on selected or spontaneous images, the thoughts and feelings they gave rise to, and the changes they underwent. We set various exercises centered on K. and N. taken singly and together from different points of view. During a critical session R. pictured both K. and N. giving art exhibits under the same roof but in different parts of the gallery. N.'s paintings were warmer and more popular, attracting crowds of admirers. He quickly became known as a true humanist with universal appeal. K.'s paintings were more difficult, more primitive, something like cave paintings, only less familiar. It was as though he had passed through the books of the

East into depths of stone ruins and brought back something hard to decipher, a kind of esoteric archeology with an aura of psychological or possibly religious significance. His works did not attract nearly so many viewers as N.'s and the few K. did attract were mostly young students. R. was annoyed and impatient with the crowds in N.'s part of the gallery and spent most of his time in K.'s area. He and the students enjoyed K.'s works without quite deciphering them.

The core incongruity was the crowd around N. and the space around K., the opposite of R.'s manifest feelings. R. at first thought he was expressing hostility toward K., getting revenge by punishing him with a sparse audience. That, however, did not satisfy the sense of density versus airiness, or closed versus open space, without remainder. As he repeatedly concentrated on the different affective weights "beneath" these images, the following line of thought began to develop. "I feel crowded by N. but have plenty of space with K. . . . but N. does nothing to crowd me really . . . he is the one who is being crowded . . . I am crowding N. . . . I have more air to breathe with K. . . . I can't crowd K. . . ." A decisive meaning of K. being always just beyond his grasp struck home: "I like K. because I can't lose myself with him . . . I swallow up my freedom in feeling I have N. . . . I can't use my freedom up with K. . . . I can always keep going toward K. . . ." That is, it was not simply R.'s having N. that made N. uninteresting. N. staled because, in allowing himself to be had, he left no room for R. to move toward him. K.'s being out of reach guaranteed the distance which makes approach possible. N.'s being within reach used up this distance, thus ending all possible approach. R. can always keep going toward K. It was the distance and not the nonhaveable *per se* which enticed and made good R.'s possibility of movement toward K. by leaving always a little more to go. R.'s basic goal was not possession but movement toward. That is, he was not trying merely to get or have. His aim was precisely the gap of nonpossession, the lack which provided the possibility for him to always keep coming back for more.

The revelation of R.'s desire to be able always to move toward, which amounts to being able always to come a little closer, constituted a momentary end-point which opened a way both back and forward.

As a view backward it transformed an unstable past of disconnected relationships into a meaningful aim. The restless one-after-another which had characterized R.'s life now took on the unitary glow of a blind, repetitive struggle toward the discovery of approach. In making this central striving explicit his urge to fail in business deepened in significance. Success had meant closing possibilities, ending distance, while in failing, R. could seem to be always starting anew. R. experienced failure as keeping approach alive.

As a view forward the discovery of the life of approach opened a program to be embodied. The work of therapy, for example, could take a direction not limited to practical-social success or failure as R. grew more sensitive to matters of character. Similarly, the idea of experimenting with new ways of being with people like K. became more attractive and necessary. To sustain a friendship with N. was, further, accepted as a challenge (here R. would have to conserve distance so N. could approach).

R.'s reversal appears to have been motivated by what was novel in the therapy relationship. In the past R. generally picked people he could probably win on his terms. This seemed to happen automatically as part of his style. The sort of relationship which obtained in therapy — the therapist, like K., was friendly but ungraspable — provided the structural form or setting underlying R.'s initially "blind" attraction to the new mode of relating represented by K. With K., R. could begin to generalize or live out specific feelings evoked by the therapy situation which combined the archaic and the wise with the future, as in the dream-fantasy above. Approach presupposes temporal integration, a reaching-out of the past through and from the present to the future. Approach is "defined" by the future. Insofar as K., like the therapist, made approach possible, he was expressive of the future. N., closing approach, symbolized the past (R. could preserve a relationship with N. only by becoming N.'s future). The temporal meaning of each relationship determined who was sought or left behind. It often is the temporal meaning of the other which determines the direction we will take with him.

4

Working with "Unwanted" Patients

The "unwanted" patient often goes through trials in trying to find a therapist who can and will work with him that are similar to those he encounters in trying to find people who are able to sustain benign interactions with him in his daily life. These patients tend to drive therapists away as they do people in general. They generally present severe narcissistic character deformations which are more than usually exasperating or repulsive. They may oscillate between an overcloying and obnoxiously negativistic manner in apparently endless repetition of extreme forms of hostile dependence. They can appear needy and demanding yet seem to present intractable resistances if one tries to help them. In some instances they may appear snakelike and cynically chilling. If they are vegetative, they are also willful and proud, even when in seemingly masochistic and silent ways. They are very sensitive to slights but seem to have long ago accepted that the best they can do is just manage to get through things. They carry a hope tinged with resentment, made heavy with an accusing sense of deprivation and self-pity. They seek relief from pain but have a high tolerance for feeling that things will never change and nothing good can happen to them. However, all this despair seems part of an atmosphere of muted want and rage. Their identity is formed by a chronic sense of injury together with a primitive union with the phallic mother — male or female — who injured them. Thus one moment they may enact the role of helpless victim and then become a terrifying active mass — impulsive, tyrannical, or biting. Their personality deformations, further, frequently express themselves in physically unappealing ways, such as unkempt obesity or severely distorting facial and postural rigidities. In these cases the actual body has become closely identified with and formed by a negative self-image.

In general, these patients tend to evoke some sense of distaste in the therapists who try to treat them. Their basically constricted ways of behaving seem to set off and accentuate their psychophysical distortions and tend to have a constricting-distorting effect on others, including the therapist. Their frequent use of denial and externalization may habitually frustrate the therapist who is primarily interested in verbal reports of inner experience. The therapist will find it difficult not to experience some form of disgust or anger as treatment develops. He may try to defend himself by becoming sleepy or bored or subtly fight to maintain his sense of boundaries in a pedagogical way. However, he cannot help these patients by remaining emotionally uninvolved. As in work with children and psychotics, suitable cognitive-affective responses are required for maximal healing to occur. The problem facing the therapist is how to provide the specific emotional responses which will facilitate the patient's growth when the instinctive responses the patient evokes are largely negative. The patient who appears gross, dull, chilling, or otherwise "impossible" and yet seeks genuine help (in however magical a way) presents a radical challenge to the well-meaning practitioner's image of himself and therapy.

The problem appears particularly acute in light of the theory of introjects. Part of the therapeutic process may involve introjecting the therapist in a way which builds up the patient's good object representations. The ego's increasing relationship with a good object offsets the power of inner bad objects and diminishes its addiction to them (Klein 1948, Eigen 1974b). If the patient needs to introject the therapist as a transitional means of building his ego, he had best make part of himself someone who likes him. Robertiello (1971) particularly stresses therapist–patient confluence as a critical factor in the success of this process. If the patient and therapist are too dissimilar on basic dimensions or harbor a repulsion or dislike of one another, referral, Robertiello suggests, is in order. The referral, Robertiello points out, ought to be to someone who can genuinely like the patient and to whom the patient does not feel too dissimilar. In this regard Henry and colleagues (1973) have demonstrated that therapist-patient similarity (religiocultural) is an important factor in spontaneous patient selection.

Unfortunately, the theoretical, clinical, and human situation is not always so clear. In the course of getting to know someone, liking may turn to dislike and vice versa. One may, also, like someone and still not be able to work well with him. In certain instances liking may tend to inhibit incisive therapeutic responses and make one's work more lax, while dislike can keep the therapist alert and add extra reason to work more carefully. My experience, moreover, has not indicated a clear correlation between liking and cure or dislike and failure. Well-liked patients have stalled in treatment or left, some possibly threatened by my liking them. And patients whom I have disliked have flourished. To be sure, the other two possibilities have occurred as well. Patients I have liked have done well and I have managed, one way or another, to get rid of others with whom I did not want to deal. Similarly, when I canvassed colleagues mixed results were reported. Many seem to have had experiences akin to mine. However, a number felt that patients whom they like do best. These therapists try to refer patients they do not like to someone who might like them, something not always possible.

Some frankly admit that they have "put in their time" and now want to see only people they enjoy. However, other therapists with no less experience still prefer, given the limits of their time, to take all comers.

A relaxed and hedonistic approach to case selection can have the good effect of helping to demystify the therapy situation and foster more open personal honesty. On the other hand, the adage that everyone is likeable to someone can often prove cruel and glibly misleading in practice. The undue "therapist-hopping" that relatively unwanted patients may be forced to go through can become too costly in every sense. In a clinical setting, for example, these patients frequently outstay several generations of therapists and are rarely taken by a therapist when the latter leaves for private practice. By means of multiple rejections the analytic world colludes in aiding these patients to continue to act out their pattern of provocativeness and cynical defeat. In spite of the apparent tenacity of their bitterness and sense of hopelessness these patients often feel lucky when they chance upon an analyst who says, "The buck stops here."

Perhaps the most fundamental consideration of all is that the distaste or dislike a patient may evoke can assume an important clinical function. It often serves as a signal to keep one's distance in spite of the patient's protestations to the contrary. It is a warning that too much closeness is dangerous and undesirable. The hard-core resistant patient may say that he wants closeness more than anything in the world and is angry with the therapist for remaining elusive. However, should the therapist give in and become obliging, a reversal frequently occurs. The patient may be forced to regain the distance the therapist gives up by becoming contemptuous of and rejecting the therapist. When, in turn, the patient becomes ungiving, he may secretly expect and want the therapist to beg and plead with him. It is as though there exists a quota of distance which must be fulfilled and spontaneous fluctuations in the balance of power conspire to ensure that space (see Eigen 1973a for an account of this phenomenon with reference to time experience).

In supervision one often must deal with the therapist's rage which is the consequence of failing to take the principle of this pattern clearly into account. A therapist may have an expectation that his warmth and concern will be responded to in kind and is hurt and furious that the patient mocks him. As the therapist consciously lives through this vicious circle enough times, he begins to telescope and develop increasing control over its negative impact. In effect, he reduces the intensity of dislike or distaste a patient can evoke in him. In so doing, however, he becomes more sensitive to the various nuances of negative feelings the patient can stimulate and his interventions become more highly differentiated. Although with successful experience it may become more difficult to genuinely dislike a patient, the therapist learns to modulate his show of liking in a way that fits the patient's ability to process positive feelings. As the therapist develops an accurate trust in himself, his contact with his sense of basic love becomes more constant but is appropriately tempered and adapted to the patient's need for hate and distance. In time the patient converts his frustrating experience of the analyst's paradoxical restraint into the beginnings of self-respect.

The present paper develops the above themes with reference to specific patients who were difficult to be with. Attention is given to the principal psychodynamics which characterize the patients, the correlative feelings and attitudes evoked in the analyst, and some of the directions taken by therapeutic responses which proved effective. In addition, general problems of case management are discussed and, finally, specific issues regarding the benefits and dangers one finds in this kind of work are raised.

An unpleasantly obese woman, who scarcely seemed to take care of herself, initiated her therapy with repetitive complaints and demands concerning everyone around her. She was filled with self-pity and chronic hatred toward herself and others. No one seemed to care about her and she less about herself or them. Her husband no longer approached her sexually and she continued to put on still more weight, feeling deprived and resentful. She seemed to cover herself with her flesh in passive defiance and frequently smelled badly. It was as though she were trying to be provocatively nauseating. Moreover, it was not her obesity itself which was disgusting, since fat women can be vibrant and appealing. It was her spirit, limp and decaying, which turned her body into an oppressive mass.

Her complaints, apparently oral, involved a profound anal component. One had the vivid impression that she experienced herself as feces and that the food she fed herself was a form of feces and she the toilet. The course of her analysis verified that her oral life was anally identified. In severe pathology the anal is often structurally more primitive though temporally later than the oral, although both dimensions tend to assimilate each other (Ehrenzweig 1967).

After several months of sitting through a repetitive verbal barrage and constant complaints, something genuinely interesting happened. The patient revealed that although she knew she was disgustingly fat and put off people with her appearance and behavior, she did not really believe or see herself as fat. In her wallet she carried a picture of herself taken ten years earlier, when she was 19 years old. Her hair was a wavy strawberry blond (not the straw sticks she now displayed) and her figure was well within normal range and attractive. This, she claimed, was the real she, the person she saw in her mind's eye throughout the intervening years and who she still believed she was. She disclosed that when she was certain she was alone she would often open her arms and gracefully dance about the room, spinning and swaying to her heart's content. Only in those moments could she feel truly herself.

As her confidence in me strengthened, her wish to show me her dance grew. She wanted me to see her as she saw herself. She began to speak with baby-face appeal and soon felt impelled to dance in session. As it turned out, her dance was as graceful as she had boasted, poignantly so. Yet for a moment while I was watching her I could not help thinking of Charlie Chaplin as Hitler performing a ballet holding a globe of the world. She danced on and I allowed myself to be drawn in, so taken with her expressive gestures and rhythms that I, too, forgot she was fat and saw only a thin, young woman. She had turned into her fantasy which, for a time, became the true reality for both of us.

Afterwards she suggested that one reason she had been unable to keep a diet was that she did not believe she was fat. She could not admit the pain of owning her bodily distortion. She broke down and wept and, frightened, begged for help. For some time she had known she was afraid without allowing herself to actively acknowledge it. Without having the means or daring to formulate it, she had been afraid that she could not tell the difference between what was real and what she only imagined. To complicate her dilemma further, her "unreal" outer form conveyed important inner realities. Her obesity gave a distorted expression to her deep narcissistic and exhibitionistic needs. It was something everyone could see. It also expressed ugly feelings about herself she could not deal with and had to keep hidden. Through her unkempt obesity she called attention to the fact that her feelings about herself and others were in danger and that she needed help.

Her analysis indicated that she had early experienced but attempted to deny a sense of damage vis à vis a traumatically intrusive mother. She tried to master her underlying intimation of weakness by simultaneously incorporating and expelling the phallic maternal image by means of an oral–anal fusion. For example, her mouth was experienced as a retentive, sucking anus which took in feces-food and expelled words. Fantasies of an oral–anal inversion also occurred in which intake occurred through the anal mouth and expulsion through the oral anus. Therapy also included working through the ego's identification with bisexual images associated with giving in to and the fight against the phallic aspect of mother. The overall context for this work was a therapeutic relationship through which object longing and anxiety related to fantasies of mutual destructiveness could be integrated. As the patient was gradually able to overcome the gross discordance between her imaginary and actual bodies, she became more likeable. Eventually she was able to tolerate and enjoy being attractive to her husband and participating in other basic life satisfactions.

Only the first two phases of a long-term process were sketched above. The analyst first waited out the discomfort, which the patient's appearance and style evoked, until a genuine gap in her defensive armor appeared. This permitted a moment of "primary identification" with the patient on the analyst's part which, in turn, made it possible for the patient to experience her disorganization and grief more openly. One, of course, moves flexibly along the distance–closeness continuum according to the patient's requirements in a particular treatment phase and from moment to moment. It is as undesirable to deluge the patient with therapeutic openness as it is to starve her with too great austerity. One provides the conditions for a variety of experiences so that the patient has ample opportunity to luxuriate in her hatred on the way to rediscovering the love on which it is based. The therapist attempts to time his use of frustration and gratification in such a way that the patient is able to bring together and begin to integrate polar experiences which were previously dissociated or overwhelming.

In a second case the patient was an isolated young woman who chronically withdrew from contact in an accusing, suspicious manner. She would look at me disdainfully as though she were above and I beneath words. Any move I might make, verbal or nonverbal, was subject to her mute scorn. Her face had an unappealing embryonic quality, as though she were a baby in a test tube, distorted by the glass through which she was seen. She often complained about a tendency to overeat, although from the neck down she was physically attractive. In contrast to the previous case, the split between her body image and physical reality led her to experience herself as too heavy, regardless of the food she denied herself and the weight she lost. Her face was amorphous except for a sharp and frequent expression of distaste. At the same time she acted as though she were "dribbling, pissing and shitting" and expected others (me) to clean her mess. The only sexual act with another person she was capable of enjoying was cunnilingus in which, finally, she could relax and feel powerful and loved. Everything else seemed intrusive and troublesome to her. In the social and vocational spheres she expected success to come to her without active effort on her part and she was highly critical, as well as envious, of the efforts of others.

Her first consistent verbal communications in analysis were to attack me repeatedly for being, as she saw it, a "male chauvinist pig." She felt I wanted her to give in to me and become the kind of patriarchal woman whom, in her eyes, I might value. As therapy progressed she strenuously fought against her urge to give herself up to me in primitive fusion, a repetition of her early relationship with an exploitative mother. She frequently threatened to leave treatment and tested me for a time by storming out of sessions when she felt overirritated by me. It was a good omen when she could tell me that the only reason she stayed with me was because her previous analysts were even worse than I and it would be too uncertain and take too much effort to look for someone new again. I received little encouragement from her and could expect only nettles coupled with her indignant desire for me to seek her out with unfailing, satisfying sensitivity. My perception that I was involved in a trying situation which demanded long-range endurance enabled me to monitor and check my irritation and counterhostility until the appropriate time came to form the latter into useful interventions. My overall feeling was that the task at hand was not a pleasant business but had to be done. We did not pretend great liking for each other but we did begin to develop a mutual patience or tolerance of a sort. She said she tolerated (put up with) me because she wanted to be helped and would have to let someone help her sometime.

She regressed to the point of having to stop her activities and lead an essentially womb-like existence in her small apartment. At first she blamed her regression on me, then on herself, oscillating between externalizing and internalizing the bad object. Finally she perceived her collapse as a consequence of her own psychic reality and historical destiny and came to understand the restorative nature of what she was going through. In time she began to rely and draw on my energy and feelings as though I were an artificial lung. She took on some of my expressions and gestures while, at the same time, her face began to fill out and to lose its squeamish, embryonic appearance. She seemed to acquire volume and tentatively began to explore what she might want to do with her life, gradually approaching life's starting line. However, while she used me to build up her good object representation, she, for some time, showed no less hatred of me. She hated me the more for the grudging dependency her nature forced her to exhibit.

When, later in her analysis, she was able to speak about some of her hidden feelings toward me, she disclosed that she had liked me from the outset. Although she had hated me and knew she had to hate me, a current of liking continued throughout most of the treatment. She revealed that by the middle of our first year together she had begun to feel a secret gratitude for the way I held together in face of her attacks ("holding the position") but she had not been able to express it for fear of sullying her use of the therapy situation. She experienced a certain integrity and as she several times said, "purity," by being able to hate without having to counteract her hatred with displays of love. At those moments the love she felt without risk of intrusion was hers alone. It was the love her mother always tried to take for herself by force or seduction. It had been important that at such junctures I did not try to expressly divine what she was feeling beyond her expression of hate. For had I done so, I would have been like her mother, picking her innermost being against her will.

Her liking me came more as an affective than theoretical surprise. It was the spontaneous liking she had been forced to keep out of her existence. Throughout much of her analysis it was necessary for her to keep me insecure concerning how she felt about me. My allowing myself to experience this induced feeling without caving in helped her to live out and begin to free herself from the mutual terrorizing which characterized her relationship with her parents. The therapy relationship was able to contain such a transference–countertransference pattern and eventually allow it to diminish.

One does not try to discourage the negative transference by prematurely interpreting it. The highly narcissistic patient tends to experience usual interpretations as violations and may harden in masochistic retreat if his sense of violation is systematically exposed. The patient makes important maturational gains by being allowed to have the new sense of energy and freedom his hate brings him vis à vis the therapist. Acceptable interpretations at this point concentrate on helping to deepen the patient's emerging sense of self, introduce the patient to the art of shifting perspectives, and provide an exhilarating taste of the dimension of meaning (Eigen 1973b). More direct interpretations of the negative transference may be used when it is necessary to slow down the pace of treatment or to provide enough of an orientation so that the patient does not feel forced to terminate. If the therapist successfully protects the negative transference, the patient in time spontaneously reveals his vulnerability and longing and himself interprets the self-protective use of his ambivalence. At this point transference analysis is ego-syntonic and the patient can genuinely use his own and the analyst's observations concerning the shifting meanings of their relationship.

A third example is the analysis of a middle-aged man who had previously passed through six therapists, one of whom he had seen for ten years. The patient had a gnomish appearance. His body appeared somewhat bent and twisted, seeming shorter than his actual size. His trunk and pelvis were pinched together and his head squeezed into his shoulders. However, a medical examination revealed no evidence of physical deformity. His chronically spastic body became grossly distorted because of his severely anxious–rigid character structure and its related body armor.

The patient claimed he was worse than before he started any of his therapies. He ominously threatened that he was getting very tired and had little energy left to continue the fight much longer. As he described it, the nightmare of his life went on and on and he felt he was nearing the point of final exhaustion. I began seeing him after his third hospitalization. He did not make the pretense of trying to find work. Previously he had managed to hold one type of menial job or another. Now he announced that he was completely succumbing to his illness. Nevertheless, he did not give the impression that he was completely giving in. He spoke at length about self-control and self-management, using energic and self-regulatory system metaphors. According to him, his past therapists had marveled at his vast store of energy and had told him, "If only you could channel it positively, what you couldn't do." He also felt he had enormous powers of intelligence which remained blocked. He had been unable to develop them because of the negative use to which his energy was put (his description).

He had a loud peremptory manner even while he complained about how badly off he was. In windmill fashion his alternating complaints, protective attempts at self-diagnosis, and expressions of hopelessness kept people in general at a distance (except his mother, with whom he lived). His rapidly shifting moods formed a protective shield around his deeper pathology. One moment he enumerated his flood of symptoms and confusional states and stressed his helplessness in face of them. Moments later his tone took on a boasting, grasping quality as he insisted he ought to be able to control them. He spoke in a monologue broken occasionally only to ask me if I thought I could do anything for him. He would continue in a nonstop fashion and point out that his last two therapists refused to see him when he contacted them for treatment. They offered no adequate explanation. However, he and his first therapist had seemed to like one another but after ten years of agreeable and supportive work the patient felt unchanged and did not wish to return. In actual fact this therapist, too, had advised him to seek help elsewhere. The patient wondered what would happen if he actually could be helped and likened his situation to someone who had spent his life in prison and perhaps was better off inside. The thought of getting better consciously frightened him. On the other hand, he yearned for relief. At some point during a typical session, usually near the end, he would return to his main question and again ask if I thought I could help him. If he paused for an answer I might say, "I don't know. We can try. What do you think?"

The most apparent impulse he induced was the urge to keep one's distance. At the same time, at first without clearly knowing why, I experienced a certain amusement with his manner and style. He presented himself in an incorrigibly loud and ill-fitting extroverted manner, with his eyes bulging and his ears extended from anxiety. As I viewed him I could not suppress images of a kind of restless corkscrew turtle. In some sense he presented himself as a morbid, comic figure.

As it turned out, my reserved amusement provided an opening for him. After asking me whether I could help him, he usually answered himself saying, "Yes. I think you can, though I don't know why I think so. I just have that feeling." At the time, of course, neither he nor I could know what the result of our work together might be. Apparently he used my silent "comic" perception to help place his pathology in a larger perspective. He was also relieved that I was not intimidated by him, or at least did not seem so. Much later he could say that my attitude made him feel that his illness was a secondary offshoot of who he really was, a felt cognition which gave him faith. My distance tinged with humor provided him with room, a reliable space which helped to offset the effects of his mother's impingement. At the same time he had to fight against this space since, given his past life, it created a threatening, although ultimately redeeming, vacuum.

My reserved amusement was, of course, a form of self-protection, at least partially. I found the sessions difficult to get through and frequently found myself clock-watching. I had to protect myself from being inundated by his flood of disorganized thoughts and feelings and the discomfort they could arouse in me. My tolerance for the negative feelings he might induce seemed low, reflecting his own use of denial. In essence, I was in danger of experiencing the attacks he had experienced together with the consequent internalized rage reactions. However, my overt response of reserve tinged with humor, while partly defensive, also provided the patient with a model for a missing function in his behavior. By means of this persona I appeared able to sustain my integrity without being destroyed or destroying, an ability which he began to introject and eventually make part of his own identity.

As the analysis unfolded, my expression and tone seemed to the patient to be more like himself than he was. He confided that my tone and face mirrored a hidden image of himself. In his words I seemed like his "secret, real self," distortion-free. By means of his narcissistic union with the projected ideal image I evoked, he could begin to experience his being without any traumatic sense of otherness. For a time we participated in an ideal union of twins from which genuine difference and relationship could gradually grow. It took some time before I was able to like him spontaneously without simultaneously having to draw back defensively. My growing ability to be with him without constantly having to keep one eye on my defenses reflected his own growing ability to make contact without hiding behind too prohibitive a barrier.

In this case the healing movement was initiated by my partially defensive persona, a dissociated system of feeling and behavior stimulated by the patient's developmental needs. Another type of schizophrenic patient, for example, might have induced a reaction of hushed reserve or respect for fragility (Eigen 1973c, 1974a). In the present instance an unconsciously induced reaction in response to a comic perception of the patient's physiognomy functioned to feed back to the patient a dissociated and poorly developed aspect of his own personality which had not previously received an opportunity to undergo adequate development. A latent and unacknowledged clown-like self image met with an appropriate bemused response. The self-hatred expressed in the image was reflected by the withholding aspect of the analyst's distance and the mocking aspect of his humor. However, the clown is also a cry for love and in this light the analyst's feeling was experienced as a playful and respectful affirmation. The patient was able to create through the analyst a response ambiguously fitting enough to satisfy the patient's multiple but specific therapeutic needs.

The patients in the above examples are, of course, very difficult. They generally externalize their problems and show very little spontaneous interest in intrapsychic processes. They have been forced to undergo gross personality distortions which were patterned after inordinately destructive early object relations. In particular, the ego of these patients exhibits a marked incapacity to process aggressive feelings in wholesome ways. The ego's hate becomes, in part, aimed against its needs and love wishes and, concomitantly, develops a reproachful attitude toward an apparently ungiving or overwhelming world. If the analyst fully exposes himself to the force field of these patients, he will tend to feel injured or drained. The patients themselves have erected barriers to avoid this by repelling those who venture near. At the same time the intensity of their deepest needs compels them to attempt to draw the other into their orbit and merge, a basically incorporative-reparative gesture. Hence the analyst, like the patient, remains in danger of feeling pulled apart by the patient's conflicting tendencies.

The patient may try to escape the tension created by poorly managed antagonistic tendencies by collapsing one or other of the poles of tension or, simply, by leaving the field. He may, for example, try to become part of the analyst, have the analyst become part of himself, or try to drive the analyst away. Since, however, in analysis the analyst remains stationary, in the end the patient drives himself away. The analyst's instinctive repulsion and indignation, often unconscious, with regard to the patient's style, products, and demands, offends the patient's narcissism and provokes retreat. On the other hand, a too nurturant attitude may make the analyst appear too eager and needy (worse than the patient) and also drive the patient away.

While the therapist's instinctive negative reactions cannot be avoided, their effects can be brought under conscious control. One aspect of the therapist's work is to transmute his immediate reactions into conditions for his own and the patient's development. The patient lives within a circle of negative inversions and requires a fair amount of frustration in order to experience ego survival. What makes therapy different from other frustrating situations in the patient's life is, for one thing, the analyst's sustained awareness of the process which is occurring. The therapist can use his negative reactions as possible cues to the dosage of frustration the patient requires at any given moment in order to feel psychologically alive. The maintenance of a trustworthy though appropriately varied quality of frustration assures the patient that the therapist is not going to overwhelm him. Although this frequently angers the patient, the result is a deep feeling of safety. The patient's sense of safety provides a ground from which he can begin to open himself to the positive contact with the therapist that he needs in order to build a good object image.

The relationship between frustration and gratification is not simple and one must live with the paradox that frustration is linked with and made tolerable by still deeper sources of gratification. As treatment progresses one may even elect to frustrate the patient in gratifying ways. For example, a highly resistant patient may be enticed as well as confused or angered by ambiguously meaningful remarks. In certain circumstances the analyst's silence can arouse the patient's curiosity and interest at the same time that it frustrates him. Or, again, the patient may find himself intrigued and stimulated by the therapist's ability to be freely both playful and serious, moving just beyond the patient's grasp.

Therapy provides a healing rather than a toxic frustration in that the patient is enabled to live out his pathology in transference within the framework of a broader, corrective relationship. The therapist, as much as possible, designs his interactions to fit and extend the patient's actual ability to benefit from contact with self or other. In order to accomplish this the therapist allows himself to be led by imagining or observing what spontaneous forms patient–therapist interactions would tend to take if inhibitions were lifted. A type of psychodrama may naturally occur as patient and therapist fluidly move in and out of the roles that are of consequence to the patient's blocks in living (for related studies see Nelson and colleagues 1968, Spotnitz 1969). For example, patient and therapist may vary exciting and rejecting roles, tantalizing and frustrating each other:

P.: I want something from you.
A.: I don't see why I should give you anything. When I don't, you want me more.
P.: Give it to me. This time will be different.
A.: If I want you to want me, I should play it cool. You'll think I don't want you to like me if I do what you say.
P.: Damn that stuff. Just give it to me. Let me worry about it.
A.: Why should you get me? When you have me, you can't stand me.
P.: Why do you always bring up past sins? What's past is past. Maybe this time will do it.
A.: Well, maybe . . .
P.: Got you [laughing foxily, smugly].

In this instance the interaction ended with a momentary closure and release. The therapist might go on playfully to admit defeat, caught liking the patient. At another time he may remain unattainable, barely slipping through the patient's grasp. Similarly, the patient may withhold and the analyst plead. Such interplays of transference-countertransference grow out of primary dramas with aspects of Great Mother figures (for descriptions of the latter see Elkin 1972, Fairbairn 1954). As the interactions progress, it becomes difficult to know who is who between patient, therapist, and parental figures, particularly with reference to erotized images of bad objects. In this transitional, inherently manic phase of treatment, the patient's progress is greatly aided by stimulating a capacity for aggressive intimacy. Destructive tendencies are infiltrated by the good object through a kind of aggressive, loving play which evokes the patient's active *élan*.

More one-sided interventions may be necessary before the patient seeks or can utilize such relatively free-flowing exchanges. Both interpretative and noninterpretative techniques which echo, model, or otherwise dramatize the patient's implicit assumptions may be used to mobilize more varied ego functioning. In one instance, for example, a 35-year-old man repetitiously complained about how bad people were to him. Everyone picked on him, a "pussy." He, in contrast, was good-hearted and would not think of harming anyone. In response to these remarks he had grown accustomed to my silence or occasional questions, which he took as sympathy. He was thus surprised when one day I agreed that he was all good and began to compliment and envy his good heart. My action stood out enough from my earlier behavior to act as an effective stimulus, provoking him to revisualize me. By then the patient had become bound to me through his need and could not simply leave the situation. Because the patient was now deeply involved with me, it follows that seeing me in a new light would lead to a shift in his self-image. At first he could not tell whether or not I was being serious. In order to remain connected with me, he had to process my apparent change of attitude. In this new context his "goody-goody" intention could spontaneously become an object of self-perception rather than merely lived. Although the patient, of course, saw through the sarcasm and expressed annoyance, a shift in cognition had taken place: "If I'm better than you, I must be kidding myself." In this instance the patient reported a visual representation of his goody-goody self flashing before him, then exploding and going up in smoke. He felt pleasantly shocked rather than pained and was impressed enough by this initial glimpse of the observing-experiencing function to take up transcendental meditation for a time.

Another patient obsessively complained that his apartment was horribly messy and filled him with disgust. Its walls were peeling and its furniture and floors were rotting. Cartons were piled up without care and cleaning was neglected. He had promised himself for years that he would correct this but habitually felt overwhelmed by the task and lacked the necessary energy. His year of treatment had brought him to the point where he could contemplate making a beginning but he continued to procrastinate and complain. Finally, based on evidence from his dreams and history, I suggested, "It seems you must keep living in your mother's ass-hole." He reacted with defensive confusion and rightly attacked me for my coarseness. However, during the week the vision of living in his mother's "ass-hole" haunted him and he was compelled to begin to renew his apartment, half out of spite toward me. For a time his impotent obsession turned into a counterphobic compulsion which permitted an advance in his capacity to act. More important, perhaps, were the fantasies and self-experiences which occurred. He began to perceive the anal self-image which governed him, particularly with reference to his mother's body. He had been fused with his mother's anality and, as he put it, could not tell the difference between his mother's ass-hole and his own. He envisioned himself contained within her powerful rectum as her anal baby, his penis her feces seeking the anal womb. He also pictured her in her phallic aspect entering him. However, the most important experience for him at this stage of analysis was his sense that he had never breathed the air outside of his mother's anus. Without his ever clearly realizing it before, the air he breathed and the atmosphere he lived in always had a faint anal scent. Now for the first time he was able to breathe air without smelling feces and genuinely begin to experience open space.

If such interventions as the above are to be maximally effective, a good deal of preparation must go into setting them up. One of the most difficult challenges in the work described is the creation of the context with regard to which the analyst's more sharply outlined interactions achieve optimal power. Much tentative trial and error goes into the highly differentiated responses arrived at for different patients. Not all responses by the analyst will be equally potent, although one may find a range of responses which will work in a given case. The quality of the patient's movement will depend, in part, on the keenness of the analyst's timing and how finely one can finger the latent meanings in the patient's verbal and behavioral communications. For example, after the patient begins to come alive, the phase of aggressive intimacy (described above) may eventually function as a resistance to the next stage. To progress past the phase of aggressive intimacy one would have to recognize and begin to work through the residual manic identification with the aggressor (the therapist) on which the success of such therapeutic role-playing inevitably depends.

A further word about technique. Although this is not the place to enter into a full discussion about the uses and abuses of the couch, it must be pointed out that Freud's distaste for being stared at by patients makes good sense in the case of distasteful patients. The couch facilitates work with such patients and in certain instances is virtually the only way that treatment could be possible. It often takes useless and destructive pressure off both analyst and patient.

For example, an extremely critical and observant woman described her mental life as "thinking in black." She tended to draw others into her blackness in subtle ways. She had a frightening–fascinating serpent stare and a chilling way of speaking. It was difficult to sit still in front of her without a hair-raising feeling. It was clear that her state was chronic and that it would be some time before real movement was possible. When I suggested that she use the couch, she questioned me severely as to why I had not taken any notes (her past therapists had) and concluded that I could not be interested in remembering what she said. She believed that using the couch would give me too good an opportunity to doze off and dismiss her (out of sight, out of mind). She made it clear that she wanted me where she could keep an eye on me. We let it drop but later she returned to the topic and asked me why I had suggested the couch. I said simply, "So you won't have to see my face."

After the session I learned from her intake worker that this patient had originally requested a therapist who was used to working with the sickest people because she feared that no one else would be able to stand her. My reversal of her feeling (which was a reversal of the feeling she induced in me) relieved her and helped her sense we might be able to work together. It supported her defense in a way which made her feel understood. The next session, however, we spent face to face. She filled it speaking about her astrological chart, which was remarkably accurate. I improvised on what she told me, joining her language, and suggested she would have to further develop and integrate her conflicting signs. She opened the succeeding session by saying, "I want to try the couch route." As soon as she lay down, the room perceptibly lightened for both of us, an all-too-great pressure immediately taken off our egos. We could begin to relax a little and allow her therapy to unfold.

In another case a young schizophrenic man was too frightened to use the couch. He would become more paranoid if he lay down. We therefore proceeded face to face. However, his range of thinking and feeling was severely limited, as was his functioning in general. The sessions became progressively deadening. Finally I could not stop myself from starting to doze off. At the end of the second session in which I did this, he managed to confront me about my behavior. I then asked him how he felt about my not being able to keep my eyes open when I was with him. He said, "I feel you don't care. You're not interested in what I'm saying. You can't stand to see me and are trying to shut out the sight and sound of me." The next session the patient asked to use the couch and for the first time he was able to use it successfully. Seeing the effects of the feelings he induced in me had relieved him. It was he who in transference had wanted to shut out the sight and sound of me, an expression of his need to retreat from and annihilate contact with others in order to avoid emotional dangers. My sleepiness mirrored his defense and validated his own lack of emotional contact in a preverbal way, the level which felt most real to him. The couch provided him with the requisite safety and privacy from which he could begin to allow treatment to follow the lines of his actual contact functioning.

Nevertheless, even with the greatly extended range of interventions the analyst now has available and the increased flexibility this gives him, no practitioner can successfully treat every person who seeks his help. There will always be patients for whom referral is the wisest or only choice. For example, in one instance I was literally driven to refer a woman to a colleague when I found that I could not adequately sustain being in the same room with her. She was an extremely interesting patient and I very much wanted to work with her. But the concentration of her kind of toxicity was too high for me to be able to tolerate. Her hatred of men was more total and searing than any I had encountered and I was not ready to deal with it at that time. I referred her to a woman therapist who had difficulty relating to men and the patient has prospered with her.

To be sure, insofar as one has opted for a life of open sensitivity, one's experience of the treatment situation progressively deepens and the range of people one can effectively work with continues to increase. Concordantly, a truly heterogeneous practice offers a powerful vehicle for expanding and deepening oneself.

What, if anything, can the therapist gain by working with patients who arouse distaste?

In a particularly disgusting scene in Jodorowski's film, *El Topo,* the hero sucks and eats a spine-chilling bug as a condition for being spiritually reborn through an old hag. El Topo gets "high" on the bug's juices, which apparently have psychedelic properties, and explicitly enacts being born through the wise old woman. The film as a whole depicts the viscissitudes in a journey through the self which is characterized by ever-deepening interactions between self-assertion and self-effacement. A certain strain of immolation or surrender is necessary in order for the hero to build up a capacity to be creatively responsive to the workings of unconscious processes. It seems like masochism only from the outside. The actual result is an enlargement of the hero's consciousness. In Winnicott's (1958, 1965) terminology, the false self is humiliated and "burnt away" in order to prepare a clearing for the true self. In the case of El Topo, the originally phallic–aggressive hero becomes enlightened by progressively assimilating his dissociated feminine side. It is, largely, androgynous and feminine (or feminine-controlled) figures that he must come to terms with in order to be transformed. Winnicott (1971), Khan (1974), and Eigen (1974b, 1975, 1976) have recently called attention to the therapeutic power one gains by integrating split-off bisexual identifications.

Therapy requires a wise combination of narcissistic wounding and gratification for deep healing to occur. Therapeutic pain is unavoidable. Whatever satisfactions one may enjoy in therapy, a certain quota of pain is attached to the working through of resistances. This, in a sense, is as true for the therapist as for the patient. An ascetic as well as rewarding vein runs through therapy for therapist and patient alike. It is an elementary part of the therapist's trade to learn how to tolerate and utilize being ignored, resented, criticized, and variously abused as well as admired. Perhaps one of the most far-reaching contributions of psychoanalysis to the concept of human relations is its theory of the way in which the helper uses the full range of his thoughts and feelings to further his understanding of the one he helps. The analyst learns to become sensitive to his positive and negative states as a source of intelligence about himself, the patient and the varied forms their relationship assumes. If this is difficult with people with whom one easily feels good, how much more so with someone whose type of ego deformation is seriously off-putting. The analyst learns to discriminate whether the negative feelings he experiences reflect his own idiosyncrasies or is an objective message about the patient's needs and character. In the latter case one can do the patient therapeutic injustice by premature referral or by trying to like him too quickly.

Certain difficult patients feel they are unlikeable and have painfully acquired objective knowledge to justify this feeling. They may find reassurance comforting but suspect it is phony and in time compulsively rebel against it. However, insofar as therapy can sustain what is distasteful about them without false moves, it provides a context in which the patient can begin to integrate and transcend his identification with attacks by a poisoned self-image. When, in time, the bad self-image becomes telescoped and loses some of its power, these patients take great satisfaction in genuinely beginning to like themselves and in helping this hard-won feeling find modes of expression which they can respect.

The corresponding liking which they now sense in the therapist is experienced as fitting and confirming their own emerging reality. New possibilities of trust and mutuality become apparent as patients clearly perceive the objective validity of what they are experiencing.

It is, of course, possible that the therapist may never come to like the patient freely and naturally. A colleague once made a case presentation of a patient who became clinically well but in a psychopathic manner which was overtly distasteful to the conscientious therapist. The therapist's dislike for the patient increased as the patient became progressively more successful in the latter's own terms. One can, unfortunately, only speculate on what the dynamics of this interaction might have been.

On the other hand, the therapist may find himself drawn into his task with a heightened interest which seems to run counter to his dominant feeling toward the patient. The forms of behavior and expression presented by the patient may exert a kind of "horrified fascination" and the therapist may adjust his vision to the requirements of the patient's world with a child's paralyzed attachment to figures in the dark. In this form of countertransference the therapist is intrigued by the grotesque, and unconsciously views the patient as a masklike point of entrée through which he, the therapist, may live a magical existence, albeit an ecstatically degrading one. His macabre-toned interest in the spectacle of his work may give rise to a conscious experience of sardonic liking which is in excess of the patient's ability to process intense attitudes and affects. However, in this case the therapist may make use of and experiment with his negatively toned interest until a volume is found which is ego-syntonic for the patient. The productive uses and meanings of such states in the therapist have received too little study in the field in general and are still in need of more detailed research.

Where the liking for the patient by both the patient and therapist is achieved by degrees and is the result of difficult work by both persons, it may be experienced as a creative accomplishment. It possesses a quality different though not necessarily better than the liking which is easily sustained from the start, gold harder than easier to find. The therapist arrives at his liking by working through his own resistances and encrusted defenses to ego–alien aspects of his personality at extremely early developmental levels. The patient who chronically tends to evoke distaste in others evokes tendencies and images of a radically archaic and primitive nature, psychic dimensions one usually can avoid or is required to survey only fleetingly in everyday life. Thus the therapist engaged in this work has unusual opportunities to encounter and integrate phobic structures embedded in his psychic foundations. The well-known danger which the analyst faces in fully opening himself to the vicissitudes of his work involves succumbing to a life-style permeated by schizoid self-effort and self-attentiveness. Even this, however, may serve as a transitional phase in the overall development of the therapist's consciousness, greatly adding to his capacity to experience and know. The ideal result is a mode of self-healing and personality growth which outstrips the use of manic defenses and subtle forms of self-hardening. Whether or not this effort is worthwhile or desirable hinges, at least partly, on individual preferences, values, and, ultimately, one's vision of life.

REFERENCES

Ehrenzweig, A. (1967). *The Hidden Order of Art*. Los Angeles: University of California Press, 1971.

Eigen, M. (1973a). The recoil on having another person. *Review of Existential Psychology and Psychiatry* 12:52–55.

———— (1973b). Abstinence and the schizoid ego. *International Journal of Psycho-Analysis* 54:493–498.

———— (1973c). The call and the lure. *Psychotherapy: Theory, Research and Practice* 10:194–197.

———— (1974a). Fear of death: a symptom with changing meanings. *Journal of Humanistic Psychology* 14:29–33.

———— (1974b). On pre-oedipal castration anxiety. *International Review of Psycho-Analysis* 1:489–498.

———— (1975). The differentiation of an androgynous imago. *Psychoanalytic Review* 62:601–613.

———— (1976). *The primal scene and psychic androgeny* (unpublished paper).

Elkin, H. (1972). On selfhood and the development of ego structures in infancy. *Psychoanalytic Review* 59:389–416.

Fairbairn, W. R. D. (1954). *An Object Relations Theory of Personality*. New York: Basic Books.

Henry, W. E., Sims, J. H., and Spray, S. L. (1973). *Public and Private Lives of Psychotherapists*. San Francisco: Jossey-Bass.

Khan, M. M. R. (1974). *The Privacy of the Self*. London: Hogarth Press.

Klein, M. (1948). *Contributions to Psycho-Analysis, 1921–1945*. London: Hogarth Press.

Nelson, M. C., Nelson, B., Sherman, M. H., and Strean, H. S. (1968). *Roles and Paradigms in Psychotherapy*. New York: Grune & Stratton.

Robertiello, R. C. (1971). Introjection of the therapist. *Psychoanalytic Review* 58:625–629.

Spotnitz, H. (1969). *Modern Psychoanalysis of the Schizophrenic Patient*. New York: Grune & Stratton.

Winnicott, D. W. (1958). *Collected Papers*. New York: Basic Books.

———— (1965). *The Maturational Processes and the Facilitating Environment*. New York: International Universities Press.

———— (1971). *Playing and Reality*. New York: Basic Books.

5

Breathing and Identity

It is surprising to think what little role the experience of breathing has played in Western accounts of personality, considering the importance of breathing in Eastern systems of personality change and the age-old association of breath with psyche, spirit, or soul. Where body functions are concerned Western phenomenology has been preoccupied almost exclusively with the experience of appetite.

Appetite traditionally has been taken as the raw material to be transformed by the higher functions of will, reason, or faith. Will is conceived as an enigmatic maverick intermediate to appetite and faith or reason, capable of siding with either the higher or lower functions. Will extends the experience of appetite through evil imaginings into the realms of pride and power. It is called upon by reason or faith to somehow transcend itself. The result of this scheme is to insist on deep-seated personality changes rooted in body experience while the means of personality change are ultimately beyond body experience. That is, the scheme supplies no systematic means of transforming appetite at the level of body experience itself.

Eastern forms of meditation make use of body experiences outside the appetitive realm as a matter of course, especially breathing. With the West's increasing consciousness of itself and self-criticism it has begun to be open to Eastern influences with regard to psychotherapy. Jung and Reich, for example, were logical outgrowths of a current already present in psychoanalysis through Schopenhauer. The various body therapies followed naturally.

However, even the therapeutic use of the body in the West has largely been assimilated to the paradigm of appetite. The body generally has been worked with in terms of what "it" wants, its basic hungers and frustrations. Whatever the profound gains in stimulating a fresh sense of openness and vital aliveness, the self appears fixated in a fight for its due against outside obstacles and its own introjects, caught in the pattern of mobilizing the "I really want" past the resistances of alien shoulds and should nots. The phenomenology of breathing has been swallowed up by appetite.

This article offers a summary and descriptive sketch of therapeutic experiences of breathing during the course of psychotherapy in which various body experiences were drawn into focus. As a sketch it is open and incomplete. In particular it omits an account of the inhibitions, conflicts, and appetitive-aggressive aspects often associated with breathing. It concentrates on the patient's less conflicted experiences which tend to distinguish breathing from appetite and calls attention to some of the effects this awareness has on ego formation and the I-feeling. The particular order in which breathing experiences are presented here is prototypical, in part a logical arrangement for ease of presentation. The range and order of experiences for different persons are, of course, variable.

When one first attends to breathing, one becomes aware of simple facts about it, its usual speeds or rhythms and normal irregularities; the urges and counterurges to shorten, quicken, or extend one's breaths; and the like. One finds breathing itself stimulates many kinds of body sensations in diverse body regions. As one breathes more deeply into one's tensions, streams of erotic sensations may be triggered off with the result that one may forget about one's breathing entirely. Feelings of power and energy rise and fall and become concentrated in specific body zones as well as remain unpredictably fluid. The person first experiences a defensive consciousness in relation to the rise of body feeling. The ego is interested in, stimulated and frightened by the unanticipated world of continuous and varied body sensations and feelings it begins to glimpse. A testing process evolves in which the ego gradually builds courage to tolerate and experiment with larger doses of being "in" it. It gradually becomes an explorer of the shifting centers and currents of body aliveness.

As the experience of breathing is slowly distinguished from the flux of changing body states it is perceived as a safety zone, a gentle regularity in the midst of unpredictable momentary or periodic fluctuations. The fearful or exhausted ego uses its experience of the predictable smooth flow of breath as a retreat and stepping stone from which to regroup and progress more deeply into the body. The ego uses its experience of breathing as a bridge to move safely in and out of the body. In so doing, it strengthens both its capacity for observation and its receptivity to perceived body aliveness. The regular inflow and outflow of breath becomes a model for the ego's growing awareness and acceptance of its dual status. As the ego gradually allows itself to participate deeply, at least periodically, in the flow of breathing qua experienced breathing, it more securely grasps its own basic ambiguity of being both without and within the body: "I am but am not my body." The experience of breathing provides the most continuously lived bodily form for the ego's fundamental experience of itself. The ego's movement toward a more delineated awareness of its experience of breathing helps it more adequately grasp its own basic structure.

As already noted, for most people breathing usually is submerged in the general experience of the body. Appetitites and mood changes most often stand out from the background of generalized body sensation. Bringing breathing into the center of awareness makes explicit a persistent bodily ground for an experience of self which contrasts with the sense of self rooted in appetite. The experience of breathing provides a concrete and dramatic reference point within body life itself from which the pervasive and partly hidden appetitive image and use of the body can be realized. Thus the sense of self is extended to encompass not only the ambiguity of being both out of and in the body, but also the awareness of being rooted in two fundamentally different kinds of body experiences. In everyday life a flexible communion between these various aspects of self-feeling takes place naturally. A certain degree of disjointedness or dissociation between them seems to be tolerated as part of the normal background of everyday functioning and is allowed to go unnoticed if mild. However, anxiety and defenses quickly increase if the disjunction becomes threatening. If severe enough, psychotic terror or radical self-questioning can occur.

Breathing goes on constantly at a fairly steady pace with momentary and periodic variations, yet it is not experienced as a disturbance under normal circumstances. On the contrary, when made the object of attention it most often gives rise to a feeling of well-being. No body experience is more thoroughly permeating yet light of touch and unassaultive. Although breathing continuously pervades almost the entire body, it is hardly invasive or intrusive. As one patient reported, "When I feel my breathing fully I feel as though I've come into the clear." Appetite, by contrast, is a more ambivalent experience. It often has a disturbing or irritating quality which may or may not also be pleasurable. The rise of appetite involves more acute and insistent sensations than the flow of breathing. In appetite there is almost always a gap between the felt want and the moment of gratification, a gap usually filled, in part, by some form of aggressive action. The zones of emphasis are more sharply etched for appetite.

When breathing is hampered, of course, acute distress results which is as pressing as any appetitive urgency. Usually, however, breathing takes care of itself and, unlike appetite, is supplied with an outside source of gratification *which is always there.* Where breathing is concerned there is usually no lack of outside supplies. The fact that there is generally more supply than demand is one basis for the deep current of well-being associated with felt breathing. In breathing the insides of the body are continuously fed by the outside world, a continuous interpenetration of bodily depths and open expanse. This basic, sustaining interpenetration provides a bodily form for communion and relatedness in life. It helps support the current of hope and trust in personality since it is virtually every moment in the process of giving one gratification.

The experience of breathing has two centers, the abdomen and chest. A differentiated awareness of the feelings associated with these body areas is gained as a matter of course while attending to one's breathing. Feelings associated with the chest may at first be experienced as clotted, painful, or sad.

Although anger, too, may be localized in the chest, simple rage and fear unqualified by sorrow or tenderness is more typically experienced as visceral. The abdomen may be allied either with the genital or chest areas, emphasizing appetitive or nonappetitive experiences. It is in the chest that one ultimately experiences simple feelings of love. The head, too, is brought into this nexus. The cool sensation of air in the nasal passages spreads between the eyes toward the temples.

As one becomes more familiar with the experience of breathing, a certain asymmetry appears to characterize the inflow and outflow of breath. More anxiety may occur with either the exhalation or the inhalation. Death and contraction are associated with breathing out, life and expansion with breathing in. However, giving and getting rid of may also be associated with breathing out and taking and keeping associated with breathing in. A momentary gap or breath stoppage occurs after each outflow or inflow, like a pendulum. In time, consciousness masters this fleeting suspension of movement and finds in it an added moment of renewal.

In the experience of breathing the ego finds support for its own sense of constancy and unifying activities. No rhythmic, continuous, and consciously accessible body experience is more constant, permeating, and unifying. Partial identification with the breathing process provides the ego with a good model of cohesion and interaction. The sense of self based on a normal experience of breathing is an unpressured sense of self which is not easily stampeded. For the sense of self structured by appetite, time is an irritant. The self structured by an awareness of breathing can take its time going from moment to moment, just as breathing usually does. It does not run after or get ahead of time but, instead, seems simply to move with it.

An apparent danger associated with the sense of self arising from breathing-awareness is based on the pronounced passivity of the experience. Patients sometimes report feeling more themselves when watching or being with their breathing than when they are active in the world. A partially schizoid perception of essential selfhood is animated: one comes to feel the sense of self associated with breathing-awareness is *the* true or real self. One may wish to taste more of or be drawn into it. This regressive pull tends to be offset and balanced by the active counterurge to realize and embody this private sense of selfhood in one's everyday life as much as is realistically possible. In breathing the experience of *being* is dominant, and the wish to do arises out of a sense of plenitude. In appetite *doing* is dominant and is based on a felt lack or threat. To be sure, breathing also involves a lack or threat but one that is instantly and effortlessly answered. In breathing one can rest assured of the strengths and rewards of passive being.

In time the self-feeling evoked by an awareness of breathing becomes one of a set of identity experiences, although a very important one. Like all other identity experiences it is subject to the processes of habituation and self-transcendence. It has, however, made a profound contribution to the person's sense of continuity and basic unity. One can, further, repair to one's experience of breathing as needed or wanted and find there a healing experience without loss of self-awareness. A self-feeling as easy and continuous as breathing, once firmly established remains an underlying thread through whatever crises or current discontinuity of identity one may have to solve.

6

The Significance of the Face

The centrality of the human face as symbolic of personality permeates the fabric of human experience. It is often observed that a full face-to-face sexual encounter is unique to human beings, an event profoundly linked with an earlier structural correlate—the rapt stare of the human infant at the mother's face during feeding. Again, as the infant develops, the appearance of a face or even mask is enough to evoke another uniquely defining quality of the human dimension—an expressively radiant smile. In a related fashion psychoanalytic concern with the "mirror" metaphor in clinical work and the psychology of the self carries an implicit reference to the human face as the center of personality, symbolically linked with reflexive mind.[1]

More generally, in many times and places the dualities that make up human experience have often been given compressed focus through representations of the human face. In Oscar Wilde's well-known *The Picture of Dorian Gray,* a hidden picture of the hero functions as a deforming mirror that reflects his deteriorating inner state while his everyday face remains composed. The more encompassing polarity-in-unity principle is implied in portrayals of the Roman god, Janus, guardian of portals and patron of beginnings and endings. He, of course, is shown with two competing or complementary faces, one in front, the other in back of his head. In this vein universal human experiences achieved a shorthand, model summary in the tragic and comic masks of Greek theater.

It is not surprising, then, that psychoanalysis must concern itself with this central symbol of personality, particularly as the constitution and development of the early self and correlated disorders of the self are increasingly brought into focus. For example, when working with highly disturbed patients or with nuclear

---

[1]The mirror metaphor has recently undergone an extremely rich development within psychoanalysis (e.g., Bion [1972], Eigen [1980a,b, 1981a,b, 1982], Kohut [1971], Lacan [1977], Winnicott [1971]). For an exquisite exploration of the mirror metaphor as expressive of reflexive mind by a non-analyst, see Elizabeth Sewell (1952).

49

aspects of character problems the cathexis of the therapist's face frequently indicates that fundamental personality change is evolving. Some patients with early disturbances are unable to create a rich and freeing image of the therapist or are unable to construct an image of the therapist's face in the latter's absence. In certain instances this incapacity is not simply a matter of repression due to "killing off the object" but suggests that the inability to experience and internalize has been impaired from the outset. The growing ability to experience and meaningfully represent the other's face in such cases is not only achieved through insights or through the recall of repressed memories but proceeds in a hidden way, emerging in dreams, or slowly as a new growth or healing process. The appearance of a sustaining and enduring image of the therapist's face may then be a crucial portent of cure at the deepest levels of personality.

It seems likely, also, that the actual (perhaps involuntary) facial behavior of the therapist plays a role in evoking and broadening the patient's capacity to experience. Considering the importance of the other's face in the formation of the self-feeling, it seems likely that certain basic ego defects may have their origins in the facial expressions (or lack of expressiveness) of the primary object. At this early level of empathic responsiveness even the quality of one's voice may be affected by such traits as the shape of the other's mouth. In an earlier paper (Eigen 1977) I have shown in detail how the therapist's feelings toward the patient may undergo spontaneous yet systematic changes during the course of the therapeutic process. The therapist's expressive gestures doubtless reflect these changes. Thus the therapist's face may be more open and expressive at one phase of therapy than another, depending, in significant part, on the patient's shifting therapeutic requirements. At certain appropriate moments the quality of the therapist's involuntary smile may indeed help offset a chronic defect or distortion partly rooted in the failure of adequate facial expressiveness on the part of the patient's primary object. In the clinical examples below this must have been especially so in the case of James who as a painter was more than usually aware of the part the object plays in bringing about imagery and felt internal changes.[2]

Three clinical examples in which aspects of the patient's self-feeling emerged and were partly consolidated through experiences involving the analyst's face will now be sketched. A historical and theoretical exploration, meant to be suggestive rather than systematic, follows the case material.

CLINICAL STUDIES

One patient, Jane,[3] entered therapy feeling painfully agitated, unreal, and empty. She drew pictures depicting alternative mind-body relations. In one scene

---

[2]Shifts in the visualization of the analyst's face often occur on the couch alone when the psychic levels of present concern are reached. However, it is not possible (nor desirable) never to see the analyst. An account of the complex interplay between facing and not facing the analyst is not undertaken here.

[3]A detailed account of this case may be found in Eigen (1980b).

a severed head and body courted each other. She drew variations in which either the head or the body seemed more inviting or rejecting. In a second scene, head and body seemed determined to have nothing to do with each other. In a third group they struggled and fought grimly or playfully. In a fourth they melted or collapsed into one another, becoming amorphous and unrecognizable.

For some time she could not represent a wholesome relationship between head and body. The first picture in which head and body fit well together followed a dream in which my face appeared more glowing than in real life. She said of my dream face, "Your face is heavenly, from another world . . . yet still you, the you I know . . . I had the feeling I could enter it or become one with it and pass through it and be more myself than ever. It was with me all the next day. It made me feel better. I saw myself in it somehow . . ."

Jane's description depicts a kind of psychological consubstatiation, the sense of being two yet one, simultaneously within and outside each other, permeable and distinguishable. She had contracted the ideal and material worlds into one point, a type of beatific vision that preserved my actual material reality while transforming it. Mind and body could come together in this safety zone which gradually could expand.

In a second case[4] a patient's experience of my face was one factor that helped resolve an aspect of a chronic split in his personality which he expressed in terms of devil images. He felt himself split into two devils. One was a body devil who liked to explode. The other was a head devil who looked on and chuckled, "Heh, heh." In an important phase of therapy my face at times seemed radiant, coherent, and good while at other times it seemed like an "ass" which tended to become fecalized and damaged. In moments of positive idealization I seemed to him the way he wished to be, the way he felt he would have turned out had his life gone well. My face then functioned as a promise of wholeness, a mirror for what he felt was best in him but had always devalued. When my face turned into an ass the patient, Frank, feared that his body devil would smear and contaminate everything good, even fecalize the entire universe. With panicky foreboding he could hear the head devil's mocking laughter egg the body devil on.

With work Frank became aware that my face seemed spoiled when he (or I) was angry. When, on the other hand, he felt well-being in the therapy relationship my face seemed brighter and caring. The question arose as to whether the good face could survive destructive attacks. In fact my face always reconstituted itself and appeared fresh and undamaged once more. It would seem to Frank that the damage would never go away or that I would take revenge, possibly withdraw, or simply disappear. He might then feel a mixture of triumph and guilt or be convinced that he was lost. His critical learning, won over and over, was that the restored face persistently surfaced, encompassing his fragility and hostility with a sense of the ultimate undamageableness of essential goodness. The devil images were contained and progressively assimilated. The aggressive energy they carried was eventually released for effective use.

A final example is James, a young painter.[5] In a critical phase of his analysis he

---

[4]An extended version of this case in a somewhat different context appears in Eigen (1979).

[5]A more extended account of this case appears in Eigen (1982).

began to see my face as a penis. He was aware that he was angry at me for insensitivities in my behavior. He hoped by his visual and verbal violence to shatter whatever walls prevented contact and to compel me into magical feats of repair or to feel defeated.

During this period he dreamt of an impassive Indian face which reminded him of the catatonic chief in *One Flew Over the Cuckoo's Nest.* He described the Indian as withdrawn but powerful. He linked me with this face and berated me for being like a stone wall. He caricatured my dead spots. After venting his fury with me for the pain I caused him because of my apparent deficiencies, he related the Indian to himself. He said, "I don't budge either. I frustrate myself. I'm like cement inside. The Indian in me doesn't blink. He just sits there and grits his teeth. I picture him breaking down barriers. That's the energy he has in him. I make myself weak and act like a monkey because I'm afraid of that power. My Indian is the prick I see in your face. Maybe you've been keeping him in safekeeping. I've got to warm him up. He has a lot of thawing out to do."

The mute Indian represents a level of stifled aggression and longing that James had been unable to reach before. However, this figure also represented an observing quality of great importance. James said ruefully, "My Indian sits and watches. Nothing escapes him. He's waiting. He's my mind-prick sitting on its ass in my head. I've been afraid to know how clearly he really sees things. It seemed safer to feel clogged up."

After several weeks of expressing and working on these feelings James dreamt of me sleeping, my face soft and open like a baby's. He was touched with my vulnerability in the dream and was tempted to feel united with me. At the same time he felt that the soft feeling was connected with a sense of his own impassive, Indian face thawing out.

ON THE EXPERIENCE OF THE FACE

Early in psychoanalytic history the experience of the face was associated with seduction and for good reason. Charcot's patient, Blanche Wittman, who called herself "Queen of the hysterics," was depicted in a painting by A. Brouillet as staring at a picture of herself having the attack she was in the process of duplicating in reality. Her sense of the fascinated gaze of the doctors is implicit in her self-satisfaction with her performance. René Major (1974) wrote of this scene:

> . . . the principal technical innovation of psychoanalysis was the removal of the therapist from the hysteric's field of vision, so that she was forced to make herself heard and was no longer before a real spectator in whose eyes she might find the desire that she sought. The patient was constrained to seek through her own words her own internal divisions and find in the analytic mirror her own image. [p. 387]

Sartre (Milner 1967) and Lacan (Kohut 1971) have deepened our understanding of certain aspects of the psychology of seduction by focusing on the psychopathic, schizoid, and paranoid dimensions associated with gazing and being gazed at. They focus on what one might call the "negative gaze." Sartre

(Milner 1967), for example, has described in detail how seeing and being seen can objectify and magnetize the self and other as both pass through the self-defeating intricacies of trying to maintain (or lose) freedom via stratagems of domination.[6]

Lacan (Kohut 1971) takes up the dialectics of alienation by elaborating on what he envisages to be the inevitably paranoid foundation of the ego, derived from the sense of dislocation the self experiences in having to make itself an other in order to be at all. When, for example, the infant sees himself in the mirror he experiences an exhilarating, triumphant sense of an externalized visual self-image (self yet other) which is under its perfect control (a coherent, bounded image instantaneously responding to its every gesture). The infant automatically uses this visual I to defend against helplessly identifying with his more vague, awkward, and imperfectly controlled bodily sense of self. A complex sense of otherness thus pervades the ego, here couched in terms of an exteriorized visual self-image versus one's partially disowned sense of body life.

To be sure, most body and mental functioning goes on anonymously and impersonally. In an important sense mental and body life present themselves to us when we arrive on the scene. In a basic sense they are our givens and, indeed, they give us ourselves. We can — we are required to — own them, always imperfectly and with residues. To some extent we are and remain other to ourselves by virtue of the very processes through which we are constituted and maintained. According to the particular dialectical tradition adopted by Lacan, we are always trying to rid ourselves of the sense of otherness, we see that the sense of otherness is rooted in a variety of sources, which makes us possible. Not all theorists, however, have adopted the position that otherness need feel toxic.

Many authors (e.g., Bion [1977], Kohut [1971, 1977], Weil [1958], Winnicott [1938, 1965, 1971]) have indicated that one's sense of self is intimately connected with early mirroring responses of significant others. The infant in large part builds his self-image in terms of how he sees himself reflected through the eyes of his parents, in the first instance his mother. Weil (1958) describes how a negative self-image is formed and repressed insofar as the mother unconsciously equates the infant's self with feces or garbage. On the other hand, good maternal mirroring helps form the basis of adequate self-esteem and the hopeful sense of possibilities. Thus the ego may have a mixture of paranoid and nonparanoid foundational experiences, the particular balance in important part dependent on the overall quality of responsiveness by the parental milieu.

Winnicott (1938, 1965, 1971) details several phases involved in mirroring processes that precede and play a role in the gradual internalization of good enough maternal functioning. He stresses the quality and timing of parental responses in the development of an alive, trustworthy, and creative sense of self.

---

[6]See Eigen (1973) for a clinical development of these themes in terms of time experience.

It is not necessary to outline his contribution here but a case vignette may prove helpful. In one example Winnicott[7] described a patient's attempt to center his image in her hand mirror while he sat behind her. By looking over her shoulder he noticed that his image was off-center and that she seemed bothered by this fact. In order to "help" her he moved his head slightly, centering himself. The patient became upset and in the next session explained to him that he had been just like her mother who chronically helped her against her will. The situation had called for his tolerating the patient's wish to keep his image off balance, a wish made difficult to tolerate by the patient's manifest attempts to center the image and her apparent frustration over failing to do so. That is, he was called upon to tolerate the patient's deliberate and tantalizing failure, a failure that symbolically succeeded in turning mother into a puppet who had to accept her own unbalanced state, a state early in life pawned off on the patient. The patient soon informed Winnicott that had he made this mistake much earlier in her treatment she might have been forced to return to hospital for a period but now, after their work together, they were both able to capitalize on his failure. Well enough timed experiences of both fitting and not fitting in with the patient gradually built up a sense of both an inside and outside syntonic other.

In the above example the patient, in part, was attempting to force the therapist-parent to build and use his or her own containing function rather than promiscuously "spill out" into the patient. Bion (1977) has suggested that an adequate sense of self partly depends on the infant's ability to assimilate such a parental containing function, a function which in the case of this patient's mother was extremely faulty. Ideally the mother absorbs and processes the infant's attitudes, fantasies, and feelings in a way which both accurately reflects and effectively refines his psychic reality. The infant is thus enabled to grow by taking in the mother's ability to rework the psychic life he places in her. Here again an enhancing intermingling of self and other occur at the heart of self-experience and personality development.

In a somewhat related manner Kohut (1971, 1977) links the development of an adequate sense of self to successful mirroring and idealizing processes. He, for example, points to the confirmation the self experiences when seeing the "gleam in the mother's eye" as opposed to the emptiness that follows when such empathic responsiveness is missing. He attempts to delineate a process wherein more gross identifications and internalizations gradually give way to the psychological capacities and functions they substitute for and help to develop. In this process syntonic otherness adds to and actually becomes part of a cohesive self-feeling. The mother's expressive gestures, particularly facial and vocal, coupled with the quality of her touch and more obvious action patterns, play a key role in spontaneously conveying to the infant the life enhancing or wounding quality of her psychic makeup.

---

[7]Personal conversation, 1967.

Levinas (1969) has developed one of the most extended accounts of the experience of the human face that has been written. He associates the birth of the human personality with a positive experience of the face. For Levinas the human face gives rise to a sense of the Infinite in relation to which one can become inexhaustibly real. In his phenomenological philosophy the experience of the other's face carries with it a sense of goodness that becomes the tonic chord or home base of the human self. Chronic deviations from this sense of intrinsic goodness are ultimately felt as irritants or, worse, deforming and alienating.

Levinas' view, which links the origin of the self with the primordial experience of the face, appears to find genetic support in the work of Spitz (1965).[8] Spitz has found that the human face or face representation systematically evokes in the infant a coherent and joyous smile, roughly by about two or three months of age. This suggests that the infant then has some form of awareness of self and other. Prior to the advent of this coherent, affectively full and focused smile (the "smiling response"), the infant, to be sure, does smile. But his smiles, when spontaneous, tend to be random and diffuse, possibly elicited by passing sensations and thrills. The infant, one might say, is conscious but not self-conscious.

It is unlikely that one can account for the emergence of the smiling response, in essence as Spitz has tried to do, wholly in terms of a biological signal theory, that is, in terms of the smile's functional value in eliciting empathic maternal responses which would ensure the infant's survival. The novelty and felt significance of the smile, the surplus of its expressive coherence, marks a dimension of responsive cognition that goes beyond the range exhausted by animal signalling and consciousness. Similarly, although phenomena of bonding or attachment may occur prior to the smiling response, they frequently also characterize animal behavior and do not in themselves provide the means for understanding how they are psychically represented once self–other awareness arises.

Another aspect of the reductionistic bias which often characterizes psychoanalysis when thinking about infantile consciousness may be seen in the tendency of analysts to reduce the meaning of the face to the breast, as has usually been done. The fact that the infant stares at the mother's face and not the breast when feeding appears to make such a reduction untenable. Although Spitz (1965) does not feel that the infantile perception in question possesses a defined enough object quality necessary to support an image of the breast per se, he, nonetheless, writes that oral perception during this period (two-three months) is the "hallmark of 'things,' "[9] (p. 92) whatever these "things" may be. This is remarkable in light of his own data, which emphasize the visual rather than

---

[8]For an excellent critique and reworking of Spitz's data see Elkin (1972).

[9]It should be noted that an earlier dating of this phenomenon would not alter the structure of the present argument.

oral-tactile element in stimulating the smiling response. The infant will smile at a distance even to the triangular representation of the eyes and nose, and it is particularly the eyes—spontaneously animated, sparkling reflectors of personality—which fascinate his gaze during feeding. It is noteworthy that the smiling response in question requires an element of distance and does not arise with the eyes closed as a result of touch alone. One might argue that self–other awareness arises in a matrix characterized by an ambiguous interplay between psychophysical closeness and distance, both of which remain critical defining dimensions of human consciousness. It is important to stress that a nontactile element is necessary for the smile expressive of self–other awareness to occur.

The functional meaning Spitz assigns to the smiling response—survival via oral coercion—grows out of his implicit phenomenology of the infant's smile. Spitz reads into the infant's smile a more or less purely manipulative, controlling intent, formalized in Freud's will to mastery. In contrast, the present observer experiences the infant's smiling response as essentially open and undefensive, an expression of alive and vibrant delight. It appears to reflect a time in which radical dissociations between thinking-feeling-action have not yet evolved. Soon enough, to be sure, the infant will smile when angry or frightened (doubtless by or around eight months). His smile will take a seductive turn, develop blank or dead spots, and eventually even harden or freeze. But it seems to me the earlier smiling response, coherent and whole, points to a nonparanoid element at the ego's foundation which, indeed, will undergo all manner of crises attached to awareness of injury and power inequalities.

In general, of all body areas the human face is most centrally expressive of human personality and exerts its prominence as an organizing principle in the field of meaning. It acts as a reference point by which all other body areas may acquire deeper personal significance. To be sure, other body areas also act as powerful experiential foci which co-refer to one another, as is witnessed when the primacy of the face is challenged (e.g., when it is fecalized or genitalized). Normally, body-oriented lines of association, such as the face-breast-ass equation, may be more or less present but are situated within a more encompassing perspective in which the face has primacy. This is in distinct contrast with most animal life, wherein perception is preeminently organized around securing physical sustenance.

In human fantasy the face and lower body areas can be properly distinguished and related or may enter into a variety of possible confusions. One finds instances in which a lower body area is displaced upward or the face is displaced downward (Freud 1916, Milner 1967, 1969). For example, a face may appear inscribed on the buttocks or on the head of a penis. The body areas involved may then appear personalized and animated. Conversely, a face may appear with anal or genital features. In optimal instances circular transpositions of face to lower body areas and vice versa can express the symbolic upward–downward flow of consciousness and energy. In such cases what may first appear simply as a top–bottom confusion may actually represent a transitional developmental advance in which consciousness suffuses the body, and the body becomes more articulately represented. In general, the therapeutic task is to convert the contaminations feared or courted by the patient into differentiated expressions of a growing mind–body unity.

THE PROBLEM OF DIFFERENTIATION

In the above discussion it was suggested that the dawning of awareness of self and other is expressed in the infant's smile in response to a human face. It was taken for granted that early self and other emerge and develop together. The face was described as the center of the infant's *visual* field, the nipple-breast a center of the *tactile* field (Elkin 1972). This double perceptual base, symbolically elaborated, provides an experiential foundation for the simultaneous emergence of both the body and mental self. Hence a dual–unity structure characterized by areas of union and distinction applies both to self–other and mind–body relations. In the above clinical examples (1) awareness of self and other included areas of union and distinction and (2) awareness of the other (and self) included both immaterial and material dimensions of experienced reality, again with areas of union and distinction.

The notion of a wholly undifferentiated state was not found to be useful as a clinical concept. In actual clinical experience areas of union and distinction are always found together. Pure union and pure distinction are abstract concepts which do not characterize living experience. In this regard experience is on the side of logical coherence inasmuch as a self with no reference point outside it could have no sense of its own existence. It seems fairer to say that a basic ambiguity — a simultaneity of areas of distinctness and union — represents an essential structure of human subjectivity, whatever developmental level. If one tries to push beyond these poles, the sense of self must disappear: to be undifferentiated and exist is not possible.

The starting point of most psychoanalytic theorists brushes up against this dilemma. Mahler (1968), for example, believes the early–most self arises with no sense of otherness ("autism") and moves to a state of fusion with the other who was not yet here ("symbiosis"). From this imaginary point separation-individuation proceeds. However, in light of the preceding considerations, to postulate a self with no other is to postulate no self at all. Similarly, without some form of awareness of self and other the notion of merger refers to a fusion of beings who do not yet psychologically exist. With this scheme regression must always be hazardous, and it must seem wiser to build "good defenses." The psychic depths are depicted in terms of isolation on the one hand, merger on the other — both boding catastrophe. It seems the safer and truer course to under-stand the basic self as participating in both areas of union and distinction at all levels of its awareness, whatever imbalance may present itself at any moment.

Only this framework provides a proper ground for the deepest, restorative regressions.

Winnicott's (1971) formulation of the transitional area describes aspects of the structure of concern here. For Winnicott the transitional object carries the meaning of that which is yet is not the other and that which is and is not self. It is like the other in mirroring the self and like the self in mirroring the other; yet it cannot wholly be reduced to either. (Winnicott, I believe, runs into his genetic and logical problems because he fails to make this essential ambiguity more radically constitutive.)

He suggests that the first (incipient) not-me, the transitional object (or area), begins to separate out from global omnipotence (Winnicott 1971). The distinction between inner and outer follows later. However, he also writes that the mother must be present enough to keep the internal representation of her alive or the transitional area could not appear and survive. Here the representation of the mother (or maternal functioning) must precede the transitional area, an apparent contradiction. Winnicott, further, believes that the sense of otherness emerges when the infant perceives that the other survives the infant's destructive attacks and wishes (1971). However, one would have had to know that the other had been there in order to appreciate the fact that the other has come through. The perception that the other survives one's destructive attacks doubtless leads to a fresh sense of otherness and oneself but assumes rather than accounts for the original constitution of self and other. For Winnicott, in fact, they are conditions for one another, mutually constitutive.

The clinical vignettes reported above suggest that the human face is experienced as self yet other, a dual unity in which both areas of distinction and union bring each other into existence. The feeling of wholeness may initially be rooted in the implicit awareness of self and other giving rise to one another, permeating yet transcending one another—a primary creative act repeated anew at every developmental juncture. Personal being is here felt to be distinct yet to exist fully and mysteriously in a state of union, each pole made possible and fulfilled by the other. Insofar as the infant lives in this subject-subject psychical reality, expressive meanings, moods, intentions, and attitudes appear to be experienced with direct, immediate transparency.

As suggested by the above case examples the human face when experienced on the deepest levels takes on a glowing quality which seems more than itself. That such experiences do not simply refer to the breast or maternal functioning, although often they may, is suggested by developmental findings and reports of patients such as those discussed earlier.

Under appropriate conditions patients may find themselves reporting experiences which may be summarized in the following way:

I see you but not just you. I am experiencing a more real, perfect version of you, a glowing-light you, inexpressibly radiant and fluid. I can go in and through you yet feel more myself than ever. It is as if I entered and passed through a highly charged yet resistanceless medium and feel newly conscious and restored. (Also see Eigen [1980a,b, 1982]).

In such experiences the other retains something of his specific, everyday personality; at the same time, he is transformed into something more or other than himself, a symbolic carrier of a translucent sense of immateriality. In such moments the ineffable is a distinguishable mental object as such. The therapist functions as a mediator between immaterial and material dimensions of existence and is in a position to be able to facilitate more wholesome interactions between these two spheres (Eigen 1979, 1980a,b, 1981b, 1982).

For the infant the appearance of a face is an indicator that another personality is present. When the child is panicked at the mother's absence it is likely that an image of her face, not her breast, brings more comfort. The possibility also exists that some double sensation of both the face and the breast touches somewhat different areas of infantile longing.

As development proceeds, areas of distinction and union of self-other and, correlatively, mind–body undergo enrichment. In pathology various combinations of these capacities are developed at the other's expense or, more accurately, typical distortions of each may be seen. Conditions in which these areas tend to overly collapse into or diverge from one another may be studied, particularly in light of the healthy capacities they are failed versions of and still aim to restore. One's sense of wholeness, in part, matures through struggle with one's pathology. As one's personality continues to develop, a rich and complex perceptual array of self–other and mental–physical self configurations proliferate, and the struggle to expand and articulate the meaning of one's sense of unity (which includes tolerance for areas of "creative chaos") gains in subtlety and structural significance. One's personality, as an open, expanding system, repeatedly engages itself in the process of seamlessly linking the multiple levels and dimensions of experience it undergoes and plays its role in creating. Ideally the perceptual glow of early childhood is not lost but deepens in nuances and latent meanings. It may be analytically rediscovered through creative regressions. The accretions and interweavings of felt significance, often hard won, come to act as both a natural brake and gateway for further self and other opening. The human face remains a central reference point through which we may read or show the results of our labors, a compressedly focused summary and pointer, poignant and triumphant. It flashes the sign of presence, its calling card, however opaque, and demands some sign of knowing from the center of the unknown.

REFERENCES

Bion, W. R. (1977). *Seven Servants*. New York: Jason Aronson.
Eigen, M. (1977). On working with 'unwanted' patients. *International Journal of Psycho-Analysis* 58:109–121.

————— (1979). Ideal images and creativity. *Psychocultural Review* 3:287–298.

————— (1980a). Instinctual fantasy and ideal images. *Contemporary Psychoanalysis* 16:119–137.

————— (1980b). Expression and meaning. In *Expressive Therapy,* ed. A. Robbins, pp. 291–312. New York: Human Sciences.

————— (1981a). On Guntrip's analysis with Winnicott. *Contemporary Psychoanalysis* 17:103–112.

————— (1981b). The area of faith in Winnicott, Lacan and Bion. *International Journal of Psycho-Analysis* 62:413–433.

————— (1982). Creativity, instinctual fantasy and ideal images. *Psychoanalytic Review* 69:317–339.

Elkin, H. (1972). On selfhood and the development of ego structures in infancy. *Psychoanalytic Review* 59:389–416.

Freud, S. (1916). A mythological parallel to a visual obsession. *Standard Edition* 14:338.

Kohut, H. (1971). *The Analysis of the Self.* New York: International Universities Press.

————— (1977). *The Restoration of the Self.* New York: International Universities Press.

Lacan, J. (1977). The mirror stage as formative of the function of the I as revealed in psychoanalytic experience. In *Ecrits: A Selection,* pp. 1–7. New York: Norton.

Levinas, E. (1969). *Totality and Infinity.* Pittsburgh: Duquesne University Press.

Mahler, M. (1968). *On Human Symbiosis and the Vicissitudes of Individuation,* vol. 1: *Infantile Psychosis.* New York: International Universities Press.

Major, R. (1974). The revolution of hysteria. *International Journal of Psycho-Analysis* 55:387.

Milner, M. (1967). *On Not Being Able to Paint,* 2nd ed. New York: International Universities Press.

————— (1969). *The Hands of the Living God.* New York: International Universities Press.

Sartre, J-P. (1956). *Being and Nothingness.* New York: Philosophical Library.

Sewell, E. (1952). *Paul Valery: The Mind in the Mirror.* New Haven: Yale University Press.

Spitz, R. (1965). *The First Year of Life: A Psychoanalytic Study of Normal and Deviant Development of Object Relations.* New York: International Universities Press.

Weil, E. (1958). The origin and vicissitudes of the self-image. *Psychoanalysis* 1:15–18.

Winnicott, D. W. (1938). *Collected Papers.* New York: Basic Books.

————— (1965). *The Maturational Processes and the Facilitating Environment.* New York: International Universities Press.

————— (1971). *Playing and Reality.* New York: Basic Books.

7

Instinctual Fantasy and Ideal Images

Recent work with disorders rooted in early developmental levels has, in some quarters, led to a recognition of the intrinsic value of ideal experience[1] in healing and creativity (e.g., Balint 1968, Kohut 1971, Milner 1950, 1969, Searles 1965, Winnicott 1971). Balint (1968) expressively describes a "harmonious mix-up of self and milieu" as the matrix from which a fully human development can proceed. Kohut (1971) writes of a foundational oneness of self and other which gradually must undergo maturation. Searles (1965) has depicted the healing power of sustaining a phase of "pre-ambivalent symbiosis" with the patient, purportedly reflective of the primary matrix in which the early-most self arises. Milner (1969) describes the value of allowing personality distortions to collapse into undifferentiated states from which a new self-feeling and relation to the world can grow. Winnicott (1971), together with Milner, places a critical importance on "illusion" in generating a true self feeling and, ultimately, linking oneself meaningfully to cultural life in general. In some basic sense the "oceanic" for these authors is no longer viewed pejoratively but as a dimension of subjectivity with hidden resources waiting for exploration and use. It is seen, essentially, as in traditional religions, as carrying a redemptive element, linked with the feeling of wholeness.

This positive emphasis on regressive states is in contrast with much psycho-analysis of the past. To be sure, Freud saw the importance of ideal states in motivating a patient for treatment. He early used the transference in just this way insofar as he relied on idealization-identification to try to influence patients. However, Freud's overall aim was to strengthen the individual so that "illusion" would not be necessary. Indeed, throughout his writings illusions were equated with weakness. The truly strong man would not need them. A formulation like

---

[1]In this chapter terms such as *ideal experience, ideal states,* and *ideal images* are usually related to some aspect of the felt sense of infinite perfection. It is understood that all experience is ideal in a broad sense, invisible, intangible.

Balint's "progression for the sake of regression," with its positive emphasis on regressive capacities and delights, is clearly not in keeping with Freud's personality and emphasis on relentless struggle. Much excellent psychoanalytic literature (e.g., Chasseguet-Smirgel 1974, 1976; Reich 1973a, 1973b, 1973c) has followed Freud in deciphering the pathological element in attachment to ideal states, relatively neglecting their healing aspect.

From Freud's materialist bias, ideal images tended to be seen as second-class citizens. On the other hand, Freud's whole contribution was a study of ideal reality, the drama of will and drives, of fantasy and sublimation, of the various facets of the mind. This ambivalence remained throughout his writings. On the one hand he felt (Freud 1950) a full biology would render psychology superfluous, but he also affirmed (1940 [1938]) that nothing could replace the struggle of human subjectivity to reflect itself for its own sake. In fact it may not be possible to draw a sharp distinction between instinctual and ideal aspects of subjective reality. Finely complex relations between drive and ego have been the subject of psychoanalytic study almost from the latter's beginning. Desire and idealization are sisters, as Freud early indicated in his writings on the overvaluation of love objects. And love and hate play an important role in generating ideal states, for example in constituting demonic or divine images with which one may unite and/or fight in many ways.

In recent literature (Kohut 1971, Stolorow 1975) instinctual fantasy is viewed in terms of its function in maintaining and building aspects of the self-image, especially the body image. The proliferating complexity of fantasy life is often linked to a multiplicity of self-images or facets of self-images (Meltzer 1973). It is not the purpose of the present paper to unravel the well-nigh impossible problems involving the status of drive and ego or self theory with relation to one another. My use of drive is preeminently focused on the role of fantasy in the formation of one's self-image.

However, the heart of this paper is concerned with the function of ideal images in clinical healing and self-formation. Although it may not be possible to create clear boundaries between instinctual fantasy and ideal images in fact, one may still suggest differences in emphasis. One may study the shifting contributions made to self-development by both instinctual fantasy and ideal images, their commonalities and antagonisms. Some highlights drawn from a single case will be presented in order to help bring out certain differences and overlaps between the functions of instinctual fantasy and ideal images in the personality development of one individual.

In the case presented below work with instinctual fantasy played a large role in alleviating the patient's presenting complaint of sexual impotence. However, it did not in itself relieve his work block. His creativity was released by means of experiencing ideal states evoked by the therapy relationship. This distinction between the clinical function of instinctual fantasy and ideal images is suggestive and has been found in other individuals. Owing to the complexity of psychic life, exceptions may be likely, if not the rule. Generalizations must be qualified by a detailed understanding of the meaning and function of processes in a given context.

The paper closes with a more theoretical exploration of the meaning and place of ideal images in psychoanalytic writings and clinical work. Weak points in current conceptualizations of ideal states, particularly revolving around notions of "undifferentiation," will be pinpointed so that a more sound foundation for working with these states may be achieved. Special emphasis is placed on ideal experiences of the human face and their structural implications for achieving personal integrity.

REPAIR OF THE PHALLIC SELF-IMAGE

The symbolic use of body organs to express felt psychological capacities has occurred from the early history of humankind on. Most vivid, perhaps, are the use of representations of genitals in religions to symbolize active and receptive powers of thought and feeling. Psychoanalysis, too, has distinguished between the literal, anatomical penis and the symbolic phallus (Laplanche and Pontalis 1973), the latter a pointer to a generic capacity beyond its reference to the literal body. The symbolic phallus generally has been equated with active power, particularly creative activity. Lacan (1977) is perhaps the most systematic of analytic writers to point out the danger of confusing the literal penis with its symbolic function. The appearance of the penis in fantasy most often communicates a message concerning the patient's ongoing conflict centering on active, creative use of power, his own and others. Erikson's (1959) concern with phallic initiative and self-assertion is only one aspect of the general theme involving personal potency, ultimately creative potency.

Nevertheless, the reduction of the problems concerning active creativity to problems centering around mere initiative and self-assertion can also have beneficial results. In the present case, James, a painter in his 20s, used phallic imagery to convey his damaged ability to be an active agent. Instinctual fantasy and symptoms were used as means to expose more pervasive problems rooted in basic feelings about himself and others. His literal and symbolic uses of phallic imagery were often confused, but in the end he used his fantasies to create a more viable self-feeling. The use of fantasies involving body functions as symbols of psychological capacities seemed sufficient to relieve his presenting sexual impotence. However, they were not in themselves effective in working through his equally disturbing presenting work block. For the latter James had to come in contact with, and own his capacity to create, ideal images, experienced as inspiration.

The present account highlights selected states of mind which made their appearance when James's father began to assume greater importance in his analysis. It omits the greater part of anal paternal fantasies (Eigen 1975–1976,

1982) and focuses on more purely phallic imagery aimed at establishing the integrity of phallic aspects of the self-image. It also omits earlier and necessary work on the patient's mother problems. It focuses on fantasies and feelings which immediately preceded James's gain of sexual potency.

Initially and for some time James experienced his father as psychologically weaker than his mother. For James, father was a passive, background figure who had given up his decision-making capacity in all important matters. His father had few outlets in personal relationships and generally bottled up his feelings. However, James saw his father as athletic and feared his physical strength. Typically, mother threatened James with paternal punishment and showed that she controlled paternal power. What normal contact James had with his father appeared to be in occasional physical games, albeit sadistically tinged.

One bizarre form in which James's father allegedly expressed affection was by getting into bed with James on weekend mornings and holding James's penis, apparently in a warm, cuddly way. This continued until the first months of therapy. James rationalized this behavior as one of the few ways his father could seek contact. In some ways he felt affirmed and flattered since his father acted this way only with him, not with his brother. He felt some pride in being the cuter, more desireable sibling whom people fussed over. In analysis it also was revealed that he experienced power in being identified with the seductive mother whom his father needed, an inversion in which his penis was the desired breast.

In James's presenting phenomenology he depicted himself as lying in bed at his father's disposal with a muted and suppressed self-consciousness, semimesmerized, a state approximating erotic hypnotization. Until therapy he did not allow himself to dwell on any of his fleeting thoughts that something might be wrong with this behavior, nor could he permit himself any coherent sense of anger for being rendered passive. He was, however, clearly angry that his father intimidated him with superior physical strength (when James was fully grown his father was four inches taller and much fuller), although he did not express such feelings directly. In spite of devaluing his father, James wanted his father to like him. When James first entered therapy he made little of his predicament with his father, and it was not until work with mother problems was underway that paternal concerns became prepossessing.

Following is the line of fantasy and dream images that appeared to be most directly concerned with mastering some of the deficits in his father relationship and establishing his own fundamental sense of potency. The first in this series involves James's apparent attempt to reverse his passivity in relation to his father.

> Dream 1: James was riding on a horse with another man. The latter in front. As the horse increased speed James got an erection. The man tried to masturbate James who countered by masturbating the man instead. James felt triumphant and pleased that the man was in his power.

> *Dream 2:* James met his father in a whorehouse. His father asked, "Will you fuck
> me?" James replied, "Get out; I don't want you." Instead James per-
> formed anal, then vaginal intercourse with a prostitute and enjoyed
> himself.

The manifest content of these dreams was highly impactful and enabled
James to taste a heightened sense of power in relation to his father. Most often
James felt weak and helpless vis-à-vis his father, this in spite of looking down on
him. In the above dreams James reversed roles and luxuriated in the sense of
power that devaluing father implicitly gave him. More important than interpreting latent meanings or clarifying the various distortions which characterized
his reactions was a newly released sense of his own potential might, even if
inflated and tinged with manic spite.

Following are excerpts from his associative stream, including fantasies evoked
by his dream images: ". . . Father used to grab me as if I were mother's teat.
Now I'm fucking him. No, I disdain to fuck him. I toss him aside . . . Father's
sucking my cock, almost chewing on it like a dog chewing on meat. Yet my penis
is hard and strong and won't be chewed up. He's chewing hard but my penis is
stronger than he is. I'm the man now." James's thoughts turned to women, whom
he tended to view as part-objects. "Making it with prostitutes would be like
masturbating. But it would be better than not making it at all." He saw
prostitutes as ". . . worthless shit—fucking them would be like fucking shit." He
remembered being inhibited at a party. He could not talk to women because the
only thing he could think of saying was, "I want your body." He summed up, "I
have a lot of hate for women but I want them just the same. I feel great I was
able to have intercourse in the dream at all."

James found the dream and his fantasies demeaning but liberating.
He readily saw that the dreams expressed the wish for omnipotent revenge
toward both his parents (and to the analyst). However, it was the first dream,
so far as he could remember, in which he had sexual intercourse. He felt badly
it had to take such a debased form but was happy it could happen one way or
another. He liked it more for its promise than actuality: it felt good to be able
to visualize himself as a person who really could have sexual intercourse. His
few attempts had failed in reality and engendered a sense of fear and
hopelessness.

However, his elation, inevitably, was short-lived. The self-representation
cannot long be kept free of contamination from degraded object representations
without chronic insulation and self-hardening. Thus the heightened self-feeling
he momentarily achieved could not be consolidated on the basis of role reversals.
The momentum of therapy necessitated that he expand his options in more basic
ways. He would have to move beyond the position of trying to be on top in order
to avoid or compensate for being on bottom. The essential quality of his self- and
object representations required further change.

A genuine step forward was expressed in the following extended fantasy produced in a session a little less than two months after the above dreams:

> An eagle takes my cock and flies off with it and gives it to an athlete. It becomes a stick in a relay race. The guy goes faster than anyone. He's thin with long hair. My penis is giving him power and energy. A bird picks the athlete up and drops him on a mountain. Now he becomes a little boy running and playing. He gets picked up by his father and gets put on his father's back. His father kisses him and puts him down. The kid runs . . . gets picked up again . . . Father keeps doing this . . . up and down . . . like masturbating . . . The kid is a penis . . . The father puts a huge penis in the little boy's ass . . . rocking the kid on it . . . The kid enjoys it laughingly . . . Then the kid has enough and gets down. He kicks his father's penis but can't escape it. He's held onto it somehow. Maybe his clothes get caught on it. He jumps up and down on it. He slides down off it like a sliding pond . . . The little boy goes swimming by himself . . . In actual life my father played with me sometimes but was tired most of the time. I missed all this. . . .

Although the fantasy appears to begin with self-punishment it announces a desire to make contact with and increase oneself through a greater power. Hostile manic aspects, the wish to dominate and possess the penis to compensate for weakness and loss or as part of a mother identification, seem less important than the resulting confirmation of both the patient's and father's phallic powers. Above all there is a positive valuation of the penis in general, even to the point of overestimation, clearly an attempt to experience some kind of narcissistic integrity through the father image. James ends by using his father's penis, now a charging (life-giving) device, as he pleases. The initial dangers have been surmounted for the moment. A sense of harmonious phallic mix-up emerges. The paranoid elements which remain now seem secondary, and James experiences some sadness over realistic loss. A relatively undefensive communion with the paternal phallus emerges in which both his and his father's integrity were sustained, at least fragmentarily. In such a situation male phalli are experienced as enhancing each other in free play. Once this principle is firmly grasped and integrated, even though specific males may temporarily appear degraded, the phallic principle itself can be relied upon to remain essentially intact and life-giving, at least potentially—an analog to basic trust in phallic terms. In the present instance the phallic communion emerged in a spirit of aggressive, buoyant play, doubtless evoked by the implicit élan of the therapy relationship.

Once phallic identification with the uncontaminated father could occur, falsehoods with regard to the ulterior mother identification became visible and distonic. That is, once James tasted the exhilirating, clean air of lively, phallic play, the extent to which he had felt tricky and sneaky without acknowledging it became clearer. He could now freely admit that he manipulated people by being clinging and cloying much as his mother did. He confessed, "I go through all sorts of changes to get people to fall in with me. I'm like a baited trap. I'm a little monkey." In wake of this experience James's mother image underwent a significant change, as reflected in the following dream.

> *Dream 3:* James's mother subordinated herself to directions given by an unknown male. James felt the man was honest and had good values. He was aware that this was the first time he was experiencing his mother as submissive or even respectful to anything beyond herself.

The prostitutes in James's earlier dreams now seemed to him to reflect his own lifelong "whorishness" which he desired to break through. A number of unseductive women began to appear in his dreams. One figure was a simple, good-natured pregnant woman who possessed what James described as "unmanipulating beauty." He felt more truly himself when he focused on her image and let the feelings it evoked spread through him. Contact with the good-mother image increased James's supplies and, dialectically, enabled him to tolerate a more radical encounter with the wounding and saving aspects of father.

The culmination of the sequence described in this section is reflected in the following dream, one of the last dreams James recalled prior to his first successful sexual intercourse:

> *Dream 4:* A man who resembled a very creative artist known to James repeatedly cut off James's legs and penis which kept growing back. Each time they were severed they grew back more strongly. It was as though the cutting increased their strength. At first James was frightened, then realized the man was doing him a favor.

Although the dream might be viewed as an attempt to deny castration anxiety, the actual movement of the case had another impetus. James saw the creative artist in the dream as a corrective father figure, one whom he could respect, like the analyst. This was much different in spirit from the contempt he had displayed for the paternal figure in an earlier fantasy in which a similar motif appeared. In the present context James felt the creative wounding described an aspect of therapy, the repeated castrations or mortifications which had beneficial results. The dream witnessed his deepening trust in the therapy situation and in his own resilience, suggestive of a genuine change in self and object representations (Job's outcry comes to mind, "Though He slay me, yet will I trust Him"). A sense of the symbolic phallus surviving attacks was developing. Sexual potency soon followed and was consolidated through further work. In James's case the emergence of symbolic phallic object constancy appeared to be a necessary condition for genuine potency. To be sure, it received support from both male and female elements in James's personality. As indicated above, changes in both father and mother images played an important role in allowing the phallic aspect of the self-image to approach integrity.

THE CAPACITY TO GENERATE IDEAL IMAGES

Work with phallic fantasy led to the repair of certain aspects of James's self-image and to a genuine gain in potency. However, it did not relieve his work block. Only when his communion with ideal images became explicit did his work block give way to a heightened sense of inspiration. Nevertheless, work with phallic fantasy did not occur without some implicit reference to ideal feelings. For example, the creative artist in Dream 4 functioned as a potentially useable ego ideal. Moreover, James's overall struggle to rehabilitate his father image included idealizing tendencies. It was, however, necessary for him to distill and effectively own his basic capacity to create ideal experience.

James's capacity to create ideal experience had become impaired owing to destructive aspects of his relations to his parents. The early ideals he had projected on his parents were returned to him in poisoned and debased forms. He learned to keep idealizing tendencies to himself, with the result that periodic bursts of chaotic inflation alternated with strong demoralizing tendencies (see Dreams 1 and 2 with commentary, for a more successful organization of an inflated state). The modification of parental images through therapy allowed his desire for ideal communion to come into the open. This was especially expressed and carried forward in his relationship to the analyst.

The explicit emergence of ideal states did not occur until James was able to acknowledge the increasing importance I had for him. As he admitted my growth of importance to him he experienced more hurt and angry feelings at my apparent personality defects, moments of self-absorption, attention lapses, and various insensitivities. In keeping with his struggle to establish a viable father image, he often couched his hostility in phallic terms. When he abusively called me names such as "prick-face" or "fuck-face" he at times imagined and even "saw" my face as a penis. Many of his more destructive wishes, for example, the wish to kick, hit, bite, or spit at, were aimed at my now penis-like face. He hoped by his show of verbal violence to shatter whatever walls prevented contact and to compel me into magical feats of repair. At the same time he feared his inner violence would damage the essential goodness he found in (or through) me. For in more benign moments he could experience my face as glowing and good.

During this period James dreamt (Dream 5) that he tried to stab an Indian in the heart with a pencil. The Indian guarded his space with a firm, unbreakable pencil of his own. James noted that the Indian's face seemed impassive and could be thinking anything. Although he felt some sense of defeat at having been repulsed, he largely felt relieved and energized, to his surprise. What began as an anxiety dream ended by his waking up feeling wonderful. Contact with the Indian had a strengthening effect and increased his sense of well being.

The Indian reminded James of the catatonic chief in the film *One Flew Over the Cuckoo's Nest*. He described the Indian as withdrawn but powerful. The dream seems to begin as a variant of the "phallic charge" theme but introduces a new and striking emphasis on the "face." He linked me with the impassive face and berated me for being like a stone wall. He caricatured my dead spots. After venting fury with me for the pain I caused him because of my apparent deficiencies, he related the Indian to himself. He said:

> I don't budge either. I frustrate myself. I'm like cement inside. The Indian in me doesn't blink. He just sits there and grits his teeth. I picture him breaking down barriers. That's the energy he has in him. I make myself weak and act like a monkey because I'm afraid of that power. My Indian is the prick I see in your face. Maybe you've been keeping him in safekeeping. I've got to warm him up. He has a lot of thawing out to do.

The mute Indian represents a level of stifled aggression and longing that James had been unable to reach before. However, this figure also represented an observing quality of great importance. James said ruefully, "My Indian sits and watches. Nothing escapes him. He's waiting. He's my mind-prick sitting on its ass in my head. I've been afraid to know how clearly he really sees things. It seemed safer to feel clogged up." In this connection the pencil duel is linked not only with aggressive homoerotic wishes but with culture and potential sublimation, associated as it is with the active and creative phallic Word or logos.

After several weeks of expressing and working on these feelings James dreamt (Dream 6) of me sleeping, my face soft and open like a baby's. He was touched with my vulnerability in the dream and felt united with me. At the same time he felt that the soft feeling was connected with a sense of his own impassive, Indian face thawing out. He thus had a double sensation of being me yet not me but more thoroughly himself. For James it was as though we simultaneously permeated one another *and* were mutually transcendent, a state characterized by mutually enhancing areas of union and distinctness. He soon found himself beginning to give formal expression to this elusively stirring quality in his painting which now made genuine progress.

James's struggle to constitute valuable ideal experiences which could endure polluting and destructive attacks was well underway. His sense of my soft aspect contrasted dramatically with my "prick face," and he feared it would not sustain harder, meaner feelings. It was critical for him to learn that both his and my sense of intrinsic goodness persistently regenerated itself and, whatever our failings, remained essentially incorruptible (Eigen 1975, p. 290). The emergent sense of goodness and well-being was experienced by James as the core of his self and of selfhood in general. It gave rise to a sense of wholeness characterized by a vibrant, glowing aliveness. It waxed and waned, now pervading more, now less of himself and others. Although it was not something he could entirely be for long, it acted as an indicator or reference point for what was best in himself and others, something experienced as precious and inexhaustible.

Contact with ideal feelings intensified James's desire for personal development and prompted creative urges. Further contact with ideal images was, in part, consolidated and carried forward by the growth of a supportive and stimulating ego ideal. As mentioned earlier the creative artist in Dream 4 was an ego ideal figure awaiting use. The analyst, by becoming a temporary model for dedicated work, attracted useable resources from James's past, including elements serviceable for creating inspiring ideal figures. As the ego ideal function gradually matured, James came to experience both the analyst and himself as under its aegis, each person potentially faithful in his own way to some basic sense of truth-goodness and the desire to grow. The inspirational quality of ideal experience initially heightened James's desire and capacity for creative work. However, its structural evolution into a viable ego ideal function helped direct inspiration into culturally meaningful forms (Eigen 1979b).

THEORETICAL CONSIDERATIONS

Although instinctual fantasy and ideal images tend to be inseparable, different directions of emphasis in their clinical functions were noted in the above case. Instinctual fantasy was most directly related to lifting the patient's sexual block. However, it was work with ideal images which decisively heightened the patient's creativity in his painting. Although these directions of function could be discriminated, work with both instinctual fantasy and ideal images was interwoven and necessary for the fullest possible correction and reconstitution of the patient's self-image and ability to utilize his energy.

In the present instance James's experience of the human face was pivotal in repairing his ability to create and effectively use ideal states (Eigen 1977, 1979b, 1980, 1982). Since instinctual interpretations were not sufficient to open this dimension, James's concern with the face is not easily explained by instinctual meanings alone (e.g., face = breast). As noted above, work with instinctual meanings cured James's sexual but not creative work problems. James's concern with the face seems better viewed as an attempt to generate a source of ideal inspiration which may utilize but cannot be exhausted by instinctual meaning components.

In this context the work of Spitz (1965) is suggestive. Spitz found that during feeding, the baby stares raptly at the mother's face, not her breasts, a phenomenon which strongly indicates that symbolic face imagery cannot be reduced to the breast, as analysts usually have done. The symbolic equation, face = breast (correlated with buttock = breast) often holds, but not always and perhaps not primarily.

Another related finding by Spitz is that the baby smiles coherently, systematically, and joyously in response to a human face or face representation as early as two or three months of age (investigators now say much earlier), apparently indicative of some basic form of self and other awareness. Prior to the emergence of this smiling response, the baby's smile tends to be random or diffuse, excited by passing thrills, sights, or tactile sensations. The affectively full and expressively coherent smile in question may be seen to occur to gestalts of the eyes and nose but not nose and mouth and does not occur through touch alone. Thus it appears that an element of distance is required for the smile expressive of self and other awareness to occur. One might argue that early awareness of self and other arises in a matrix characterized by an ambiguous interplay between psychophysical closeness and distance, both of which remain critical defining dimensions of human subjectivity.

Spitz's conclusion that the smiling response can be viewed entirely in terms of "oral perception" (p. 92) contradicts his own data, wherein a nontactile, distance element contributes something distinctive. It can equally be argued that the emerging sense of self and other involving a distance element gives coherence and organization to what otherwise would be diffusely insistent tactile-proprioceptive-kinesthetic sensation streams.

It is also unlikely that one can account for the emergence of the smiling response, again as Spitz has tried to do, wholly in terms of biological signal theory, that is, in terms of the smile's functional value in eliciting empathic maternal responses which would ensure the infant's survival. The novelty and felt significance of the smile, the surplus of its expressive coherence, marks a dimension of responsive cognition which goes beyond the range exhausted by animal signaling and consciousness. It may be that before the smiling response the infant can be said to be conscious (e.g., like an animal) but not self-conscious (i.e., in some way aware of its "going on being"). Similarly, although phenomena of bonding or attachment may occur prior to the smiling response, they also characterize animal behavior and do not in themselves provide a means for understanding how they are psychically represented once self and other awareness arises.

The teleological form of biological signal theory masks a basic decision with regard to the implicit phenomenology attributed to the infant's smiling response. For Spitz the infant's smile is essentially manipulative and controlling, bent on "coercing" the environment. However, to the present observer the smiling response in question appears to be open and undefensive, neither tricky nor tough. It reflects a state in which thinking-feeling-action have not yet undergone radical dissociations. The infant seems to responsively smile, his whole being alive with a certain vibrant delight, more suggestive of spontaneous joy in being-cognizing-doing than a simple focus on control (although the two need not be mutually exclusive). It is not long before the infant begins to inhibit expressions of affect out of fear and guilt. By 8 months, I believe, the infant may be seen to smile when frightened or angry. Its smile may then take on a seductive–manipulative turn or, still worse, develop dead areas or became blank. Chronic breaks in thinking-feeling-action become consolidated and defenses begin to proliferate. The full, open experience of the Other's face (reflected in the baby's full, open smile) becomes toned down, distorted, even lost. In certain extreme instances the capacity to represent the human face may become seriously impaired. The appearance of the analyst's face in fantasy or dreams may portend healing on very early levels for such individuals.

The above portrayal assumes that the sense of self and other arise together. There are sound logical and clinical reasons for this belief. Gestalt psychology, for example, has shown that perception cannot occur in psychologically empty space, a phenomenon which includes self-perception. A self with no reference point outside it could have no awareness of its own existence. In essence, one's sense of self and other function as figure and ground for one another, each a condition of the other's possibility.

In actual clinical experience areas of union and distinction are always found in some mixture or conjunction, and it is likely the original self shares this quality as well. Since pure states of fusion or detachment are not found in actuality (they are intellectual abstractions), there is no reason to postulate them as characteristic of the early-most self. It seems fairer to say that a basic ambiguity — a simultaneity of areas of distinctness and union — represents an essential structure of human subjectivity, whatever developmental level. If one tries to push back beyond either of these constitutive poles, the sense of self must disappear.

However, current theoretical discussions centering on ideal states tend to relate the latter to some notion of "undifferentiation." This loose usage does not stand up to rigorous analysis. Strictly speaking, to be undifferentiated and exist is not possible. Undifferentiation must always be a relative notion, implying some quality of differentiation, if it is to have any meaning. An alternative which takes some variant of "primary narcissism" (e.g., "autism") as its starting point is equally problematic if the sense of self can only exist in a relational or differentiated experiential field, whatever imbalances of self/other emphasis may exist.

In this regard Mahler (1968) believes that the early-most self arises with no sense of otherness (autism) and moves to a state of fusion with the other who was not yet there (symbiosis). From this imaginary point separation-individuation proceeds. However, in light of the preceding considerations, to postulate a self with no other is to postulate no self at all. Similarly, without some form of awareness of self and other the notion of merger refers to a fusion of beings who do not yet psychologically exist, and thus cancels itself out.

Winnicott (1953) presents a somewhat similar problem when he suggests that the first not-me, the transitional object, begins to separate out from global omnipotence. The distinction between inner and outer follows later. However, he also writes that the mother must be present enough to keep the internal representation of her alive or the transitional area could not appear and survive (Winnicott 1953). Here the representation of the mother must precede the transitional area, an apparent contradiction. Winnicott (1969), further, believes that the sense of otherness emerges when the infant perceives that the other survives the infant's destructive attacks and wishes. However, one would have had to know that the other had been there in order to appreciate the fact that the other has come through. The perception that the other survives one's destructive attacks doubtless leads to a fresh sense of otherness and oneself but assumes rather than accounts for the original constitution of self and other. For Winnicott, in fact, they are conditions for one another.

In the present view the correlative constitution and elaboration of the sense of self and other is taken to be the primary creative act of human beings, repeated with varying quality and emphasis on every developmental level. Further, in my belief it is the implicit awareness of the generative experience in the act of giving rise to the original sense of self and other — with areas of distinction and union — which most basically evokes the experience of wholeness. The sense of wholeness is ever threatened by the shifting imbalances and conflicts between polar tendencies toward distinctness and union. However, genuinely harmonious and unifying moments can occur throughout the course of one's development, ideal moments which function as reference points for and nourish faith in a sense of one's ultimate integrity.

An adequate developmental theory would attempt to give an account of the evolving qualities which characterize the coexisting areas of union and distinction as these necessary aspects of human subjectivity undergo enrichment. This includes the study of how these intrinsically related structures interact and under what conditions they appear to become relatively dissociated from or collapse into one another. In pathology individuals attempt to create a spurious sense of wholeness by emphasizing one of these terms at the other's expense or, more accurately, distorting each in typical ways.

Terms like *autism* or *symbiosis* refer to differences in emphasis along the isolation-union continuum. They represent characteristic ways individuals attempt to create an illusion of wholeness, spuriously or as the result of developmental deficiencies. By firmly grasping the principle that at every point subjectivity is characterized by some mixture of distinctness–union, one can refer distortions in either direction to the normal capacity they implicitly aim at and often seek to restore. However, if one tends to absolutize these poles, as Mahler's scheme appears to have done, the therapist would have to be frightened at risking the deepest (potentially restorative) regressions. For, according to Mahler's scheme, if the patient goes back far enough he is left with the choice of being isolated or merged, in either case nonexistent. In light of this scheme no wonder emphasis is so often placed on building good defenses rather than risk becoming lost in the imagined vacuum of the psychic depths. The deepest regressions can be maximally wholesome only if one owns the ambiguous psychological presence of self and other at each turn, whichever occupies the foreground in a given moment or developmental phase.

The experience of the Other reached by means of restorative regression in the therapy situation is rich with creative ambiguity. The analyst's realistic identity was preserved but something was added which also made him seem more or other than his usual self. A sense of boundless immateriality pervaded the subject's experience; the ineffable was a distinctive part of his mental object. In an earlier paper (Eigen 1980) I summarized such experiences from the viewpoint of the patient in the following way:

> I see you but not just you. I am experiencing a more real, perfect version of you, a glowing-light you, inexpressibly radiant and fluid. I can go in and through you yet feel more myself than ever. It is as if I entered and passed through a highly charged yet resistanceless medium and feel newly conscious and restored. [p. 439]

In such experiences a sense of being thoroughly alive in both immaterial and material dimensions of experienced reality (the "dual unity" applied to mind-body) was reparative. To simply reduce one of these subjective aspects to the other (e.g., the ineffable = mother) collapses the structural integrity of the achievement. Ideal experience is a basic human capacity and emerges spontaneously in the course of human development. Since in some sense it is free floating and can merge with virtually any material object, it cannot be reduced to any single object or set of objects with which it comes to be identified. It is a generic capacity and its relation to particulars is riddled with problems. To explain the felt sense of infinite perfection or an intimation of immaterial boundlessness solely in terms of their material occasions (mother, breast, father, penis, etc.) seems at best careless; it assumes what it needs to understand.

In the case of James and in the summary example quoted earlier, ideal images of present concern centered on the analyst's face. The patient sensed himself to be one with yet also distinct from the analyst, a two-in-one dual unity in which both poles of human consciousness were upheld. This basic ambiguity of human life was carried forward by the ego ideal which in its dual capacity acts as a subjective object mirroring one's own creative urges while it simultaneously reflects the endlessly inspiring Other, the intended object pole of all authentic, creative strivings.

The ambiguity touched upon in these occurrences perhaps finds its most focused structural analog in the infantile feeding situation. In this situation a nontactile sense of the face is the center of visual experience, while the nipple-breast is the center of tactile experience (Elkin 1972). This perceptual distinction, symbolically elaborated, may suggest that the human ego has a double foundation from its inception, simultaneously a physical and mental self, dwelling both in material and immaterial dimensions of experienced reality. It is likely that when the baby is panicked at the mother's absence it is not an image of the breast but of her face which brings most comfort. The possibility also exists that some double sensation of both the face and the breast touches different areas of infantile longing.

REFERENCES

Balint, M. (1968). *The Basic Fault.* London: Tavistock.

Chasseguet-Smirgel, J. (1974). Perversion, idealization, and sublimation. *International Journal of Psycho-Analysis* 55:349–357.

_____ (1976). Some thoughts on the ego ideal: a contribution to the study of the "illness of ideality." *Psychoanalytic Quarterly* 45:345–373.

Eigen, M. (1974). On pre-oedipal castration anxiety. *International Review of Psycho-Analysis* 1:489–498.

_____ (1975). Psychopathy and individuation. *Psychotherapy: Theory, Research and Practice* 12:286–294.

_____ (1975-1976). The differentiation of an androgynous imago. *Psychoanalytic Review* 62:601–613.

_____ (1977). On working with "unwanted" patients. *International Journal of Psycho-Analysis* 58:109–121.

_____ (1979a). Common failings in analysis and therapy. *Psychotherapy: Theory, Research and Practice* 16:246–251.

_____ (1979b). Ideal images, creativity and the Freudian drama. *Psychocultural Review* 3:287–298.

_____ (1980). On the significance of the face. *Psychoanalytic Review* 67:426–444.

_____ (1982). Creativity, ideal images and instinctual fantasy. *Psychoanalytic Review* 69:317–339.

Elkin, H. (1972). On selfhood and the development of ego structures in infancy. *Psychoanalytic Review* 59:389–416.

Erikson, E. (1959). *Childhood and Society*. New York: Norton.

Freud, S. (1940 [1938]). An outline of psycho-analysis. *Standard Edition* 1:144–207.

_____ (1950 [1892-1899]). Extracts from the Fliess letters. *Standard Edition* 1:177–280.

Kohut, H. (1971). *The Analysis of the Self*. New York: International Universities Press.

_____ (1977). *The Restoration of the Self*. New York: International Universities Press.

Lacan, J. (1977). *Ecrits: A Selection*. New York: Norton.

Laplanche, J., and Pontalis, J-D. (1973). *The Language of Psycho-Analysis*. London: Hogarth.

Mahler, M. (1968). *On Human Symbiosis and the Vicissitudes of Individuation*, vol. 1: *Infantile Psychosis*. New York: International Universities Press.

Meltzer, D. (1973). *Sexual States of Mind*. Perthshire, Scotland: Clunie.

Milner, M. (1950). *On Not Being Able to Paint*. New York: International Universities Press.

_____ (1969). *The Hands of the Living God*. New York: International Universities Press.

Reich, A. (1973a). Narcissistic object choice in women. In *Psychoanalytic Contributions*, pp. 179–208. New York: International Universities Press.

_____ (1973b). Early identifications as archaic elements in the superego. In *Psychoanalytic Contributions*, pp. 209–235. New York: International Universities Press.

_____ (1973c). Pathologic forms of self-esteem regulation. In *Psychoanalytic Contributions*, pp. 288–311. New York: International Universities Press.

Searles, H. F. (1965). *Collected Papers on Schizophrenia and Related Subjects*. New York: International Universities Press.

Spitz, R. (1965). *The First Year of Life: A Psychoanalytic Study of Normal and Deviant Development of Object Relations*. New York: International Universities Press.

Stolorow, R. (1975). Towards a functional definition of narcissism. *International Journal of Psycho-Analysis* 56:179–185.

Winnicott, D. W. (1953). Transitional objects and transitional phenomena. *International Journal of Psycho-Analysis* 34:89–97.

_____ (1969). The use of an object and relating through identifications. *International Journal of Psycho-Analysis* 50:711–716.

8

Creativity, Instinctual Fantasy, and Ideal Images

INTRODUCTION

Creative activity is profoundly rooted in a fundamental ambiguity of human experience: the fact that we can experience ourselves as both embodied and disembodied at the same time. The basic tension between two worlds or dimensions of experience has been recognized by psychoanalytic thinkers in such concepts as *body ego* and *observing ego* (Freud 1923, Greenson 1967), *somatic ego feeling* and *psychic ego feeling* (Federn 1952), *body self* and *mind self* (Kohut 1971), and *body ego* and *transcendental ego* (Elkin 1972). We move within and between these two poles, now immersed in thought, now in body experience. In extreme states of dissociation the observing function becomes split off from immediate experiencing (Federn 1952). More generally the flow of interest flexibly shifts in emphasis as cathexes fluctuate in characteristic ways. In optimal instances the ego's double experience of itself reflects a natural division or differentiated unity. At such moments one may take oneself for granted or experience oneself as "whole" in harmonious well being. Creative activity frequently appears to be motivated by the intention to reconcile these two primary poles of human experience. It may be prompted by the wish to reduce the tension between them or represent an expressive overflow of their felt harmony.

Milner (1969, 1973) and Ehrenzweig (1971), in particular, point out various ways the ego symbolizes its shifting states of tension and harmony as it moves through different worlds of experience. The ego, for example, may represent its own self-experience and, more broadly, its sense of psychic creativity by means of androgynous god images (Ehrenzweig 1971). It may, too, express its implicit awareness of its dual nature by means of images which portray various degrees of mind-body separation and union. Thus images of facial features superimposed upon a lower body area or vice versa can, we shall see (Milner 1973) intimate something of the ambiguous interplay between representatives of mental and physical aspects of experience.

The quality of analytic outcome may be related to whether and to what extent a patient can allow symbols of psychic creativity to emerge and, finally, be integrated with body experience. In an earlier paper (Eigen 1973) I described patients who were able to absorb a healing experience of the ego reflecting itself in a disembodied and isolated way, albeit within the context of the therapy relationship. Some patients find it difficult to go beyond the confines of body imagery and values while others find it more difficult to enter the body and live in it fully. In the present paper a patient, F., who eventually was able to produce symbolic experiences of creativity itself is contrasted with another patient, B., who could not allow himself to transcend body-oriented ego experiences. Both patients exhibited severely resistant character disorders and both ostensibly entered treatment because of sexual impotence. In each case impotence was cured. However, the quality of cure in F.'s case was inestimably better inasmuch as he was able to move far beyond symptom relief.

Although both patients possessed a gift for meaningful, spontaneous imagery, only F. systematically produced transference images of creativity as such. What was particularly significant in F.'s growing capacity to experience symbolic expressions of psychic creativity was his ability to create ideal images which he could attach not only to self and other representations but to an evolving, useable ego-ideal. The mind spontaneously creates ideal images which enter into varied points of tension and harmony with representations of material reality. The ability to sustain the tension between representations of ideal and material realities is an essential condition of creative growth and work. A vital ego-ideal provides an ideal pole of experience which attracts representations of material reality which are relevant for its purposes. Thus the ego-ideal may come to act as a nodal point for the convergence and transformation of symbolic expressions of ideal and material experience. Insofar as the ego-ideal helps to stimulate and support creative activity it often also serves as a symbolic mirror of creativity itself. For example, F.'s ego-ideal, as will be seen, ultimately mirrored and represented his experience of creativity. With the support of the therapeutic relationship the newly restored ego-ideal was able to withstand both cynical attacks and threats of fusion. By so doing it was enabled to undergo the maturation requisite for it to play a significant role in the process of integrating ideal and material dimensions of experience, a never-ending ideal of growth.

Although ideal visions vary in specific content they normally convey some sense of infinite or absolute perfection (Bion 1970). In order to facilitate discussion a generic term, *ideal imago,* will be coined to represent what is constant in the consciously and unconsciously intended ideal objects of cognition. The developmental course of the ideal imago, particularly with reference to the ego-ideal as a symbolic expression of creative experience, is discussed following the case presentations.[1]

---

[1]For related work on ideal feelings and images see Eigen 1979a, 1980a,b, 1981, 1982.

Case of B.

B. had been married over a year and only on several occasions had he been able to have sexual intercourse, and then with premature ejaculation. He could sustain erection and achieve orgasm during mutual masturbation which was his usual sexual activity. If he placed his penis near his wife's vagina during masturbation he lost his erection almost instantaneously. He had had very little sexual activity prior to marriage. B. initially said he functioned well enough in other areas of his life.

B.'s central concern was to preserve his marriage. Before marriage he had been extremely isolated. He had lived alone with his mother. His wife was his first deep contact outside of his family and they fast became inseparable. She accompanied him to sessions and remained in the waiting room. Before sessions I often found them holding one another and after sessions they usually embraced. He could not relinquish this behavior throughout his analysis. They clung to their island of safety with a vengeance, a defiant oneness, at once formless and determined. There was something proud in their dependent isolation, as though they were saying, "What you see is a hard-won creation: Hands off!" Other persons seemed to be enemies.

In much of the early part of his therapy B. ventilated long-held-back fantasies and feelings about his mother. He had lived alone with her from the age of 4 until age 30, when he married. His father left home when B. was 4 and died five years later. He depicted his father as weak and futile, constantly demeaned by mother. In B.'s view his father's strongest moment was his leaving. He felt his mother turned his father into a vegetable and, in effect, killed him. B., afraid of his mother, became outwardly polite and compliant. In his words, "I learned to play dead in order to avoid my father's fate." At the same time he felt a longing for mother, tinged with protective worry. He frequently was excessively anxious over her well-being. His wish to appear good was threatened by "bad thoughts," obsessive intrusions. He periodically broke out with uncontrollable fits or temper tantrums and occasionally smeared himself with feces until age 8. He had erratically soiled throughout childhood. He spent much energy warding off his hate.

Once he began to realize that in analysis he could voice whatever he wished his obsessive stream began to emerge. In many of his fantasies, previously short-circuited, his mother injured herself. When as a child he learned that parts of heaven sometimes fell to earth he feared that a meteor would fall upon his mother in the night. He remembered at one point having been convinced that he saw trees begin to break and fall as she walked under them. He also felt a need to be her protector and accomplished this by touching himself secretly without anyone noticing, thus neutralizing evil forces. In still more frightening fantasies he was responsible for her imagined, almost hallucinated injury. He recalled trying to make her fall down by closing his eyes and tensing his muscles as tightly as possible. He squeezed himself with all of his might wishing she would collapse. His mental efforts were sometimes so intense he was convinced she did fall because of him.

In sessions he developed a magical world based on comic book heroes from his childhood. His mother was Wonder Woman in danger whom he, Superman, would save or vice versa. He also would be Plastic Man and she Plastic Woman. They could stretch their limbs as far as they pleased in order to find and protect each other. At other times they competed with each other in heroic and treacherous acts, alternately saving and endangering one another. In one fantasy series they turned into all-consuming monster blobs who menaced each other but finally recognized each other's true super identity in the nick of time. They could reverse as well as change identities, he the female and she the male.

He experienced much relief in letting his fantasy life unwind. Keeping it in check had caused great tension. However, he did not view me favorably. He split his love and hate, reserving the former for his wife. He claimed to have an all-loving relationship with her but viewed me as a villain who wished to break up his marriage. Yet he did not seriously consider changing to another analyst. He commented with hostile self-satisfaction, "You're [the mental health field] all alike. You can never let a marriage be because you're all so miserable yourselves." It seemed as though he came to analysis in order to find someone to hate. His anger most often was shown in intellectualized backbiting but at times more direct irritation broke through. He preferred to be icy and aloof and tended to blame me when he felt needy. He was in the transference bind of hating but needing therapy and took to acting as though it were my fault that he needed to be in session. When he was able to express some of his anger a little more directly he admitted, "I would have exploded if I didn't come here. Even if you don't know what to do with me it's a relief to pass part of my nervousness on."

If I tried to explore the way he split his feelings he became more defensive. At the same time his attacks on me tended to loosen his psychic flow so that more remembering and imagining could occur. In particular, permission to express his angry feelings seemed to enable him to explore his feminine identity more thoroughly, as though feeling his might allowed him to express some feared wishes.

He recalled a period in his childhood in which he dressed in his mother's clothing. He felt urges to do this again and for a time acted out his wish with his wife's clothes and some women's outfits he bought for himself. He admired himself in the mirror and explored many imaginary autoerotic possibilities, such as sucking his own nipples, sucking his penis, and having sexual intercourse with himself. He successfully fulfilled his oral fantasies in his dreams. For a brief period he enjoyed the inflated thought that he was an androgynous being capable of fertilizing and giving birth to himself. In one session he went so far as to feel that the world was a giant embryo within him which resembled him.

Such images expressed B.'s envy of and wish for fusion with the maternal object together with his attempt to feel more powerful than she. They also reflect a basic need for self-building. The apparent defensiveness of his imagined self-containment was partly a way of furthering contact with himself. In the safety of a self-created womb one may dare to consider the potential birth and regrowing of oneself in both one's male and female aspects. A regression to a sense of self-creation is sometimes needed in order to generate and maintain a fuller sense of self.

A particularly significant aspect of his self-creation fantasies involved anally generating his legs and penis from his feces. In a vivid set of images his body at birth was only partially formed. His head and upper torso were most prominent. He created his legs and penis last. They emerged as a fecal tail from his anus and gradually became properly differentiated. With the emergence of feet and penis—

symbolic carriers, respectively, of self-support and self-assertion — as aspects of his body ego, his self-birth fantasies diminished.

The anal drama expanded to include parental figures. He imagined smearing himself with feces using material from his fecal feet and penis. He painfully acknowledged that he had always felt like a "bag of shit." The fecalization of his body had two aspects: his body was both "made of shit" and covered with it. In being feces he was a part of mother which was just like father. He felt that both he and father were made from mother's feces, "pieces of mother's shit." Smearing himself with feces was smearing himself with father. The self-demeaning role of his father had been concretized and fixed by a fecal metaphor by means of which B. had structured his paternal longing. Smearing himself with feces as a child took on new meaning in light of this. It represented a fight to hold onto father any way he could, even if both of them were reduced to part-objects of mother's body.

He experienced the provocative, spiteful, and exhibitionistic spirit of his fecal bravado. In it he asserted that what his mother found useless he found valuable. He and father remained degraded maternal creations but it was a defiant degradation. His awareness of his need to identify with the fecal father in order to have a father at all was sufficient to initiate the pain of real loss. He was able to sustain, at least transiently, a mood of mourning over paternal deficit and failure. A correlate of this movement was that B. was able to openly experience positive feeling toward me for a time. The mechanism of splitting diminished long enough for some psychic readjustment to occur before his basic defensiveness reasserted itself.

B. could now maintain an erection during sexual intercourse but suffered from premature ejaculation. The latter cleared up after work with dreams and fantasies concerned with the relationship between oral and phallic androgyny. In one of the most important of these sequences B.'s penis was lined with teeth which he deposited in a woman's vagina during intercourse. In this image the *vagina dentata* derived from him. This was followed by a dream in which a woman's vagina appeared to be toothless and spongy, possibly needy. B. thought, "If I enter it, it will suck up my power." The question that now formed was who would be toothless, he or she. In vigorous protest he imagined his whole body as a giant mouth bursting with teeth. Nevertheless, the opening of his penis seemed to be a hungry mouth, toothless and gummy. The problem became one of owning both might and need without reducing one to the other. In his dialectic with maternal power he had projected both his teeth and wish for merger onto the vagina, a projective need reinforced by his mother's inability or refusal to grant him what was his: only she could be hungry and have teeth. He was testing out the possibility that he had the right to be needy and dangerous too.

His withdrawal of negative projections from the vagina created space for the emergence of a more positive projective–introjective process. The vagina, at least temporarily, could be experienced more in accord with its containing function and as a model symbolic container for psychic contents as well as for penises and babies. By contact with the vagina the penis now could become a vehicle for the transfer of power whereby it assimilates something of the vagina's containing function and resilience. That is, contact with the vagina as a symbolic container, even if in a rudimentary way, permitted a more profound acknowledgment of the male and female aspects of the phallus. B. now experienced his penis in both its penetrating and containing aspects. He recalled a time in childhood when he wondered whether men could have babies. He oscillated between anal and phallic birth fantasies. He also thought that the penis was a baby that men were continuously having. For the first time in adult life he became conscious of respecting his scrotum and testicles as containers of the ability to propagate. This led to positive feelings for both the hard-rigid and soft-flexible aspects of his genitals. The soft–hard polarity, expressed above in images of gums, teeth, feces, and weaponry, now could be further integrated in genital terms.

One extreme consequence of his assimilating vaginal capacities in terms of the phallus was a striking set of fantasies in which he imagined his penis as an androgynous god. Hitherto his mother had claimed most of the god power. His state of mind might be summarized, "I can be god as well as or better than she." One might be tempted to interpret B.'s affirmation of the bisexual phallus as a narcissistic attempt at encapsulation, a defiant denial or, certainly, an identification with the maternal aggressor. Nevertheless, what is most central in this movement is the attempt to assimilate and transcend maternal power. It expresses a primitive and tentative consolidation of the wish to be and do, however defensively, and it is this which requires the greater emphasis.

It is worth noting, in passing, that B.'s gain in ability to have sexual intercourse was accompanied by a shift in time experience. Previously he had felt rushed, often without clearly realizing it. He had to hurry in order to evade impending dangers. He also complained that things went by too quickly. He would try to go faster in order to catch up to the rushing moment only to find himself speeding ahead of himself and events. However, when he would slow down things seemed to move too quickly again. He always felt "behind" or "ahead" but never just "with." He once sarcastically said that he "could not come fast enough." By assimilating aspects of maternal power he was able to make and give himself time. He felt a greater fit between his inner time sense and his sexual rhythms.

When B. became reliably potent he terminated analysis. From his point of view treatment was successful. In addition to satisfactory sexual functioning he experienced fewer somatic disturbances, increased confidence, and a wider range of daily options. The results were more than he had hoped for. Nevertheless, he regrouped his defenses and consolidated his gains behind splitting and projective identification strategies. He continued to idealize his wife while I remained the wayward and at times malevolent intruder. His sense of mastery was reinforced by a partial fusion with the idealized image he projected onto his wife. At the same time he installed the analyst within his system as a containing focus for bad parts, at best a kind of internalized outhouse. By using the analyst as a permanent psychic draining system B. achieved a manic superiority over the bad mother but at the cost of a fuller integration. What goodness he received from the analyst he experienced as his own without gratitude or acknowledgment.

In addition, no genuinely independent father principle was established. B. accomplished his gains by reducing the analyst to a useable element in his matriarchal psychic system. Masculinity was almost entirely defined with reference to the maternal body. His use of images assumed a quasisymbolic function. He did not fully enter the image as a symbolic possibility through which he could be radically transformed. In an important sense his use of his mental processes was well controlled. He participated in his capacity to imagine only enough for the desired, circumscribed gains to occur without opening himself to more risks than were necessary to reach his goal. He was not willing to sustain the more profound disruption necessary for a fuller creative development. He thus appeared to use his psychic processes as things or objects in order to achieve tactical ends rather than as signifiers of a more developed quality of selfhood, an end in itself.

Case of F.

F.'s presenting complaint also was sexual impotence. He had been in therapy twice before with other workers. His past complaints had been severe anxiety and depression. He was a chronic drug user who impulsively rotated between marijuana, amphetamines, barbiturates, heroin, and alcohol. His past therapists attempted to regulate his addictions by prescribing controlled drug regimes. He had received a mixture of supportive and insight therapy and had achieved some semblance of order in his life. He was a professional rock musician who worked, dated, and had friends. He adapted to and took for granted a chronic moodiness and background feeling of low grade despair. He showed strong idealistic and cynical attitudes side by side. His idealism seemed to be coupled with a moralistic bitterness pervaded by a sense of having been gypped. He sided with what might be characterized as a "magnanimous pessimism" with a tone of hurt pride and compulsively attacked any inclination to feel good.

In his first sessions he wondered whether his prolonged drug usage caused his impotence. He defiantly confessed that if it did he could or would not break his addictions. They were too much a part of him. He stated with some irony, apparently using "therapy language," that he wanted a magic cure that left the life he built up for himself intact. He seemed untouched by the cloudy, drift-along, and at times almost slurred quality of his style.

Once F.'s analysis began he allowed painful obsessive defenses to emerge first. He secretly believed he was being punished for sinful wishes and behavior. He felt he transgressed God's will and was suffering the inevitable consequences. This was one reason he no longer complained about his reduced state and learned to "make do."

His main crime was that he had induced his wife to have sexual intercourse with his best friend. He tortured himself for years with fantasies of his wife having sex with his friends. He enjoyed elaborate masturbatory rituals in which he prolonged the excitement these ideas brought him. Only through such fantasies did he achieve full orgasmic relief which he described as "explosions." He felt his wife eventually left him because he was basically a monster. He also felt guilty that his wife's or daughter's clothes at times became part of his rituals. He felt such thoughts and actions alienated him from the human community. He dreaded but lived for these degrading, ecstatic moments and spoke of them with a tone of depressive helplessness tinged with gloating.

An early resistance took the form of wanting to argue over the religious basis of his hopelessness. F. compulsively tried to convince me that God never could accept him, that he was irredeemable. After a time he mentioned a friend from high school who became a priest, an active homosexual who was intensely interested in

Buddhism. I asked what would happen if he spoke with his friend. He felt certain his friend would condemn him. At the same time he was fascinated that someone could be so aberrant yet still be a holy man. F. rationalized that priests were allowed to do "funny" things because they were closer to God but ordinary folk like himself were lost.

He began meeting with his friend, who was accepting and insightful. He helped F. begin to face his punitive picture of God and supported my view that F. had God and the devil mixed up. When in sessions F. began to verbalize "God's voice," mocking laughter could be heard behind its demands and accusations. F.'s God turned into a devil, either mischievous and impish or rasping and hating. F. initially tried to maintain a stance of defensive amusement with his devil-self but broke down in horror. With the disclosure of his partial identification and possibly fusion with the combined god–devil image he found himself unable to clearly distinguish between the divine and demonic in his experience of himself and others, something which seemingly had been clear to him before. He was forced to become aware of a deeper psychic reality. Although this placed him in a more acute predicament, he experienced immediate relief from the obsessive sexual fantasies about his wife and daughter which had plagued him for years.

He terrified himself with his new religious perplexity and at one point broke out in fever. The perseverating quality of his predicament began to subside as an underlying fecal self-image became more conscious during his illness. In a transitional image F. saw himself as a Jesus made of feces, blessing others with the fecal material which composed his body: "a shit-smearing Jesus," in his words. This image expressed both his covert megalomania and his sense of unworthiness. By being the divine fecal child he felt both spoiled and saved, an experience of power mixed with the thrill of humiliation. Through the fecal blessing he could be identified with mother and her special son, a "lovable little shit." He thus turned his self-hatred into provocative activity in which others received what he became, an essentially boundless revenge ("I can turn anything into shit").

In another set of fantasies, the fecal Jesus image was replaced by a little girl who urinated fiercely from a standing position.[2] The urine turned into liquid feces that streamed from her body openings. She seemed to F. "like a fountain pissing shit from every pore." F. experienced the "shit pissing little girl" (his description) as a primitive act of self-assertion, a furious show of might. It was a cathartic letting go. After experiencing the affect carried by this anal–phallic image F. was able to maintain an erection during fellatio. In this context fellatio made him feel clean. He pictured his partner as a cat licking his fecal body parts as though they were part of herself. By feeling himself as a cherished part of her he could momentarily feel redeemed.

In other images the cat turned into a lioness. F., though more paranoid, remained passive and covertly identified with her power. In fellatio his passive needs were met directly while dissociated active tendencies were experienced vicariously. At the same time by licking him ("licking shit") the maternal figure was

---

[2]A study of the image of a female urinating from a standing position, particularly with reference to female orgasm, may be found in Eigen (1977b).

debased. In this drama his active side was devalued while his masochistic aspect was elevated. However, contact with the phallic little girl aroused in him an inkling of his own active potential. In fact he experienced himself in a superior and dominant position at least mentally, since his partner did as he wished. In terms of body zones he felt his activity bottled up in his sphincters and more than once used the phrase that "he had his prick up his ass."

When F. was successfully able to sustain oral sex he terminated analysis. Termination and return to treatment became a recurrent pattern. The rise in good feeling threatened his chronic depressed and masochistic position. He was used to a lower level of stimulation and the increase in pleasure tended to have a disorganizing effect.

Soon after he returned to analysis he elaborated his first explicit transference fantasies, the threat of which was doubtless a major factor in his having left. F. was having difficulty maintaining the integrity of the analyst's face and body. In a vivid quasihallucination he saw the analyst's face turn into buttocks with mouth as anus. At the same time he imagined the analyst's face inscribed on the anal zone, "a face below." A mutual transposability of face and anal region emerged, a facial–anal fusion. F., further, found that he could convert any part of the analyst's body—or the human body in general—into an anal image. For example, he imagined the analyst as an anal breast, a container of fecal food. In a further development the breast had an anal mouth filled with a fecal nipple, simultaneously sucking and sucked on. The analyst was both anal mother and fecal child, at once an elevated and degraded creator and creation. Most importantly, the analyst's face seemed cohesive and radiant or dim and cracked depending on the patient's and sometimes the analyst's mood or momentary psychic position.

The initial feeling F. expressed concerning these images was anxiety. He also showed curiosity. The crises F. was undergoing centered around his doubts as to whether the cohesive or "good face" could support and give coherence to anal fusion and attacks. Insofar as the "face-ass" identity[3] implied a failure to properly differentiate and coordinate components of the self-image, F. experienced his position as precarious and his fantasies as threatening. Contact between face and anus could contaminate and spoil the face.

At the same time imaginary contact between face and anal area can have a positive function insofar as it reflects a growing, reciprocal relationship between mind and body. The face, symbolic of human personality, may act as a reference point by which body areas acquire deeper personal significance. In a similar context Milner (1973) suggests that the "face-ass" merger expresses a twin movement in which consciousness (represented by the face, particularly the eyes) is at once embodied and suffuses the body. The circular transposition of face to anal area and vice versa expresses the symbolic upward–downward flow of conscious-

---

[3]The vernacular, "ass," seems most aptly descriptive of the entire anal zone, inclusive of buttocks, anus, and in some instances rectum. More generally, crude usage is inevitable in work with disturbances at the psychic levels addressed here. McDougall (1974a) offers a complementary description of what may occur if such raw imagery fails to be evoked.

ness and energy. In pathology either of these poles may be too much absorbed by or detached from the other. This might result, for example, in either overliteralizing or overspiritualizing the body and in collapsing or making an abstraction of consciousness. In psychic unity the face as human signifier retains its prominence as an organizing principle in the field of meaning but is, nevertheless, one of many experiential foci which flexibly co-refer to one another. The therapeutic task is to convert the contaminations feared or courted by the patient into differentiated expressions of a growing mind–body unity. This is most effectively aided by the patient's increasing awareness of affective meaning in the therapy relationship.

The use of imagery is one way to experience the connection between thinking and feeling. Images give rise to both. However, images may also be used to maintain isolation. For example, F. tended to experience his rush of imagery with generalized anxiety softened by curiosity. The full range of thought and feeling they might evoke was avoided at first. They initially took on an appearance similar to screen memories, vivid but still. It was when he was able to connect the rise of images to his feelings in the therapy situation that they came most alive with meaning and affect. Spontaneous imagery for F. was both a way of expressing and keeping distance from the importance the analyst was beginning to have for him. He began to admit pain at perceived slights or neglect on the analyst's part. It was when he felt hurt or angry that the analyst's face appeared to be filled with cracks, holes, or otherwise damaged or deteriorating. When he experienced a taste of well-being the analyst's face appeared brighter and caring. The analyst's face always reconstituted itself and appeared fresh and undamaged once more. For a time this drama repeated itself incessantly. It would seem to F. that the damage would never go away or that I would take revenge, possibly withdraw or simply disappear. He might then feel a mixture of triumph and guilt or be convinced that he was lost. His critical learning, won over and over again, was that the restored face persistently surfaced, encompassing his fragility and hostility with a sense of the undamageableness of essential goodness.[4]

F.'s use of imagery reflected a sensitivity which had remained relatively uncultivated because it had not been able to find an effective interpersonal form. He had had to dampen his sensitivity rather than continually risk feeling overwhelmed. In the context of the therapy relationship F.'s feelings for the therapist and his capacity to imagine could stimulate each other and lead to a further unfolding of both. This eventually resulted in a deepening of his relationship to the various phases of his life.

As F.'s fantasy life evolved he made and sustained the distinction between fecal and urinary images, thus breaking through his pan-anality. A dream summarizes this phase of work. In it a devil offered F. heroin with the promise that it would help F. The devil had a fecal smell and fecal material oozed from his body surface. F. hesitated. He felt angry and repelled. The devil told F. he would die if he refused. This frightened F. so that he began to urinate. As his urine gathered force

---

[4]A related description of a patient's experience of God is recorded in Eigen (1975a, p. 20). Elkin (1972) offers an account of the Primordial Other which may underlie such phenomena.

he thought of cleaning the devil with his urinary stream or perhaps wash the devil away entirely.

Upon waking F. feared the anal devil would try to hide deep in his bottom. If he tried to drown or flush the devil out it meant irrigating his own insides with his urine. This led F. to remark with black humor that his way of helping himself was to "piss up his own ass," a grim metaphor for his self-destructive bind. He associated feelings of congealed hatred with the devil whom he now saw as his bad self. The urinary stream was a display of incipient phallic power which in the dream remained clean, uncontaminated by the fecal object it opposed. In this context the urinary image was an intrapsychic advance, whatever the remaining mix-up between cleansing and polluting forces.

Following the image of the uncontaminated urinary flow from his own penis, historical associations came more freely. F. recalled having been tied to a bed by an older female cousin when he was under five. She teased him in various ways. Afterwards, throughout middle childhood, he felt humiliated by the laughter of little girls and he withdrew in impotent rage. He related a number of incidents in which girls taunted him and he withdrew rather than risk greater defeat. When alone he had rageful fantasies in which he beat the girls. In time his sense of outrage faded. Instead he appeared to eroticize his aggressive feelings and found himself excited by the sight and touch of women's clothing, first an older sister's. He developed orgasmic rituals based on a fantasy of being teased.

In adolescence F. acted out homosexual feelings on a number of occasions without basically doubting his essentially heterosexual orientation. He associated images of his father with his homosexual urges. He pictured his father as weak and needy, a man who swept the floor at his mother's command. When F. found that his homosexual episodes failed to establish a proper paternal object he abandoned them in despair. It was then he started taking drugs and succumbed to his fecal self-image. Although drug addiction may be an oral disorder it, like many oral problems (Ehrenzweig 1971, Eigen 1977, 1984), frequently is structured in anal terms. In street language, for instance, drugs are referred to as "shit" while abstaining from drugs is known as "staying clean." F. described his drug taking as an attempt to create a world of his own by "eating his own shit." In one self-denigrating fantasy F. stuffed his feces back into his anus and commented, "Even my ass eats shit." When he explored his attempt to be self-contained it seemed as though he were trying to nourish himself by stuffing his fecal penis into his anal mouth.

F. remembered having received enemas in early childhood while his mother ritually held him firmly on her lap, his penis pressed against her clothed belly. Either she or his father administered the enemas. F. would feel rageful humiliation and ecstatic pleasure. He felt as if he would die and experienced his bowel movements as orgastic explosions, an orgy of masochistic satisfaction. The described sequence of dying and orgastic explosion amounted to a perversion of the rebirth experience.

He could recall splitting into two demons in these orgastic moments. One was his body demon madly exploding. The other was his head demon, an onlooker who grimaced and chuckled, "Heh, heh." In sessions the head demon's laughter turned into images of a woman who wished to incorporate his penis through fellatio. F. felt helpless but also fused with her power, secretly controlling. Her oral striving condensed maternal intrusiveness, F.'s active and passive wishes, and his feared punishment. In talking about this image F. remembered scenes in which his mother displayed a ruptured navel when he was a small child. It seemed to pop out like an erection, as though the incorporated phallus was showing. It also seemed like an umbilical cord. F. felt repulsed and wished to rip it off. It infuriated him that his mother repeatedly rejected her doctor's recommendation to have it removed by an operation. Her masochistic exhibitionism maddeningly stifled him. His strong impulses horrified him because, as he expressed it, "Cutting off my mother's belly-cock would be cutting off my own life-line." Maternal castration anxiety (Eigen 1974) merged with separation anxiety.

After recovering the above memories and elaborating fantasies and feelings associated with them F. reported significant changes in his devil images. The body demon became a prankish little boy who harbored erotic-aggressive urges toward mother's body. Maternal longing became a meaningful issue. At the same time the head demon — previously also a castrating woman (above) — turned into a little girl who laughed at F. each time he achieved an erection. The derisive girls of childhood had become a symbol of castrating and self-castrating contempt.

After exploring the above thoughts, feelings, and memories, F. became potent during genital intercourse and left treatment once more. His life had been going relatively well. He was enjoying both his personal relationships and his work. However, within half a year of termination he experienced a suicidal depression which forced him to seek help again. Once in analysis he revealed that he had magically expected potency to solve all of his psychological problems. The discovery that he could be potent and still have disturbances was vastly disillusioning.

He now had several dreams in which he was flying and enjoying the expansive, resistanceless feeling he had hoped sexual intercourse would bring. He confused complete narcissistic fulfillment with sexual gratification. This failure in reality testing pointed to a wish for limitless union with the Great Mother. His collision with reality had been so devastating because an opposite process had been initiated by analysis. The analytic work prior to his termination contributed to a growing decathexis of the Great Mother image. F. felt wounded by the experiential gap and sense of emptiness associated with becoming disengaged from a highly charged identification or merger. He sought to ward off the threat of further individuation by leaving therapy. The narcissistic injury he tried to avoid might be summarized, "After so much, this is all I am?" His collapse forced him to return to therapy and come to terms with the depressive loss and deflation of becoming merely human.

However, the entry into the human world is also vastly liberating. The pain of mourning the loss of an identification or idealized magical power is compensated by the release of energy previously tied to the mother–god image. The hidden megalomania implicit in such a fusion is converted into a useable sense of power. The ego is threatened but also exhilarated by the mounting sense of aliveness linked with an increase in personal creativity.

F. gave tentative form to his heightened sense of creative potential in an image of a history teacher similar to a teacher he liked in high school. This kindly and encouraging man once had presented an alternative which seemed radically different from F.'s own degraded father and homosexual acting out. F. had thought he would like to become a history teacher also. This was his first memory of an active and appealing ego ideal. He had almost forgotten about it over the years. This man was the only unambivalent figure F. had presented. His image for some time symbolized for F. the hope of living up to his potential. However, this one source of support had not been enough to sustain him. He found he lacked the inner resources to go to college. By the time he completed high school he was already immersed in a drug culture and soon acquiesced bitterly and finally numbly to his reduced life-style. Now and then flickers of what he might have been or once wanted to be crossed his mind but that was rare. The emergence of his old ideal came as a surprise to him but fit his overall increase in self-feeling.

He had never respected himself for being a musician. For him it was a dirty business, part of the drug world. He would say of himself and his friends, "We're just a bunch of animals." He felt he did not use his mind as a musician as he imagined he might if he were a history teacher. He knew that music could be more stimulating and meaningful but for him it was "just coasting." He now gave himself to his revived interest in history and permitted himself to begin to think and feel everything he could about it. He had dreams in which he appeared as a history teacher or his former history teacher appeared in a positive role. In one dream he read a history book of Western civilization as he traveled through Europe. In the dream he was animated and absorbed, more present than he normally was in everyday life.

His ideal image of a history teacher was different in a number of respects both from himself and his high school teacher. The face was brighter and clearer. It evoked a sense of breathing fresh air. F. felt "cleaned out" thinking about it. The fantasy figure's eyes were particularly important. In F.'s words, "They're just nicely there. They don't pierce me or try to draw me in. They seem content just seeing and feeling. They're not up to anything funny. You can be OK with them." F.'s attachment to this image preserved the promise of wholeness. It tended to energize, give direction, prod, and soothe. The ego-ideal functioned as a good mirror for what F. felt was best in him but had devalued. He once said of his idealized image of the history teacher, "He's the way I might have turned out if things had been right . . . the way I should turn out . . . the real me. . . ."

F. made abortive attempts to return to school. He took some courses that interested him but did not complete any. He found that becoming a history teacher was a good idea in theory but that it no longer actually appealed to him. He was libidinally more involved with music. He felt disappointed at not finding school more appealing and began to mourn his never-to-be-achieved old ego-ideal. In so doing he discovered that what being a history teacher *meant* to him was more important than actually becoming one. He began to transfer the good feelings he tapped in contacting his neglected ego-ideal to the idea of working more seriously as a musician. This enabled him to admit the deeper significance music always held for him. He felt he previously disparaged music, for one thing, because it came easily to him. Since he did not have to work hard at it he felt it could not be worth much. Consequently he failed to invest it with the work required for real accomplishment. He really loved playing and had been ashamed to admit it. In a profound sense music had been a Good Mother for him. He often succored and nourished himself by playing. He deprived himself of fuller satisfaction by not cultivating his talent. In thinking what he might yet do as a musician he felt some relief at not having to become something which was foreign to him, such as a schoolteacher.

It gradually began to dawn on F. that all of the feelings evoked by his ideal image were his and could be applied to anything he did. He experimented with the ideal feeling he had discovered and at times could turn himself on at will by contacting it. When he was able to tune into it he felt clearer and brighter. As his ability to tolerate good feelings increased his drug intake spontaneously diminished. He almost entirely stopped heroin and pills. Marijuana and alcohol continued, markedly reduced. He began to face more of his ambivalence about becoming a person. Experiencing himself more meant that he would have to take more responsibility for who he was and who he might become.

F., almost predictably, again left treatment. He returned after a shorter time than usual and with greater awareness of what he was doing. He could remark, "Maybe next time I'll be able to just talk about leaving without having to do it." He was involved in a serious relationship with a woman whom he also considered leaving. He used the gratification he received from this relationship to attack the analyst and used the more rare air of analysis to attack his partner. Fear of closeness bordering on paranoia oscillated with moments of intimacy. His ability to tolerate more friction in the therapy relationship enabled him to contain disturbances better in daily life.

Oedipal material became more important in the transference. F. had dreams in which he compared himself with the analyst. In them the analyst was admired by women for his superior strength, intelligence, and creativity. The women represented the mother and F.'s own feminine longings. In a further dream he admitted the analyst's superiority of experience but still felt humanly equal with him. He could now say, "I fled therapy so I wouldn't have to face coming to terms with you." This meant coming to terms with the father principle. A flexible shifting back and forth between narcissistic and object transferences was necessary in order for F. to build and test his capacity for experiencing many possibilities on the closeness--distance continuum. Insofar as oedipal problems came into focus F. could visualize and be energized by the challenge of integrating passive and active aspects of his creative wishes (for related examples of the relationship between psychic androgyny and the oedipal situation see Eigen 1974, 1975b, 1979a,b, 1980a,b).

Nevertheless, F. was only at the beginning of being able to consolidate the capacity to tolerate feelings of well-being and effective power. He was still easily flooded by self-demeaning outbreaks and panicky intimations of underlying deadness. He had made gains which enabled him to experience momentary feelings of wholeness which provided a basis for a gradual shift of his basic ego identification. He could endure attacks on himself and others without having to destroy the feeling life he was beginning to permit himself to build. The range and intensity of feelings available had increased in variety and subtlety. He experienced a sense of renewal. He thus had some framework from which to risk productive leaps into disorganizing areas. This phase of the growth process involved an intricate interplay between a comforting-stimulating relationship to the *ideal imago* and frightening-depressing encounters with flaws in his psychic structure.

DISCUSSION

Although both patients accomplished more than they anticipated in therapy, the quality of the outcome in the case of F. clearly was superior. B. never seemed to decisively rise above an essentially self-contained addiction to maternal part-objects. Even sexual intercourse remained inherently autoerotic in spirit for him. He maintained a clinging relationship with his wife which sealed off the possibility of otherness. No transcorporeal idealizations arose nor was father ever defined truly independently of mother's body. Potential symbols of autonomous selfhood were either lacking or manifested themselves almost entirely within the context of body-ego meanings where they remained embedded.

F., in contrast, was able to create images of the analyst's face and ultimately cathect an ego-ideal which assimilated positive maternal and paternal qualities. For F. revived contact with ideal images and, particularly, the ego-ideal, was profoundly healing. In instances of serious personality impoverishment contact with ideal images can genuinely nourish the ego, build supplies, and restore hope, as well as stimulate and support the wish for meaningful work. Kohut (1971) has recently emphasized ways in which ideal images spontaneously arise in narcissistic transferences and ultimately add to the personality's overall well-being and ability to function. The therapeutic impasse with B. provides an instance in which resistances to an idealizing transference were not surmounted. B.'s gains largely came through contacting aspects of the grandiose self. F., in contrast, more flexibly moved between self and idealized object cathexis. This greater elasticity enabled him to develop beyond the defense of splitting. With F. both sides of dissociated polarities could be gathered into the transference so that the transition from splitting to ambivalence could be made. Without such a development the most far-reaching assimilation of identifications or, in Kohut's phrase, "transmuting internalizations" could not adequately occur.

In F.'s case the affective coloring and heightening of F.'s visualization of the analyst's face suggests the highly charged tone with which the infant must view the human face since for the infant the human face or face representation has been found to be a central and organizing focus of perception (Elkin 1972, Spitz 1965). The infant's systematic and coherent gaze and smile in relation to the human face has been correlated with the emergence of self and other awareness (Elkin 1972, Spitz 1965). Thus F.'s dramatic perceptions of the analyst's face may well establish contact with the foundations of selfhood. F.'s development appears to confirm this belief. As F. evolved the *ideal imago* proceded to be transferred onto the therapist as a maternal, then paternal ideal and, ultimately, as an ego-ideal which both incorporated and transcended maternal and paternal qualities. The capacity of the human mind to spontaneously create ideal images undergoes development through prematernal, maternal, paternal, and transparental phases. Similar developmental phases with reference to ideal images have been traced by Pumpian-Mindlin (1969) and Blos (1974).

Analysts such as Reich (1973a,b,c) and Chasseguet-Smirgel (1974, 1976) have pointed out the harmful role a pathological ego-ideal may play. In these instances there is either (1) a short-circuiting of the distance between the ego and its ideal so that work is no longer a felt necessity or (2) an impossibly demanding ideal which renders all work futile. A proper relationship to one's ideal leaves room enough to be able to move a little closer to it at the same time one participates in it through empathic vision.

Freud (1914) warned against confusing the ego-ideal with sublimation but noted that the ego-ideal can prompt sublimation. Blos (1974) has attempted to delineate some aspects of the positive motivating appeal of the ego-ideal, particularly in its role of creative inspiration. Both Freud and Blos emphasize the importance of the father principle in sublimation and creativity. In this regard McDougall (1972, 1974b) and Chasseguet-Smirgel (1974, 1976) have indicated that patients who are "pseudocreative" or who have failed to attain genuine psychic generativity are frequently patients who have excluded the father principle. In basic ways such a patient's "ego is its own ideal" (Freud 1914) in a primitive and undeveloped sense, stunted by mother fusions. In the course of his analysis F. affirmed the integrity of the father principle in ways that B. did not. This involved a basic modification of the structure of the ego-ideal which for F. became paternal. However, a purely paternal ego-ideal, the mature end point for Aarons (1970) and Blos (1974), was a transitional phase in F.'s development. F.'s more developed ego-ideal absorbed both maternal and paternal qualities. It did not only stimulate unceasing approach but gave some of the encouragement and support that made approach possible. The musical activity itself which formed part of the content of F.'s ego-ideal provided a comforting mothering function in addition to presenting a challenging, "limitless future."

As the ego-ideal undergoes further development, the primal couple is transformed into a symbolic expression of the active and receptive aspects of the creative process in general. Identifications with mother and father proper are transcended by assimilating the various active and passive currents each represents. Insofar as this is accomplished more direct encounters with representations of the ideal imago as such, no longer fused with individual personalities, becomes possible. The self once again may emerge as its own ideal but with a richly developed structure and a new, coherent meaning.

REFERENCES

Aarons, Z. A. (1970). Normality and abnormality in adolescence. *Psychoanalytic Study of the Child* 25:309–339.

Bion, W. R. (1970). *Attention and Interpretation*. London: Tavistock.

Blos, P. (1974). The genealogy of the ego ideal. *Psychoanalytic Study of the Child* 29:43–88. New Haven: Yale University Press.

Chasseguet-Smirgel, J. (1974). Perversion, idealization and sublimation. *International Journal of Psycho-Analysis* 55:349–357.

_____ (1976). Some thoughts on the ego ideal: a contribution to the study of the "illness of ideality." *Psychoanalytic Quarterly* 45:345–373.

Ehrenzweig, A. (1971). *The Hidden Order of Art.* Berkeley: University of California Press.

Eigen, M. (1973). Abstinence and the schizoid ego. *International Journal of Psycho-Analysis* 54:493–498.

_____ (1974). On pre-oedipal castration anxiety. *International Review of Psycho-Analysis* 1:489–498.

_____ (1975a). Psychopathy and individuation. *Psychotherapy: Theory, Research and Practice* 12:287–294.

_____ (1975b). The differentiation of an androgynous imago. *Psychoanalytic Review* 62:601–613.

_____ (1977). On working with "unwanted" patients. *International Journal of Psycho-Analysis* 58:109–121.

_____ (1979a). Ideal images, creativity, and the Freudian drama. *Psychocultural Review* 3:287–298.

_____ (1979b). Female sexual responsiveness and therapist feelings. *Psychoanalytic Review* 66:3–8.

_____ (1980a). On the significance of the face. *Psychoanalytic Review* 67:427–442.

_____ (1980b). Instinctual fantasy and ideal images. *Contemporary Psychoanalysis* 16:119–137.

_____ (1981). The area of faith in Winnicott, Lacan and Bion. *International Journal of Psycho-Analysis* 62:413–433.

_____ (1984). On demonized aspects of the self. In *Evil: Self and Culture,* ed. M. Eigen and M. C. Nelson, pp. 91–123. New York: Human Sciences Press.

Elkin, H. (1972). On selfhood and the development of ego structures in infancy. *Psychoanalytic Review* 59:389–416.

Federn, P. (1952). *Ego Psychology and the Psychoses.* New York: Basic Books.

Freud, S. (1914). On narcissism: an introduction. *Standard Edition* 14:73–102.

_____ (1923). The ego and the id. *Standard Edition* 19:13–66.

Greenson, R. (1967). *The Technique and Practice of Psychoanalysis.* New York: International Universities Press.

Kohut, H. (1971). *The Analysis of the Self.* New York: International Universities Press.

McDougall, J. (1972). Primal scene and sexual perversion. *International Journal of Psycho-Analysis* 53:371–384.

_____ (1974a). The psycho-soma and the psychoanalytic process. *International Review of Psycho-Analysis* 1:437–459.

_____ (1974b). Anonymous spectator. *Contemporary Psychoanalysis* 10:289–310.

Milner, M. (1969). *The Hands of the Living God.* New York: International Universities Press.

_____ (1973). *On Not Being Able to Paint.* New York: International Universities Press.

Pumpian-Mindlin, E. (1969). Vicissitudes of infantile omnipotence. *Psychoanalytic Study of the Child* 24:213–225.

Reich, A. (1973a). Narcissistic object choice in women. In *Psychoanalytic Contributions,* pp.

179–208. New York: International Universities Press.

———— (1973b). Early identifications as archaic elements in the superego. In *Psychoanalytic Contributions*, pp. 209–235. New York: International Universities Press.

———— (1973c). Pathological forms of self-esteem regulation. In *Psychoanalytic Contributions*, pp. 288–311. New York: International Universities Press.

Spitz, R. (1965). *The First Year of Life*. New York: International Universities Press.

9

Ideal Images, Creativity, and the Freudian Drama

Creativity thrives on the interplay between ideal[1] images in the mind and the hard facts of life. The sense of the ideal marks the discovery of mind. Some sense of ideal reality runs through the history of thought and makes it possible, whatever shifts in meaning and function it undergoes. An ideal may act as a vector, pointing in one direction or another, making visible a range of facts or meanings previously unnoticed. It stimulates processes of selective sensitivity and reorganization. It may exhaust its powers and grow stale, a deadweight or sterile box. Plato's Idea of the Good, Aristotle's Unmoved Mover, St. Paul's perfect, personal Love, Galileo's thought experiment on "pure" motion—all are time capsules which evoke ways mind experiences, organizes, and uses its ideal sense of itself and its objects. Galileo's actual experiments were mixtures of ideal vision and observed fact. He symbolizes an attitude which has expressed itself in the infinitesimal calculus applied to motion and gadgets from the telescope to rocket ship (reflectors of consciousness which changed it). Nowadays it is no longer unusual to see the idealist in the empiricist and vice versa.

What ideal vectors governed Freud's creative thinking? What role did they play in the constitution and dynamic function of psychoanalytical symbols of creativity? What limitations did his materialist attitude impose on his treatment of the ideal pole of creative strivings and healing? These and related themes will be explored here informally.

THE IDEAL OF VIRILE HETEROSEXUALITY

An ideal of heterosexual intercourse, largely modeled on the prevailing culture's image of virility, dominated Freud's (1950) early thought. Anything less than

---

[1]"Ideal" may refer to some sense of perfection (beatific feeling, goal, or standard) or to the immaterial quality of thought and mental life as such. Its use throughout this paper is kept somewhat free floating, the overall "feel" determined by its context.

vital, sexual performance resulting in orgasm might (in combination with other factors) result in nervous illness. Such "failed" sexual acts as masturbation, coitus interruptus, or use of condoms were associated with illnesses like psychasthenia and "actual neurosis," reflections of congenitally low vitality and sexual damming. In essence, ideal virility was used by Freud as a principle of classification at once taxonomic, etiological, and clinical (recall the famous "fantasy" Rx Freud quoted from Chertok: "penis normalis — repeated dosage").

The ideal of vital sexual intercourse remained a conceptual organizer in one form or other throughout Freud's writings. At times genital intercourse appeared to function as a figure for generativity as such, psychic as well as biological, a meaning emphasized by later analysts (e.g., Meltzer 1973, Milner 1950). As Freud's views developed, he felt the chief obstacle to heterosexuality (i.e., creativity, literal or symbolic) was homosexual libido. Accordingly, the key to creativity was the sublimation of homosexual libido. Freud believed that his own life demonstrated this principle. As he worked through his transference to Fliess, he felt or envisioned the sublimation of homosexual libido which had been tied to his father. In so doing, he was enabled to move from creative block to breakthrough, paralleled by a loss of sexual interest. In his own words, creativity remained the one activity which made his life worth living.

By implication, then, and allowing for past disclaimers, for Freud (1908) aborted creativity must be linked with an inability to sublimate homosexual libido:

> The forces that can be employed for cultural activities are thus to a great extent obtained through the suppression of what are known as the *perverse* elements of sexual excitation. " 'Civilized' Sexual Morality and Modern Nervous Illness." [p. 189]

In this context, it is not surprising to find that Freud's greatest case histories are concerned with the inability to achieve or sustain heterosexual genital functioning together with failure to resolve creative block. The nuclear imagery in his cases is strikingly similar.

SODOMIC RAPE: A FIGURE OF ABORTED CREATIVITY

Freud's greatest case histories (Rat Man, Wolf Man, Schreber) have a common core image. In the Wolf Man the drama rushes toward a dream which Freud translated into Father entering Mother from the rear. In the Rat Man the core fantasy fear involved rat burrowing into anus. Schreber's feared-courted longing was to be possessed by his doctor god and, finally, by God himself. All, explicitly or by innuendo, involved rape by sodomy and war between passive-active, male-female tendencies.

Sodomic rape, as a paradigmatic image combining power and helplessness, may be viewed on many levels. One can envision as a kind of prototype the very early danger of being flooded by sensations of various sorts, possibly even in the womb (Bion 1979)—"stimulus rape." The embryo-infant-child soon learns to dampen and filter stimulus input to a manageable level. However, stimulus sensation speedup or shutoff may occur in a variety of conditions. Certain phases of schizophrenia and artistic creation may involve massive stimulus streaming. It is as if protective barriers have been somewhat lifted and the individual feels inundated by wave after wave of intense experience. Some individuals may try to protect themselves from their own sensitivity by turning off their attentional capacity. From early on, our mental equipment gives rise to images, thoughts, and feelings it cannot handle well. We scare ourselves with the imaginings we produce but cannot adequately process. Our mental creations are often ahead of our ability to assimilate them in meaningful and useful ways. In this sense we are at the mercy of the very psychophysical processes which constitute and sustain us.

For Freud the sense of helplessness beginning in infancy determined the profoundest longings of humankind, universally expressed in religion. Freud's vision of the depths of human helplessness formed the background which eventually led to his asserting a primacy of masochism in psychic life, the "death wish" (albeit clothed in biophysical terms). At the same time he adopted a basically phallocentric view of early development; in essence, we all begin our lives as "little boys" (libido, too, is "masculine," the activity of desire). Winnicott's (1971) work involves similar problematics at another level of meaning. He opts for a primacy of *being* over *doing:* we begin life as "little girls." At the same time he stresses the positive role of "ruth-less" aggression in the infant's early sense of vital aliveness. A kind of atomistic elementarism is deeply embedded in psychoanalytic thinking with the consequent tendency to impute primacy to one element of a system, only to be forced to reverse perspectives when the context shifts. In contrast, Taoist thinking describes a *primary reciprocal relation* between activity–passivity, a basic interweaving or polarity-in-unity.

The Freudian primal scene (essentially sodomic rape) expresses destructive or paralyzing distortions of this activity-passivity reciprocity, whether between individuals or within the same subject. It was, in part, the primal scene image superimposed upon the vision of infantile helplessness which stimulated Adler's "masculine protest." This latter, when transposed back into the Freudian network, became the drive to mastery, a concept with which Freud linked such diverse phenomena as the persistence of pathology, nightmares, and play. In this context, aggression appears to be a life drive (in opposition to Freud's formal theory), a meaning explicitly brought out by Greenacre (1971a) and Winnicott (1958, 1965, 1971). Nevertheless, in the strict Freudian vision, aggression against the self ultimately exerts the stronger pull and drains off the mastery thrust.

It is but a small step for the will to mastery to become sexualized through its link with pain and pleasure. The active and passive subjects identify with one another; we are all partners in giving and experiencing pain. In sadomasochism proper, the pleasure of masochism finally seems the more intense and exercises the greater gravitational pull. Was Freud mirroring the tidal swings of his civilization? The West began the "modern age" with a mentally-physically appropriative attitude (the "rape of Nature," world, all otherness) and progressively finds it has been raping itself, hapless in face of the forces unleashed.

It is, however, through the Marquis de Sade (e.g., 1967) that a further dimension of the primal scene may be read. In Sade male domination–control and female submission–obedience are equal terms in an essentially nonentropic steady state system. Role reversals would not alter the form or overall distribution of energy. Sodomite and sodomee make each other possible and neither seems to have the final word. The text is additive; more of the same could always happen (Barthes 1976). The last word, if any, belongs to the narrator, the voice of polite lawlessness, a variety of Bion's (1962)-K. Unlike Freud, Sade seems untroubled by any bias toward death or life but has rather stepped aside from both.

Nevertheless, it is Sade's uncompromising rigor in making power and pleasure interchangeable that allows the true subject of his discourse to be glimpsed: His Majesty the Baby. The nearly seamless union of power and pleasure in the Sadian text mockingly mirrors Winnicott's "primary creativity" or Kohut's "grandiose self" and "sodomized" therapist: the baby god of creation and his earthly servants. The partners in the Sadian scene caricature the double directionality of infantile tendencies: omnipotence–dependence, active–passive, sadistic–masochistic, male–female. The most decisive of these pairs is an anal transposition of the first: control–submission, each aglow with its own nuances of megalomania.

MEANINGS OF ANALITY

The Sadian pleasure sites are mouth, anus, penis: the sites of the Freudian child. It is a polymorphous universe essentially sans vagina. In the Sadian scene the anus is by far the dominant object, the noema for the phallic subject. If the bearer of the penis is likened to a sun god, all Sadian penises, nonetheless, orbit around a still more irresistible asshole sun. Is the Sadian scene after all testimony to the primacy of a "death wish," with apparent phallic domination (life) a defense against greater, deeper, more mysterious anal powers (death)?

The phallus for Freud, as for Sade, becomes much more than the literal, anatomical penis. It functions as a symbol for sovereign power and creative activity. It carries ideal, numinous power, phallic Divinity (viz., Freud's reference to Hindu genital sculpture in *Leonardo*, nowadays turned into the "logophallo machine"). However, unlike Sade, in Freud's great cases the phallic ideal is portrayed as always in danger. The patient's unconscious attachment to the anus threatens phallic integrity. Whereas the Sadian penis is affirmed by absolute and unqualified anal submissiveness ("Let thy will be done"), the power of the Freudian phallus is short-circuited by anal desires. In this sense the patients described by Freud are not Sadian enough.

Freud described the child's first theory of birth and sense of creativity in anal terms: shitting as personal gift and making babies. As development proceeds, anality remains the background of creativity, but ultimately gains its sanction when integrated within a primacy of genitality. It is, circularly, assimilating what is positive in anality which contributes to the primacy of genitality. For example, the subject must be able to sustain and utilize rushes of anal sensations if these are not always to be feared as villainous. The sense of emotional fullness and power attached to anal awareness may be symbolized in dream life by the rich interior of a church or wheels which help one go somewhere. In a dream of one of my patients, a priest reached into her rectum and pulled out an arabesque fecal piece to be used in a ceremony (for details see Eigen 1975–1976). This gave expression to a process of deep repair of a bad self-image (Allen Ginsberg's assertion of the holiness of the body and its products applies here, the body as "literal" and as language of the self).

The cases Freud described were unable to assimilate positive anal feeling-life properly. They were caught in a chronic war between "prick" and "asshole." Sadian "cooperation" was impossible for them, as was the Freudian "sublimation of homosexual libido." They were plunged in profound conflict, uncertainty, and self-doubt, far from Sadian know-how. Nor could they settle for the perverse compromise of a "fecal penis": idealization of excrement, pseudocreativity, magical fabrication rather than engendering (Chasseguet-Smirgel 1974). Their anality was in spirit somewhat more like that described by Burroughs (1959), whatever the thrills and black humor: hell itself (more Dante than Milton). Freud's patients were quite aware of the filthiness of their own shit, indeed could not rise above it.

The Sadian asshole is above all clean (including the feces). It is the control-submission rather than excremental aspect of anality which is emphatic. Anality is not idealized so much as made antiseptic. In essence, the Sadian asshole is a kind of hollowed-out penis, an "anti-vagina" or clean, corrupting force no vagina can survive. That the Sadian asshole does not exist except as a figment of mind (a language production which may be an inversion of the Immaculate Conception) is banal. What is crucial is that in principle it can and must not exist. Although not idealized, *it functions as a counter-ideal — not to the penis (Freud's problematics) but to the whole of creation.* Sade's pricks and assholes are at peace with each other. They form an unnatural alliance not merely against but beyond Nature and even beyond God (in intent). In positing themselves beyond every lawful power in this universe, they function as embodiments of Bion's-K, pure "without-ness," denudation as such. In the end Sadian sadomasochism is outside of Freud's all too humanly felt "death wish" which still is law bound. In Sade, if a law should be acknowledged it is at the same time mocked and finally nulled (viz., generational law: "He says he knew a man who had fucked three children he had had with his mother, whence he had a daughter he had married to his son, so that by fucking her he was fucking his sister, his daughter, and his daughter-in-law, and he was making his son fuck his sister and his stepmother"; quoted by Barthes 1976, p. 138).

Freud was saved from Sadian trans-lawfulness by his ideal of heterosexuality, an ideal rooted in Nature and in the prevailing culture, eventually raised to the level of a paradigm for creative action. The path lay through the discovery of the vagina and the struggle to differentiate it from the anus, thereby making the penis–vagina combinative possible. If the phallus is far more than an anatomical penis, so must also be its proper partner, the symbolic vagina. The differentiation of vagina from anus marks the advent of a new, lawful dimension: the possibility of generativity in principle (Chasseguet-Smirgel's 1974 "engendering" rather than "making").

The Sadian world excludes vaginal reality by choice. This is in marked contrast with the homosexual asshole as, for example, described by Burroughs (1959). The latter contains muted vaginal longings. Burroughs's homosexual asshole (his term) is governed by a principle of undifferentiation: asshole contains elements of mouth and cunt. It may contain elements of almost anything but eyes, the distancing apparatus attached to a cut-off machine brain (e.g., Burroughs 1959, "Ordinary Men and Women"). From a structural viewpoint Burroughs is right to pick the anus as organ of undifferentiation, and this is not merely because the possession of an anus fails to distinguish between the sexes. Anal identifications involve greater ambiguity than either oral or genital models with reference to self–other differentiation in general. In deep pathology anality tends to assimilate orality and genitality rather than the reverse (viz., Ehrenzweig 1971, Eigen 1977). Orality tends to explode itself with the inevitable discovery of the breast outside. Anality always lacks such clarity, hence its basic doubt and obsessional strivings. Burroughs guards his inherent sense of lawfulness by keeping the eye away from the anus, thereby affirming a distinction between mental and body ego. Burroughs's man may turn into an asshole rather than a breast, but his observing ego will note him doing it. By contrast, Milner's (1969) schizophrenic draws eyes inside the anus, collapsing the difference.

By making *woman's* asshole the primary sexual object, Sade is emphasizing the import of his *choice*. The homosexual has no such choice with regard to openings. His premises carry their own built-in limitations (anus, mouth). Sade, by deliberately excluding the vagina, can carry his protest to infinity. The anus as primary sexual object does not merely reflect undifferentiation or infantile regression or even masculine protest. For Sade it becomes *the principle of transcendent reversal*. He can choose to reverse the order of things, turn everything "ass backwards" (infantile negativism raised to Bion's-K). His devil is a tidy gentleman compared to Burroughs's fierce anal search because he sets the stage for what feels itself to be an ideal transcendence, a nullity of sheer will, a pure superiority–inferiority beyond all content.

The Freudian journey is epitomized in the case of Schreber, a judge who was never Freud's patient but who laid bare his psychotic soul in an autobiography that intrigued Freud. During the course of his psychosis, Schreber feared/wished to be sodomized by his doctor, then similarly ravished by God (whom he also confused with his doctor). He tended to experience his own wishes as attacks, as indeed he was actually attacked by his brutal father while growing up. Paradoxically it was when he could symbolically (in delusional fantasy) realize his feared wish that submission turned into surrender (to God) and consequent remission of his psychosis. His movement was from unconscious anal addiction toward a freeing psychological vagina. In this he echoed the Judaic structure, the feminine relation of man toward active, creative God (man the receiver; Israel, the Bride of God). Following Burroughs's homosexual language: "Allah fucked me, the All Powerful. . . ." from tight- to loose-assed. The Freudian enterprise aims at nothing less than to reinstate the vagina as a symbolic possibility in Western civilization (the vagina which implies phallus in a way that anus and phallus cannot imply each other), hence affirming and preserving the category of the fecund, true complementarity over mere "cooperation" (ironically, adaptation). In human terms healing calls for a corrective primal scene, a traversible arc from copulation à tergo to face-to-face, a reversible perspective symbolic of paradox and creative movement.

THE MOTHER-INFANT IDEAL

Since Freud much psychoanalytic thinking has focused on the mother–infant relationship preceding "anality" and "phallicity." In this context, feeling memories of infinite or divine perfection are referred back to moments of mother–baby psychosomatic "fit" or intunement (e.g., Balint's "primary love," Winnicott's [1958, 1971] and Bick's [1968] maternal "holding," Bion's mother as psychic container, Kohut's maternal mirroring). Art tends to be viewed as an attempt to recreate some sense of this early ecstatic union or, at least, reflect the vicissitudes of its rupture. In essence, psychoanalytic reductionism is moved a step back, from father to mother. By uncritically maintaining that the first object is the mother, the *fact* of ideal images is taken for granted and not genuinely integrated into psychoanalytic epistemology (even if this *fact* is often intuitively used with great clinical power, left hand ignoring right).

Kohut's (1971, 1977) formulations provide a good illustration of the problem which arises when ideal and material realities are implicitly confused (not united). He is one of a growing group of analysts to place great importance on the constructive use of ideal feelings in the course of therapy. Oceanic states are no longer to be taken as second-class citizens but as a source of inspiration and sense of wholeness, a kind of "home base" of the human self. He describes an early sense of oneness in which ideal feelings come to fluctuate between self and other, a fluidly oscillating god sense ("I am God" and/or "You are God"). The mother, other actual people, and one's own body come to be differentiated out of such primary ideal states. The experience of an actual mother (in whatever imaginative–realistic forms) is a developmental achievement, one made possible by undergoing inevitable separation–disillusionment processes. A goal of therapy is to help mediate reversible passage between ideal moments (whether focused on self, other, both, or the "between") and the pain necessary upon repeatedly discovering the "hard facts of life" (unyielding otherness, materiality). In optimal conditions one develops the capacity to be able to flexibly undergo and process both "ideal" and "realistic" dimensions of experience in a rich, well-nigh unlimited variety of ways.

In keeping with the prevalent psychoanalytic tradition, Kohut uncritically describes the first ideal other as the mother, an error easily fallen into from the viewpoint of adult perception. If the mother as mother (or part of mother or maternal functioning) is gradually discriminated from early ideal images projected on or fused with her, the critical implication is that the creation of ideal images precedes the perception of mother *qua* mother or, at least, cannot be derived from her.

Kohut's attempt to give ideal images their due as a source of creative inspiration and healing brings to the fore basic problematics inherent in Freud. For Freud, ideal feelings always involved something in disguise (e.g., mother, father, sex, hostility, etc.). Although he states (Freud 1914) that an idealized object (in particular, the ego ideal) may spur creativity, he nevertheless stressed its possible interference in the actual work itself. In most Freudian literature the defensive and pathological uses of ideal images have been stressed (e.g., Reich, 1953, 1954, 1960), at best emphasizing their importance as "compensations." Kohut is thus in the untenable position of emphasizing the import of normal, inherently undefensible ideal states for creative and healthy development while lacking a critical anthropology suitable for the task.[2]

Ideal images play a central role throughout the Freudian corpus. They are virtually omnipresent — complexly interacting with or against instincts and reality. Ideal qualities in one form or another appear as part of the object pole of instincts. In Freudian dramas *instincts seek an ideal imago*. If instincts or instinctual signifiers are intrinsically fluid and mobile, so are their intended objects (not their aim). But as desire is the noetic constant, the noematic nucleus

---

[2]For a discussion of related problems in the work of Mahler and Winnicott, see Peterfreund (1978), Grotstein (1977), Eigen (1980a,b), Eigen and Robbins (1980). I have elsewhere discussed in detail how the need to account for creativity in psychoanalytic healing and everyday life has led to successive revisions in psychoanalytic theory (Eigen and Robbins 1980). For an in-depth psychological account which attempts to do justice to the anthropological-epistemological status of ideal images, see Elkin (1972).

of this shifting "X" which is desired carries an ideal glow. In Freudian dramas the ideal imago variously saturates one's own body, ego, mother, father, and on to a wide range of possibilities (e.g., feces, feet, science, nation, God).

A goal of analysis is to unmask the hidden god sense displaced or mixed up with some mundane reality. The question of who or what carries the god sense of how one's ultimate sense of power is distributed at a given time is critical for understanding the nature of the subject's distress and the direction of his movement. In work at the deepest levels of character it is necessary to search out and clarify the subject's relation to his power source with its ideal penumbra (or core) and chart how the subject maintains and gives away power in complex ways.

By a sleight of hand Freud linked desire with ideal images without crediting the capacity which produces the latter. Yet it is the copresence of both terms which defines creative, human consciousness. In systems language they are correlatives, neither reducible to the other. In the course of therapy it is possible to help the individual become aware of the play of "divine-demonic" ideal images in his life. By distilling out and making the *ideal imago, as such,* the object of one's attention, one may acquire a greater capacity to enter fruitful communion with it. In optimal instances one does not simply become free from it but through it. One draws on a power that previously seemed enslaving.

In the West God was to function as the one living Reality which possessed the qualities of the ideal imago as such, thereby objectifying it. In Bion's language, he was to be the one container for human desire who could not be exploded by it. Freud was one of those meant to whittle God to the bone, then detonate and see what, if anything, survived. A radical filtering process. The shattered ideal bits and pieces, although many are inert, are still bursting into action and language in our times.

REFERENCES

Barthes, R. (1976). *Sade, Fourier, Loyola.* New York: Hill and Wang.

Bick, E. (1968). The experience of the skin in early object relations. *International Journal of Psycho-Analysis* 43:13.

Bion, W. R. (1962). *Learning from Experience.* London: Heinemann.

_____ (1979). *Memoirs of the Future III: The Dawn of Oblivion.* Perthshire, Scotland: Clunie.

Burroughs, W. S. (1959). *Naked Lunch.* New York: Grove.

Chasseguet-Smirgel, J. (1974). Perversion, idealization and sublimation. *International Journal of Psycho-Analysis* 55:349–357.

Ehrenzweig, A. (1971). *The Hidden Order of Art.* Los Angeles: University of California Press.

Eigen, M. (1975–1976). The differentiation of an androgynous imago. *Psychoanalytic Review* 62:601–613.

_____ (1977). On working with "unwanted" patients. *International Journal of Psycho-Analysis* 58:109–121.

_____ (1980a). On the significance of the face. *Psychoanalytic Review* 67:426–444.

_____ (1980b). Instinctual fantasy and ideal images. *Contemporary Psychoanalysis* 16:119–137.

Eigen, M., and Robbins, A. (1980). Object relations and expressive symbolism. In *Expressive Therapy,* ed. A. Robbins, pp. 58–94. New York: Human Sciences.

Elkin, H. (1972). On selfhood and the development of ego structures in infancy. *Psychoanalytic Review* 59:389–416.

Freud, S. (1908). Civilized sexual morality and modern nervous illness. *Standard Edition* 9:189.

_____ (1914). On narcissism: an introduction. *Standard Edition* 14:73–102.

_____ (1950 [1892–1899]). Extracts from the Fliess papers. *Standard Edition* 1:179–199.

Greenacre, P. (1971). *Emotional Growth,* vols. 1 and 2. New York: International Universities Press.

Grotstein, J. (1977). The psychoanalytic concept of schizophrenia: II: Reconciliation. *International Journal of Psycho-Analysis* 58:427–452.

Kohut, H. (1971). *The Analysis of the Self.* New York: International Universities Press.

_____ (1977). *The Restoration of the Self.* New York: International Universities Press.

Meltzer, D. (1973). *Sexual States of Mind.* Perthshire, Scotland: Clunie.

Milner, M. (1950). *On Not Being Able to Paint,* 2nd ed. New York: International Universities Press.

_____ (1969). *The Hands of the Living God.* New York: International Universities Press.

Peterfreund, F. (1978). Some critical comments on psychoanalytic conceptualizations of infancy. *International Journal of Psycho-Analysis* 59:427–441.

Reich, A. (1953). Narcissistic object choice in women. *Journal of the American Psychoanalytic Association* 1:22–44.

_____ (1954). Early identifications as archaic elements in the superego. *Journal of the American Psychoanalytic Association* 2:218–238.

_____ (1960). Pathologic forms of self-esteem regulation. *Psychoanalytic Study of the Child* 15:288–311.

Sade, The Marquis de. (1967). *The 120 Days of Sodom and Other Writings,* ed. A. Wainhouse and R. Seaver. New York: Grove.

Winnicott, D. W. (1958). *Collected Papers.* New York: Basic Books.

_____ (1965). *The Maturational Processes and the Facilitating Environment.* New York: International Universities Press.

_____ (1971). *Playing and Reality.* New York: Basic Books.

10

Soft and Hard Qualities

"Soft" and "hard" are universal expressive qualities that inform all our experience. We sense their interplay in the margin of our awareness throughout our lifetime. Their varying dissociations and interpenetrations color and texture our thoughts, feelings, sensations, and actions. They permeate objects of concern at every level of our existence and are subtly woven into the atmosphere of subjectivity as such. Without them our psychophysical existence would be more bland and dimensionless.

This theme is given a distilled representation in the Taoist yin-yang symbol, the *Tai-chi-tu*. But even this most coherent symbol of polarity-in-unity is too geometric to do justice to the subtle, interpenetrating flow of these qualities in moment-to-moment living. To be sure, hard and soft often do set each other off. They may oppose or complement each other in rather clearly distinguishable ways: for example, the erect penis and adaptable vagina, hard-headedness/soft-heartedness (or vice versa), and the like. But even (especially?) in sexual intercourse it becomes most difficult to know clearly where the softness and where the hardness, as they melt into and permeate one another, ineffably fluid. The rock gradually dissolves in the water, but the water can no longer be described simply as soft.

The qualities soft and hard are virtually omnipresent building blocks of personality. At each moment of development the self senses both itself, its capacities, functions, and objects in terms of soft and hard resonances. Its organizational capacities are partly steered by an implicit awareness of the soft–hard contours of sensed mental and physical realities. Blocks and distortions in the perception of these qualities and their shifting emotional meanings both reflect and perpetuate developmental deficiencies. Many individuals often are relatively insensitive to or misinterpret these vital cues of psychic movement.

The therapeutic task of helping patients to "experience their experience" is aided by the therapist's sensitivity to the incessant and complex interplay of soft and hard currents in mental life. These currents may act as moment-to-moment cues of psychic possibilities, which often go unheard or unheeded. Most patients tend to run roughshod over them or distort their meanings in accord with persistent, rigid patterns. Individuals are usually filled with too much anxiety noise to truly feel and value the subtle expressive forces which ever form part of the background of existence. Occasionally patients make inflated use of background qualities and turn what could be "news of difference" into chronic, narcissistic shields. The creative recognition of the flow of softness–hardness qualities also may threaten areas of affective flattening built up as protection against dangers associated with psychic fertility.

In the present paper I record some aspects of the struggle involved in keeping oneself open to fresh perceptions of the meaning and use of softness–hardness cues in personal development. I focus on the appearance of softness–hardness qualities in dream life and how these qualities reflect actual or potential shifts in self-feeling. The patients involved often tended to disregard or ward off experiencing the genuinely new nuances of self-feeling to which their dreams might give rise. It was largely up to the therapist to sustain the integrity of the dreamer's attempt to create perspectives outside well-worn destructive circles or stereotypes — until the patient could increasingly own this function. The meaning-making processes described here do not claim to be the only or right ones. Any number of possible avenues might have led to development. What is perhaps most important is the personal faith and investment in meaning creation itself, a communal process in which we stimulate each other's appetites for meaning and creative shifts in self-feeling.

DREAM 1

Jane was a patient who had passed through many therapists and was caught in a vicious, destructive process. Her productions tended to be frightening and her interpretations relentlessly sadistic. Her therapies ran the gamut from classical analytic to behavioristic, and included ego psychological therapy and work which emphasized the importance of anger. I opted to incessantly shift meaning perspectives in surprising (to her and me), elusively stimulating ways. My touch was light and supportive even when damning. Following is one example of the way I sometimes managed to bail her out at the last moment, when a saving meaning would dawn on me just in time.

Jane dreamt that she opened a tin can of cat food. She took out the food and served it on the sharp edge of the tin can.

To her the dream could mean only one thing: one more ruthless indictment, a testimony to her hopelessness. In fact, during the past year she had bought a cat, her first pet. And since living with her the cat had become progressively crazy, as she knew would happen. If the cat represented some part of herself, it was treated no better, lucky if it survived. It seemed the hour would end meaninglessly when the polar dimensions brought together in the dream hit me: the juxtaposition of sharpness and nourishment.

"What's wrong with being cutting?" I began. "I dig my cutting edge." I wondered if she wasn't depicting me, a combination of food and sharpness. Of course, she was referring to this duality in herself, qualities which in her mind tended to cancel each other out. In me she could see them a little more developed and coordinated. I really do value both. How can something cutting be nourishing and vice versa? The thought pulled the session out of the hat, a little like lifting the heroine off the train tracks just as the locomotive is bearing down. The drama, in one form or another, was repeated endlessly — until the way I operated became something she wanted, and she began to duplicate it. Within several months of this particular dream, Jane's cat began to show improvement.

Months later, in Jane's next cat dream, Jane appeared solicitous and helpful, but no matter what she did the cat was angry. It was clear that there was nothing she or anyone could do to help her angry cat. It was just plain mad. Jane became noticeably more open and free after this realization. It was as though the cat had her tied in knots inside and now she could let the animal go a little more.

About half a year later the cat appeared again in a series of dreams in which I took a book off a shelf and found a passage for some students (Jane being one), followed by simple and lovely oriental buildings. The cat was full and beautiful, really cat-like. Something cat-like ran all through the various figures. Jane spoke about my cat-like mind. "You perch here and there and when I think you're trapped you're somewhere else." We spoke, too, about our love of Beauty and Truth. Jane's love of culture was growing. There was a moment of sharing.

A week or so before Jane had these last dreams — unknown to her — Fred Astaire became part of my mental ego ideal for the first time. I was watching a movie of his on television with my girl friend, who said, "It's like he's oiled all over, every part of him." I applied this to the way I wanted my mind to work. Things became more seamless between Jane and me. The stitches were dissolving.

DREAM 2

A fairly vegetative, middle-aged woman, Kaye, a veteran of clinics, had been striving to get her life together. She was a rather mushy and amorphous person who often gave in and felt walked on in life. At the time of the dream reported here she was preoccupied with bad feelings about her body.

In her dream Kaye saw and enjoyed a soft carpet. While she relished it, she noticed some spots where the hard floor was visible. She stared at them curiously.

In session Kaye raised the theme of being walked on, and we discussed ways she felt that we walked on each other. Still the bottom line was her feeling that her vagina and body as a whole were defective. She castigated herself and even entertained the thought that her self-directed anger might have caused the carpet holes. She felt marred.

In a sense I could not disagree with her. She felt and was damaged, grossly so. On the other hand the dream offered an alternative statement by bringing hard and soft together. I remarked that part of her problem was that she wanted to be all soft — yet it was probably by accepting a certain hardness that authentic softness was possible. In the dream itself Kaye had not been deprecating — only curious, as in making a discovery. It was of no use to view the hole in the carpet in terms of everyday notions of damage. The dream, rather, was showing a solid, underlying ground hidden by a soft cover or persona. It was, of course, Kaye's task to value both in right relation.

Kaye attacked me for setting an impossible task, but for the moment looked and felt lighter. She enjoyed an exhilarating taste of shifting perspectives and the possibility of meaning.

DREAM 3

During her therapy Elaine made great strides in work and friendships with women but was still at sea with men. She began therapy in the wake of a broken five-year relationship. After a period of isolation she began dating, only to discover that she related to men in terms of an ideal sexual model and did not care to know men as they really were. Those who fit her model were "space cadets," emotionally distanced like her father. She saw herself as warm and giving.

At about the time her problems with men were coming more into focus, she dreamed of a baby girl who had big, sharp teeth and venereal disease. Elaine was a therapist in training and so had no trouble producing "associations" related to wanting to have oral phallic power, or herself as the big, bad, sexual wolf. She was confused, though, as to why the baby had venereal disease.

After focusing on the top-bottom contrast and staying with the confusion, I shared the following gestalt. "Therapy has helped you build up your teeth. You've gained a certain toughness and can really bite into things. But teeth after all are hard and rigid—unyielding. In the dream there's something wrong with your soft side."

After this remark Elaine readily related the venereal disease to her oversexualization of relationships. With her hard side she stared at and confronted her defect. She was not really receptive to men; they existed almost wholly as objects of use. She did not want to truly know and feel them. She wanted them to penetrate only her vagina, not *her*. She had fine teeth but lacked, so to speak, a healthy psychological vagina.

Her attention gradually turned to me, and her face softened. She wanted to be open to me and to get to know me as well as I knew her. She felt me enter her— my face her mental focus. For some moments my face became so meaningful that it scared her, but she also liked it. Here there was no touching, only intimacy with distance. She could not tolerate much of it before breaking contact. She felt the need to become cold and hard and shut me out and in some way behave toward me like a "space cadet." Now she was like the men who left her, and in a sense she was right to protect herself against the fusion. I was Elaine and she her father. She felt herself alternately quivering and stiffening. She relaxed again and experienced the muted play of softness and hardness in my automatic shifts of expression. The oscillation became a glowing tremolo. We were both within and outside each other at the same time, permeable yet mutually transcendent. For long moments soft and hard blended in new, wordless configurations. Who could tell their difference? Yet each was given its due.

11

The Area of Faith in Winnicott, Lacan, and Bion

The basic concern of this chapter is what I am calling the *area of faith* in the work of Winnicott, Lacan, and Bion. By the area of faith I mean to point to a way of experiencing that is undertaken with one's whole being, all out, "with all one's heart, with all one's soul, and with all one's might." At the outset I wish to avoid quibbling over whether such experiencing is possible. My methodological strategy is to let what I mean by area of faith stay open and gradually grow richer as the paper unfolds.

Winnicott, Lacan, and Bion have attempted sophisticated and intensive depth phenomenologies of faith in travail. For them, I believe, the vicissitudes of faith mark the central point around which psychic turmoil and conflict gather. In the hands of these authors, further, the area of faith tends to become a founding principle for the possibility of a fully human consciousness, an intrinsic condition of self–other awareness as such.

In Winnicott the area of faith is expressed in his descriptions of transitional experiencing (1953), and taken forward in his later work on object usage (1969). Since much work has already been published on transitional experiencing, my main concern will be with object usage.

In Lacan the area of faith is associated, at least in its developed form, mainly with the Symbolic order and his notion of the "gap." After discussing the underlying play of faith in these conceptions we will begin to see how Lacan and Winnicott heighten and extend each other's overlapping positions.

We will center our discussion of faith in Bion on his work on O, his sign denoting ultimate reality. Bion's concepts clustering around O appear to provide the most flexible and general framework with which to understand Winnicott's and Lacan's basic concerns. Nevertheless, when these three authors are brought into relation with one another, the dimension of faith appears enriched by an interweaving of vistas which are not mutually reducible. Metaperspectives on these views open still more vistas.

THE AREA OF FAITH IN TRANSITIONAL EXPERIENCING
AND OBJECT USAGE

The area of faith in Winnicott's transitional experiencing and object usage may be brought out more clearly by contrasting it, as Winnicott himself has done, with the Kleinian introjective–projective fantasy world. In Winnicott's scheme, transitional experiencing and object usage, respectively, point to a realm prior to and beyond Kleinian introjective–projective dramas. In the following discussion time sequence is less important than formal differences between phenomenological dimensions.

In transitional experiencing the infant lives through a faith that is prior to clear realization of self and other differences; in object usage the infant's faith takes this difference into account, in some sense is based on it. In contrast, the introjective–projective aspect of the self is involved in splitting and hiding processes, an inherently self-bound psychic web-spinning in which the possibility of faith is foreclosed. How these diverse experiential universes relate to one another is a complex problem which will be worked with only tangentially in the present paper. My immediate concern is the way object usage takes the life of faith in transitional experiencing forward, and the role introjective–projective processes play as a foil to this unfolding. In order to accomplish this, I must, in turns, discuss transitional experiencing, object relating (the introjective–projective world), and object usage. My aim is to show how faith evolves from transitional experiencing through object usage, in part by transcending (or undercutting) introjective–projective ordeals and barriers.

Transitional Experiencing

Winnicott situates transitional experiencing between the early emergence of consciousness and the infant's growing awareness of otherness outside himself.[1] In the transitional area self and other are neither one, nor two, but somehow together make up an interpenetrating field. The core of transitional experiencing has to do with an inherent fit between the infant's creativeness and the world. It is a fit that is lived and taken for granted, a faith that the infant lives out of without radically questioning its basis. In Winnicott's words,

> the essential feature in the concept of transitional objects and phenomena . . . is *the paradox*: the baby creates the object, but the object was there waiting to be created and to become a cathected object . . . We will never challenge the baby to elicit an answer to the question: did you create that or did you find it? [1953, p. 89]

---

[1] I have elsewhere (Eigen 1980a,b, Eigen and Robbins 1980) discussed the weakness in Winnicott's starting point and will not take this problem up here. What is critical for the present discussion is the structural link between transitional experiencing and object usage that distinguishes these areas of experiencing from introjective-projective operations.

The infant here lives in an atmosphere of creativity, participates, as it were, in a creativity bath. The question of where to locate the self and object is slippery. The transitional object carries the meaning of that which is, yet is not mother and that which is, and is not self. It, like mother, mirrors the self and like the self, mirrors mother. Yet it cannot be reduced to either. Insofar as the transitional object is a first not-me, it is so without any sharp sense of exteriority. It is perhaps an incipient other, otherness in the process of being born, not yet wholly other. It is expressive of a primary creative process at the origin of symbolic experience and is itself a vehicle for creative experiencing. As neither wholly self nor other nor wholly outside these terms, it is itself symbolizing experiencing emerging as such.

In an important sense, while the infant is living through creative experiencing, it neither holds on to anything, nor withholds itself. It may grip a teddy or blanket as a mother or self substitute for security, but this is not the heart of the transitional area. Transitional phenomena are not primarily tranquilizers. Objects held onto as tranquilizers mark a rupture between the infant and the realm of creative experiencing, which it may seek to close by self-soothing practices. In the transitional dimension creative experiencing is open and fluid, if also profoundly heightened. Apparent possessiveness and perseverations here, in part, provide an opportunity for intensifying the feeling of creativeness, of digging deeper into the immersion process, rather than simply reflecting compensatory needs. For Winnicott, in contrast to Freud and Klein, creativity permeates psychic life and is involved in the very birth of self and other, a process more fundamental than substitute strivings. Creativity is itself a primary term of human experiencing. For Winnicott, the defensive use of creativity is a secondary development and not the home ground of the human self (Eigen 1981b, Eigen and Robbins 1980).

Object Relating: The Unit Self

Winnicott (1971) contrasts transitional experiencing (and object usage) with object relating through projective–introjective operations by a unit self. He describes this latter mode of relating in the following way:

> In object-relating the subject allows certain alterations in the self to take place, of a kind that has caused us to invent the term cathexis. The object has become meaningful. Projection mechanisms and identifications have been operating, and the subject is depleted to the extent that something of the subject is found in the object, though enriched by feeling. Accompanying these changes is some degree of physical involvement (however slight) towards excitement, in the direction of the functional climax of an orgasm . . . Object-relating is an experience of the subject that can be described in terms of the subject as an isolate. [p. 88]

Winnicott tends to situate this way of object relating as an intermediate phase between transitional experiencing and object usage. The object is meaningful but not yet experienced as wholly other. Rather, the subject continuously tends to bring any incipient sense of otherness into the circumference of its omnipotence. The self is an isolate here not because its sense of exteriority is overdeveloped, but because any promptings toward this sense collapse into the orbit of autarchic projective–introjective operations.

In the world of the unit self the subject grows through the continuous cycle of putting self in others and others in self. In projective–introjective identifications the self may disguise itself as another and another as oneself. The mind may capitalize on its invisibility and defensively play such cross-currents off against each other. Through these operations the psyche can split itself, making secrecy and hiding possible, together with all the subtleties linked with self-deception.

Winnicott associates physical excitement with this area of the self, since introjective–projective identifications help mold erotic sensibility. Introjective--projective processes pave the way for structuralizing ego deformations associated with the erotization of mental functions. They make possible seductive and tantalizing expressive styles, which assault the true self feeling and intensify the life of bad faith.

The unit self, wherein unconscious lying becomes possible, stands in marked contrast with the rapt immersion of transitional experiencing and, we shall see, the clean air of object usage. For Winnicott the picture of a closed system perpetuated by a self-encapsulating network of projective–introjective operations, functions to help set off what life may be like when one feels free of this subjective bubble, when one is not closed in on oneself.

Object Usage

For Winnicott object usage occurs with the explosion of the introjection–projection circle and, reciprocally, occasions this explosion. The subject is reconstituted through a fresh realization that all is not self in disguise and, as in transitional experiencing, tastes a wholling innocence, although on a new plane. In transitional experience the unit self, the self as isolate, is as yet irrelevant, and in object usage it is undercut or transcended. In the former there is the freedom prior to a clear-cut sense of sameness or difference, and in the latter the freedom brought about by news of difference.

In transitional experiencing the baby's sense of freedom was linked to a limitless feeling of wholeness, prior to raising the question of absolute limits. The new awakening in object usage involves the realization that the other is in some basic way outside one's boundaries, is "wholly other." And while this may precipitate disorganization and dismay, it culminates in quickening and enhancing the subject's sense of aliveness. It opens the way for a new kind of freedom, one *because* there is radical otherness, a new realness of self-feeling exactly because the other is now felt as real as well. The core sense of creativeness that permeates transitional experiencing is reborn on a new level, insofar as genuine not-me nutriment becomes available for personal use. The subject can *use* otherness for true growth purposes and, through the risk of difference as such, gains access to the genuinely new.

Winnicott links this new sense of otherness with the subject's realization that the object survives his destructive attacks. For Winnicott it is the subject's dawning awareness of the limitations of his all-out destructive attacks (which once seemed boundless), that creates the experience of *externality* as such. In one of Winnicott's (1969) summaries, he describes this process in terms of the analytic situation in the following way:

> This destructive activity is the patient's attempt to place the analyst outside of omnipotent control, that is, out in the world. Without the experience of maximum destructiveness (object not protected) the subject never places the analyst outside and therefore can never do more than experience a kind of self-analysis, using the analyst as a projection of a part of the self. [p. 91]

One cannot take Winnicott's description overliterally. One would have had to know the object had been there in order to appreciate its survival. Winnicott's description assumes and does not account for the original constitution of the object. What is at stake, however, is a fresh sense of what an object (and self) can be. The object that survives is *qualitatively* not the same object present at the attack's outset. The object that survives is one that could not be destroyed, whereas the object first attacked is one which the subject felt could or even should be. What is emerging is the sense of externality as imperishable living fact and principle. As living fact it is the Other as personal subject outside one's grasp. As principle it is a structural category which gives all beings, including oneself, the meaning: "potentially other," a being vulnerable to the transformations genuine difference can bring. It is this intersection of profound vulnerability and saving indestructibility that brings the paradox of faith to a new level.

Perhaps Winnicott's (1971) most memorable expression of the faith he points to is the following:

> This subject says to the object: "I destroyed you," and the object is there to receive the communication. From now on the subject says: "Hullo object!" "I destroyed you." "I love you." "You have value for me because of your survival of my destruction of you." "While I am loving you I am all the time destroying you in (unconscious) *fantasy*." [p. 90]

What is happening is the "continuous" destruction of the fantasy objects (the introjective–projective world) and the birth of the real object, the other subject outside all of one's psychic web-spinning. This "real" is not quite Freud's "reality." Although it carries an urgency somewhat akin to necessity, it is not a reality one can adapt to in order to manipulate. It is a sense of the real that explodes all adaptive and manipulative attempts in principle. It is an all-out, nothing held back, movement of the self-and-other feeling past representational barriers, past psychic films and shells, a floating freely in a *joyous shock of difference.* At this moment one is enlivened and quickened through the sense of difference. One is sustained sheerly through the unfolding sense of self–other presencing, a presencing no longer taken for granted but appreciated as *coming through.* This may be something akin to Job's and God's wrath turning into joyous appreciation of one another's mystery, a newfound trust, wherein anything outside of the faith experience at that moment must seem unreal. The real here is self and other *feeling real* to one another, breaking past residues of depersonalization–derealization. In contrast, the Freudian reality basically requires some degree of depersonalization for adaptation and mastery to be possible. The category of mastery is irrelevant to the kind of self–other awareness at stake in the moment of faith, where all that exists of importance is the fact that we are real together, living in the amazing sense of becoming more and more real, where destructiveness makes love real, and love makes destructiveness creative.

Winnicott stresses that the destructiveness that creates the sense of externality is not essentially hostile (1971). This destructiveness, rather than reactive anger, seems to be an inherent part of developmental struggle. Winnicott recalls Greenacre's (e.g., 1952) examples of violence intrinsic to hatching processes, typical of a chick breaking out of an egg. In such instances one tries to move ahead with all one's might.

However, this general observation about the nature of developmental struggles does not appear to exhaust what Winnicott is trying to convey when he speaks of destructiveness creating externality. When Winnicott says that the object that survives the subject's destructive attacks is "in process of becoming destroyed because real, becoming real because destroyed" (1971, p. 90), he means to suggest that these two facts, *the new sense of reality and the new sense of destruction, bring each other into being.* The texture of this argument is necessarily circular for what is involved is the emergence of a new experimental dimension in which each of the terms co-create each other. A quantum leap is in progress in which destruction creates the real at the same time that the real invites and sustains the subject's attempts to cancel it — a continuous process wherein self and other are freshly recreated through one another.

It is important that Winnicott takes this step beyond the simple notion that the creative destructiveness at stake is the pushing past the old by the new, a natural movement from one stage to another. For if the destruction began on the footing of the old order, the introjective–projective world, there could be no basis for affirming the all-out wholling-in-differentiation experience that object usage implies. Destruction *within* the introjective–projective sphere tends to involve splitting and concealing processes. No all out risk-taking is possible within this system. The movement toward object usage, rather, involves the destruction *of* the introjective–projective order *and,* at the same time, contact with a sense of the real outside it: both these events are interwoven and produce each other.

Hence Winnicott's statement, "the subject does not destroy the subjective object (projection material), destruction turns up and becomes a central feature so far as the object is objectively perceived, has autonomy, and belongs to "shared' reality" (1971, p. 91). It is the projective world that is "continuously" destroyed at the same time that the real is "continuously" born and vice versa, and both of these happenings are necessary for the real as such to be experienced. If there were no projective system, there would not be this fresh sense of the real, and the reverse holds as well. From this viewpoint, projective operations and the sense of the real require and feed each other, a type of figure-ground for one another. The object is being destroyed in fantasy and *as* fantasy and is felt as real because of this, at the same time its realness makes *fantasy* destructiveness possible. The realness of the object comes into being as a fantasy being destroyed at the same time it participates in an order beyond fantasy. The subject here, as in transitional experiencing, grows through paradoxical rather than dissociative awareness.

It is the survival of the object qua object, with its integrity intact, that is crucial. And by survival Winnicott stresses the importance of the object's not retaliating, for the latter would maintain the object within the subject's magical hold. As I noted earlier, the object that comes through the subject's attack is not, qualitatively, the same object that it was at the attack's outset. The object that comes through is outside the subject's grasp, whereas the object attacked is within it. In the moment that leads to object usage *both of these phases are maximized.* What is constituted is an experiential world which embraces both fully, one forever breaking through the other. In this complex system *an all out wholling feeling keeps breaking through diverse splits and compromises, neither term reducible to the other.*

We can deepen our sense of what Winnicott has achieved through his object usage formulation by realizing that Winnicott has expressed two different views concerning the importance of the other qua other, of which object usage was his most recent. His earlier account (1963) centered around the *capacity for concern* and reworked, but basically retained, the Kleinian guilt dynamics that characterize the depressive position. In contrast, Winnicott's object usage is a joy-base account of the growth of otherness. We will now allow the dynamics surrounding object usage and the capacity for concern to confront and heighten each other.

Object Usage and the Capacity for Concern: Joy and Guilt

It appears that Winnicott may have conflicting views concerning the subject's basic relation to the other *qua* other. We have studied Winnicott's account of the constitution of externality in which the object maintains itself outside the subject's destructive orbit. This culminates in a freeing feeling of subject and object difference, which ensures the category of the new. However, Winnicott (1963), following Klein, earlier rooted the subject's recognition of otherness (i.e., others as whole subjects) in guilt over hurting the loved other. This earlier account asserts that a genuine sense of otherness and guilt arise contemporaneously. The subject moves from anxiety to guilt and concern by being able to hold ambivalence and feel he can contribute something to the object in reparation.

In this earlier paper, "object usage" is linked with the ruthless expression of instinctual drives, excitement states toward the object. The infant goes all out at the object and the latter must see to it that it survives. Here the mother is object of the infant's instinctual desires, very much the Freudian and Kleinian libidinal object.

At the same time, the infant feels protective toward the aspect of mother that protects and cares for it, the holding environment mother. It is the coming together of these "two mothers" in infantile perception that evokes the wish for reparation, the birth of concern. The infant tries to help the holding environment mother by modulating its libidinal–destructive attacks on the exciting mother, the two now perceived as the same person.

A quote from Winnicott (1963) will suffice to show that his later object usage and earlier capacity for concern accounts contained many common elements, reworked in different ways.

> A sense of guilt is anxiety linked with the concept of ambivalence, and implies a degree of integration in the individual ego that allows for the *retention of a good object-imago along with the idea of a destruction* of it. Concern implies further integration, and further growth, and relates in a positive way to the individual's sense of responsibility, especially in respect of relationships into which the instinctual drives have entered. [p. 73, italics added]

Winnicott's later account also involves a simultaneity of destruction, love, and survival, but *without a need to make reparation*. The core affect of this later account is joy, not guilt. The infant feels grateful because it can destroy and love the object and the object survives. The feeling is that integrity is really possible without compromising self or other. The subject appreciates the other *qua* other for intrinsic reasons, without the self-splitting that guilt may occasion. In the kind of unity of destructiveness and love Winnicott depicts in his later object usage account, love is alive and strong enough to use destructiveness creatively, rendering guilt superfluous.

In the Kleinian guilt-based account, the primacy of joy could not truly be understood. It would be rationalized as a manic defence, part of the paranoid position, or associated with the joy that arises when one makes amends. It would have *no place in its own right, as an intrinsic part of self–other awareness as such*.

In the reparation account, I believe, a subtle form of megalomania, that undoes the possibility of otherness itself, is left undetected. If the infant needs to repair the mother because of the imaginary damage he has inflicted upon her, he remains caught in his own psychic web-spinning. *There can be no true otherness where the infant is concerned for mother because of a fantasy of destructiveness that he tries to undo.* It is precisely this fantasy that continuously is exploded in Winnicott's later object usage formulation, allowing otherness to emerge fully. The concern based on guilt is mired in fantasies of mastery and control, whereby even love functions in controlling ways, if only as a defence against hate. The need to be good in order to make up for being bad is a very different moment from the freedom of loving for its own sake. In the object usage formulation, joy is not defined by a background guilt, but is an intrinsically undefensive feeling.

In his object usage formulation, Winnicott appears to move beyond his earlier thought and provides a ground for human concern which is not anxiety-derived. The later account provides a basis for a nondefensive appreciation of otherness which may grow into concern. One might come to guard this otherness in order to protect the richness in living it offers. Both the "I destroy you" and "I love you" of object usage are valued as rock-bottom givens, primary inclinations of the human heart. They are spontaneous feelings toward others, not discharge mechanisms. This *I love you* does not make up for *I destroy you,* but turns the latter to good use. Together they constitute a sustained reaching-out, a hope, a joyous gambit. In saying this, however, I do not want to minimize the importance of guilt dynamics in actual living. A fuller working out of relationships between object usage and the capacity for concern dynamics is beyond our scope here. My wish is to point out a distinction which makes an important contribution to the way a subject feels about himself and others.

The object usage, and capacity for concern, accounts both draw on object relational possibilities inherent in Freud's theory of drive fusion. Both are ways love and hate are structured in relation to one another. In the object usage account, the primacy of love does not rely on any added notion of ego mastery or adaptive control in order to handle destructive wishes. Within the framework of the primacy of love, hate finds its own limits and adds to, because encompassed by, joyous creativeness. There is no such faith in the capacity for concern account, where one recoils at one's own evil, and remains fearful of what the monster within can do. Both are genuine and necessary human experiences. The latter may provide sobering self-restraint, but it is not the true freedom faith can bring.

THE AREA OF FAITH IN LACAN

In order to begin to approach the ways Lacan and Winnicott differ, and from the perspective of their differences explore how they enrich each other, we must first say something of Lacan's three orders of unconscious mind and their relation to the phenomenon of the "gap." Lacan depicts three orders of unconscious mental events: the Real, Imaginary, and Symbolic. Each will be taken up with an eye toward understanding them with reference to the faith dimension.

The Real, at least in one of its profiles, may be viewed as a repressed awareness of lived experience (Lemaire 1977, Lowe 1980). The originary world of spontaneously lived experience, the primordial interweaving of subject and object as, for example, described by Merleau-Ponty (1962, 1968), undergoes repression and becomes subject to increasing distortions through secondary revisions. This repressed awareness is a complex one, including both the originary subject–object interlocking *and* the latter's rupture, lived experiencing before and after the trauma of separation. We will leave open for now exactly what the nature and status of this separation is. Lacan points to our sense of incompleteness and dissatisfaction which he variously refers to in terms of separation from mother at birth or the break-up of an early, mute dual union of baby and mother through the advent of language (the latter associated with law, social order, father, the castration complex).

It is the spontaneously lived contrast between subject–object interlocking *and* rupture that the Imaginary seeks to escape or undo. The Imaginary seeks to close all genuine gaps or fill them with mock or parody gaps, such as reactive withdrawal or oppositionalism, creating an illusion of self-sufficiency. Toward this end it employs mirroring or projective–introjective identificatory operations. Through these operations the subject can create an exteriorized (mainly visual) image of himself as an actor who masters anxiety by eliciting admiration/ hostility from both his own self and world as audience. He becomes, as it were, an imitation of himself (and others) by molding his reactiveness in terms of image forms that aid his quasispurious sense of self-sufficiency. The subject supports his defensive use of mastery by seduction and power techniques which increasingly alienate him from his most profound feeling life. As he rivets himself to his exteriorized self-image, he more and more filters himself through its projections, and takes in those reactions of others most relevant to his self-mesmerization.

For Lacan it is the Symbolic that explodes the closed system of the subject's introjective–projective world. The Symbolic responds to the subject–object interlocking and rupture inherent in the Real by trying to represent this state of affairs, not annihilate or foreclose it. It builds on primordial experiencing and takes it forward, enriching it through the dimension of meaning. It does this not by simply returning to primordial experiencing (which, in any case, comes under the governance of primal repression), but by accepting the gap within the Real, and between the Real, Imaginary, and the Symbolic. One requires a certain faith to tolerate and respect the gaps through which the life of authentic meaning unfolds.

Lacan associates the advent of the Symbolic with language and links the structure inherent in language with social structure, lawfulness (logos), the phallus, the father principle, the Other. The Imaginary tries to use or manipulate language so as to reinforce the subject's tyrannical illusion of mastery, his omnipotent self-encapsulation. The Symbolic provides a way out of self-enclosure through the subject's surrender to the life of meaning, the play of language, and the emergence of effective insights which outstrip his control. The gap between what is hidden and the pulsation of insight is respected and worked with, rather than delusively escaped or filled in. The subject is genuinely recreated through his participation in the movement of language, through his interaction with the Other, bearer of the Word (namely revelation).

The Symbolic and Imaginary orders intersect in complex ways, feeding and opposing each other. An important example of their irreducible co-presence, often used in Lacanian texts, is Freud's (1920) description of the child who throws a spool of string out of sight, and himself brings it back in view, the famous *Fort! Da!* anecdote in *Beyond the Pleasure Principle*. On the one hand the child tries to symbolize the lived fact of interlocking and rupture: his mother's absence and return. On the other hand he tries to subdue this fact by representing her as under his control: his demand can bring a representation of her to him. In this latter case he does not so much encompass the complex pressing issue so much as seek to undo it. He substitutes Imaginary victory over the persistent difficulty of presence–absence, instead of taking up the (perhaps impossible) challenge of symbolically sustaining both terms in noncontrolling expectancy (a risk of faith). The bad faith in the subject's attempt at Imaginary triumph is his wish to turn the gap into something he can discount.

Lacan, Winnicott, and Kleinians (namely, Meltzer 1973, Segal 1978) agree that human subjects cannot be fully constituted without access to the symbolic. It is through the subject's realization of the symbolic dimension that meaning can freely evolve. However, the Kleinian path to the symbolic is through the subject's capacity to value positive introjective identifications. For Lacan, as Winnicott, the symbolic function is rooted outside introjective processes. He situates the Kleinian introjective–projective fantasy realm in his Imaginary order, the megalomanic subject caught up in identificatory or mirroring processes.

His critique of American ego psychology rests on somewhat similar grounds, although far more brutal. He rigorously attacks the idea of a cure based on a positive identification with the analyst, the line of development usually summed up as "introjection-identification-internalization." According to Lacan, good internalizations tend to function as psychic tranquilizers, benignly socialized versions of "master-slave" dynamics. They help offset the personality's tendencies to paranoid–depressive anxieties by muting the risks a more profoundly grounded autonomy entails.

From Lacan's perspective, I believe, Kohut's (1971, 1977) presentation of his self psychology exhibits a similar problem. Kohut's picture of cure stresses the installation of a benign superego as an internal self-esteem regulating system. The transmuting internalization of the good analyst into a good superego (psychic structure) leaves the ego something of a child in relation to his good internal object, in effect subject to the tyranny of goodness. The good superego may be counted on to make the ego feel better, even to guide it better and provide inspiration, but may seal off the possibility of a more profound regression, and a fiercer, more thorough search.

For Lacan, introjection-identification-internalization do not account for the

Symbolic (the path toward "cure"). Symbolization transcends them and makes them possible. They are limiting modes *of* symbolization and presuppose the more general creative activity they grow out of. They may help, but also often hinder the full play of meaning, one's search for emotional truth. They often fill in gaps within and between orders (the Real, Imaginary, Symbolic) with doses of premature goodness, foreclosing glimpses of what one must face. One must trust that through the gap between himself and the Other (the Unconscious, the Real, the Symbolic), creative play will save him. The subject's search for the truth about himself evolves by listening to a live play of meaning that always exceeds his grasp. Here faith is necessary. One cannot master the real, or life of meaning in any fundamental way. One can only try to participate in one's own revisioning through impact and revelation, with all the openness and intensity of insight one can muster.

COMPARISONS BETWEEN WINNICOTT AND LACAN

For Winnicott the symbolic begins at the level of lived experience, prior to language. Language itself grows out of the matrix of preverbal *symbolizing experiencing* and carries threads of the latter to new heights. In transitional experiencing primordial symbolization takes the form of an affective cognition in which self–other awareness creatively thrives. *Self–other awareness is itself the core of symbolizing experiencing* and perhaps remains humankind's most creative activity at various levels of developmental complexity. In terms of preverbal symbolizing experiencing, self and other are neither felt as identical nor experienced with any sharp division. Winnicott and Milner (1980) have at times expressed this phase of consciousness in terms of overlapping circles.

Winnicott's symbolic experiencing thus begins at the level of Lacan's Real. However, it does not exhaust the Real. For the latter includes the double fact of subject–object interlocking *and* rupture. The events in Lacan's Real are more nearly encompassed by Winnicott's transitional experiencing *and* object usage. The latter deals with the realization of subject and object difference earlier than language.

A comparison like this raises difficulties and cannot be exact. For Lacan, the unconscious—in the first instance, the primal repressed lived awareness of interlocking-rupture—is instituted by the advent of language. However, the Real also continuously eludes language. It is the reference to lived awareness that evocatively links Lacan's Real with Winnicott's transitional experiencing and object usage. For Winnicott, however, transitional experiencing and object usage are *not* essentially linked with repression. They are ways the subject lives all out through the feeling of wholeness (a paradoxical wholeness). Winnicott is saying that there are modes of experiencing which are both lived and symbolizing at a preverbal level, and which cannot be understood in terms of self-splitting processes. This is one of several differences between these authors which, we will see, cluster around deeper phenomenological commitments.

Another important divergence is that Winnicott's formulations do not imply the same sense of radical rupture that pervades the tenor of Lacan's account. Even in object usage, where externality is radically encountered as such, the feeling tone is one of basic goodness of "news of difference" (Bateson's 1979 phrase), not catastrophe. In Winnicott the movement is one of dramatic unfolding rather than traumatic im- or propulsion. In his account a sense of basic harmony makes divergence revitalizing rather than essentially menacing. There is something seamless even about Winnicott's radical otherness. In Lacan the agonistic element is more emphatically stressed in the rupture of *juissance* and the latter's ironic reappearance in the life of meaning.

Winnicott (1965) expressed his alliance with the thread of connectedness, for example, in his work on the capacity for concern:

> We often discuss separation-anxiety, but here I am trying to describe what happens between mothers and their babies and between parents and their children when there is *no* separation, and when external continuity of child-care is *not* broken. I am trying to account for things that happen when separation is avoided. [p. 78]

This passage was written before Winnicott clearly distinguished the *use of the object* (1969) as personality nutriment from libidinal use of the object, as well as from the holding environment mother. However, his later account also retains a primacy of connectedness, wherein some form of subject-object togetherness persists in the midst of subject-object difference. In healthy development of object usage, the "I destroy you" is encompassed by "I love you." The tension between these two terms generates useable rather than disruptive aliveness, a joyous quickening.

Lacan is more preoccupied with the rent in the heart of the real and the gap within and between orders of mental life instituted by language. The subject can turn this gap to good account by understanding it as the clearing where cultural creativity thrives. Nevertheless, the subject's main preoccupation is with this rupture and a considerable part of his striving for (and through) meaning involves seeing through ways he tries to avoid or foreclose the rifts that meaning brings. For Lacan the trick seems to be to catch on that we are continuously symbolizing some lack which our symbolizing activity itself both institutes and transcends.

Winnicott and Lacan agree that the Imaginary (e.g., introjective-projective dramas) marks the self's attempt to master trauma in a false way, usually through the subtle assertion of some mirage of self-sufficiency. The urge to exert control over what must not be merely "controlled" cuts oneself off from one's most basic creative promptings. At some level the Imaginary occludes the sort of profound self-responsiveness that results in genuine personal evolution. One tries to control rather than open oneself to the transformation of dialogue, of interaction. For Winnicott, separation is part of the faith journey, an all-out symbolizing experiencing at the preverbal level. For Lacan good faith is a matter of respecting the basic gap within lived awareness, as elaborated, enriched, and transcended by verbal symbolizing capacity. In both these cases something other than control and identificatory dimensions (namely, the wish to stay on top or fuse) uplifts the self.

The Human Face

It is, I suspect, Lacan's basic distrust of the visual that, in part, leads to his situating the symbolic primarily in language. For Lacan vision is the site of seduction *par excellence*. In his account it is above all through the visual self-image that the Imaginary works. He uses, for example, the baby's self-recognition in a mirror (at roughly six months of age) as a paradigm of self-alienation. The perfect responsiveness and clearly articulated boundaries of the mirror image provide a magical sense of control and cohesion that far outstrip the facts of everyday experience. The mirror or visual me, the actor for an audience, comes to be used as a defense against authentic body feelings, especially one's vulnerability and insufficiency.

The infant's relationship with its mother easily exploits this tendency. The infant's and mother's gaze capture each other. The infant grows by imitating but at the same time loses contact with its own subjective pulse. For Lacan it is through symbolic discourse, the living Word, that baby-mother seductiveness is purified. Here visual control is futile. What counts is emotional truth, self-disclosing meaning (Heidegger's full rather than empty speaking, Husserl's statements spoken with "evidence"). The talking cure on the couch is a methodological strategy aimed at rendering visual control (the life of mimicry) futile and fostering awareness of one's basic situation. In this phenomenology, listening undercuts the power of seduction.

Winnicott, in contrast, emphasizes the positive (nonparanoid) aspect of the baby's visual experience. In optimal circumstances, baby and mother mutually mirror one another's *personal* qualities, so that one's sense of self is confirmed and evolves. An enhancing intermingling of self and other occur at the heart of self-experience.

For Winnicott, like Lacan, seduction is an alienating event. He has written (1971) that nothing is more treacherous for the developing self than tantalization, seduction to extreme. Seduction impinges on the infant's ongoing being, provoking the development of a False Self system. Vision may be misused to steal intrusively or to engulf, but is not necessarily or primarily employed this way. From Winnicott's viewpoint, Lacan's paranoid–seductive mirror me is a key way the self's use of sight may go wrong. It offers an excellent portrayal of an imaginary, false self which stains the human condition. Still, our seeing and seeing through also play a positive, nondefensive role in the texture of our lives. We can grow through a fundamentally fertile symbiosis between Word and vision, albeit one easily aborted or distorted. The human ego appears to have a mixture of paranoid and nonparanoid foundational experiences, the particular balance, in important part, dependent on the overall quality of responsiveness by the parental milieu (Bion 1977, Eigen, 1980a,b, 1981, Eigen and Robbins 1980, Kohut 1971, 1977, Weil, 1958, Winnicott 1958, 1965, 1971).

Both Lacan and Winnicott in some way link the origin of the early self with the primordial experience of the face, although each presents a different phenomenology of this basic experience. For Lacan it is paranoid–seductive, for Winnicott a matrix of true self-feeling. Spitz's (1965) work also links the early emergence of self–other awareness with the infant's response to the face or face mask. By roughly two or three months of age (perhaps earlier), the infant may spontaneously break out into a coherent, joyous smile to a face stimulus (eyes and nose must be represented). Like Lacan, Spitz reads a seductive or controlling (adaptive mastery) element into this smile. He feels this smile is primarily geared toward inducing maternal responsiveness. I find this smile more radically joyous, expressive of delight in recognizing personal presence. As Spitz also points out, it is part of a system of self-and-other mutual reverberation and resonance. To view this full and focused smile merely in terms of its value for ensuring survival says little of what kind of being survives *this* way, and scarcely does justice to its surplus of expressive meaning.

To live in and through a smile marks the advent of a radically new sort of consciousness, some extra *x* of subjective quality. In earlier papers (Eigen 1980a,b,c, 1982, Elkin 1972) I have suggested this smile is the home base of the human self, the felt criterion for what is most basically sensed as emotionally right or wrong. Soon enough the infant may smile when frightened or mad, signaling seductive intentionality or splits between thinking, feeling action (Lacan's Imaginary, Winnicott's False Self). However, the *primary smile* in question expresses all-out, spontaneous living through faith (more basic than splitting), the primordial underpinning for the possibility of rebirth throughout a lifetime. This nuclear joy kernel, I believe, is inexhaustible. So, it seems, is suffering. Over and over, like Job, the true smile at the center of human consciousness attempts to come through the struggles self-feeling must undergo.

The fact that the primordial human smile and the vision that evokes it support conflicting phenomenologies, both of which carry a ring of truth, dramatically brings out the challenge we face in discovering how thoroughly duality permeates us. In what way can we say that our sense of wholeness comes through our dual view? Can duality open out from or toward wholeness? Everywhere we look doubleness proliferates. Does our dual view keep our struggles for wholeness honest—cynical? The intrigue between our sense of wholeness and duality is intensified in Bion's formulations. Through his notation "O" he takes on our need to engage ultimate reality, without compromising any conflicting experiential dimensions which may help or hinder us in this enterprise.

BION: FAITH IN O

Bion uses the sign, O, to denote ultimate reality (namely, absolute truth, the godhead, the infinite, the thing-in-itself). For the psychoanalyst the O (ultimate reality) of psychoanalytical experience is what might be expressed as the emotional truth of a session. Strictly speaking, as psychoanalysts we live in the faith that emotional truth is possible, even necessary as a principle of wholesome psychic growth. In itself the emotional truth at stake may be unknown and unknowable, but nothing can be more important than learning to attend to it. This is paradoxical: an unknowable is to be the focus of our attention. Our faith in something important happening when we reach out toward the unknowable sustains the attention that clears a working space for truth. Our intention to attend to the evolution of emotional reality does make a difference in how we come to feel about ourselves as development proceeds. For better or worse, the individual who addresses this issue cannot be the same, in the long run, as one who does not.

Bion rigorously distinguishes the faith dimension, *the* locus of psychoanalytical experience, from all other events in human experience. Bion sees faith not only as a condition that makes psychoanalysis possible, but as the latter's *primary methodological principle*. In order to attempt to clarify this, he systematically distinguishes faith from knowledge and tries to work out the relationship between these two capacities. In this, we will see, he followed Kant, but with a shift of emphasis.

Bion grounds his thinking on the distinction between being and knowing and draws, from epistemological considerations, implications about the human condition. Being and knowing require each other. For us the being of knowing and knowing of being are inextricably intertwined. Our knowing I-feeling permeates the heart of our existence and makes it what it is. Nevertheless, the distinction between being and knowing is no mere intellectual exercise. We are not in the same qualitive space when we focus on knowing and when we focus on who we really are. In the former attitude we may gain knowledge about ourselves, but *knowing about* may or may not contribute much to genuine emotional change. If *we* are to develop as whole persons, the actual truth of our emotional realities must evolve. This state of affairs may be condensed in a paraphrase of one of Bion's (1977) cryptic orphisms: "One cannot know O, one must *be* it" (p. 27).

The O of who we are may evolve to a point where we feel we know something about it. The evolution of O gives rise to formulations which aspire to express it. It is through discourse that we try to communicate about O. Without our knowing discourse the mere muteness of our being would cave in on itself. We hope, too, our formulations not only reflect O, but facilitate its evolution. If our formulations are good enough approximations of O, they may act as vehicles through which we become more at one with our own movement. However, for this to occur we must be aiming ourselves toward O, not mere knowledge.

> It [O] stands for the absolute truth in and of any object; it is assumed that this cannot be known by any human being; it can be known about, its presence can be recognized and felt, but it cannot be known. It is possible to be at one with it. That it exists is an essential postulate of science but it cannot be scientifically discovered.

No psycho-analytic discovery is possible without recognition of its existence, at-one-ment with it and evolution. [1977, p. 30]

Our formulations are couched in terms derived from sensuous experience, but the emotional truth we seek to express is not sensuous or spatial. It is not localizable anywhere. When speaking about psychic reality spatial references are metaphorical or analogical. Emotional truth is inherently intangible, invisible, or ineffable (i.e., consciousness sees and hears but can't be seen or heard). We use terms derived from sensuous experience to point to a realm beyond the latter. Our pointing is always an approximation, a guess, a conviction.

O does not fall in the domain of knowledge or learning save *incidentally*; it can "become," but it cannot be "known." It is darkness and formlessness but it enters the domain K [knowledge] when it has evolved to a point where it can be known, through knowledge gained by experience, and formulated in terms derived from sensuous experience; its existence is conjectured phenomenologically. [1977, p. 26, italics added]

We develop a phenomenology of intimations of emotional truth formulated with conviction and with the realization that we may be wrong. We aim in faith to connect with what is beyond our representations, as we use our representations to light up the mystery of who we are. We live parallel lives with ourselves in our being and knowing, and develop a critical trust in possible points of intersection, if intersection were possible. Communion with O is an imaginative adventure, not an acquired certainty to be taken for granted. This realization helps keep us honest, at the same time that it provides fresh stimulus for inspired groping.

The fundamental distinction between Faith in O and all other attitudes is brought out most dramatically in Bion's discussions of the "good therapist" and the container (e.g., 1970). The good therapist wants to help the patient and may learn all he can about the latter toward this end. However, the desire to help and know can get in the way rather than prove useful in a profound sense. Such activity may block the openness of mind necessary for inklings of the emotional truth of a session to form. Wanting to help and know can saturate the space in which O might evolve. The therapist who, even with the best intentions, is caught up in a subtle controlling or mastery stance toward the emotional reality of a session, is in danger of stunting perceptive listening and shutting out subtle currents of creative movement.

Bion's famous dictum, that the analytic attitude is one of freedom from memory and desire, must be understood in terms of the faith–mastery polarity, particularly with regard to his critique of the wish to know. He opts for a primacy of perception and attention over memory and knowledge as the analyst's most basic working orientation. In his view, the intention to attend and perceive rather than remember and know or impose a helpful scenario, is the more fruitful attitude for creative unfolding. Knowledge, to be sure, spontaneously enters the process of freshly forming *gestalts* expressive of psychic reality.

However, in the frame of mind designated by faith in O, one does not hold on to either what one knows or one's formulations, but is more deeply anchored (better, freely floating) in hopeful contact with the thing itself.

Even functioning as a "good container" can present a danger for perceptive vision (1977, pp. 28-33). It is important to stress this because in analytic writings the positive aspects of the mind's containing function is usually emphasized (Eigen 1980b, Green 1975, Grotstein 1979). In the latter instance, for example, thoughts or feelings the baby cannot process are evacuated into the mother, who contains and detoxifies them by her own mental functions (memory and reverie) and feeds the baby usable responses. More generally, the mind as container is more concerned with regulating the balance of pleasure and pain than with emotional truth. Ideally, the individual grows in his ability to contain and successfully represent his painful states along with his wish to feel good.

However, an orientation toward pleasure–pain regulation (here the containing function working through introjective–projective operations) tends to mitigate against intunement with movement of O. Attention to the emotional truth of situations must have a certain independence of pleasure–pain considerations. One cannot regulate the movement of truth. Rather, one seeks to modulate oneself in relation to requirements that truth discloses. The containing function, at bottom, seeks to influence the movement of O in ego desirable directions, in fathomable and manipulable terms. It aims to cut one's ultimate reality to ego size. Ordinary good adaptations may make life manageable, but may diminish chances for profound psychic transformation. The natural attitude, however supportive and useful, is not the analytic attitude and can interfere with the most far-reaching kinds of therapeutic encounters. To try to control where truth will lead is to put oneself above truth, and so, in part, shut out the potentially reorienting effects of the latter. To maximize the possibility of contact with what is most important for becoming at one with oneself, the subject must relate to truth with faith.

Below are several quotes from Bion (1977) relevant to our primary concern in this section, the distinction of the faith dimension (*the* analytic attitude) from other inclinations.

> for me 'faith' is a scientific state of mine and should be recognized as such. But it must be "faith" unstained by any element of memory or desire. [p. 32]

> The evocation of that which provided a container for possessions, and of the sensuous gratifications with which to fill it [e.g., the pleasure of helping or being helped], will differ from an evocation stimulated by at-one-ment. [p. 33]

> It may be wondered what state of mind is welcome if desires and memories are not. A term that would express approximately what I need to express is "faith"—faith that there is an ultimate reality and truth—the unknown, unknowable, "formless infinite." This must be believed of every object of which the personality can be aware: the evolution of ultimate reality (signified by O) has issued in objects of

which the individual can be aware. The objects of awareness are aspects of the "evolved" O and are such that the sensuously derived mental functions are adequate to apprehend them. For them faith is not required; for O it is. [p. 31]

In sum, the starting point for psychoanalytic work is the analyst's capacity to be at one with O. To paraphrase Bion, the more real the psychoanalyst is, the more he can be at one with the reality of the patient. The learnings and formulations that go into our acts of communication are necessarily derived from past sensuous experience and must be taken as analogies to be purified of the very terms employed. All formulations are, in part, signs of their own limitations. They are pointers, expressive vehicles of access, and undo themselves if they serve their purpose. The therapeutic *gestalt* that grows out of evolution of O is not a memory of past learning, but a present speculative seeing, a felt link with emotional truth that may be relevant for the latter's further evolution. If the analyst is able to sustain Faith in O and tolerate the development of formulations that reflect O, he may legitimately hope for a therapeutic outcome in which the analysand becomes more at one with himself, that is, his own evolution.

DOUBLENESS AND MYSTERY:
BEYOND THE DEPRESSIVE POSITION

The tension between two or more orders of experience permeates the thought of Winnicott, Lacan, and Bion. A basic tension in all of these writers is that between true and false turns of mind. Taken together, their approach is both Kantian and Biblical, yet distinctly psychoanalytic. The dynamic tension within and between different orders of mental life is a formal, as well as descriptive, characteristic of Freud's thought (Bass 1980, Lowe 1977, 1980). The theme is ancient and restless, its turns unpredictable. The vicissitudes of faith involve the struggle not only to know but in some way be one's true self, to take up the journey with all that one is and may become, and to encounter through oneself the ground of one's being. This is undertaken with the knowledge that we are mediate beings, that certainty is beyond certain reach, but that anything short of this attempt portends disaster and is self-crippling. The undertaking itself involves one in continuous re-creation.

Although Winnicott, Lacan, and Bion develop the theme of faith-through-doubleness in their own individual ways, there is a point at which they converge. The faith dimension is a common vertex through which they move along differing paths. In the present section I will try to situate some of their key differences in the light of their central crossing. My interest is not in reconciling (reducing?) these theorists so much as seeing ways they help set each other in motion. My development draws on but is not limited to earlier sections. Some further summary and amplification of aspects of their thought is necessary in order to bring out the full flavor of how they fill out and challenge each other.

Winnicott

Winnicott assumes life is primarily creative and in infancy this creativity unfolds in phases with proper environmental help. For him a certain similarity, perhaps continuity, persists from biological to psychological spheres. However, this apparent monism quickly shifts keys. Human life, as it is lived, is shot through with antimonies. For example, he contrasts a basic True Self with a False Self, the latter a self-protective personality distortion. The true self feeling involves a sense of all-out personal aliveness, more than simple animal aliveness because it includes an awareness of being or feeling *real*. It thus requires a lived recognition of being the self one is, that this felt presence is one's true being. This connects with Bion's insistence that truth is necessary for wholeness and emotional growth. Falsity pollutes one's self-feeling, even if one has become used to it, or even takes it as the norm.

For Winnicott, the true self feeling is essentially undefensive. It may be defended and under pressure shrink or start to disappear (Eigen 1973). But it is most basically unarmed and characterized by the feeling of genuine wholeness. In Winnicott's account the sense of wholeness evolves from a period of self–other harmonious mixup (to use Balint's 1968 phrase), through self–other distinction, and thrives on both these tendencies. At all points it (the sense of wholeness) is threatened by countertendencies toward disruption and perversion, especially tyrannical (False Self) introjective–projective fantasy operations whereby the self-feeling becomes demonized. With reference to the above account (pp. 2–18), Winnicott's False Self tends to correspond with what he termed the unit self, the self as an isolate, Lacan's Imaginary. He describes central aspects of the True Self's foundational journey in his accounts of transitional experiencing and object usage.

In the resulting dualistic clinical picture, truth and falsehood vie in the human soul. For Winnicott the essential battle is over one's sense of realness: does one feel real to oneself or merely a phantom or splinter self? The main problem that pervades his clinical writings is depersonalization and the profound self-splitting and self-anesthesia that underwrite it. Both he and Bion link authentic wholling processes with trueness. This may be viewed as an assumption, a faith. From their viewpoint it is also profound description.

For Winnicott life requires violence (hatching processes). However, he believes that in human life, optimally, this occurs within a primacy of love. His object relations rewriting of the drive fusion theory opts for a primacy of unity-in-differentiation. For example, in his account of the use of the object we have seen that an *I love you* spontaneously arises in the wake of the *I destroy you,* and this *I love you* makes destructiveness creative. In this instance, the two together lead to a fuller, richer awareness of self and other, a revitalizing sense of otherness as such.

In sum, Winnicott's aim was to place the living sense of feeling true or false to oneself at the center of human experience and thinking. He did this by raising the issue of how these two psychic tendencies meet the perennial vicissitudes of connection and otherness. The particular psychoanalytic turn given to these issues involved a detailed account of the interaction of love and destructiveness within the context of subject-to-subject interactions at originary phases of the self's history.

Winnicott's True Self was apparently meant as a phenomenological expression, but it may also function as a *formal principle of personal growth*. (Eigen 1973, Winnicott 1958, 1965, 1971) believes that the True Self is in some sense absolutely private, incommunicado. However, not only is it inaccessible to everybody but oneself; it may be somewhat beyond the subject's reach as well. The subject both participates in true self feeling at the same time that he strives toward (more of) it, an inexhaustible paradox built into the very structure of self feeling. The true self feeling may become defensively abused, so that true and false self mix-ups arise (evil seems good, and good evil). In such instances some overall skew or offness in the personality will press for recognition, until the core subjective quality of what it feels like to be a person gets set right or is given up on (Evil, be my good). In this context, a Winnicottian (given, as Khan 1979 says, that there's no such thing) therapy aims at working through the individual's profound depersonalization in a way that makes access to true self feeling possible. Nevertheless, even within the domain of true self feeling itself, mystery remains in fact and principle. More approach is always possible.

In both Lacan and Bion the subject's reaching after the true and real *explicitly* becomes a formal principle for full, personal evolution (in Bion, at least, it also is meant descriptively). The fundamental status of the need to generate meanings which reflect or bring the subject into accord with the truth about himself defines the tenor of these men's writings. This hunger for emotional truth is frequently at war with the ego as an adaptive mechanism (or system).

Lacan

Lacan (1977, 1978, Lemaire 1977) seems to say that there is some primordial state of affairs that psychic life seeks to represent and deal with throughout its history. What this state of affairs is we cannot know. We can only create myths that function as markers for the unknown it is. The principal myths for Lacan involve the rupture of some fundamental union, that is, the separation from mother's body at birth, the break-up of baby-mother dual union with the advent of language. These wounded unions leave the infant with a propensity to feel incomplete and insufficient, with a need or lack which becomes translated as desire. The human venture is the history of desire as it ceaselessly loses and rediscovers itself through the identificatory and symbolic registers. The imaginary order perpetrates endless misreadings, while the Symbolic makes as honest an attempt as possible to represent the basic situation beyond our grasp, the proposed wounded union.

The basic structure of Lacan's views, like Freud's, involves some basic state of affairs or fantasy, some basic *x* behind a ceaseless flow of transpositions which reflect or deal with it more falsely or truly. Lacan associates truth as such with the unknown state of affairs itself, the Real, from which we are barred from direct access by primal repression. The latter is instituted by our insertion into language, the basic medium of rupture. We may try to create a spurious image of wholeness, an Imaginary self-sufficiency. But we also strive to represent, as best we can, the *sense* of our division as it unfolds through the very gaps we are attempting to read. These three unconscious orders, The Real, Imaginary, and Symbolic, are not reducible to one another. They express categories that form the basis of humankind's perennial date with conflict.

Bion, Lacan, and Winnicott

For Bion (like Lacan, Freud, and Kant), the ultimate reality of the self is beyond the reach of knowledge. However, for Bion, openness to the unknown is *the* formal and working principle by which psychoanalysis must proceed. Lacan also posits the unknowable. However, he tends to link it with a basic situation that has undergone repression, and reads psychic life in terms of its transforms. For Bion this would constitute one mode in which the unknowable can show itself. His position, I believe, is far more radical.

Bion's O has *no psychological locus at all*. Its status is not confined to any category one can possibly postulate concerning psychic life, yet it is assumed to be the ground of them all. No starting or ending point can be envisioned for O. It is always evolving. As we aim to express the emotional truth of a session, we cannot know ahead of time what this truth will look like. It may take the form (Lacan's, Freud's) of elemental situations traveling in disguise via condensations and displacements (Lacan's metaphor and metonymy). Or it may take as yet unperceived forms which require fresh methods of approach.

Lacan, too, stresses the importance of not oversimplifying the complexity of psychic life. The path of meaning is unpredictable, nor can one bottle the Real in one's representations. Both he and Bion stress the necessity of a doubleness of vision as an intrinsic part of one's working method. In this regard, Bion speaks of "binocular vision," a metaperspective the subject continuously adopts on the interplay and barriers between conscious and unconscious processes. Lacan talks of the different languages employed by consciousness and unconscious mental orders. One reads unconscious meanings as one might a palimpsest or different sides of an obelisk. The emphasis in both writers is on what sort of attitude makes a simultaneous reading of a plurality of dimensions possible. However, Bion leaves it open, in principle, as to what constitutive forms such a reading might look like. There are no working limits placed on the nature of O and its evolutions. One is not constrained to read emotional truth in terms of an unchanging situation. In Bion's view, what Lacan might call the basic situation (the x that is transposed, say, via metonymy), itself may be an evolved form capable of undergoing further evolution.

Lacan's entire panoply can be situated within a framework that, in Bion's vision, may be represented as evolutions of O or barriers against this evolution. As a formal concept Lacan's Imaginary represents barriers against the evolution of O. His Symbolic expresses and possibly facilitates this evolution. The status of the Real is more ambiguous. Is it a lived dimension outside of meaning? Is it instituted by meaning? Is it both inside and outside of meaning? In Lacan's writings it is all of these in different contexts. As the primal repressed instituted by meaning, it eludes meaning and is expressed in disguised forms through meaning.

Derrida (1978) also has challenged the structure of Lacan's thought on the basis of this ambiguity. He, somewhat like Bion, questions the need of postulating, even as a myth, a static basic x with which meaning is forever preoccupied. Like Lacan, however, he views the structure of language as the defining dimension of human subjectivity and equates meaning with languages. If, he argues, language is the privileged phenomenon that makes human subjectivity what it is, and psychic life is the play of signifiers, there is no reason to look to a basic x outside of language. Such a looking would be senseless and impossible. Meaning feeds on meaning from its inception. If human psychic life *is* the life of meaning, no situation extrinsic to the latter can be used to start it off.

Bion's position differs in important respects from both Lacan's and Derrida's. As mentioned earlier, his O is not necessarily an ever-recurrence of the same. It is, also, meaningful in a more profound sense than language. For Bion, the subject seeks to express his emotional reality *through* language. The latter may help feed the movement of his emotional truth but is not identical with it. In this regard, life may be richly meaningful for the preverbal baby, as witnessed, for example, by the radiant self–other awareness expressed in the smiling response.

If, given Bion's framework, the life of meaning goes deeper than language, language is one way (or series of ways) that meaning can be organized. The language operations charted by Lacan may be included by and even reshape the unconscious but do not exhaust the latter. They portray crucial ways a subject can be a subject, privileged ways meaning operates. For Bion emotional truth is not confined to language, nor does it have a static basis. Its evolving quality spreads out in all temporal directions. We open ourselves to meet it. Our formulations try to express what in faith we trust our gesture contacts.

In this context, Winnicott's transitional experiencing and use of the object represent evolutions of O. They are formulations of preverbal events alive with felt meaning, areas of lived truth linked with the unfolding of self–other awareness. What is suggested is the emergence of new experiential dimensions (new basic situations) rather than convolutions of a repressed x. The formulations themselves are made in the hope of helping the subject to discover and move in accord with his own meaningfully lived reality in an ongoing way.

All three authors, Winnicott, Bion, and Lacan, express the subject's struggle to live faithfully, together with impediments to this endeavour. Their central concern is the subject's radically reorienting relations to lived truth as it moves through vicissitudes of meaning. This is a struggle that incorporates yet transcends identificatory/introjective–projective/internalization processes, and so goes beyond the depressive position, the path of symbol development in Kleinian thinking.

As discussed above, Winnicott's transitional experiencing and object usage constitute a world of experiencing at once symbolic and actual. The latter two orders permeate and support each other in a kind of seamless unity, giving rise to an unfolding of fresh experiential dimensions. In object usage the introjected other is ceaselessly destroyed in loving communion with a more radically freeing sense of otherness, an otherness intrinsically experienced with joy, not depressive guilt. Introjections form part of a larger psychic field which they may interfere with or subserve. In part, they are consolidating measures that are there to be transcended.

Lacan's style is more ironic. For him the distinction between self and other (correlatively, consciousness and the unconscious) is constituted through language. The life of meaning echoes the rupture of mute union, a rupture that meaning itself is. The subject is at war as to how he is to relate to his predicament. He may try identificatory (Imaginary) ways to fill in or escape the gaps he finds in himself and between himself and others. Or he may struggle to discover ways of representing the truth of his condition to himself, thereby achieving a modicum of transcendence. This latter achievement in symbolic decentering may not exactly be joyous (although it involves the *juissance* of meaning), but it is not Kleinian introjective depression.

Introjective depression tends to save the subject from a more far-reaching and dizzying view of his meaning-creating capacity. The subject's meaning-creating capacity provides a metaperspective on the category of introjection (and internalization). Indeed, introjection requires a perspective beyond itself. The subject moves between his identificatory capacity and his capacity to see through the latter. For Lacan, irony is the guardian of the subject's good faith. Through ironic consciousness the subject recognizes that he is too complicated to be wholehearted in any definitive sense, at the same time that he moves from or toward whatever wholeheartedness is possible along a radically decentered path.

Bion's writings combine the most radical sincerity and irony. The subject who is attentive to evolutions of O is decentered from himself. He focuses on O. All aspects of his psychic life (in the strict sense, anything that implies possession: i.e., one's knowledge, desires, habits, pleasures) are distinguished from realizations that grow from the evolution of O. Even then, what the subject perceives may or may not express the prepotent truth about the emotional reality at hand.

Nevertheless, he continues focusing on what he hopes is O and meets the turbulence that comes his way. His reward is not the certainty of being right or wrong at any given moment, but the profound change of quality and reorientation he finds himself undergoing as an experiencing subject.

Introjective–projective operations, from the present perspective, fall into the realm characterized by possessiveness. The subject tries to make something part of himself or the other. This involves controlling operations which may interfere with perception of emotional truth. When Bion does describe the evolution of O in a session as a movement from projective (fragmenting) to introjective (wholling) states, these latter terms depict a phasic unfolding that spontaneously occurs within an overarching openness toward O. Neither phase is courted or held onto. The subject directs himself with his whole being toward O. The projective–introjective movements that happen as a matter of course are not themselves the primary method or aim.

What is crucial is *how one relates to* whatever one may be relating to. In Bion's view, the basic analytic attitude or way of relating is to keep aiming toward O. If, for example, one's emotional reality or truth is despair, what is most important is not *that* one may be in despair, but one's attitudes *toward* one's despair. Through one's basic attentiveness one's despair can declare itself and tell its story. One enters profound dialogue with it. If one stays with this process, an evolution even in the quality of despair may begin to be perceived, since despair itself is never uniform.

What evolves in analysis is no mere knowledge about content, or pleasurable ways of interaction, or more successful adaptations. These may be involved but are not primary. The most precious gain is the evolution of openness toward experiencing, or, as Bion writes, "experiencing experience," a process in which something more is always happening (or about to). The essential freedom analysis brings is the analytic attitude itself, the liberation of the capacity to focus on O.

IDEAL EXPERIENCING: GOD, MOTHER, FATHER

In sum, Winnicott, Lacan, and Bion carry on Freud's theme of the self in conflict with the constituting dimensions through which it lives. My emphasis has been on a sense of wholeness which, nonetheless, continuously evolves through struggles which threaten to deform or occlude it. The paradoxical complexity of a wholling tendency that thrives on coming through tendencies toward depersonalization and dispersal, bears witness to the category of mystery as a basic dimension in which we live (Lowe 1977).

In Winnicott's account, the sense of wholeness passes through phases in which the distance between self and other is taken for granted (transitional experiencing) and is acutely experienced (object usage). In Bion's work Faith in O represents a wholling attitude (linked with attention and creativity) that evolves, in part, by suffering through the divisions and disruptions psychic life is prone to. Whatever wholling principle exists in Lacan's thought ironically enters with the subject's realization of the impossibility of wholeness. Realization itself is a wholling as well as divisive act, even as it realizes its divisiveness.

The concerns of these authors converge on a central interest: creative experiencing — what makes it possible or hinders it (formally and descriptively). They chart detailed ways in which creative experiencing involves paradox, mystery, or faith expressed through dialectical thinking. In effect, each tries to develop something of a phenomenology of creative experiencing. In so doing, these authors begin to sustain a radical encounter with what is the primary quality of experiencing as such: its intangibility or immateriality.

As mentioned earlier, experiencing as such is not spatially localizable, yet it is that through which space awareness arises. An apparently unknowable, imperceptible dimension makes knowing and perception possible. Freud, of course, acknowledged the phenomenological immateriality of mind (at certain points he even tried to derive our primitive sense of space from the immaterial psyche's sense of its own depth). However, by a sleight of hand he played down crucial aspects of this realization in the working out of his formal theory (Eigen 1979, 1980a,b, 1981). This is most readily seen in his treatment of "ideal states," a basic form ideal experiencing can take.

Ideal states often refer to a sense of infinite perfection, whether beatific (divine) or horrific (demonic). Such ideal moments together with the images associated with them play a central role in the Freudian corpus. They are virtually omnipresent, complexly interacting with or against instincts and reality. Ideal qualities in one form or other appear as part of the object pole of instincts. In Freudian dramas, *instincts seek an ideal imago*. Desire is a noetic constant. The noematic nucleus of the shifting x desired carries an ideal glow. In Freudian dramas the ideal imago variously saturates one's own body, ego, mother, father, and so on to a wide range of possibilities (e.g., feces, feet, science, nation, God).

In most Freudian literature the defensive and pathological uses of ideal images have been stressed, at best emphasizing their importance as compensations (Chasseguet-Smirgel 1974, Freud 1914, Reich 1953, 1954, 1960). For Freud, ideal experiencing usually involved something in disguise (e.g., mother, father, sex, hostility, etc.). The capacity which produced ideal images tended not to be credited in its own right, but seen as a derived form of something else (Eigen 1979).

I believe the authors discussed in this paper, more than most psychoanalytic writers, systematically attempt to take up the problem of ideal experiencing in its own right, as a spontaneously unfolding human capacity related to existential concerns (for a discussion of where Kohut 1971, 1977, falls short, see Eigen 1979). Their critique of the identification-introjection-internalization track preserves what is valuable in the Freudian analysis of the defensive function of ideal images, but distinguishes this line from the inherently positive capacity it defensively deploys.

These authors attempt to differentiate the positive and negative aspects of ideal experiencing without reducing one to the other. Winnicott, for example, distinguishes the sense of wholeness (an ideal state) linked with True Self from perversions of ideal feelings linked with False Self (see Khan 1979, for excellent descriptions of perverse ecstasies involving a demonized sense of wholeness). In the former instance, ideal moments of dual union may be regenerative and not primarily defensive (Eigen 1980a,b,c, 1981, 1982, 1984). Undefensive and defensive use of ideal states complexly intermingle in actual living. Neither term of this ongoing tension is absent for long, although either may dominate in any given instance.

In Lacan, both the Imaginary and Symbolic orders may function defensively. But the latter seeks to open out to Truth, while the former moves to foreclose the latter. Truth-seeking requires a metaperspective on defensiveness as such, and so, in principle, moves in contact with a more profound vision than the defensiveness it is caught in. In Bion, as indicated earlier, truth functions as an intrinsic principle of emotional growth and is not basically a defense against anxiety (although it *may* be so employed). Faith in O is an undefensive, open attentiveness to the emotional reality of a subject, his truth, and comes in fierce conflict with inclinations that fight against it (the latter includes introjective or projective tendencies toward premature wholeness).

All three authors maintain the critical importance of not confusing creative experiencing with introjection (or internalization) of mother and father images or functions. The sources of creative experiencing run deeper than internalization and go beyond it. If one reads these authors carefully, one discovers that *the primary object of creative experiencing is not mother or father but the unknowable ground of creativeness as such*. Winnicott, for example, emphasizes that what is at stake in transitional experiencing is not mainly a self or object (mother) substitute, but the creation of a symbol, of symbolizing experiencing itself. The subject lives through and toward creative immersion (including phases of chaos, unintegration, waiting). What he symbolizes and seeks more and more of is the absorption of creative experiencing and the way this latter makes use of objects through successive waves of self–other awareness. Maternal or paternal object relations may subserve or thwart this experiencing but must not be simply identified with it. A similar argument could be made for the subject's immersion in the life of meaning as described by Lacan, or Bion's Faith in O.

By emphasizing the positive aspect of ideal experiencing as an irreducible term of human experience, these authors make it difficult to permit any facile "mother" or "father" reductionism. The latter, for example, may be seen most dramatically in the tendency to equate God with father (Freud) or mother (Klein). The primary ideal object cannot be reduced to either. The mix-up between God, parents, and self is a basic and perennial problem in human life, and psychoanalysis contributes much in charting this confusion. However, the terms of this dilemma can not be collapsed into one another without deception. If parents and self are, in part, gradually distinguished from idealizations, they cannot account for the capacity to idealize. They are occasions which enable this capacity to operate in developmentally sound or ill ways (Eigen 1979, Elkin 1972, for a psychoanalytic account which tries to give ideal states their due in an epistemological–anthropologically sound context).

Winnicott's, Lacan's, and Bion's emphasis on understanding the capacity to produce ideal images in its own right is no empty formalism. These authors are wary of traditional idealist–empiricist bifurcations. As psychoanalysts, following Freud, they chart the vicissitudes of ideal experiencing vis-à-vis the hard facts of life, from early infancy on. However, they do not obscure the irreducible co-presence of different orders of experience, or try to explain one in terms of the other without reciprocity. I believe they explicitly bring out and heighten the problems at stake in a psychic field wherein ideal experiencing and a spatial object world permeate and withdraw from one another. It is the irreducible (irreconcilable?) co-presence of immaterial and spatial dimensions of lived experience (reflectively elaborated) that defines human consciousness. In systems language they are correlatives. They require each other but cannot be equated in life as we know it so far.

I have tried to indicate ways in which three psychoanalytic writers have begun to chart systematically the interplay of variant experiential dimensions without compromising any of the basic terms involved. So far as I am aware, this is a radically new enterprise within psychoanalysis proper. It has been more usual for one of these terms to be made primary at the other's expense, or at least, in some way for primitive terms of experience to devalue each other. Whether or not the kind of project the approximations discussed point to can work, or will prove to be wishful thinking, remains to be seen.

The authors discussed made highly sophisticated attempts to articulate the faith dimension, a critical faith which functions both as a formal condition that makes psychoanalytical experience possible and, descriptively, as a specific state of mind (i.e., the psychoanalytic attitude). I wonder if the structure of their attempts does not connect in spirit, at least partly, with the biblical injunction for a snake–smart brain and dove–gentle heart. The wholling tendency expressed here is a differentiated one. It is not primarily based on mastery or control, although circumspection comes into play. It grows most basically through a faith in a spontaneous play of experiencing and meaning which aims to express and unfold what is most real for the subject, his emotional truth or way of being a subject, who one is.

REFERENCES

Balint, M. (1968). *The Basic Fault*. London: Tavistock.

Bass, A. (1980). The double game: psychoanalysis and deconstruction. Unpublished paper presented at the National Psychological Association for Psychoanalysis, New York.

Bateson, G. (1979). *Mind and Nature: A Necessary Unity*. New York: E. P. Dutton.

Bion, W. R. (1970). *Attention and Interpretation*. London: Tavistock.

_____ (1977). *Seven Servants*. New York: Jason Aronson.

Chasseguet-Smirgel, J. (1974). Perversion, idealization and sublimation. *International Journal of Psycho-Analysis* 55:349–357.

Derrida, J. (1978). *Writing and Difference*. Chicago: University of Chicago Press.

Eigen, M. (1973). Abstinence and the schizoid ego. *International Journal of Psycho-Analysis* 54:493–498.

_____ (1979). Ideal images, creativity, and the Freudian drama. *Psychocultural Review* 3:287–298.

_____ (1980a). Instinctual fantasy and ideal images. *Contemporary Psychoanalysis* 16:119–137.

_____ (1980b). On the significance of the face. *Psychoanalytic Review* 67:427–441.

_____ (1980c). Expression and meaning: a case study. In *Expressive Therapy*, ed. A. Robbins, pp. 291–312. New York: Human Sciences.

_____ (1981). Guntrip's analysis with Winnicott. *Contemporary Psychoanalysis* 17:103–117.

_____ (1982). Creativity, instinctual fantasy and ideal images. *Psychoanalytic Review* 68:317–339.

_____ (1983). A note on the structure of Freud's theory of creativity. *Psychoanalytic Review* 70:41–45.

_____ (1984). On demonized aspects of the self. In *Evil: Self and Culture*, ed. M. C. Nelson and M. Eigen, pp. 91–123. New York: Human Sciences.

Eigen, M., and Robbins, A. (1980). Object relations and expressive symbolism: some structures and functions of expressive therapy. In *Expressive Therapy*, ed. A. Robbins, pp. 73–94. New York: Human Sciences.

Elkin, H. (1972). On selfhood and the development of ego structures in infancy. *Psychoanalytic Review* 59:389–416.

Freud, S. (1914). On narcissism: an introduction. *Standard Edition* 14:73–102.

_____ (1920). Beyond the pleasure principle. *Standard Edition* 18:7–64.

Green, A. (1975). The analyst, symbolization and absence in the analytic setting (on changes in analytic practice and analytic experience). *International Journal of Psycho-Analysis* 56:1–22.

Greenacre, P. (1952). *Trauma, Growth and Personality*. New York: International Universities Press.

Grotstein, J. (1979). Who is the dreamer who dreams the dream and who is the dreamer who understands it? *Contemporary Psychoanalysis* 15:110–169.

Khan, M. M. R. (1979). *Alienation in Perversions*. New York: International Universities Press.

Kohut, H. (1971). *Analysis of the Self*. New York: International Universities Press.

_____ (1977). *The Restoration of the Self*. New York: International Universities Press.

Lacan, J. (1977). *Ecrits: A Selection*. New York: Norton.

_____ (1978). *The Four Fundamental Concepts of Psychoanalysis*. New York: International Universities Press.

Lemaire, A. (1977). *Jacques Lacan*. London: Routledge and Kegan Paul.

Lowe, W. J. (1977). *Mystery and the Unconscious: A Study in Thought of Paul Ricoeur*. Metuchen, NJ: Scarecrow.

_____ (1980). Evil and the unconscious: a Freudian exploration. *Soundings* 43:7–35.

Meltzer, D. (1973). *Sexual States of the Mind*. Strath Tay, Scotland: Clunie.

Merleau-Ponty, M. (1962). *Phenomenology of Perception*. London: Routledge and Kegan Paul.

———— (1968). *The Visible and the Invisible*. Evanston, IL: Northwestern University Press.

———— (1977). Winnicott and overlapping circles. In *The Suppressed Madness of Sane Men*, pp. 279–286. London: Tavistock, 1987.

Reich, A. (1953). Narcissistic object choice in women. In *Psychoanalytic Contributions*, pp. 179–208. New York: International Universities Press, 1973.

———— (1954). Early identifications as archaic elements in the superego. In *Psychoanalytic Contributions*, pp. 209–235. New York: International Universities Press, 1973.

———— (1960). Pathologic forms of self-esteem. In *Psychoanalytic Contributions*, pp. 288–311. New York: International Universities Press., 1973.

Segal, H. (1978). On symbolism. *International Journal of Psycho-Analysis* 59:315–319.

Spitz, R. (1965). *The First Year of Life*. New York: International Universities Press.

Weil, E. (1958). The origin and vicissitudes of the self-image. *Psychoanalysis* 1:3–19.

Winnicott, D. W. (1953). Transitional objects and transitional phenomena. *International Journal of Psycho-Analysis* 34:89–97.

———— (1958). *Collected Papers: Through Paediatrics to Psycho-Analysis*. London: Tavistock.

———— (1963). The development of the capacity for concern. *Bulletin of the Menninger Clinic* 27:167–176.

———— (1965). *The Maturational Process and the Facilitating Environment*. New York: International Universities Press.

———— (1969). The use of the object and relating through identification. *International Journal of Psycho-Analysis* 50:711–716.

———— (1971). *Playing and Reality*. New York: Basic Books.

12

Guntrip's Analysis with Winnicott

Guntrip's (1975) account of his psychotherapeutic journey is one of the deeply moving portrayals in analytic literature. By all usual standards he was not a clinically ill person. He functioned creatively in his work and personal life. His major presenting symptom — a background sense of unreality — was apparently marginal, one most people would put up with or try to ignore. However, he was one of those individuals who could not let any sense of offness rest. There was a sense in which he was not able to compromise or settle for anything less than becoming a whole person — even if this goal is necessarily elusive.

What gives Guntrip's case an added dimension is that his two analysts, Fairbairn and Winnicott, were among the most creative in the profession — and that he sensitively and creatively charted his pilgrimage. We look over his shoulder and try to catch a glimpse of who these men were and how they interacted with one another. By studying their work we must inevitably increase ourselves, even if our view is speculative and fragmentary.

Glatzer and Evans (1977) recently have raised the question "what went wrong?" in Guntrip's therapies. They feel his paper contains a veiled reproach for the shortcomings of his therapists and unconsciously portrays the lineaments of "therapeutic misalliances" (Langs 1975). Glatzer and Evans find that Guntrip's therapeutic work missed his baby hostile omnipotence and sibling rivalry. They believe that his therapists provided gratifications which masked these critical psychodynamics.

In the present paper I hope to qualify and amplify Glatzer's and Evans's findings. My main interest centers on problems in Guntrip's relationship with Winnicott — Guntrip felt the stakes highest there. After some introductory comments I will try to extend the meaning of Guntrip's hidden omnipotence, thus adding to Glatzer's and Evans's work. However, their view of Guntrip's theoretical position seems too limiting and their own theory too narrow. I believe it would have led to a technical error opposite to Winnicott's and perhaps even to greater therapeutic failure. I will consider these points in detail as this essay develops.

REVIEW OF GUNTRIP'S HISTORY

I will not give a detailed summary of Guntrip's history. It can be found in his original paper and in Glatzer and Evans. Nevertheless, some orienting comments seem necessary.

Guntrip linked his background sense of unreality to his amnesia for events surrounding and antedating the death of his younger brother, Percy. Percy died when Guntrip was three-and-a-half. Apparently Guntrip was supposed to have seen his brother die in the arms of their psychotically depressed mother.

In the course of analytic work Guntrip became aware that his mother had been at least four different mothers. The earliest maternal object was a good enough mother, or so Winnicott had postulated. Winnicott had supposed this to account for the preeminently positive cast to Guntrip's personality. Winnicott's own empathically comprehending presence evoked feeling memories which Guntrip took to be related to good mothering from the earliest phase.

A second mother was the empty, absent mother, apparently inertly depressed after her second child. Here was the affectively dead mother who was unable to support life. It was supposedly in her arms Percy died—and it was her blank face Guntrip had recalled through a dream evoked by Winnicott's death. Guntrip felt it was the good maternal presence animated by Winnicott's personality which formed a reference point which made reexperiencing maternal emptiness possible. In part Winnicott's death stood for the good mother turning into the emotionally absent one.

The third mother was the bad, intrusive mother analyzed with Fairbairn. Here was a mother Guntrip felt he remembered, the mother he had actively hated and fought, one he would never give in to. He gradually came to see this fight as a defense against a deeper emptiness.

His fourth mother was more neutral and dated from a later period in childhood. This corresponded to the time his mother had became successfully involved in her own business. Having something to occupy her took pressure off Guntrip and left him to his own devices. He no longer had to spend so much energy warding off her invasiveness. His mother in this phase was energetic and industrious, perhaps a model for Guntrip's "latency" style industry ever after.

It was with Winnicott that Guntrip felt most deeply understood. Winnicott reflected back to Guntrip how the latter kept himself feeling alive by doing and was terrified of being. It was Winnicott's death that finally precipitated the dreams which Guntrip believed cured his amnesia. In the most critical dream Guntrip believed he saw what was his dead brother in the arms of a faceless woman, experienced as his blank, empty mother. It was after the lifting of this amnesia that Guntrip felt cognitively whole, as if all the pieces had finally come together.

THE TRANSFERENCE AND COUNTERTRANSFERENCE BIND

Glatzer and Evans (1977) suggest that Guntrip took control of the therapy situation, and, in effect, stayed out of therapeutic reach. In the first instance he structured the overall therapeutic situation by means of a self-determined goal — the lifting of his amnesia. Other evidence for Guntrip's controlling attitude included his need to work only with a like-minded theorist, his critical disputatiousness in defense of his theoretical viewpoint, and his compulsive keeping of detailed records of sessions. His therapists apparently colluded with him by accepting his terms rather than analyzing them. Glatzer and Evans believe that beneath Guntrip's controlling and distancing behavior was a deeper infantile megalomania, a "primary narcissism" which experienced the external world as essentially wounding. They suggest that Guntrip's unconscious hostile omnipotence was expressed in his need to blame his mother for his personality difficulties and in veiled death wishes toward his brother. They argue that in crucial ways Fairbairn and Winnicott reinforced Guntrip's narcissism instead of analyzing it. For example, the writers point out that Winnicott tended to play a good mother role instead of working with Guntrip's wish for an all good mother and the inevitable angry frustration which must follow.

Indeed, Winnicott told Guntrip how much he enjoyed him as a patient. Somewhat tongue in cheek he added that Guntrip might be too good; Winnicott had never worked with anyone who kept such elaborate notes and remembered more about sessions than he. Nevertheless, he truly appreciated Guntrip. The angry, resistant patient before Guntrip had given Winnicott a rough time. Guntrip was a bright spot in the day. Winnicott was careful to add he did not *need* Guntrip to do this, but in fact Guntrip did make him feel good. Winnicott felt confirmed by Guntrip.

If Winnicott played good mother to Guntrip so also did Guntrip play good mother to Winnicott. In this regard Winnicott also played the baby role and received good narcissistic mirroring from the gleam in Guntrip's maternal eye. Guntrip's omnipotence was expressed not simply by enacting the baby but also the mother (benevolently controlling). It seems to me that part of the good feeling experienced by Winnicott was an induced countertransference reaction requiring containing and reprocessing. It reflected a psychic structure in which omnipotent baby–mother functions are part of the same system of role reversals. In this light Guntrip's compulsive playing good mother throughout his life may be seen as contributing to his overactiveness.

That Winnicott did not feel altogether at ease in this situation was reflected in his periodic attempts to evoke in Guntrip an awareness of baby rage. Winnicott repeatedly wondered where Guntrip's baby sadism and ruthlessness were, Guntrip dodged the issue by pointing to the old-fashioned Freudian drive language Winnicott used at these times. At such instances Guntrip felt Winnicott betrayed the object relations viewpoint; Winnicott was not Winnicottian enough. Guntrip's criticism was not in itself simply evidence of resistance. The patient often sees things the therapist doesn't and must come to own what his mind produces. If the patient cannot in some way consciously represent to himself his therapist's countertransference, there is danger that the latter will become an enslaving part of the patient's superego. In this context Guntrip's disputatiousness may function as a differentiating technique.

However, in not being able to let the problem of baby anger go, Winnicott appears to be humanly and clinically correct; and correct in Guntrip's own object relations terms. Winnicott knew only too well how all human beings inevitably fail one another. He based some of his best clinical descriptions on this awareness (Winnicott 1971). If his view of Guntrip's early life is plausible, the shift from mother-1 to mother-2 must have initially evoked a rageful protest before the danger of giving up could take over. Yet, oddly enough, Guntrip protested that rage would be unnecessary if mothering were only perfect. It appears that Guntrip was trying to mold his actual emotional reactions in light of an idealized theoretical possibility: how it might be in a perfect world. In this he seems to be using his idealized version of object relations theory as a defense against living through how things actually are from moment to moment. Glatzer and Evans saw in Guntrip's idealizing use of theory a mask for primary narcissism, a viewpoint which I find overly reductionistic and which I discuss below.

Winnicott clearly understood that rage is part of babyhood and that Guntrip failed to tap critical aspects of the baby self the latter so wished to contact. Guntrip did not express anger in any convincing way in either of his therapies — not even playfully. Winnicott's attempts to help Guntrip face this lack were fobbed off by induced feelings of liking Guntrip. It is difficult to truly want to deal with anger in someone who is gratifying one. The atmosphere of mutual mirroring-liking contributed to muting anything unpleasant which could spoil the gratifying communion. As Glatzer and Evans (1977) point out, it was precisely this gratification which failed to become an object for systematic analysis. Guntrip's omniscient mother–baby stance was able to stay undetected.

REPARATIVE TENDENCIES

Whatever the limitations of Guntrip's therapy, there also were genuine achievements. Glatzer and Evans argue that Guntrip's controllingness (hidden primary narcissism) precluded any true acknowledgment of dependency. For example, they state that Guntrip's avoidance of his baby omnipotence made him unable to see or come to terms with his mother as a person with problems in her own right. He remains like one ". . . constantly blaming, shifting the responsibility for his neurosis on to the mother and blinds himself to the fact that however bad she may have been, she could not have been without some redeeming quality" (Glatzer and Evans 1977, p. 97). In contrast, Guntrip writes that his early history ". . . lingers as a mood of sadness for my mother who was so damaged in childhood that she could neither be, nor enable me to be, our 'true selves' " (Guntrip 1975, p. 155).

It appears that deep mourning work was going on and Guntrip expressed gratitude to his therapists and wife for helping him undergo it (Guntrip 1975). With at least one area of his personality (an aspect of Fairbairn's central ego?) Guntrip seems to have come to a meaningful reconciliation and transcendence of "the traumatic legacy of the earliest formative years, as it seeps through or erupts into consciousness" (Guntrip 1975). This strikes me as a genuine advance, without denying the area of grandiosity detected by Glatzer and Evans and amplified above.

OPPOSING VIEWS OF THE EGO OR SELF

In my opinion Glatzer's and Evans's overstatement of their insight is rooted in a more basic opposition between their and Guntrip's view of the nature and origin of the human self. Guntrip views hate as reactive to failings by primary objects. The implication of this view is that if love were perfect there would be no hate. It is a profoundly Christian psychology. Love is deeper than hate and without some experience of love as a point of reference hate would not make sense.

Glatzer and Evans question this. They argue "that there can be no such thing as primary love" (1977). They quote Freud, Ferenczi, Jacobson, and Mahler to show that in psychoanalytic formulations the birth of the subject's knowledge of the external world is coincident with his hatred of it. "Hate as a relation to objects is older than love" (Freud 1915, quoted by Glatzer and Evans 1977, p. 88). Further, they envision the earliest self as a self-contained pleasure ego, a kind of "egg" which reacts to stimuli outside it ragefully. The pleasure principle is viewed as prior to the reality principle and constitutes a "psychical system shut off from the stimuli of the external world . . . able to satisfy its nutritional requirements autistically" (Freud 1911, quoted by Glatzer and Evans 1977, p. 88).

Glatzer and Evans present their position as if it had been validated. However, their epistemological premises are questionable and there is much experimental work which points in another direction. There is no substantial evidence that early object perception is necessarily hate motivated or that awareness of self and other may arise independently of each other. Logically and experientially, awareness of self and other are conditions for one another; each makes the other possible (Eigen 1980, Elkin 1972, Peterfreund 1978). Many psychoanalytic theorists now believe that pleasure and reality principles presuppose each other and necessarily arise together (Bion 1962, Grotstein 1977, Meltzer 1978, Rycroft 1968). There is also a growing emphasis on the intrinsic order which character-izes primary process thinking (Eigen 1983, Green 1977).

To select hate as the primary moment of a subtle experiential flow is simply to assert one's own phenomenological prejudice. Clinical and life evidence can be marshaled for either view—primary love or hate. Otherness may be experienced as syntonic or distonic depending on a variety of conditions. The most basic reaction to the external world need not be paranoid. Many authors (Bion 1962,

1963, 1970, Eigen 1980, Kohut 1971, Lichtenstein 1977, Weil 1958, and Winnicott 1971) have described the importance of early maternal mirroring in self-formation. The Other may be experienced as syntonic or distonic depending on the quality of its psychic nature and functioning in a given context. The ego may have a mixture of paranoid and nonparanoid foundational experiences, the particular balance in important part dependent on the overall quality of responsiveness by the parental milieu.

GUNTRIP'S NARCISSISTIC TRANSFERENCE:
A TECHNICAL PROBLEM

From the present viewpoint Winnicott was technically correct to let a mixture of mirror and idealizing transference elements develop. Guntrip could not have entered therapy otherwise. He needed someone in whom he could see what he took to be the best in himself, a confirming ego ideal or twin figure. Both Fairbairn and Winnicott offered such a possibility. *Guntrip needed to see reflected in someone else an inherently positive viewpoint concerning the foundations of selfhood.*

This need was far more than a defensive intellectualization. Guntrip's search for a like-minded theorist was a search for someone whose thinking reflected a certain core feeling or vision about what a human being most basically is. Analysts who viewed the self as essentially paranoid (here Glatzer and Evans) could never have been accepted by him as a true mirror of essential selfhood. Such a disagreement between Guntrip's and Glatzer's and Evans's viewpoints ought not be dismissed by the latter as simply Guntrip's resistance to analyzing his omnipotence. Hidden omnipotence—in this case omniscience seems more accurate—cuts both ways. Glatzer's and Evans's own basic view of the human ego is an unsubstantiated and perhaps unverifiable absolute statement, a negative stereotype which carries its own alienating possibilities. Each view may cover some aspect of psychic reality and may be more or less defensively deployed.

Glatzer's and Evans's view throws into relief the failure of the therapy couple (Guntrip and Winnicott) to objectify certain meanings inherent in their mutual mirroring. However, without this mirroring there could have been no therapy at all. If Guntrip could have brought himself to enter therapy with Glatzer and Evans, his angry omnipotence might have emerged more radically. The complementary problem might then have been the lack of any agreed-upon criterion with which to distinguish his infantile anger from his justifiable outrage at an inimical view (with its self-feeling correlates) of what makes the self possible.

A Note on the Missing Father

Guntrip and Glatzer and Evans agreed with Winnicott's observation that Guntrip did not have an Oedipus complex. Guntrip's father had not been important or powerful enough for this position to be reached. His father frequently was absent but when he was home he tended to support his son in face of maternal attacks. The father, to some extent, was pictured as benign and helpful, a nourishing mother. Overall he was represented as a background figure.

It seems to me that an important part of Guntrip's missing rage must also relate to the absent father. A stronger paternal presence might have gone some way toward offsetting maternal trauma (Eigen 1974). It would have offered some alternative perspective outside the mother world. It is part of the function of parents to help save the child from the negative aspects of each other. If, further, Guntrip had a stronger father to love and struggle with, he would have had more of a chance to go through a negative oedipal phase. He might have allowed himself to integrate passive feelings with father which remained locked out of reach from mother. Winnicott's position would have reinforced the omission of whatever concealed longings Guntrip may have had in this area.

Here again a countertransference factor may have been operative. Winnicott (1978) depicts a benign relationship with his own "good tempered" father but says of the latter: ". . . it is probably true that in the early years he left me too much with all my mothers. Things never quite righted themselves" (p. 24). There was not much room for the direct expression of anger in his household—it would have seemed odd or out of place. The few angry moments he experienced made a great impression on Winnicott and played a crucial role in his later theorizing (Winnicott 1971). Although Winnicott's father played a helpful role in Winnicott's few isolated angry outbursts, he apparently remained more in the background than was desirable. Winnicott's personal sense of identity remained somewhat skewed as a result of a felt deficiency on the father side. It seems likely this deficit played a role in his work with Guntrip. Both Guntrip and Winnicott played out their symbolic exchange in a purely mother-bound world.

I believe that had Guntrip's therapy with Winnicott gone on long enough, it would have foundered, exploded, or eventually broken open over the above issues. The tension generated between them by Winnicott's theoretical positive valuation of anger would likely have led to growth for both parties once the therapy *struggle* began. If they saw it through they would likely have had to face the realization that a preoedipal solution was not enough. Megalomania can not be overcome without healthy, creative intercourse between the parental objects of one's internal world.

REFERENCES

Bion, W. R. (1962). *Learning from Experience*. London: Heinemann.
_____ (1963). *Elements of Psycho-Analysis*. London: Heinemann.
_____ (1970). *Attention and Interpretation*. London: Tavistock.
Eigen, M. (1974). On pre-oedipal castration anxiety. *International Review of Psycho-Analysis* 1:489–498.

————— (1980). On the significance of the face. *Psychoanalytic Review* 67:426–444.

————— (1983). A note on the structure of Freud's theory of creativity. *Psychoanalytic Review* 70:41–45.

Freud, S. (1911). Formulations on the two principles of mental functioning. *Standard Edition* 12:213–226.

————— (1915). Instincts and their vicissitudes. *Standard Edition* 14:159–208.

Glatzer, H. T. and Evans, W. N. (1977). On Guntrip's analysis with Fairbairn and Winnicott. *International Journal of Psychoanalytic Psychotherapy* 6:81–98.

Green, A. (1977). Conceptions of affect. *International Journal of Psycho-Analysis* 58:129–156.

Grotstein, J. (1977). The psychoanalytic concept of schizophrenia II: reconciliation. *International Journal of Psycho-Analysis* 58:427–452.

Guntrip, H. (1975). My experience of analysis with Fairbairn and Winnicott. *International Review of Psycho-Analysis* 2:145–156.

Kohut, H. (1971). *The Analysis of the Self*. New York: International Universities Press.

Langs, R. J. (1975). Therapeutic misalliances. *International Journal of Psychoanalytic Psychotherapy* 4:77–105.

Lichtenstein, H. (1977). *The Dilemma of Human Identity*. New York: Jason Aronson.

Meltzer, D. (1978). *The Kleinian Development*. Perthshire, Scotland: Clunie.

Peterfreund, E. (1978). Some critical comments on psycho-analytic conceptualizations of infancy. *International Journal of Psycho-Analysis* 59:427–441.

Rycroft, C. (1968). *Imagination and Reality*. London: Hogarth.

Weil, E. (1958). The origin and vicissitudes of the self-image. *Psychoanalysis* 6:3–19.

Winnicott, C. (1978). D. W. W.: a reflection. In *Between Reality and Fantasy*, ed. S. A. Grolnick and L. Barkin, pp. 15–33. New York: Jason Aronson.

Winnicott, D. W. (1971). *Playing and Reality*. New York: Basic Books.

13

Breaking the Frame: Stopping the World

BREAKING THE FRAME

Paradigmatic interventions, by modeling aspects of the patient's implicit assumptions, may help the subject get outside himself and the narrow world he is addicted to. They can dramatize in emotionally meaningful ways unconscious imperatives the patient lives or fails to live by. This might take the form of gross caricature on occasion, but, I believe, is most effective when subtly varied, sensitive to modulations of the subject's quality of awareness. These responses, at their best, often are ambiguously overdetermined, "a sort of cryptogram, an encoded message which touches upon but does not make manifest the meaning of the patient's productions" (M. C. Nelson 1966, p. 188). From Don Juan's perspective, "the worst thing one can do is confront human beings bluntly" (Castaneda 1973b, p. 10; quoted by M. C. Nelson 1976, p. 351). Such a tactic is easily assimilable by the subject's defenses. One would need to generate situations that stimulate the subject's reach and lead him toward the gap that makes approach possible (Eigen 1973, 1977, Nelson et al. 1968).

A more general principle that paradigmatic therapy makes its own particular use of involves the art of shifting "sets" or frames of reference. A frame of reference is a system of relations that forms a context for understanding and interpreting reality. An attitude, for example, may function as a frame of reference which organizes the impact of experience. Toxic introjects may contribute to the rigid and spoiling quality of unconscious attitudes that constrict and torment a person or group. They (toxic introjects) contribute to processes that select and distill in deformed ways what may or may not be taken as real, often at inestimable cost for an individual or even entire cultures.

Our basic assumptions are mirrored all around us. They find expression in our products, in all we are and do. Some areas of cultural endeavor explicitly try to bring to light the assumptions that govern us. Psychotherapy can be one such attempt. At its best it attempts to do this in emotionally meaningful ways that allow the quality of experiencing to evolve. In touching our lived assumptions in a uniquely person-to-person way, it can affect the way we relate to our experiencing in general, our "experiencing of experience" (Bion 1962). The ways it may do this seem to be infinite (Matte Blanco 1975). Psychic events involve systems of relations and no obvious end to relational hierarchies or interactions can be envisioned. Everywhere one looks multiple perspectives continuously move in and out of one another, rubbing, teasing, clashing, fusing, collapsing, potentially stimulating further revisualization. I do not know rules that exhaust the ways in which this is done.

The therapeutic framework may also be described as a complex frame of reference which potentially shapes and is shaped by structures of experience. What constitutes a therapeutic framework is an area of research which invites continuous exploration. Some representative attempts to investigate structures of the analytic situation may be seen in the work of Racker (1957), Little (1951), Khan (1960), Searles (1965), Balint (1968), Winnicott (1971), Viderman (1974), Green (1977), Arlow (1963), Limentani (1977), and Langs (1978). A perusal of this literature suggests that what makes for a therapeutic setting or framework is far from settled. What *can* be said is that a profound appreciation for the subtle and complex ways therapist and patient affect each other keeps growing.

My own work is a fairly eclectic psychoanalytic therapy which draws on a wide range of sources. The clinical vignettes I give below, therefore, must not be taken as examples of paradigmatic therapy in a strict sense, but as informal illustrations of therapeutic encounters involving shifting emotional sets. In each case the therapeutic framework was broken, exaggerated, or otherwise worked with in ways which led patient and/or therapist to a new awareness of each other and of basic issues.

Clinical Vignettes

A variety of interpretive or noninterpretive interventions may be beneficial or harmful, depending on the requirements of the situation and the qualities of the patient, therapist, and surrounding circumstances. In one case, at a certain phase of work I found myself filled with an intrusive desire which led the way. Dee was a 12-year-old girl diagnosed as epileptic and schizophrenic. When I met her she was in a state of vegetative collapse, incontinent, and unintelligible. Her *grand mal* seizures were poorly controlled by medication and she was believed to be suffering from progressive brain deterioration. Throughout the time I knew her her mother felt her problem was nutritional and could not give up on trying to get me to cure Dee with Tiger's Milk, home-baked bran cookies, and other magical, oral supplies (Dee had been ill since she was 5 and had not responded to her mother's prescriptions). From time to time Dee and her father managed to play cryptic games of his invention; one favorite was that he would draw for her a snake going into a hole.

I have recounted this case in more detail elsewhere (Eigen 1984) and, at the risk of doing violence to this material, must focus here on only one episode. It was at a point when Dee and I had begun to more deeply notice each other's presence; our silences seemed to thicken. I increasingly felt a hostile, provocative quality in her muteness. The full impact of her heightened silence seemed to act like a vacuum, exerting a suction-like force on me. I conceived an urge to put my hand in her mouth. I was aware of the hostile, sexual connotations of this, as well as the possibility that I was simply unable to tolerate the anxiety of a void state, which I hoped to fill with defensive mothering. But I also felt this wish expressed a linking gesture, however tainted, and I finally gave in to it. (Dee was one of my first cases at a treatment camp over twenty years ago; I might not be so physically brave today.)

She eventually turned her head to look at me with dismay, the most direct and emphatic look of recognition I had yet experienced from her. She tried to collapse and ignore what was happening, but I kept my fingers in her mouth. Almost without warning she stood to her full height, stared at me with outrage, and screamed. I maintained my hand in position as best I could without choking her and she hit me. She was hitting me with all her might but I didn't feel any pain. After all the time I had spent banging against the wall of her unresponsiveness, I felt only joy. She reared up in indignant majesty and beat me to her heart's content, pummelling any part of my face or body she could contact. She looked righteous and queenly and radiant, a mixture of imperious incredulity and chagrin: "How dare you affront Her Majesty!" It was the first physical exercise I had seen her take outside her seizures. After this episode tangible progress in her treatment began to be made. This compulsive exorcism expressed outwardly the force she had exerted to be stuffed, together with the ways her parents relentlessly exploited it. However, this drama now took place within a context dedicated to therapeutic struggle which could better contain and work with her explosive hunger.

In this case nonverbal psychophysical happenings imposed themselves on the therapy situation through the therapist in ways that turned out to be potentially meaningful and useful. In the following example I was able to shift vertices on a more verbal level and in a less intensely gripping emotional field. A supervisee spoke about a woman patient who worried him. She had been successfully operated on for an inner ear tumor. The tumor was benign and her hearing loss minimal, but she became progressively more withdrawn and inaccessible.

Her chronic psychological position was fragile and her relationship with her therapist had been a light in her life. While in hospital she told her therapist (who visited) how often she thought of him. Her life remained otherwise desolate and painful. Once out of the hospital she found it difficult to get to see her therapist. She didn't know why. Nothing either of them tried worked. She continued coming but her functioning in sessions as well as in the rest of her life deteriorated sharply. The therapist became alarmed and feared hospital care might be necessary. He was a sincere man who wanted to help but felt more and more helpless.

The core of his therapeutic approach (not on my advice) was to build a positive and trusting relationship which could be a rallying point for the patient's reorganization. He tried to help her with her day-to-day life and pointed out ways in which past patterns interfered with present functioning. The positive atmosphere he created left little room for either his or his patient's negativity. He had tried to kindle her trust and in fact had begun to succeed. He had been so successful that in her idealization of him she expected he might take care of her physical illness as well. In this he failed miserably. There had been nothing he could do about the tumor or the painful circumstances around her operation. She had been invaded from within and he could not protect her. The very processes which made and maintained her seemed destructive. And he was as helpless in face of them as she. This triggered massive disillusionment with all possible support sources. The fact that her operation seemed successful meant nothing next to this rupture with her primary transference figure. She was caught in the grip of an ultimate question with no way to express it: is there a primacy of good or evil in the way life is composed?

I suggested that he comment on how disappointing it must be for her to discover how little he could help when it really mattered and to suggest that her collapse of faith in his ability to come through was driving her mad.

He was upset and was silent for a short time. Then he asked, "What will she have left if I take our relationship away?"

"What difference will what you call a relationship make if it destroys her?" I asked.

"You mean if I threw her back on herself she'd have her Self to rely on?" he asked with what seemed to be grim hope.

"Why should her Self be any more reliable than yours? When it comes to this kind of 'relying' aren't we all in the same boat?"

"Well, then—what is there?"

As I silently mulled over what response to make I felt myself looking at him with an expression that conveyed a mixture of I Don't Know, yet also Faith.

"I feel scared," he said. "It's a relief; more honest. I get an image of myself as a bridge suspended over an abyss. I—It might break anytime. Yet it's strangely comforting."

The above examples implicitly raise the issue of one's relation to multiple experiential dimensions which threaten yet potentially enrich each other. In her work on Castaneda, to which we will now turn, Marie Coleman Nelson focuses on the broader, underlying issue at stake: *the mystery of personal liberation of a self traversing a multi-dimensional universe.*

Stopping the World, Resistance, the Nagual

In a series of books Carlos Castaneda (1969, 1973a,b, 1974) purports to describe his apprenticeship to Don Juan, a Mexican Yaqui Indian Sorcerer and "man of knowledge." Whatever the validity of Castaneda's account as an anthropological document in the narrow sense, it raises crucial, perennial questions about human nature, what life is about, and the proper meaning of selfhood. Castaneda charts a visionary expansion of consciousness which renders him more acutely sensitive to his own personal autonomy and more responsive to the nuances of existence as a whole. As part of this reorientation, he was called upon to move beyond the familiar directive cues by which he steered his life, the cultural interpretations of reality he lived by. Castaneda, following Don Juan, gives the term *stopping the world* to this suspension of attachment to collective views of reality, a process that creates space for new apprehensions and behaviors to emerge and be tested out.

In her paper on Castaneda, Nelson describes stopping the world in the following ways,

> Engaging in specific acts and exercises, under tutelage, which undermines pre-established definitions of the world. An important component of stopping the world is learning to suspend one's habitual internal dialogue. [p. 336]
>
> Stopping the world involves the mastery of certain acts which generate sensory experiences that defy explanation according to the scientific principles which prevail in our ordinary reality. [pp. 338–339]
>
> . . . sorcerer's apprentice and analysand are each obliged to "suspend judgment." This, in effect, means abandoning the familiar directive cues by which they have interpreted their lives. Both processes [sorcery and psychoanalysis] emphasize the immediacy of experience, and in the capture of the moment the perpetual search for causation is suspended. [p. 355]

In practice the experiences generated are far more but not less than sensory. Like psychosis, they grip the whole individual, set challenges, are terrifying or ecstatic, precipitate despair or inspiration. But they are highly specific and exacting, requiring keen observation, intunement, and coordinated action. All of the individual's powers and wits are engaged in intense, flexible attentiveness. The individual sees through the cues (perceptual, feeling, procedural, belief, reverence, emulation) he has directed himself by, and begins the new, positive work of becoming a hunter, a warrior, acquiring power (knowing oneself), obtaining an ally, and, the culmination, achieving a separate reality (B. Nelson 1964, M. C. Nelson 1976).

A crucial outcome of apprenticeship is growth in the ability to assimilate and use id powers, the *nagual*. From the sorcerer's viewpoint, the *nagual* may be irrational but is not basically chaotic—it is a form of consciousness with its own mysterious order. In its hands space and time seem like toys but the result is highly meaningful. Primary process omniscience (*nagual* consciousness is "aware of everything") is not mainly viewed in terms of pathology or as something to outgrow, but is tied to a basic capacity to utilize boundlessness. An important area of current psychoanalytic theorizing revolves around problems implicit in the overlaps and differences between the *nagual* and the id (viz., Eigen 1980–1981, 1984, Green 1977, Grotstein 1979). For example, the conceptual difficulty involved in deriving an orderly ego from a chaotic id has led to fresh perceptions of the mysterious order that pervades psychic life at early levels, prior to the rule of spatially fixed boundaries (Matte Blanco 1975).

In the preceding sections I used the term *breaking the frame,* to refer to operations and processes which led to *stopping the world.* Don Juan regularly introduces an element from outside the system at hand (current adaptation level), a "third term" which throws the experiential field into imbalance. In Castaneda's case Don Juan usually achieved this by administering exposures to the dimensions of the *nagual*. Only thus could he dissipate Castaneda's natural-istic rationalism. At the same time he indicated how a father might stop a child's autistic or antisocial orientation and bring him to a new sense of *tonal*-social reality. In both instances enough support also is given to make the turbulence associated with emotional change tolerable. Still, a leap is repeatedly required, and nothing can save the apprentice from grappling with this fact.

In discussing the similarity of Kierkegaard's and Don Juan's methods of undercutting frameworks, Nelson (1976) summarizes,

> . . . truth can only emerge through the activation of dialectical tension between dichotomous paradigms emphatically rendered, and . . . the generation of such tension by means of what in the moment may appear as falsehood serves the cause of a larger truth in the long run. . . . [pp. 358–359]

Nelson's concern with multiple realities is supported and extended in the work of Bion (1962, 1963, 1965, 1970). Bion has attempted what may be the most general, epistemologically sound psychoanalytic approach to the mystery ex-pressed through stopping the world. His revision of psychoanalysis speaks to the lack Nelson observes in her comparison of psychoanalysis and sorcery. He is among the handful of analytic writers who have tried to penetrate to the center of such problems, or at least face their difficulty without giving up on them. In the present essay we will turn to some of his formulations clustering around "O."

Bion (1970, 1977) uses the sign, O, to denote ultimate reality. Depending on one's frame of reference (philosophical, religious, scientific) O may be expressed in different terms (the godhead, the infinite, the thing-in-itself). In psychoa-nalytical experience O might be viewed as the emotional truth of a session. In a strict sense, we can never know emotional truth with certainty, yet faith in the possibility of emotional truth seems necessary as a principle of wholesome psychic growth. We develop intimations and convictions about what is going on with ourselves and others. We may try to find a language for what we sense, and our acts of expression can alter our awareness of who we are. Psychotherapeutic interventions grow out of conscious and unconscious hypotheses concerning an emotional reality at stake. All interventions reflect underlying interpretations of the nature of psychic reality. Interventions of any kind express a faith. Their quality expresses the quality of one's faith, one's groping, one's vision (also see Eigen 1981). Ordinary good adaptations may make life manageable, but may diminish chances for profound psychic transformation. The natural attitude, however supportive and useful, is not the analytic attitude and can interfere with the most far-reaching kinds of therapeutic encounters. Communion with O is an imaginative adventure, not an acquired certainty to be taken for granted. To try to control where truth leads is to put oneself above truth, and so, in part, shuts out the potentially reorienting effects of the latter.

For Bion the heart of psychoanalytic methodology hinges on the attitude taken to certain epistemological conditions that make psychoanalysis possible. Like

Freud, he acknowledges the Kantian insight that ultimate emotional reality as such is beyond certain reach. At the same time, in true biblical (and scientific?) spirit, he aims, all out, to reach it and hopes his formulations, or interventions of any sort, carry it forward. The analyst hopes his therapeutic behavior grows out of and intersects with the emotional reality of moment. If the analyst is able to sustain Faith in O and tolerate the development of expressive forms that reflect O, he may legitimately hope for a therapeutic outcome in which the analysand becomes more at one with his own evolution. Perhaps the essential freedom analysis brings is the analytic attitude itself, the liberation of the capacity to focus on O (also see Eigen 1981).

The Trickster and Beyond

Is an all-out aiming toward O, the emotional truth of a session, compatible with paradigmatic therapy, which may appeal to trickery? Nelson makes a case for the use of tricks in working through resistances. She, for example, quotes Don Juan telling Castaneda, "If we wouldn't be tricked we would never learn. . . . The art of a benefactor is to take us to the brink. A benefactor can only point the way and trick" (M. C. Nelson 1976, p. 359; Castaneda 1973b, p. 257).

Again, she quotes (1976) Benjamin Nelson's comments in his introduction to Kierkegaard's *The Point of View for My Work as an Author.*

> His [Kierkegaard's] deeds and works become a series of contrived camouflages and "deceptions," illustrating the adventures of his pseudonymous heroes and heroines (his *alter egos*) among the blandishments in every sphere of human existence. . . . The author's guide and teacher through all these byways was the wondrous Socrates who had devoted his life to setting an example and embodying a paradigm, compelling his indifferent contemporaries by his odd acts and odder questions to know themselves so that they might pursue the good in deepest inwardness. [pp. 359–360]

To be sure, Kierkegaard felt that faith in Christ took one beyond Socratic thoughts and models, for example, in making temporality, the significant moment, crucial. It was always the decisive moment of conversion — stopping the world, the turning, the rebirth — at which he aimed. But he *was* an acknowledged donner of masks with incisive purpose. For Kierkegaard philosophy was, in part, profoundly theatrical, and the role he played, he prayed, was God's trickster.

As pointed out earlier, Don Genaro was a trickster on whom Don Juan repeatedly called to stop the world for Castaneda. Don Genaro was, indeed, a showstopper, a performer of cosmic theater. There was, too, a precision to his "supernatural horseplay." Don Juan's use of it grew out of an understanding of Castaneda's condition and phase of development. It grew out of his knowledge of emotional truth in a given situation. It aimed, in part, at evoking awareness of what unsuspected forms truth can take.

How far can beneficent trickery take the individual in a time when a lethal mixture of business and show business, the Trickster as fraudulent consciousness *par excellence,* is a presiding image over all? Can a paradigm of the Trickster break its own framework? Does the creating of such a paradigm imply its self-transcendence, or does it inevitably collude with the evil it mimics?

We would at this point require a more thorough phenomenology of the devil in modern times — tricky business indeed (viz., Eigen 1984, Grotstein 1981). If such knowledge were embodied in a paradigm, the devil might see his own reflection. Would he or the mirror break? Would they compromise? Assimilate each other? Or would a lingering, or lasting, or freshly achieved awareness of some Third Term save the day?

REFERENCES

Arlow, J. (1963). Conflict, regression, and symptom formation. *International Journal of Psycho-Analysis* 44:12–22.

Balint, M. (1968). *The Basic Fault.* London: Tavistock.

Bion, W. R. (1962). *Learning from Experience.* London: Heinemann.

————— (1963). *Elements of Psycho-analysis.* London: Heinemann.

————— (1965). *Transformations.* London: Heinemann.

————— (1970). *Attention and Interpretation.* London: Tavistock.

————— (1977). *Seven Servants.* New York: Jason Aronson.

Castaneda, C. (1969). *The Teachings of Don Juan: A Yaqui Way of Knowledge.* New York: Ballantine Books.

————— (1973a). *A Separate Reality: Further Conversations with Don Juan.* New York: Pocket Books.

————— (1973b). *Journey to Ixtlan: The Lessons of Don Juan.* New York: Simon & Schuster.

————— (1974). *Tales of Power.* New York: Simon & Schuster.

Eigen, M. (1973). The recoil on having another person. *Review of Existential Psychology & Psychiatry* 12:52–55.

————— (1977). On working with "unwanted" patients. *International Journal of Psycho-Analysis* 58:101–121.

————— (1980). Instinctual fantasy and ideal images. *Contemporary Psychoanalysis* 16:119–137.

————— (1980–1981). On the significance of the face. *Psychoanalytic Review* 67:427–441.

————— (1981). The area of faith in Winnicott, Lacan and Bion. *International Journal of Psycho-Analysis* 62:413–433.

————— (1984). On demonized aspects of the self. *Evil: Self and Culture,* ed. M. C. Nelson and M. Eigen, pp. 91–123. New York: Human Sciences.

Green, A. (1977). Conceptions of affect. *International Journal of Psycho-Analysis* 58:129–156.

Grotstein, J. S. (1979). Who is the dreamer who dreams the dream and who is the dreamer who understands it: a psychoanalytic inquiry into the ultimate nature of being. *Contemporary Psychoanalysis* 15:110–169.

————— (1981). Forgery of the soul: a psychoanalytic inquiry into evil. In *Evil: Self and Culture,* ed. M. C. Nelson and M. Eigen, pp. 203–226. New York: Human Sciences.

Khan, M. (1960). Regression and integration in the analytic setting. *International Journal of Psycho-Analysis* 41:130–146.

Kierkegaard, S. (1848). *The Point of View for My Work as an Author: A Report to History*. Ed. B. Nelson. New York: Harper and Row, 1962.

Langs, R. J. (1978). Validation and the framework of the therapeutic situation. *Contemporary Psychoanalysis* 14:98–124.

Limentani, A. (1977). Affects and the psychoanalytic situation. *International Journal of Psycho-Analysis* 58:171–182.

Little, M. (1951). Countertransference and the patient's response to it. *International Journal of Psycho-Analysis* 32:32–40.

Matte Blanco, I. (1975). *The Unconscious as Infinite Sets*. London: Duckworth.

Nelson, B. (1964). Actors, directors, roles, cues, meanings, identities: further thoughts on "anomie." *Psychoanalytic Review* 51:135–160.

Nelson, M. C. (1966). More than one way to skin a cat. *Israel Annals of Psychiatry and Related Disciplines* 4:185–197.

———(1976). Paths of power: psychoanalysis and sorcery. *Psychoanalytic Review* 63:333–360.

Nelson, M. C., Nelson, B., Sherman, M. R., and Strean, H. S., eds. (1968). *Roles and Paradigms in Psychotherapy*. New York: Grune & Stratton.

Racker, H. (1957). The meaning and uses of countertransference. *Psychoanalytic Quarterly* 26:303–357.

Searles, H. F. (1965). *Collected Papers on Schizophrenia and Related Subjects*. New York: International Universities Press.

Viderman, S. (1974). Interpretation in the analytical space. *International Review of Psycho-Analysis* 1:467–480.

Winnicott, D. W. (1971). *Playing and Reality*. New York: Basic Books.

14

Dual Union or Undifferentiation?

Marion Milner's work belongs to a particular psychoanalytic genre, yet has its own special uniqueness. Perhaps what most typifies this genre is its valuation of a dimension characterized by soft boundaries between self and other. The connection rather than division between subject and object is emphasized. Terms like oneness, undifferentiation, merger, or fusion are often used to express the valued state. Balint (1968) spoke of a "harmonious interpenetrating mix-up" of self and other, together with a boundless expanse. In varying ways writers as diverse as Winnicott (1971), Kohut (1971), and Mahler (1968) have stressed the importance of fusion or oneness in early development. Ferenczi (1933) and Federn (1926) are among the most important precursors of this tendency.

Milner is emphatic in her unwavering positive evaluation of such experiences. She would not refer to early self-other undifferentiation as a "limbo," as Mahler sometimes does. The relationship she cultivates to such states is one of extreme trust, as if the chaos they represent implicitly contains a profoundly spontaneous ordering process. She stands nearly alone in psychoanalysis in seeing plenitude rather than distress as the central source of personal growth. The workers she overlaps with include Balint (1968), Rycroft (1968), Winnicott (1971), Ehrenzweig (1967), Kohut (1971), and Loewald (1980), but it can properly be argued that none has achieved the apotheosis of plenitude she has.

I do not wish to imply that either classical psychoanalysis or Milner is naive concerning the complexities of experience. Both deal with the interplay of pleasure–reality and idealization–disillusionment, but with a certain difference in emphasis. For example, the term "pleasure" could hardly do for the kind of beatific moment Milner points to. Neither instinct nor usual object-relations theories (concerned with mother, then father) interweave ideal feeling with body experience the way she does. Similarly, current self theory comes close but does not quite develop the point that symbols most basically symbolize vicissitudes of psychic creativeness.

In the present paper I wish, first of all, to bring out the nature of Milner's psychoanalytic phenomenology revolving around psychic creativeness. I believe it to be a rare achievement and one worth a detailed study not usually given to it. At the same time my exposition must involve a critique. For I believe a close analysis of Milner's position is generally applicable to the genre she illustrates. In essence, the role of such concepts as fusion or undifferentiation in psychoanalysis must be grappled with and, if possible, elucidated. Finally I will present some guidelines which, I believe, provide a sounder way of speaking about such states. It may be that as we live with this dimension some of its contours become more visible.

My strategy is to focus on the appendix to the second edition of *On Not Being Able to Paint* (Field 1950). Her position is most succinctly and richly summarized in this seventeen page appendix, one of the high points in psychoanalytic writings on creativity. However, I will begin with a brief sketch of certain ideas drawn from her earlier and later work. This overview does not pretend to be complete, but simply provides an orienting background for the close reading to follow.

BACKGROUND SKETCH

In *A Life of One's Own* (1934), published under the pseudonym of Joanna Field, Milner reflected on her diary, in which she wrote about the event each day which most affected her. The results often were surprising. Stereotypes of what should be most important began to dissolve, as her real interests slowly made themselves known. This was followed by a companion book, *An Experiment in Leisure* (1937). An important finding of these ventures involved the process of surrender and symbols related to it. Processes which seem masochistic to the surface ego may actually open the way to new realities. Thus images of dying, dismembered, or tortured gods (Jesus, Apollo, Prometheus, Osiris) can reflect a crucial phase in psychic creativeness. By a certain inner gesture the subject can let his more usual, narrow focus drop away and contact a deeper order. This may seem a kind of death to one's accepted sense of self, yet turns out to be a liberation. The deeper order, paradoxically, is characterized by more permeable boundaries between self and other, even to the point of subject–object union. Although the experiential flow tapped may seem wild and confusing, a heightened sense of meaning and wholeness often results.

Milner's publications in the next several decades (e.g., 1945, 1952, 1955, 1956, 1969) reflect the reworking of her basic concerns in psychoanalytic terms and vice versa. Although psychoanalysis helps to enrich our understanding and appreciation of the phenomenon of creativity, it also undergoes transformation through its encounter with the latter. Milner found that instinct theory and ego psychology do not touch her most pressing concerns. Concepts related to drive reduction and adaptation seemed to miss a vital dimension. Creativeness is not simply employed for defensive functions, but is a condition of subjectivity as such. Milner postulated a primary creativeness, explained by nothing outside itself. If a heightened sense of subject–object union is an illusion, it is a crucial one. It helps give life meaning and is valued for its own sake. Primary process thinking seems to thrive on the dissolution of usual boundaries and reflects deep ordering principles. In clinical terms, regression is less to be feared than courted for its restorative possibilities. As noted earlier, this type of thinking was in the air. Its impact on psychoanalytic thought has been far-reaching. One of our tasks is to begin to come to grips with its characteristics.

A further preliminary note. Milner (1969) wrote a detailed portrayal of her work with a schizophrenic which covered nearly two decades. The main theme of the book was the birth of the patient's self, in part by helping the patient to tolerate subject–object fusion. In his foreword to this book Winnicott writes, "I have been fortunate in that I have been one of those who have known both Marion Milner and the patient over a period of decades, and I have watched both of them with amazement as they let time pass by while a process tending towards wholeness or health was taking its own time to be realized" (p. ix).

The patient's art was an integral part of the therapeutic process, yet Milner voiced some regret that as the patient moved into life, her interest in drawing diminished. This is not an unusual finding in much psychoanalytic work. Rank (1932) put the matter in extreme terms when he concluded that one must choose between personal relationships and art. In part he saw art as a parasite on life. Milner (1956, 1957) herself voiced some of the difficulties she experienced in the conflict between the aloneness of creative work and her need for communion. Much psychoanalytic work with creative persons has centered on problems related to a sense of early object loss (whether an actual or fantasy object). As pathological responses to the sense of loss are worked through, the drive to create often loses its bite. More generally, much in psychoanalytic history seems to justify Rilke's fear of losing his angels if his devils were tampered with.

Few theorists have given the basic place to creativeness that Milner has, yet this has not enabled her to solve the above dilemma. Can one find clues in her formulations to explain this lack, or is one asking the impossible? To what extent can personal healing and creativity go together? Must either the creative or personal self lose? An analysis of the structure of Milner's thought may help throw some light on this and related issues.

Exposition of the Appendix to *On Not Being Able to Paint*: A First Glimpse of the Area to be Explored

In doing free drawings Milner was impressed with how order grows out of seeming chaos. She notes the difficulties in finding a language to talk about creative processes and tentatively defines psychic creativeness as the capacity for making a symbol, whether for feeling or knowing. For her symbolic capacity has prelogical and nonverbal roots deeper than ratiocination. Moreover, the way we (prelogically) think about creativity partly determines the way it works in us. Her first approach to the problem area at hand begins to gather momentum with the following statement:

> Thus the content of the free drawings seems to me to illustrate not only the anxieties associated with "creative capacity," but also different ways of thinking about that capacity—and thinking about it in terms that are derived from those bodily functions which become the center of interest at different stages of infantile development. [pp. 148–149]

It is part of the modern art ethic that human creative capacity seeks to explore itself by developing symbols of its own processes. The emerging self-consciousness of the artist becomes part of the work itself. Milner links the idea that symbols symbolize what goes into their making with the philosophies of Cassirer and Langer. Langer (1942, 1953), in particular, emphasizes the role of feeling as the root of expressive symbolism. Symbols are concerned not only with dangers but inherent joys.

Psychoanalysts have tended to relate symbolization to instinctual drives and fantasy, object loss, psychic splits, reparation, various ego attitudes, and the like. A paramount emphasis has been psychodynamics revolving around anxiety and guilt. To be sure, the psychoanalyst does not claim that his concerns exhaust the entire range of symbolic activity, but that he explores areas easily overlooked. Milner's focus on symbols as an intrinsic expression of primary creativeness may seem to place her outside of psychoanalysis. At the same time she seems solidly a part of psychoanalytic tradition in her association of symbolic capacity with body functions. She states that the thinking creativity does about itself is most basically through terms related to the body. In this she appears to follow Freud's dictum that "the ego is first and foremost a body ego."

Psychoanalysis has developed what is perhaps the most thorough depth phenomenology of body symbolism yet evolved in the history of thought. Nevertheless, psychoanalysis itself is part of a larger revolution in epistemology in which dimensions which had been treated as second-class citizens are given a certain primacy (i.e., sensory organization, the perceptual field, the body or body subject, imagination, unconscious operations). It remains to be seen to what extent Milner develops her ideas within a psychoanalytic framework. She seems both inside and outside the latter at the same time. Does she add to, revise, or bypass it? Or perhaps she is part of a movement within psychoanalysis which forces the latter to rethink its foundations.

Anality and Creativity

Milner amplifies a particular vein of psychoanalytic thinking by beginning her investigation of prelogical ways of thinking about creativity by focusing on anality. Freud called attention to the child's fantasy that babies come out of mother's anus. An unconscious link seems to exist between creativity and defecation, that is, to make something. Milner emphasizes the mix-up between the experience of making and what is made.

Creative blocks may sometimes be linked to early confusions between the orgastic giving of the body products and the products themselves. This original lack of discrimination results in an idealization of products followed by disillusionment once the nature of one's products is perceived. In Milner's words,

> I find clinical evidence which seems to show that, particularly in poets and artists who are inhibited in their work, there has been a catastrophic disillusion in the original discovery that their feces are not as lively, as beautiful, as boundless, as the lovely feelings they had in the giving of them. Thus the infant's disillusion about its own omnipotence, its gradual discovery that it has not created the world by its own wishes, cannot be discussed fully without also considering its disillusion about the concrete bit of the outside world that it literally does create; that is, the infant's own body products. [p. 150]

It is the moment of undifferentiation which Milner emphasizes. The patient's fear of passivity reflects a dread of a perceptual letting-go tied to total incontinence, "a return to an extreme of undifferentiation between all the openings of the body and their products . . . which, to the conscious ego, would be identified with madness" (p. 150). The patient longs for and wards off undifferentiation, a blissful surrender which is terrifying to one's realistic adaptations.

In this context, ideal feelings (idealization, beatific feelings) must not be understood simply as a defense against ambivalence or as an expression of narcissism. The problem, rather, is to disengage orgastic ideal feelings (in part, Winnicott's "ego orgasm") from blind identification with specific objects (also, see Eigen 1979, 1980a,b, 1981a, 1982). To paraphrase Milner, no real object (except, traditionally, God) can be what the whole soul desires. Nevertheless, ideal feelings can be profound sources of inspiration and healing. What is required is a growth in sophistication. The person must come to see that his ideal feelings are not one with his products (or medium), at the same time one values both dimensions. In creative work a tension must be tolerated between ideal feelings and the facts of life. It is, in part, this tension which art explores. The result of psychoanalysis should be a more vital and effective interplay between ideal feelings and the capacity for work. In Milner's terms, one works to symbolize orgastic, ideal feelings, a plenitude at the core of experience.

Primal Scene and Omnipotence

Another traditional psychoanalytic theme which Milner reworks involves the meaning of masturbatory fantasy. The child not only seeks to control the parents within as a way of dealing with dependency, but uses these objects for thinking about his own creative capacities. This occurs after some relinquishing of omnipotence with growing awareness of parental genital function. Doubts about the goodness of the parental creative function, or about one's ability to cope with the feelings it arouses, lead to doubts about the goodness of real creative forces inside oneself or the goodness of the baby which results from internal intercourse (p. 152). The issue here revolves around the possibility of having trust in creativeness, one's own and others. Unconscious conflicts over masturbatory fantasies express this basic concern, and ought not to be understood simply in terms of instinctual anxiety or omnipotence.

Omnipotence (at least the sort we are concerned with here) must be understood in the light of the self's concern with creativeness and the use of expressive symbols rooted in body experiencing. I wish to quote at length a passage in which Milner gives some hints of what a symbology linking creative omnipotence and body feeling might look like.

> Such a scheme would have to take into account, for instance, the stage at which to open one's eyes was felt to be a fiat of creation, a saying 'let there be light', which resulted in there being light . . . or the time when the opening of one's bowels was not distinguished from the opening of one's eyes, so one really did believe one's faeces were the same as the world one saw, one felt oneself to be a dancing Siva creating the world; or the time when to masturbate was to create a heaven (or a hell) with the dance of one's own limbs. For there seems to have been a time when even the faculty of consciousness itself was felt to be entirely creative, to be aware of anything was simply to have made it; all one saw was one's own, as Traherne said, and it was one's own because one had made it. And in this setting it is Mother Nature who is the disillusioner, who seems to rob one of one's own creativity; it is nature that is responsible for the fact that one's faeces are such a small and stinking and dead bit of the world. So she can come to be felt, in certain settings, as the Blasting Witch who shrivels up the landscape; as well as the powerful but helpful Grey Lady of the Angry Parrot picture. [p. 153]

Here again the emphasis appears to be on a basic lack of differentiation between the subject's own capacities and the world of objects. An ineffable glow or horror is associated with omnipotence in the realm of physical experience. Conflict and struggle is intrinsic to the structure of existence and cannot simply be attributed to the effects of external bad objects, although the contribution of the latter is undeniable. Disillusionment is part of evolving awareness and limits must be negotiated. Again, an ineffable or primary sense of creativeness struggles to express itself in the vicissitudes of embodiment.

The Timeless Moment and Paradox

As noted earlier, Milner relates moments of "no-differentiation" to orgasm. Even simple techniques of muscular relaxation can evoke a certain orgasmic quality. By directing attention to a source of tension one may evoke intense feelings which spread through the body. At certain moments consciousness can suffuse the whole body which may become, as Milner quotes the psalmist, "clothed with light as it were a garment." All matter can be suffused with subjectivity. For example, a good dancer gives the impression that there is maximum intensity of being in every particle of the living flesh and muscle and skin, the body itself having become the objective material suffused with subjectivity; and in good sculpture the whole mass of "dead" metal or stone has been made to irradiate the sense of life (p. 157).

Such moments of no-differentiation, in which consciousness suffuses materiality, may be timeless. It is perhaps in her celebration of the timeless moment that Milner's prose approaches its greatest intensity. She writes,

> Thus the artist surely amongst other things that he is doing, is making available for recall and contemplation, making able to be thought about, what he feels to be the most valuable moments in this feeling life of psycho-physical experience. And in his concern for the permanence and immortality of his work, he is not only seeking to defy his own mortality (as analysts have said), he is perhaps also trying to convey something of the sense of timelessness which can accompany those moments. He does in fact make tabernacles to house the spirit, with the result that others can share in his experiences, and he himself can have a permanent record of them after the high moment of transfiguration has passed; and it may be a high moment of rage and horror and pain as well as of joy and love. So that broadly, what the painter does conceptualise in non-verbal symbols is the astounding experience of how it feels to be alive, the experience known from inside, of being a moving, living body in space, with capacities to relate oneself to other objects in space. And included in this experience of being alive is the very experiencing of the creative process itself. [p. 159]

Milner adds that in such moments what is crucial is that a new thing is being created or endowed with form. Object loss as an explanatory concept posits an object and takes the creation of the latter for granted. Milner depicts a rhythm in which fusion or con-fusion of subject and object oscillates with a sense of boundary and division. Her emphasis is on the moment of creative fusion which generates fresh powers of perception and new symbols. In this context, rage may not simply reflect the imperiousness of instinct or narcissism, but be part of a fight to protect spontaneity, a protest against the premature rupture of oneness in which creativity is rooted.

She notes the necessity of speaking paradoxically about this area of experience. A symbol is both itself yet transcends itself (via its reference). We speak of undifferentiation from a differentiated position. "The Tao of which we speak is not the real Tao." Through the language of paradox we touch the logic of nonlogical thought. Reverie and absent-mindedness help open up this realm of being. Psychoanalysis can provide a safe setting for the feared yet courted con-fusion of me and not-me to occur in fruitful ways.

Critique

We are always on shaky ground when approaching a position which emphasizes nondifferentiation, since supporters of the latter can always claim to be misunderstood. The critic may be criticized as lacking the requisite sensibility or dismissed as too well defended against such states. Nevertheless, the mystique of nondifferentiation must be faced. Those who write about this state are in touch with an experiential dimension of exquisite importance to themselves and others. But do such descriptive terms as nondifferentiation, fusion, oneness, and the like, really do justice to that which is being contacted? When Milner writes that what is crucial about such moments is the creation of something new, doesn't she most basically mean a new sense of self and other?

In a strict sense, existence and undifferentiation are incompatible. In life as we know it, whatever is, is in some way differentiated. However, differentiation is not incompatible with soft and changing boundaries or a sense of union. Perception itself is characterized by permeability. Connectedness, interweaving, or permeability require rather than exclude difference. It may be necessary to end the opposition of difference and union tendencies which characterizes so much of psychoanalytic thinking. The sections which follow amplify this and related subjects.

The Revolt against Cartesianism

Milner's work is part of a reaction against the subject–object split exacerbated by Cartesian philosophy. In the latter the essential division is between mind (consciousness, subjectivity, the cogito) and body (physical world). In Descartes' system, the mind is free, whereas the body is a machine. They interact as two radically different orders of creation. The body as machine enters consciousness as an object. Subjective awareness or consciousness is something other than the body. The former is our only avenue of access to anything and guarantor of our existence.

Freud's assertion that the ego is first and foremost a body ego turns the Cartesian viewpoint upside down. Merleau-Ponty (1962, 1963) reworks this idea in ways which underscore some of its far-reaching implications. Merleau-Ponty distinguishes between the lived body and body as object. In the former case, the body is a subject or subjectivity in one of its modes. The lived body is part of the fabric of awareness and not simply a bounded object which faces a distinct subject as "other." Subjectivity has bodily depths which antedate and underlie discursive thought.

Freud's body ego and Merleau-Ponty's body subject are not identical concepts. Merleau-Ponty's body subject is not primarily based on or limited to the pleasure ego vs. repression ego tension. Its emphasis is on the interweaving of subject and world which characterizes perception and behavior. Pleasure and repression orientations constitute particular subsets of organizational possibilities, although well-nigh ubiquitous ones.

Both Freud and Merleau-Ponty are part of a larger cultural movement which has been reevaluating the epistemological role of the body. For the larger part of the history of Western thought, the body has been a second-class citizen. It has been associated with the ephemeral, animal, or machine, something to be used and transcended. There were materialisms, but either idealism swept the day, or the two locked in holy wars. It was, paradoxically, the scientific investigation of the body as machine which played an important role in establishing the body as an organizing center of subjectivity. Spontaneous ordering processes were discovered at every level of life. The distinction between Descartes' two orders of being blurred. If mind was spontaneous, so was body; if body was machine, so was mind. Sensory organization intrinsically ordered itself. Mental events like inference were unnecessary to explain the basic structure of the perceptual field. Time and space as experiential structures were investigated in their own right. Therapies proliferated which based themselves on lived bodily awareness.

Although Freud's work both reflected and spurred this trend, it did not really leave Descartes' cogito behind. Freud's enterprise is a theory of mind. The body is postulated as (ambiguously) outside the mind but a primary source for what the mind represents and experiences. The body itself takes on different nuances of meaning in Freud's writings. It is described in terms of physiological, chemical, and neurological processes—the physical basis of psychology. For example, Freud suggests that the development of our sense of time may be linked to the periodicity of neural firing; sexual arousal is partly a function of hormonal irritation, etc. At the same time he stresses the *animate* organism, the striving of living beings to reproduce and survive (goals which may conflict: ego vs. sexual instincts). To a certain extent drives are psychological translations or transformations of biological pressures. Mind develops partly to handle these pressures in the light of various physical and social realities.

The two ways of speaking about the body (physical processes of an organism and organism as animate) tend to fuse in Freud's picture of how the mind evolves. For instance, it is the stimulation of cortical complexity by the pressures of the outside world which leads to the development of perception and memory (Freud 1940). At the same time such growth is needed in order to discriminate and inhibit the spontaneous hallucinatory activity which arises in connection with autocthonous inner drives (representations of subcortical pressures). The two ways of speaking about body and mind (which Freud sometimes separates and sometimes fuses) are parts of a basic circle which underlies Freud's ambivalent attitude toward psychology (that it would some day be superfluous, that it would always be needed). Physical-biological explanations may be made of mental life, but it is mental life which makes them. In this sense the cogito is necessary in principle: consciousness is our only avenue of access to anything (Gurwitsch 1966, Freud 1940).

To be sure, in contemporary life the lived body is part of our consciousness, and so are various approaches to unconscious processes. What a different sort of cogito we seem to have now. It has been vastly broadened rather than abandoned. We seem to have returned to St Augustine's appreciation of the excruciating mystery of subjectivity in all its forms. Part of the excitement of reading Freud comes from this arousal of the sense that we may glimpse multidimensional tensions at the dawn of our psychic universe.

Milner's emphasis is on the experiencing subject with regard to subject–object interlocking and the lived body. Her descriptions are riddled with problems inherent in portraying body life and consciousness of heightened feeling. She either ignores or is oblivious to such problems in favor of calling attention to certain experiences she feels are important. Yet her distrust of intellect and celebration of nondifferentiation exploits difficulties she glosses over. It is as if she fears something will get lost if she thinks too clearly.

My own feeling is the opposite. I believe the area of experience she aims to contact can shine more brightly the more clearly one thinks about it. Admittedly, it is not thought alone which is at stake, but the very quality of experiencing. Still, fuzzy thought often begets fuzzy experience, and the intense heightening Milner values may lose its features.

Orgasm and the Sense of Psychic Creativeness

A basic "sleight of hand" which characterizes Milner's writings is the shift she makes from physical to more purely psychic awareness without calling attention to the change of levels her discourse undergoes. Thus she states that art is concerned with symbolizing physical orgasm, yet also uses the latter to symbolize aspects of creative experiencing. This circle is itself a legitimate and perhaps inescapable one, but its implications must be spelled out. Milner tends to collapse these levels as if discrimination between them were superfluous.

More specifically, Milner refers to three facets of experience which the subject tries to conceptualize through nonverbal symbols: (1) physical orgasm; (2) the feeling of aliveness, especially bodily aliveness; and (3) the experiencing of the creative process itself. To sum up in her words,

> my patients often produced idealizations . . . which seemed to be an attempt on their part to externalise, to find a way of conceiving, thinking about, one particular aspect of their own creations: that is, the experience of orgasm, whether genital or pre-genital. [p. 149]

> in the analysis of the artist . . . in any patient, the crucial battle is over the 'language' of love, that is to say, ultimately, over the way in which the orgasm, or the orgastic experiences, are to be symbolised. [p. 151]

> what the painter does conceptualise in non-verbal symbols is the astounding experience of how it feels to be alive, the experience known from inside, of being a moving, living body in space, with capacities to relate oneself to other objects in space. And included in this experience of being alive is the very experiencing of the creative process itself. [p. 159]

Although these three aspects of experience may be inherently related, to overlook their distinctions from one another can be misleading. Surely Milner cannot mean that the experience of physical orgasm and psychic creativeness are identical. If at times they may be, the individual often is torn by conflicting tensions between them. In traditional terms, flesh and spirit may be very much at war. Freud formalized this division in his early duality of sexual and ego instincts, one concerned with the survival of the race, the other of the individual. Conflict between these currents may lead to neurosis, but also to creativity. With a shift of aim sexual energy may be used artistically. At times Freud emphasized the harmony between ego and what came to be called id, but in pathology and creative activity conflicts between them are crucial.

The structure of Freud's thinking reflects and is an apologia for an ascetic dimension in human life. To a certain extent, individuation moves against the natural pull of instincts. Symbolic experiencing seems to require tolerance of deferral or postponement, although instinctual fulfillment may still be sought in a roundabout way. By contrast, Milner's emphasis is on plenitude rather than deferral. The thrust of her work appears to present an alternative to ascetic conflict theory. Aesthetic acts symbolize orgasm and are psychic orgasms. The harmony and interweaving of levels is emphasized. She focuses on what experiential levels have in common, rather than on differences, partly as a reaction against too great an emphasis on the latter in the past. Her work helps to provide a corrective to an overemphasis on conflict, but goes to the other extreme of underplaying natural divisions.

The blurring of levels in Milner's presentation may also be rooted in an ambiguity in the way we experience feelings in general. Feelings have physical and ineffable aspects and either may be emphasized. Changes in respiration, heart rate, perspiration, body temperature, and the like, may accompany emotions. Our bodily being may be experienced differently as a function of affect changes. Centers of subjectivity which correspond to emotions may be located in more literal or symbolic ways. A Zen master may "think with his belly," the hero of Moravia's *Two* was led by his penis, an encounter group leader may insist on gut feelings, certain bioenergetic therapists emphasize the heart center, and so on. In these and related instances the intimate connection between feelings and body is emphasized.

On the other hand, certain feelings may lift us out of the body. In states of profound absorption the body may fall away or be forgotten. It may fade into the background of awareness, no longer a concern or interest. Awareness of the lived body is only one dimension our encounter with feeling life may take. At the other end of the spectrum is St. Paul's description of the moment of grace when, transported by ineffable joy, he does not know whether or not he has a body. Picasso remarked that, when absorbed with painting, he leaves his body at the door as an Arab removes his slippers at the entrance of a mosque. To be sure, the body experiencing Milner describes is also ineffable. In a very real sense orgasm itself is ineffable. Nevertheless, her descriptions of our sense of psychic creativeness do not always require reference to body-oriented states.

The most important direction of Milner's work may be distilled and reformulated in the summary statement that a primary concern of symbolic life is the sense of psychic creativeness, whether or not with reference to the lived body. Either embodiment or transcendence may be emphasized. I suspect no creative experience is totally without either. To call such moments orgasmic is metaphorical and perhaps more than metaphor. Those who experience them may find them more meaningful than anything else life has to offer. In the light of such moments, physical orgasm itself may be lifted to an entirely new dimension. It is but one term in an experiential trajectory far beyond it.

Psychoanalytic Epistemology, and Aspects of Clinical Theory

As is well known, there is a sense in which the structure of Freud's thought is basically Kantian. The unconscious is a concept. If it is postulated as a reality it has the status of a thing in itself beyond certain knowledge. We conjecture about it by inferences. That Freud means the unconscious to be more than a conceptual system is also clear: the unconscious is the true psychical reality. In either case Freud attributes far-reaching characteristics to unconscious processes, such as the suspension of the law of contradiction. Most pressing for our concern is his dictum that the (unconscious) ego is first and foremost a body ego. As noted above, this is part of a more general cultural movement which gives a certain epistemological value and even primacy to the body. A specific contribution of Freud's is to stress the repressed body-mind (id, aspects of ego) and the return of the repressed through derivatives.

Milner's work is part of the Freudian and broader cultural emphasis on the body–mind, although her way of dealing with body symbolism (impossible without psychoanalysis) does not require the postulation of the specifically Freudian (repressed) unconscious. She reinterprets body events in terms of a central experience: the subject's sense of creativeness. Symbols associated with psychosexual dramas are also understood in terms of their ability to express aspects of the sense of creativeness. Body life in general is viewed with reference to the ways it contributes to the sense of creativeness and the expressive symbolism associated with the latter. Milner does not deny the validity of repression, but finds it superfluous to what she wishes to investigate.[1] I have tried to spell out some of the implications of her formulations and to correct a conceptual blurring of experiential levels in her work.

A further reason Milner's work cannot easily be situated within Freud's is because she fails to distinguish systematically between unconscious and conscious dimensions. Although many of the symbols she cites have unconscious

---

[1]One might think it possible to situate Milner's focus within a Freudian framework by saying she studies symbolism from a specific self or ego perspective. Ehrenzweig (1967) tried to do just this and the result is a fertile failure which deserves discussion in its own right.

referents, the most central reference of all is to a state of heightened consciousness: the sense of creativeness. Perhaps the sense of creativeness may be unconscious or conscious, repressed or unrepressed. The principal point is that there is no essential reason why it should be one or the other. In terms of theory, either will do. In Milner's framework, a certain unity of unconscious and conscious life is rooted in the psyche's concern with its own essential nature, that is, creativeness. An implication one may draw is that the distinction between conscious and unconscious is less important than the quality of either or both (how creativeness fares throughout the psyche's multidimensional life).

In sum, Milner's focus on the sense of creativeness associated with body experience does not require repression as a cornerstone. I have also suggested that her position minimizes the logical importance of the distinction between conscious and unconscious operations, since her descriptions of psychic creativeness (her ultimate concern) may characterize either. Nevertheless, Milner does share Freud's bias that the ego is first and foremost a body ego. This is a bias which appears to be uncritically accepted by much of the psychoanalytic field. The adoption of this viewpoint has led to much fertile work. For example, Milner's inclination to link psychic creativeness with body experience has led to explorations of genuine interest. Nevertheless, one must ask if and to what extent such an assumption is justified, and how things might look if alternative assumptions were entertained.

Federn (1926) believed that the mental ego precedes the body ego and makes the latter possible. For example,

> Mental ego feeling . . . is the first to be experienced by the child; ego feeling related to the body and to perceptions conveyed through the body comes only gradually. [p. 35]

This is an astonishing remark for a psychoanalyst and has radical consequences for a theory of mind and self. It is a return to Descartes' cogito (if ever the latter were really left) on a deeper level.

Federn calls attention to many supporting phenomena. After sleep mental ego feeling often awakens before body ego feeling. In certain forms of depersonalization mental ego feeling remains after body ego feeling disappears. Federn's logical and phenomenological point is that I-feeling only gradually encompasses the body. It takes time and development to discover I must be where my body is. Even then shifting boundaries of I-feeling continue. I-feeling may expand to embrace the universe or contract to a point which places all outside it (including and at times, especially, the body). The I-feeling as such has a certain primacy. It spreads through the body and stamps it with I-ness, but may withdraw again when unduly threatened.

A search of the literature indicates that few psychoanalytic writers have taken the implications of Federn's position seriously, although many acknowledge some of the phenomena he addresses. An exception is Elkin's (1958, 1972) depiction of dramas between the primordial self and other, prior to the infant's awareness of having a body. He charts the vicissitudes of ineffable experiencing as it moves toward embodiment.

It may be necessary to distinguish diverse sources of ego- or self-feeling without reducing one to the other. Support for the double (or multiple) rootedness of self-feeling is found in the recent acknowledgement of the importance of infantile gazing (and hearing) as well as touching (Eigen 1980a,b, 1982, Elkin 1972, Spitz 1965, Stern 1977, Zelner 1982). The simultaneous input of both distance and contact senses throws the infant into different worlds of experience which must be co-ordinated. I suspect the theoretical controversies, concerning whether vision or touch is the more powerful organizer, have had their stormy history because of the radical contribution of both. Bion's (1977) playful descriptions of the difficulties involved in achieving common sense draw on the kinds of experiential worlds we pass through under the sway of different sensory modalities. My own observations suggest that when not tired, hungry, or otherwise uncomfortable, the infant responds in tune with a visually coordinated field. His sense of self tends to collapse with the loss of visual support (I must omit here a discussion of the world of audition and the defensive use of vision). Problems in achieving the right balance of distance–closeness in any situation are partly rooted in the shifting sense of self and other connected with vision and touch.

The theoretical collapse of distinct sources of self-feeling can lead to clinical confusion. For example, when Milner's (1957, 1969) schizophrenic patient fuses anal and visual elements, the sun or eye located in the anus, Milner takes this to be an example of undifferentiation prior to differentiation. My belief is that such a fusion represents a perverse reworking of spontaneous distinctions. Rather than reflect a phase of structural undifferentiation, I believe it a deterioration product linked to the threatened collapse of self-feeling which is normally fed and sustained by the tension between different experiential dimensions. The fecalized or spoiled self (a shit or garbage self; Eigen 1977, 1982, Meltzer 1973, Bion 1977) tends to pull down and debase personality functions. In terms of the anus–sun fusion which Milner depicts, solar consciousness (associated with vision, light, distance) is brought down and undone. The specifically visual contribution to the sense of self collapses and is, so to speak, absorbed or sucked up by the asshole.

I can see the potentially positive use of such situations only when directional distinctions are implicitly sustained. For example, it is possible to say (here reworking Milner) that the sun-in-anus is not simply a fecalization of consciousness, but an attempt of consciousness to suffuse the body: first, as a growth toward embodied selfhood (Milner says as much) and also as an attempt to take a look inside the anus, that is, to experience body feelings and perceive pathology. Rather than celebrate nondifferentiation, such imagery can be used to dramatize elemental urges to see and be. The various roles both mental and physical aspects of self-feeling play in any situation must be brought out rather than conceptually reduced to undifferentiation. Clearly, one must respect Milner's (1969) achievement with her difficult patient. Hers is one of the best clinical accounts in the literature. But I would like to advance the hypothesis that, in part, the loss in intensity of her patient's creative drive may be related to interpretations stressing undifferentiation as the subject's psychic starting point, rather than maintaining the tensions (and harmonies) between distinct yet interlocking dimensions (also see Eigen 1979, 1981b, 1982).

Dual Union

Perhaps nowhere is the issue of original undifferentiation more crucial or basic than in trying to envision the early starting point of the sense of self and other. As suggested earlier, Milner emphasizes the importance of undifferentiation as a reaction against a too great cultural stress on discursive thinking. She values experiences with loose boundaries, where merger of self and other is possible. To be sure, she describes how, in optimal conditions, differentiation and undifferentiation oscillate and feed each other, each playing a role in a basic rhythm. However, she does not seem to entertain the possibility that a sense of distinction between self and other can occur on early, preverbal levels. The result in her work is a polarization of distinction and merger, with the former equated with later, more superficial, and the latter with earlier, deeper, levels of being.

There is no reason to suppose that our sense of separateness and connectedness do not arise together and make each other possible. Theorists swing back and forth, making one or other of these directional tendencies primary at the expense of the other. To put it in dramatic terms, I do not think the sense of oneness can be what it is supposed to be, unless there is someone who is undergoing it and who can appreciate it. It is perhaps more appropriate to speak of a two-in-oneness or one-in-twoness. Pure merger and isolation are abstract terms which do not characterize living experience. Areas of union and distinction occur together, with one or the other more emphasized in a given situation. In this context, Christian conceptions of a triune God or communion (co-union) appear to reflect a genuine advance in mystical and psychological description. Here a sense of division and union coexist fully, neither possible without the other. Whatever its theological function, it would seem this kind of formulation expresses basic structural requirements a theory of the self (or ego) must meet. It points to a profound, preverbal realm of interaction wherein self and other co-constitute one another as distinct and united.

I would like to use the term "dual union" to refer to the simultaneous presence of both distinction and union dimensions. My use of this term differs from Mahler's (1968) insofar as I believe this basic experiential structure characterizes the self throughout all its developmental levels. Mahler uses the term loosely to describe two types of primary undifferentiated states: an autism in which a subject exists without an object, followed by a symbiosis in which subject and object are fused. Her descriptions point to possible extremes of boundary shifts (especially in pathology), but it is not clear that they can be said to describe the essential structure of the early self. Her descriptions lack specification of the conditions which make the sense of self (or other) possible. A self without an object would not be able to experience its own existence. Gestalt psychology shows us that a differentiated field is necessary for perception to occur, and this includes self-perception as well. A self with no reference point outside it could have no sense of its own existence. Similarly, pure fusion of self and other without some sense of distinctness would utterly cancel any sense of self and other.

What is valuable about Mahler's descriptions of these early phases may be preserved and corrected by seeing them as expressions of extremes toward which the permeable self can swing. In each case the self (or object) tends toward a vanishing point, whether one of impoverishment or, paradoxically, fullness. In pathology such extremes are associated with profound terrors, such as Bion's (1977) "nameless dread" or Winnicott's (1974) "ultimate agonies." However, as Milner's or Balint's work emphasizes, they may provide a basis for extraordinary richness and regeneration.

Freud did not conceive of a dual union structure in an explicit way and such a concept may be foreign to his style. However, aspects of his thinking are related to it. Although he spoke of objectlessness (autoerotism) in infantile development, he also stressed that instincts sought objects, if only for drive satisfaction. More importantly, he depicted an ego which was both separate yet given to identifications. Ego functions include perception, memory, and the sense of the ideal. The ego itself is an ideal reality both one with and distinct from itself and others. It simultaneously interweaves identificatory/idealizing and realistic aspects of experience. It lives in and through both these dimensions in complex ways. Take away either and the ego itself, as conceived by Freud, would disappear.

The simultaneity of difference and union appears to be a basic structure of human experience. Wherever we tap into the self's biography we find these two directional tendencies in some type of relation to one another. A sense of division yet seamless oneness characterizes the sense of self and other, mental and body ego, temporality, metaphor, the relationship between universal and particular, and many other phenomena. In theoretical discussions we have been prone to assign primacy to one pole of a co-constitutive relationship, a decision or slippage which is bound to affect our perception of clinical events.

Problems and Directions

Terms such as union, permeability, connectedness, identification, interweaving, and the like, express an interactive bias, yet not all require the concept of ego or self (a rigorous explication of the nuances of these terms is needed, but is beyond our present scope). Psychoanalytic and other developmental theorists have been lax in systematically distinguishing between experience, consciousness, and self-feeling.

For example, Grotstein (1981, 1982) emphasizes what he calls the self's dual track of separation and identification. He charts vicissitudes of separation and identificatory tracks as they undergo evolution. The term dual track is mechanistic sounding and conveys a rigidity which I do not think Grotstein means. However, the sense of the simultaneity of distinctness–union tends to get lost in his tracking vicissitudes of separate lines. This leads to confusions in his formulations which may be more than verbal. Thus he continues to speak of an undifferentiated self even after formulating a dual track theory, an inconsistency difficult to understand. Further, no genetic distinction between self and experience is made, so that his references to self could as easily apply to womb, pre-womb, birth, or postbirth moments. His best descriptions concern the development of the human self in infancy, but lack an explicit criterion with which to distinguish between the latter and what we share with all sentient beings.

A similar oversight is found in the work of psychologists who use experiments and microphotography to study early development. Often the phenomena they study (e.g., bonding, early dyadic interaction, object preference) might apply to puppies or chicks as well as human infants. No self need be postulated of the perceptual and behavioral patterns found in the first weeks or month or so of life.

Sandler and Rosenblatt (1962) focus on the subject's representational world. Self and object representations can, in principle, be charted throughout one's lifetime. However, Sandler believes the early sense of self must be obscurely rooted in a primitive body ego (Sandler et al. 1963) and so shares in the epistemological and phenomenological problems discussed earlier. Hermann's (1936, 1980) notion of dual union also suffers from an uncritical belief that the early intersubjective self is a body ego. He freely moves back and forth between speaking of animal and infant behavior without considering what steps may be necessary to make the leap from animal consciousness to the infant's early sense of self and other. His sensitive descriptions of what he calls dual or double thinking (the tendency to hold opposite viewpoints simultaneously) would gain in power by a clearer analysis of the dual roots of self-feeling (mental and physical dimensions).

The early self may move though many worlds of experience. An ineffable sense of self and other may interweave with the usual perceptual field with varying shifts of emphasis. A hard and fast distinction between immateriality and materiality cannot be said to hold for early infantile awareness. It is likely that both experiential dimensions feed the sense of self and other in basic ways. We do not know with any certainty when the specifically human sense of self (in contrast with animal consciousness) and other arises, although there is evidence of its presence in the smiling response (a uniquely human phenomenon) by two or three months (Eigen 1980a,b, Elkin 1972). The permeability and interactiveness common to all life is raised to a new power characterized by radically shifting boundaries and intensity (the expansion, contraction, rise and fall of self-feeling). How to coordinate the diverse experiential worlds one encounters or passes through remains a basic problem throughout life.

Milner's work suggests that we can dip into this fluid matrix and experience a heightened intensity which makes life feel profoundly meaningful. She uses the language of undifferentiation and plenitude to describe such events. Writers such as Bion (1977) and Lacan (1977, 1978) emphasize the importance of a gap or no-thingness which runs through human experience (see Eigen 1981a). The reversible or double perspective of everythingness and nothingness links up with the traditional mystical paths of the *via affirmitiva* and *via negativa,* or presence and absence (Sewell 1952). The dual union structure contains both moments and may be used to express and explore the mystery in which difference–union or gap–plenitude are co-constitutive.

The theme of the reciprocity of identity–difference has been a perennial one in religion and the arts. While it has been recognized as fundamental for psychoanalysis (e.g., Bion 1977), the latter has skirted its rigorous development.[2] Psychoanalytic writers tend to exploit the double directional tendency of human experiencing without crediting it as a primary capacity. I have used Milner's work as an entrée to this area because she uses the language of undifferentiation to describe the sense of creativeness. My analysis has tried to show that undifferentiation assumes a dual union structure (of self–other, mental ego–body ego). The epistemology of the latter is sounder than that of the former, although the law of contradiction is suspended in both.

REFERENCES

Balint, M. (1968). *The Basic Fault.* London: Tavistock.

Bion, W. R. (1977). *Seven Servants.* New York: Jason Aronson.

Ehrenzweig, A. (1967). *The Hidden Order of Art.* Berkeley, CA: University of California Press.

Eigen, M. (1977). On working with "unwanted" patients. *International Journal of Psycho-Analysis* 58:109–121.

_____ (1979). Ideal images, creativity and the Freudian drama. *Psychocultural Review* 3:287–298.

_____ (1980a). On the significance of the face. *Psychoanalytic Review* 67:427–441.

_____ (1980b). Instinctual fantasy and ideal images. *Contemporary Psychoanalysis* 16:119–137.

_____ (1981a). The area of faith in Winnicott, Lacan and Bion. *International Journal of Psycho-Analysis* 62:413–433.

---

[2]A notable exception is the work of Matte Blanco (1975), which I hope to discuss elsewhere.

_____ (1981b). Maternal abandonment threats, mind–body relations and suicidal wishes. *Journal of the American Academy of Psychoanalysis* 9:561–582.

_____ (1982). Creativity, instinctual fantasy and ideal images. *Psychoanalytic Review* 69:317–339.

Elkin, H. (1958). On the origin of the self. *Psychoanalytic Review* 45:57–76.

_____ (1972). On selfhood and ego structure in infancy. *Psychoanalytic Review* 59:389–416.

Federn, P. (1926). Some variations in ego feeling. *International Journal of Psycho-Analysis* 7:25–37.

Ferenczi, S. (1933). Confusion of tongues between adults and the child. In *The Selected Papers of Sandor Ferenczi: Problems and Methods of Psychoanalysis,* vol. III, pp. 156–167. New York: Basic Books, 1955.

Field, J. (M. Milner) (1934). *A Life of One's Own.* London: Chatto and Windus.

_____ (1950). *On Not Being Able to Paint.* London: Heinemann.

Freud, S. (1940). An outline of psycho-analysis. *Standard Edition* 23:144–207.

Grotstein, J. (1981). *Splitting and Projective Identification.* New York: Jason Aronson.

_____ (1982). Newer perspectives in object relations theory. *Contemporary Psychoanalysis* 18:43–91.

Gurwitsch, A. (1966). *Studies in Phenomenology and Psychology.* Evanston, IL: Northwestern University Press.

Hermann, I. (1936). Clinging—going in search. *Psychoanalytic Quarterly* 45:5–36.

_____ (1980). Some aspects of psychotic regression. *International Journal of Psycho-Analysis* 7:2–10.

Kohut, H. (1971). *The Analysis of the Self.* New York: International Universities Press.

Lacan, J. (1977). *Ecrits: A Selection.* New York: Norton.

_____ (1978). *The Four Fundamental Concepts of Psycho-Analysis.* New York: Norton.

Langer, S. K. (1942). *Philosophy in a New Key.* Cambridge: Harvard University Press.

_____ (1953). *Feeling and Form.* New York: Charles Scribner's Sons.

Loewald, H. (1980). *Papers on Psychoanalysis.* New Haven: Yale University Press.

Mahler, M. (1968). *On Human Symbiosis and the Vicissitudes of Individuation.* Vol. I: *Infantile Psychosis.* New York: International Universities Press.

Matte Blanco, I. (1975). *The Unconscious as Infinite Sets.* London: Duckworth.

Meltzer, D. (1973). *Sexual States of Mind.* Perthshire, Scotland: Clunie.

Merleau-Ponty, M. (1962). *The Phenomenology of Perception.* London: Routledge and Kegan Paul.

_____ (1963). *The Structure of Behavior.* Boston: Beacon.

Milner, M. (1945). Some aspects of phantasy in relation to general psychology. *International Journal of Psycho-Analysis* 26:143–152.

_____ (1952). Aspects of symbolism in comprehension of the not-self. *International Journal of Psycho-Analysis* 33:181–195.

_____ (1955). The role of illusion in symbol formation. In *New Directions in Psycho-Analysis,* ed. M. Klein et al., pp. 82–108. London: Tavistock.

_____ (1956). The communication of primary sensual experience. *International Journal of Psycho-Analysis* 37:278–281.

_____ (1957). *On Not Being Able to Paint.* 2nd ed. New York: International Universities Press.

_____ (1969). *The Hands of the Living God.* New York: International Universities Press.

Rank, O. (1932). *Art and Artist.* New York: Knopf.

Rycroft, C. (1968). *Imagination and Reality.* New York: International Universities Press.

Sandler, J., Holder, A., and Meers, D. (1963). The ego ideal and the ideal self. *Psychoanalytic Study of the Child* 18:139–158. New York: International Universities Press.

Sandler, J., and Rosenblatt, B. (1962). The concept of the representational world. *Psychoanalytic Study of the Child* 17:128–145. New York: International Universities Press.

Sewell, E. (1952). *The Structure of Poetry.* Hertford, England: Stephen Austin & Sons.

Spitz, R. (1965). *The First Year of Life.* New York: International Universities Press.

Stern, D. (1977). *The First Relationship.* Cambridge: Harvard University Press.

Winnicott, D. W. (1971). *Playing and Reality.* New York: Basic Books.

———— (1974). Fear of breakdown. *International Review of Psychoanalysis* 1:103–107.

Zelner, S. (1982). The organization of vocalization and gaze in early mother–infant interactive regulation. Unpublished doctoral dissertation. Yeshiva University, New York.

15

The Structure of Freud's Theory of Creativity

The title of this paper is already oversimplified. It is debatable whether Freud's thought contains a unified theory of creativity in any proper sense. The fertile climate and texture of his thinking stimulates interpretative gestures at the interface of psychoanalysis as a creative phenomenon and creativity as an object psychoanalysis seeks to understand. In studying creativity psychoanalysis tries to understand processes which give rise to itself. Freud's celebration of the mystery of creativity is not free of his characteristic ambivalence. As Ricoeur (1976) points out, he tries to appropriate by psychoanalytic concepts what he claims is beyond them.

It was above all in Freud's descriptions of creativity that two views of psychic life met, passed, opposed, or dialectically engaged each other. There was no phenomenon Freud was more invested in. Creative work was the one activity Freud considered to have made his life worth living. One might expect whatever alternative views he entertained on the basic nature of psychic life to emerge there. It was in fact on the issue of creativity that a radical difference persisted between what might be called Freud's formal and informal theories. In his informal theory psychic life was seen as basically orderly; an intrinsic order pervaded psychic life from its earliest beginnings. In his formal theory order was imposed on a more basic disorder or chaos, an epistemological position that, we will see, reflected his view of social life.

ON THE BASIC ORDER OF PSYCHIC LIFE

In his early work on hysteria Freud indicated that a basic coherence or fit existed between immediate experience and the symbolic language that reflects it. He pointed to an early coherent union between cognition, affect, and expressive language. For example,

> In taking a verbal expression literally and in feeling the "stab in the heart" or the "slap in the face" after some slighting remark as a real event, the hysteric is not

taking liberties with words but is simply reviving once more the sensations to which
the verbal expression owes its justification . . . and hysteria is right in restoring the
original meaning of the words in depicting its unusually strong innervations.
Indeed, it is perhaps wrong to say that hysteria creates these sensations by
symbolization. It may be that it does not take linguistic usage as its model at all, but
that both hysteria and linguistic usage alike draw their material from a common
source. [Freud 1893–1895, p. 181]

In suggesting that neurosis and language arose from a *common source* Freud
pointed to an original empathic experiencing, a sensed union of cognition and
affect—the ground of artistic sensibility as well as neurotic sensitivity. It would
seem that for Freud this original realm of experiencing was characterized by its
own intrinsic order, an order reflected in its products. For example, in the
passage quoted above, the ineffable experiencing of hurt or angry feelings was
viewed as intrinsically connected with sensed bodily states and expressive
metaphors.

However, in Freud's formal theory the individual's psychological foundation
was described as irrational and chaotic, eventually epitomized by the id concept
(Freud 1926). This primitive lack of structure, to be sure, may be viewed as
relative, since the id is characterized by a form of thinking (primary process),
structural complexes, and the genetic layering and dialectical play of instincts
(Laplanche and Pontalis 1973). Nevertheless, the irrational-passional foundation/
rational-organizing superstructure model did tend to characterize Freud's
thought and was clearly rooted in that aspect of Western philosophic-literary
tradition which viewed man as a "rational animal" (Freud 1923). Freud
radicalized this tradition in his descriptions of the power of the irrational and
chaotic foundation of human psychic life. He took scornful satisfaction in
proclaiming that his psychoanalytic discoveries constituted a grand and crucial
blow to Western man's ego, a narcissistic injury of the first order to Western
civilization.

CREATIVITY AND FREUD'S ATTITUDE TOWARD
THE MASSES

Nowhere is Freud's double attitude concerning the basic order–disorder of
psychic life more focused than in his understanding of creativity. Freud and his
followers when speaking informally often linked creativity with a fundamental
generative order, for example, the "creativity of the unconscious" (note Sachs's
[1942] book title, *The Creative Unconscious*). It was this tendency in Freud that
attracted artists to psychoanalysis and played a role in structuring certain
currents of artistic work throughout this century. On the other hand, his formal
theory of creativity maintained and developed the irrational foundation/rational
superstructure model—par excellence. It was precisely by means of the privileged status granted to creativity in his theory—expressed in the concept of

sublimation, a capacity reserved for the very few—that Freud found the mechanism with which to distinguish the mentally disciplined cultural elite from the impulsive masses. While psychoanalytic theory may be viewed as an apologia for creative life, practical psychotherapy, by contrast, must adapt itself to the lesser capacities of most individuals. It must try to help most people find pleasure enough within their unfolding means, making livable the frustrations inevitable to any human existence plus those frustrations attendant upon forever being excluded from the creative heights. The masses of people, in effect, must be helped to find some constructive compensation or outlet for their "creativity envy" and settle for sex and children, a workable combination of repression and acting out. Some few individuals may be truly helped to free their creative potential from their destructive attacks upon it. However, given this view, only in the most rare and optimal therapy are both personal healing and genuine creativity released.

THE SPLIT BETWEEN THEORY AND PRACTICE

Given the basic structure of Freud's thought, particularly with reference to creativity, it now seems inevitable that a split between psychoanalytic theory and practice must follow. The essential issue hinges on the meaning or place of creativity in the life of most people and whether the psychic roots of creativity are orderly or chaotic (or, more precisely, what interpretation is to be given of the kinds of order that characterize the foundations of creativity). If in practical psychotherapy one seeks to release what is healing in psychic nature, one cannot characterize this nature as essentially chaotic. In deep healing one always addresses oneself to an inherently orderly, creative process, even if, for a time, that order is elusive. The practical psychoanalyst soon learns that he is caught between a theory that excludes creativity for most people and the need to heal, which involves addressing oneself to the creativity at the heart of every person. This is part of the reason why the informal Freud, the sage, may sometimes sound as if he contradicts his formal constructions.

Such problems have led many workers to attempt to heal the gap between theory and practice by viewing the most fundamental strata of the mind as orderly and creative. Psychic life is viewed as creative as such. In some basic sense creativity is seen as normative for all people and pathology as creativity gone wrong. In this viewpoint healthy development and creativity are necessarily linked.

Theoretical and clinical positions have arisen which, in effect, take as their starting point what Freud once called the *common source* of language, neurosis and creativity in general, a common source with its own intrinsic order reflected in the forms (whether experiential, behavioral, or cultural) which give expression to it. Such terms as "primary symbolism" or "primary affective logic" (Green 1977) grow out of an attempt to emphasize and increasingly describe the mind's inherent order. A practical consequence of this view is to expand the precise use of regression in healing processes insofar as one can rely on an underlying and fertile creative order to sustain one's efforts. Of particular interest is the primordial generative activity that leads to awareness of self and other (with areas of distinction and union) (Eigen 1980, Grotstein 1978, Peterfreund 1978), for surely this awareness is the most essential creative act of humankind. The sense of wholeness may be most basically rooted in our awareness, if only implicitly, of generative activity as such.

REFERENCES

Eigen, M. (1980). On the significance of the face. *Psychoanalytic Review* 67:426–444.
Freud, S. (1893–1895). Studies on hysteria. *Standard Edition* 2:3–305.
———— (1923). The ego and the id. *Standard Edition* 19:3–68.
———— (1926). Inhibitions, symptoms, and anxiety. *Standard Edition* 22:77–174.
Green, A. (1977). Conceptions of affect. *International Journal of Psycho-Analysis* 58:129–156.
Grotstein, J. (1978). Inner space: its dimensions and its coordinates. *International Journal of Psycho-Analysis* 59:55–61.
Laplanche, J., and Pontalis, J-B. (1973). *The Language of Psycho-Analysis.* New York: Norton.
Peterfreund, E. (1978). Some critical comments on psychoanalytic conceptualizations of infancy. *International Journal of Psycho-Analysis* 59:427–441.
Ricoeur, P. (1976). Psychoanalysis and the work of art. In *Psychiatry and the Humanities,* ed. J. H. Smith, pp. 3–33. New Haven: Yale University Press.
Sachs, H. (1942). *The Creative Unconscious.* New York: Sci-Art.

16

Demonized Aspects of the Self

There is a Moment in each Day that Satan cannot find,
Nor can his Watch Fiends find it; but the Industrious find
This Moment & it multiply, & when it once is found
It renovates every Moment of the Day if rightly placed.

William Blake, *Milton*

PREVIEW

For many of us it appears that the devil has survived natural science. Although logically impossible, in the hearts and minds of many he has, too, survived God. My years of clinical experience teach me that the devil is very much alive as a *psychic reality,* as a potent organizing and driving force in the self-feeling of our age. He emerges with predictable regularity in sensitive depth analysis of individual patients, and his face may be plainly seen in events throughout the world.

When I speak of a devil self, I can feel myself being both apologetic and provocative, but also true to phenomenological events that arise in the course of depth-oriented therapy. Given half the chance, patients sooner or later may well report having at some point in life made a pact with the devil. They are somehow nagged by a sense of selling out for survival or power, to get by or to triumph. (There is almost always some mixture of getting and giving up, tinged with self-justificatory lying.) If nothing this drastic, they may still report having seen devil images or heard evil whispers, which they attributed to imagination and determined to ignore.

I do not think it unusual for hidden demonic aspects of therapist and patient to agree to slip through and past each other's gaze. If the therapist does not cavalierly collude in pooh-poohing such messages, significant erosions of self-feeling can be revealed. Without this acknowledgment, the struggle toward integrity may never begin to be undertaken at the deepest levels of personality.

Early psychoanalysis tended to understand psychic devils in id–superego terms. Theorists now add demonized ego structures and mean this in a strong sense. Advances in the past several decades have dramatically enlarged the picture of the baby self. It is in the primordial arena of baby mind that the devil first sows his seeds. The organizing capacities of the ego may undergo disruption and deformation early in life, to the extent that the very I-sensation, the sense of self, may feel tainted to a person. Entire areas of the baby's intentional field may invisibly take a skewed direction that begins to plague the individual's consciousness and threatens to pervade his or her life with misery and horror.

The self gives in and sides with demonic promptings as a way out. Without support, it cannot build up a tolerance for wholesome integrity. One may begin to side with the aggressor and identify with unconscious demonic aspects of the mother or father, or become cynical and confounded by self-doubt when caught in chronic double-bind situations that reward perverse mental operations. The self may not understand what it is doing when this happens. It somehow blanks out and returns corrupted (and corrupting), repeating an agonistic, self-poisoning process time and again. Yet there is also a knowing, an inkling of what one is undergoing, what one is doing to oneself. It is something like changing clothes in the dark, with texture the only clue to difference in garments, except that the very texture of one's soul is at stake.

I will illustrate this with a vignette.

An analysand who began getting better started talking about a fear of dying in great pain. She claimed it was not merely death, but painful death she was most frightened of. In spite of continued work, this communication persisted obsessively with diminishing returns for some time. While sitting with her one day, I went blank, and while she was agonizing I felt something. I began to see a baby staring into space. Soon it would die and in some sense not even know it had been alive. When I again became aware of the patient, she was talking about having an operation. She was sure she had cancer (she was really in fine physical health) and would die on the operating table. She pictured a horrendously painful scene. "But you would be in no pain, no pain at all," I mused. "You'd die anesthetized." We were both taken a bit back by my offhand remark. For her dread was actually of dying without knowing it. The "great pain" had been something of a ruse, a mastery attempt.

My baby fantasy fit. For she, too, quickly realized that her fear was of being alive without knowing it, and of dying without ever truly having realized she was alive. It was a feeling she could now report having had ever since she could remember, except that she had lacked words for it. Dreams of operations followed and provided her with an expressive language and with imaginative access to sensations of emotional "operations" in infancy and childhood (as well as with me), "operations" at the heart of her self-feeling.

In one dream a baby was operated on by mad doctors who turned the baby mad. The doctors and soon the baby were monomanic, as devils must be. The nightmare went on for another instant, and as she woke her chilled feeling faded into "Who, me?" She sensed a sort of "going away," a kind of mental blackout before the operation was completed, and again a caesura before the finishing touch, the final gesture of waking innocence. The therapy "operation" of course had its demonic quality, but she and I could try to speak about this. We could try to subject it to continuous processing. The "Who, me?" devil was now labeled, however. A particular shade of psychic shock and invisibility was less available for subterfuge.

The insight that demonization begins in infancy is reflected in popular renditions (movies, stories) of devil babies. Although aesthetically puerile, such scenarios have their area of truth — profoundly so — as do the recent rash of Draculas and far more prosaic monsters, all with demonic-baby qualities. (Science fiction creatures and machines, both good and evil, now exhibit baby features in most explicit ways.) The gap between adulthood and infancy increasingly narrows. More and more we tend to see babies everywhere throughout the fabric of adult activity, or perhaps one is simply noticing that adults and children do not greatly differ in their basic feelings. It is no accident that, for the first time in human history, grown-ups (especially psychoanalysts, but also certain historians and philosophers) can spend the greater part of their adult professional lifetime thinking about childhood. There is a sense in which we can say we have entered the Age of the Baby and that sectors of humanity are now as intent on decoding babyhood as they are the origins of the universe.

In depth therapy one can study the emergence of transformations of demonic ways of thinking–feeling (the two interweave) in what appear to be reworkings, via fantasies, of very early developmental levels. By degrees the subject lays open his or her inner world for scrutiny, and one may witness, as it were, the birth of good and evil psychic elements as these pulse through awareness, often with much of the same fluidity that characterizes aspects of infantile experience. Once contact is established with this mercurial intentional field, one becomes alert to the hairbreadth nature of the changes going on, the moment-to-moment reversals and jumps thrown up for potential self-perception.

My main concern in this Chapter is to describe some of the transformations satanic images undergo in relation to what I shall loosely call *baby mind* (the meaning of which will become clearer as this essay develops). In certain cases it is *my* perception of the demonic, rather than the patient's, that gets things rolling. I argue that in such instances I respond to subtle messages transmitted by the patient; for here, as in many instances of working with areas of very damaged self-feelings, the patient's only true way of letting me know who he or she is may be through physiognomic cues that affectively press me. How the clinician relates to realizations of his or her own permeability (and of the patient's) is crucial in determining the direction of defensive operations in the therapeutic partnership.

After three introductory cases, really fragments of cases, meant to evoke a concrete sense of the territory involved, I will relate the devil to the snake symbol and the anal mind. I believe that one of the great contributions of psychoanalysis to the evolution of human consciousness is its extension of our awareness of body as expressive symbol for emergent psychic capacities. We can create a virtual nosology of oral, anal, and phallic devils (strictly speaking, there are no genital ones; see Eigen 1979c). I will focus on demonized anality—which is really the disease of modern times, far more frightening than pan-phallicism, which in itself could not lead to ubiquitous spoiling. It is the snake wrapped up in the anal mind that is perhaps, above all, the villain here (Eigen 1979c).

The depiction of anal structures is followed by a foray into the phenomeno-logical psychology of murder and addiction. I have chosen these phenomena because they appear to be representative externalizations of tendencies that pervade people's inner lives and the historical atmosphere they breathe. In general, the case examples in this Chapter have been selected because I believe they express, if only implicitly, broader currents with which people are struggling.

In the final section I present a highly selective overview of certain transfor-mations demonic images have undergone since very ancient times and conclude with a further discussion of the hold the image of the baby has on modern consciousness. Again, I have tried to select aspects that seem relevant to humanity's historical impasse—or transition. My method is informal, really a series of sketches, as it is throughout this Chapter. Nevertheless, I intend these evocations with a certain expressive rigor, albeit characterized by quirks that some people who spend much time thinking about babies tend to develop.

Three Case Fragments

1. Smith, a professional man and experienced patient, began therapy with me in the wake of a heart attack. Not long before, I had seen him at a social gathering where he had been lively and stimulating, so I was quite unprepared for the crumpled, sunken heap who limped into my office. I thought of Yeats's "tattered coat upon a stick" and of the Bowery horrors, although he showed no sign of the self-pity or resignation of the derelict. A most striking impression was that through all his limpness this man looked like sneering steel, a lascivious and grimly set devil.

At first I felt sheepish about perceiving him this way. It did not seem right to so experience one who was convalescent. Since, however, the perception persisted, I thought it best to stay open to what I might learn from it and see where it would go.

In our first session Smith announced that he did not care if he lived or died. He had achieved relative success at the price of a chronic, background depersonaliza-tion that now pervaded his whole being. In the past, when his sense of unreality threatened him, he had offset it with intense homosexual encounters with young men. The mutual idolization (see Khan 1979, for the *idolized self*) at the heart of these experiences constituted his most fulfilling erotic moments. These episodes abruptly ended with a sense of unreality, freeing Smith to return refreshed and revitalized to his everyday life. Throughout the years he had been committed to his marriage and family, although he had remained emotionally distant. He described himself as playing parent to all the children in his life. He lived out (or avoided living out) his baby self through identification with others.

His relationship with his "children" was adhesive as well as aloof. He would elicit and partake in fusion with his body self while a corner of his mental self remained far away and out of reach. The youths he attached to himself glowed with the promise of a limitless future, yet were deeply disorganized. Through them he was able to projectively act out aspects of good body feeling. That some of them suffered breakdowns was rationalized by Smith, who continued to offer himself as nurse. He ignored, too, the somatizations he became subject to from middle age onward and referred to these bodily defections with a trace of contempt. It was as though his own body were beneath his notice, its very capacity for disease a proof of its inferiority. A mean obliviousness to his body self seemed part of his demonic appearance.

I felt it cruel and senseless to express my devil perceptions, although I wondered if it might really be more cruel not to do so. For some time I simply monitored my reactions. Nevertheless, my own awareness of them sensitized me to any such thoughts the patient might express, so that his tentative probes would not be wasted.

Indeed, after a few months Smith revealed that he sometimes saw devil images when he was tired and closed his eyes. Inquiry revealed that his consciousness of evil presences went back indefinitely. He was in the habit of averting his attention from such impressions and dismissing them. Just a few days earlier he had glimpsed a devil in a store window while he was shopping, only to discover in amazement that it was his own reflection. (It is not true that the devil never appears in a mirror; sometimes bits of self-knowledge do come through.)

With encouragement, Smith tried to slow down and focus on such images. At certain moments his devil seemed, in his description, "fiery yet stony, not at all fluid. A frozen fire. His eyes are fixed, immobile, his body a stiff, rigid machine." He was an androgynous male with "erect, pistol breasts; a leering machine mother. Only devil babies could survive."

These images combined both personal and archetypal elements. To a certain extent aspects of his actual father and mother (as well as stray features from other figures who caught his interest) were incorporated in them; however, where known persons were concerned, distorted elements of his own facial appearance eventually became dominant. He began to recognize that his devil images in part represented important aspects of a lost I-feeling, an I that had contracted and hardened almost to the point of insensibility. The devils mirrored the torment of his I-anesthesia, a fiercely numb paralysis of hopeless rage (see Chapter 8).

Smith's reveries were carried forward by a series of significant dreams that brought the issues involved to new levels. One dream series opened with a terror of burglars and killers. Ominous figures lurked outside, and Smith doubted he could keep them out. Next a baby appeared and began screaming, "Fire!" It seemed almost a demon screaming. A woman in a nearby building opened and closed windows and alternately filled and emptied her apartment of various objects. The baby's bloodcurdling scream faded away.

Such dreams may be variously approached, but we took the following line: The sequence opens with paranoid threats quickly followed by a baby's scream. The open expression of terror and outrage suggests that there still is hope of compelling a response. The mothering self, however, cannot function as an adequate container for infantile explosiveness, absorbed as she is in her own internal space and boundary problems. She is caught in her own obsessive repetitions, unable to coordinate opening–closing, emptying–filling. The baby's unmanageable feelings demonically spiral, then fade into nothingness.

In deep, imaginative activity Smith gradually opened himself to the painful scream of the baby self. To a certain extent, his devil was a frozen scream. The full experiencing of sensations of screaming had a thawing-out effect. Smith wept uninhibitedly for the first time in adult memory. He became more sensitive to the momentary oscillations, the fadings in and out of the sense of vital aliveness, including the quiet urges to scream that often pass through the day unnoticed. It began to dawn on him just how much of his life was spent in silent screaming, and he was more aware of the many ways he avoided listening to it.

In fantasy, this patient saw his heart attack as a baby screaming or at times as a devil in a tantrum. The devil images now made him feel mighty and alternated with terror and helplessness. He felt in touch with currents that come from the same place babies do. These feelings often felt clean but could also leave a macabre taste, a sign of "something off." The latter indicated that a better quality of interplay between feelings of might and weakness was necessary.

As Smith progressed in his work with primal scream awareness, a complementary theme emerged and interacted with it. A wholesome female element made its appearance in dreams of little girls. In the best of these dreams a little girl played happily, enjoying being. When my patient focused on this little girl, she brought him delight and relaxation, which felt good but maddeningly threatening. At first Smith tried to keep an internal grip on himself by anal-phallic self-tightening. By such internal constriction he warded off fears of rape, flooding, and annihilation, but also hope. He could not imagine how this girl could possibly defend herself against danger, yet when he could really contact her the dangers disappeared. Nevertheless, he desperately fought against her and struggled to see her as merely passive, worthless, or out for sex. With firm therapeutic encouragement, the intrinsic goodness of the little girl reliably resurfaced, and he started to learn to defend her against envious internal aggressors. He came to see his little girl aspect as the least demonic quality he had yet produced. He felt more clearly how he had repeatedly driven himself, mind and body, to the breaking point, partly so that acts of catastrophic self-violence might carry him past his lifelong numbing. (This latter, in part, was the result of his denial and maltreatment of his feminine component.) The little girl was not numb, but she could emerge only after the repressed baby scream could be heard. The devil quality of Smith's appearance markedly diminished after he began to value his little girl.

2. Dee was a vegetative pubertal girl diagnosed as epileptic and schizophrenic. She took slight notice of her surroundings. Most of her time was spent in front of a television, occasionally masturbating. She did not feed herself and was incontinent. Sometimes Dee walked a bit if someone physically supported and "pushed" her along. Her speech was unintelligible to anyone but her mother and to a nurse who infantilized her. In spite of medication she often had *grand mal* attacks one after another and was believed to be suffering progressive brain deterioration. It would be charitable to liken her to a Raggedy Ann doll. She was one of my first cases, twenty years ago at a treatment camp, when I was fresh and eager and lived by miracles.

Dee seemed most alive to me in her seizures. It was the only time her skin had color: her body filled out, and she became a mass of explosive movement. The seizures went through several phases from rigid stiffening through spasmodic shaking to utter limpness. Among the things I thought of were self-gripping, rocking, orgasm, and death. She uttered scarcely a sound through the entire event.

She was thought to be unconscious through all this, but I felt someone looking out, mentally alive in the midst of earthquake, silence, and paralysis. I was stunned at believing I saw staring through her eyes a devil, a malevolent core of consciousness at the heart of her apparent oblivion. It was a searing look, pure hate, a mocking laser. As I looked more closely, I believed I saw malicious glee and ghastly suffering combined, but also something regal and haughty and even prankish, as though the devil were sticking his tongue out and defiantly saying, "OK, let's see what you can do." At the same time this presence was walled off and electrical.

I spoke about my feelings in supervision, but they continued to build. One day, as Dee started a seizure and flashed her spiteful leer, I found myself screaming, "You bitch!" The *grand mal* instantaneously stopped, and she glowered. I believe her real progress with me dated from this episode.

She started to notice me, and a new quality entered her ignoring of me. She had to put more effort into blanking me out, something she previously did without trying. She was used to treating me (and herself) as though my (and her) visibility made no difference. I (she) might as well have been plasticine or stone or made of air. She assumed nonpresence. Now, however, the same fixed stare that previously characterized only her seizures began to spread to other moments as well. It was a compressed glower, and the tension gave her face a hint of color.

My sense of isolation with her deepened precisely because her "walled-offness" seemed a more active, visible force. She was not absent merely by default. I looked at this force looking at me looking at it, a dense and uncompromising sliver of fierce consciousness. Her body now seemed like an iron lung for this mental parasite, but somewhere I sensed suffering and longing.

At some point during this period, I dreamt that Dee was underwater without knowing how to swim. I was trying to teach her. Her parents held her under each time she tried to surface, yet refused to let her either swim or drown. She already showed signs of decomposition but quickly reached out to me.

Since this was my dream, it referred to the hapless Dee in me, crippled at least in part by tantalizing parental egoism, lost but not utterly without hope. Perhaps my own Dee could yet learn to navigate the unconscious, which in the actual Dee seemed chaotic beyond repair. My striving to build adequate psychic processes from the debris of parental failure (perpetuated in my own self-feeling and behavior) reflected a basic drive that in Dee was stillborn. My psyche used Dee to tell my story, but I also dreamt this dream for her. I wondered if she were not in some way using my capacities to create in me an image she needed but lacked the resources to create herself. In such a situation the therapist may seem to lend to the patient what the latter above all requires, a functioning psyche committed to developmental struggle.

After my dream our silences grew still thicker. I fancied Dee might be trying to counteract her vulnerability for having appeared in my dream. Something about her mood, a kind of "oppositional complicity," a sly triumph or pleasure over making herself known in unseen ways, also egged me on. I felt as if I had stumbled upon her secret broadcast system, and I sensed a highly charged psychic field otherwise glossed over. On this channel, however delusional, the devil constantly broadcasts news of self.

On feeling the full impact of Dee's heightened silence, I conceived an urge to put my hand in her mouth. Again, I talked over this impulse in supervision and was well aware of its hostile and sexual connotations as well as its impatient and possibly defensive mothering. I also felt it was a linking gesture, however negative. (I must admit I find it a bit hard to think I would do this today.) At first she did not seem to notice, and I simply waited. For an instant I experienced her like the proverbial woman who smokes during sexual intercourse. She eventually turned her head to look at me with dismay, the most direct and empathic look of recognition I had yet experienced from her. She tried to collapse and ignore what was happening, but I continued thrusting my fingers into her mouth. Almost without warning she reared to full height, stared at me with outrage, and screamed. I maintained my hand in position as best I could without choking her, and she bit me. I could tell she was biting me with all her might, but I could not feel any pain. I felt only joy. She rose up in indignant majesty and beat me to her heart's content, pummeling any part of my face or body she could contact. She looked righteous and queenly and radiant, a mixture of imperious incredulity and chagrin: "How dare you affront Her Majesty!" It was the first physical exercise I had seen her take outside of her seizures.

Afterward she seemed more open, alert, and light, with signs of self-satisfaction, like a cat licking herself, almost smug. For the moment her covert and barren SOS signals turned into a bright "I've been here all the time." Her seizures diminished (not without setbacks, to be sure), and her skin tone continued to improve. Within a month she spoke understandably, largely fed herself, and eagerly walked with help, although all her life processes were rusty.

The "rustiness" was replaced by a subtle quality that for me was the most dramatic of all. Dee's features and body texture underwent a certain softening, at times glowingly so. When she rested, her limbs curved lyrically, far more sensuously, as though she were now capable of enjoying the languorous spread of bodily sensations. At such times her body no longer seemed cold but visibly responded to shifting atmospheric currents. Although movement of every sort remained difficult and awkward for her, she nonetheless had a tonal grace. She was both more active and noisy and also quietly alive with nuances.

This profoundly gentle change was reflected in a dream figure of mine who now appeared: a man's face, simply there, a pure resonant passivity expressively waiting. This face had an unintrusive look one could trust; evoked by the change in Dee, it doubtless reflected a quality that had informed my work all along but of which I was unaware. I suspected it also mirrored what was most positive in Dee's mutilated passivity. The dream heightened my awareness and made me more appreciative of a very valuable kind of passivity, a most precious capacity indeed (possibly Dee's lasting contribution to my sense of self).

Before moving on I wish to say a few words about Dee's early object relations. She had indeed a serious neurological illness, but this did not run its course in vacuum. It became manifest in kindergarten, where she could not endure separation from home. Her seizures worsened, and she was forced to remain home or institution-bound. Her mother hoped nutrition was the key and clung to this notion throughout the time I knew her. She spoke of Dee in the same way one might speak of a flower or dog or nice day. Her tone was one of intrusive, intellectual intimacy, a mixture of benign impersonality and muted collusiveness. Both she and her husband were well-situated professionals. He claimed he had not learned to speak before the age of nineteen. He mouthed truisms with cryptic intensity, but his wife was tolerant. On occasion they enjoyed telling me about games Dee and her father played together. The content of one letter from him during Dee's first month at camp was such a game. I will recount it without comment, as it speaks for itself.

The letter was made up of a series of cartoons with captions. Picture 1: snake on left, hole on right; caption, "The Snake and the Hole." Picture 2: snake approaching hole; caption, "The Snake Goes Toward the Hole." Picture 3: snake entering hole; caption, "The Snake Goes in the Hole." Picture 4: snake's tail still visible as it vanishes; caption, "The Snake Disappears into the Hole." Picture 5: only the hole; caption, "The Hole." Picture 6: chaotic lines trailing off into blank page; caption, "And Then There Was Nothing." At the bottom, "Love, Daddy."

3. Paul was driven into therapy by sexual impotence. His life in general did not work well, but this he was willing to put up with. He tolerated a low-grade adjustment for some good moments. He worked, moved in and out of relationships, got by. He was used to a chronic, muted depression that tended to serve a self-soothing, tranquilizing purpose: it helped insulate him from the disorganization that accompanied more intense states. He was now deprived of sex, one of the main functions that made the motions of living worthwhile, and he wished it restored without things getting stirred up too much.

Paul preserved some pockets of affective intensity by means of perversions. His most intense life experience, he reported, had been manipulating his wife and best friend to sleep together while he watched. The marriage broke up afterward, precipitating in Paul a near psychosis. He was rescued by a regime of drugs and supportive therapy and recurrently sought help to be pasted together when disruptions threatened. I was his third therapist in this scenario. He had not remarried.

His preferred perverse routine; his "ritual," as he called it, involved creating a romantic atmosphere with candlelight and music and masturbating for hours using women's stockings, panties, or shoes (preferably his ex-wife's or daughter's). The ritual culminated in what he described as "explosions," intense orgasms that after a glow left him drained. He felt fulfilled and then defeated; he experienced an ecstatic relief that turned "shitty." Some time might pass without his repeating this ritual, but it easily could be stimulated by unmanageable doses of excitement or defeat in daily life.

Paul was raised by a chronically ill mother who used her illness to dominate the household. He felt sexually tantalized by three older sisters. When he was four, one sister initiated a "game" in which she tied him on a bed and did a striptease. This game lasted on and off for about two years, until the girl's interest turned to boys outside the household. Soon afterward even the sight of one of her discarded stockings was enough to send Paul into a near frenzy of arousal.

Paul repeatedly turned to his father for help in being lifted beyond his inner chaos. His father's presence was kindly and mild but lacked the strength necessary to set this wayward household in order. The patient's awareness of his father's weakness degraded his own personality and intensified an underlying despair. It is important, however, to stress that he did not give up on his father easily. His persistent and unsuccessful efforts to induce his father to help him played a significant role in his consequent breakdown. Nevertheless, throughout his illness the background memory of his father's quiet warmth supported some self-mothering, however depressive.

Paul's therapy was difficult and complex and is studied in more detail elsewhere (Eigen 1982). I wish to focus here on demonic aspects of perverse mental structure and the changes these underwent, especially as a result of detailed work on a highly charged memory. In early childhood Paul was repeatedly given enemas. The ritual consisted of his being held firmly by his mother across her lap while she or his father administered the enema. Paul's penis pressed upon his mother, and this pleasure fused with anal sensations and culminated in rageful, humiliating, yet ecstatic states. He felt he would die and felt the bowel pressure mount to orgasmic explosions. The repeated cycle, dying–orgasmic explosion, functioned as a perverted prototype of the rebirth experience.

He recalled splitting into two demons in these scenes. One was his body demon, madly exploding. The other was his head demon, a grimacing onlooker chuckling, "Heh, heh." In one set of fantasies in session, the head demon's laughter turned into a woman who wished to suck up his penis with an anal mouth. Paul felt hopelessly fused with her power and at the same time secretly controlling. While speaking about this image Paul recalled scenes in which his mother displayed a ruptured navel when he was a small child. It popped out like an erection but also suggested the umbilical cord. The patient felt repulsed and wished to rip it off. His mother's repeated rejection of her doctor's advice to remove it by an operation infuriated him; her masochistic exhibitionism maddeningly stifled him. As he put it, "Cutting off my mother's belly-cock was cutting off my own lifeline." Maternal castration anxiety merged with separation anxiety (Eigen 1974, 1975–1976, 1979a,b).

Instead of saving him by preventing the enema scenes, his father functioned as his mother's helper. Paul stared at his father in pleading, horrific disbelief: "Surely you will turn against her and save me." In another elaboration Paul imagined his father taking *her* over his lap and giving *her* an enema or spanking. He continued to try, in thought if not in fact, to make his father become a stronger, fuller person. He hoped to correct this lapse in fatherhood even if he himself were somehow forced to do his father's business. This wish had been fervently translated into the primal scene enactment, in which Paul's friend had "fucked the shit out of" his wife (Paul's language), the scene that had announced Paul's breakdown. Following this episode his wife (= mother) vanished, completing her symbolic transmutation into feces. In general, the patient's perversions condensed a wish for his father to subdue the maternal power which at the same time Paul was merged with.

His actual fetish objects (women's underpants, stockings, shoes) functioned as highly charged symbols of maternal power. Their small size and well-bounded form made them easy to control and set limits to permeability and fusion. The function of the fetish in his case was not so much to deny that mother has no penis (Freud's view) but to dramatize possible control over the overwhelming phallus (= active power) she has. *The fetish is an attempt to externalize and gain power or mastery over mother's phallic aspect* or at least to mitigate one's crushing sense of helplessness in relation to it. Indeed, in families like Paul's, the mother's phallus is often the only psychically potent one.

By containing mother's phallic power in a passive object (the clothing) at his disposal, Paul achieved via perversion what his father had failed to do. Thus through perverse activity he tried to make good his father's lack. He was both his father's better and proxy, working at father repair through the self-as-double. The pervert goes about his father's business the only way he can in his mother-bound world. In light of this finding, formulations of perversion that play down the role of paternal yearnings (Khan 1979) or stress the pervert's collusion with mother against father (Chasseguet-Smirgel 1974) appear oversimplified. The subject indeed has collapsed into mother-bound collusion, but at the same time tries to transcend maternal power with whatever father elements he can fabricate or salvage. He both identifies with and tries to rise above the maternal power he is locked into. *The fetish becomes a weapon with which to beat mother at her own game,* an attempt to seize victory from defeat.

In mind–body terms, the head ego keeps itself above the mother–body fetish. It triumphantly controls (see Chapter 9). At the same time the body ego is fused with the fetish, losing and heightening itself through merger with maternal power. In some way the head ego demonically hardens itself. It is always in danger of spiraling off into sheer nullifying activity, into a no-saying to all *material* existence. The body ego reaches its null point by mimicking surrender, a macabre mixture of incorporative lust and dissolution. The head demon may finally be driven to allow no mother at all within the compass of its self-feeling, whereas the body demon may allow no mother at all outside it.

In passing, let me note, perhaps paradoxically, that among the significant transformations Paul's devil images underwent, aspects of the body devil issued as a spontaneous, puckish little boy, a "cute little devil" who liked fooling mother. Aspects of the mental devil turned into the bright, tempting girls of Paul's childhood who made the little boy-self feel dumb. These images derived from two different nuclei of self-assertion in conflict with each other, still a difficult but potentially far more healthy predicament.

Summary Comparisons: Smith, Dee, Paul

By means of partial comparisons, let us explore further some of the typical structural dynamisms that characterized the three patients, Smith, Dee, and Paul.

In Smith's case an occultly transcendent mental self invisibly stayed aloof from, yet operated through, mothering capacities. By playing Big Mama, Smith surreptitiously fused with the young homosexuals — the "babies" — he attracted. His body self, and at times his mental self as well, functioned as a magnet for the hunger of others, while a detached sector of his mental self enjoyed body aliveness vicariously, through projective identification. The image of aliveness procured by servicing (or being serviced by) the "divine child" in others warded off the muted depersonalization involved. His own negativism was not clearly apparent so much as silently operative in his determination to avoid contact with people who could not be deified. He was unconsciously set against threats to his idolatrous position and willing to put up with a life pervaded by blandness and dedicated to maintenance of the status quo.

His body ego, stultified by his gloomy round of work and perverted climaxes, exploded in rebellion against such tyranny with a clearing-out process — the heart attack — that almost led to death; in so doing it led to subsequent therapeutic help.

Dee's bodily seizures had an element of autistic obliviousness and may well have been dominated by negative hallucinatory pressures that exploited her physiological weakness. Here, too, explosive rage was at the same time an evacuative dissolution. After a number of seizures she would start from scratch, as though purged. At such moments she seemed both piercing and far away; a hate-riveted focus and empty attentional lapse seemed to bind rival areas of her being. I could easily picture her as sending out, through her seizures, recurrent SOS signals — as a searingly contracted consciousness using body-ego rudiments to periodically break into visibility. I felt she was emitting messages of hate and longing in the only way left to her, a baby's helpless fit. The time between messages seemed to be given over to gathering strength until enough momentum accumulated for another all-out try.

The split between Paul's mental and physical self had been chronically sedated by depressive vagueness. It was both condensed and played out intensely in perverse activities. These enactments momentarily provided him with a heightened sense of unity wherein conflicting tendencies not so much harmonized as participated in a ritually contained war. His relationship to the fetish simultaneously expressed currents of assertion and surrender, albeit in deformed ways.

In all three cases inaccessible mental operations remained ensconced in evasive surges of hate-governed control and longing, a relentless negativism often coupled with explosive dissolution and fearful sensations of melting. Similarly, confusional blanking-out was punctuated by fierce, elusive slivers of self/object clarity. As I suggested earlier, where psychosexual imagery was concerned, this mixture of elusiveness and rigidity was most often expressed in anal terms.

The mental and often the physiognomic correlates of many of these operations also may be characterized as devious and "snakelike." Patients such as I described here embody the mythic struggle between primal innocence and primal evil and actualized the age-old symbolism associated with the myth. In the light of these clinical observations, the appellation *snake-in-the-grass* cannot be taken lightly. So we shall proceed to consider the snake symbol and the anal mind, particularly with reference to demonized mental and physical self-dynamisms.

The Serpent Self

Western symbology had adopted the snake of all creatures as most expressive of demonic qualities. The functional and structural qualities of the snake well suit it for this use. Representational meanings evoked by the snake apply to all psychosexual phases and span mental and physical processes in a rich variety of ways. The snake is also linked with fertility through its cyclic shedding of skin, a classic emblem of renewal.

The serpent's fangs often express oral sadistic or, better, unyielding superego components. The capacity to bite and poison may parallel the baby's sense of spoiling the breast (Segal 1978) and, reciprocally, of being contaminated by it. The sense of self as basically poisonous or poisoned is often symptomatic of a degraded self-image, a "fecal" or "garbage" self (Weil 1958) instilled by faulty parental mirroring. Such a deranged self-feeling may become a way of life if the mother is unable to contain and reprocess the bad feelings the baby puts into her (Bion 1977). In this case the mother has failed to separate the milk from the shit, with the result that the baby is forced to take in what he or she is trying to eliminate. He or she may come to feel that what is poisoning him or her can never be gotten rid of as it finally becomes built into the sense of identity.

The hypnotic eyes of the snake express mental–spiritual power. The transcendant quality of the snake's unblinking gaze, coupled with its bodily relation to cyclic time, may symbolize wisdom. This autarchic, affectless, mesmerizing stare may also express the schizoid, tyrannical aspect of the self. One patient referred to this Svengali quality in her own eyes as the "evil sorcerer." When her mental snake invisibly entwined itself around its prey by its own secret magic, her eyes literally bulged with tension (and, we learned, her anal sphincters contracted). She feared her eyes would pop or explode with mentalized hate and others would find her both forbidding and fascinating. This demonic aspect of the self mocks more serious, heartfelt tendencies that it seeks to debase and enslave.

The snake evokes experiences that link mental and physical dimensions. Its sudden darting movement suggests the flash of thought, and its gliding, an almost immaterial quality, a weightless merging with the surround. Its very movement parallels that of breathing: a rippling upward through the body. The sinuous ease with which it probes its medium projects a sense of electrifying power. It is as though it assimilates qualities of the surround and in some way becomes as invisible and ubiquitous as air. A frightening illusion about the snake is precisely its apparent defiance of containment outside itself; like an atmospheric condition, it is its own container, absolved from any mitigating context. Small wonder that this unpredictable creature, mysterious as breath or wind, symbolic of ineffable and numinous movement, all the more uncanny because it is tangible, captures people's imagination. One half-expects it to remain concealed, out of sight, like a penis or thought itself.

The snake's sinuous motion also suggests the tongue, one of the baby's most important cognitive instruments and weapons. The tongue is slippery and elusive, flexible and extendable, capable of fluid modulations of softness and hardness. It is darkly anchored, its source imperceptibly disappears into bodily depths; it links head and body. It lightly darts, and flattens or narrows to a point. It is ever ready to like or dislike what it meets. Through its capacity to taste, it conveys an elemental yes or no with authoritative immediacy, a vestigial root of evaluative mind. It presents itself as a model for flexible discernment in contrast to the unyielding (and unfeeling) rigidity and bite of teeth. The sense of self that takes the experience of the tongue as its model is likely to be receptive and searching in ways that link both head–body and self–other. In contrast with anal rigidity, it integrates libidinal strivings in a spontaneously object-seeking way, at once erotic, tender, and tempting.

I have omitted anality in this overview of the snake as expressive symbol of psychic capacities. It is the anal snake that, above all, organizes demonic mental structures, and it is to this symbol we now turn.

Anal Mind and the Hooped Snake

No body area is a more highly invested pivotal point for associations than the anus, especially in pathology. Common language verifies that oral and genital meanings tend to find symbolic expression more easily through anal representations than through each other (e.g., in the implication of the curses "Go fuck yourself" and "Up yours!"). The various facets of anality appear to play the most extensive role in knitting the body together in the realm of meaning; there are, for example, such well-known psychic equations as tongue-nipple-feces-penis-baby, face-breast-buttocks, teeth-feces-penis, breast-buttocks-testicles, and mouth-anus-vagina.

The anal area lends itself to organizing more undifferentiated psychic processes than do either the oral or the genital structures, not only because the anus per se establishes no distinction between the sexes (Ehrenzweig 1967; Eigen 1977, 1979c) but also because anal identifications permit greater ambiguity than either oral or genital models with reference to self–other differentiation in general. For example, oral fusion tends to self-destruct with the inevitable discovery of the separateness of the breast. Anality, which produces, expels, and reproduces its own product with or without an object, always lacks such clarity, hence its linkage to basic doubt, repetition, and obsessive strivings. The subject must tolerate the fundamental ambiguity that pervades anality and find creative ways of making use of the associated identity feelings.

The quandaries are many for the growing ego. Are feces part of the body self? How does one coordinate their initial overvaluation with subsequent repudiation? Where do they come from? How? They invade the passive subject from inside, yet the active subject has some say over their passage. At times it is impossible to know whether the anus is expelling or taking in, inasmuch as shitting can feel like sucking (the yogi recommends breathing from one's asshole). The baby fluidly displaces top–bottom and in–out (Eigen 1974, Meltzer 1973). Demonic inclinations take advantage of this potential for confusion.

In deep pathology, anality tends to assimilate orality and genitality rather than the reverse, although their influence is reciprocal. Anal images tend to function as signs of spoiling, staining, toxicity, the miasma of evil itself. When Weil (1958) tried to express features of the repressed bad self, which he theoretically located in early oral mirroring, he spontaneously used anal language (a "fecal" or "garbage" self). I have described patients immersed in primitive processes who, when exhibiting ravenous oral traits, tend to view their bodies in sewer or toilet terms (Eigen 1977, 1981a). The food becomes spoiled as fast as it can be consumed. The fecalization of oral and genital aspects of the self-image has been described by many psychoanalytic authors (e.g., Chasseguet-Smirgel 1974, Meltzer 1973, for recent examples).

Anal signifiers have long been favorite tropes of the demonic. The psychophysical experiences of anality easily give rise to expressions that reflect demonized ego operations. Sweet, innocent buttocks present themselves as virtually the softest and least defensible part of the human body, an ideal camouflage for hidden, filthy operations. The sphincters operate hidden from view under the auspices of an invisible, controlling mind. (The brain–asshole connection is reflected in many common expressions, e.g., being a "smart-ass," a trait long associated with snake and devil.) Some of these features were reflected in the following dream:

> A woman sits next to the subject at a bar, then gets up to leave. As she walks away her whole head and body appear merely to be buttocks and legs. The buttocks have a face and the eyes give the subject a startling, knowing wink on the way out. In this instance the subject was becoming aware of his anal omniscience.

Coupled with this innocuous facade and hidden control is potential explosiveness. One cannot sit on life (the throne) indefinitely. The phallic power of planes and bombs or missiles is symbolized by anal meanings, such as flying shits ready to lay waste to pieces of populations. Similarly, the nipple–phallic aspect of weaponry ("I'll fill you full of lead") implicitly refers to a fecal feed, unmistakably clear in its result, a person "wasted." A pan-fecalization of values underlies the megalomanic superiority demonstrated through weaponry.

The ancient image of the hooped snake that eats its tail, the symbol of eternity in time, succinctly summarizes the structure of anal pathology that concerns us here. The coiled body suggests the controlling sphincters (mind over matter within matter). The mouth–tail contact suggests tendencies toward rapacious oral–anal fusion, while at the same time the eyes remain transcendent, overlooking. This image neatly expresses the typical pathological structure of our times: the body ego's wish for fusion coupled with a detached, impersonal mental ego, both in some sense tyrannical. The once flowing and flexible tongue–mind (the positive snake) has become relentless, rigid, and diffuse, a nooselike circle tightening toward explosion or, worse, a spiraling adaptation downward and final leveling-off in vindication of a cynical self. The hole in this image is the tightening sphincters, emblem of spoiling and decay rather than of true engendering.

In accord with an ancient tradition, Jungians see in the hooped snake a mandala, a symbol of wholeness. It should be noted, however, that the mandala as psychic integrator is a product of stationary rather than nomadic people, a relatively late symbol in the human adventure. The Age of the Circle arose with the spread of mother goddess figures; with the centrality of Mother Earth fertility dramas, the barnyard, the farm, and, finally, the city-state.

The circle was more than womb. It announced the birth of geometric thinking and its decisive epiphany: humanity's eventual awareness of mind as such. Geometry pervaded life from handcraft to heavenly bodies and the very form of the earth one walked on. The Age of the Circle (and its partner, the cross) portended the growing geometrization of life that people are at present beginning to defy. The Industrial Age is perhaps its most recent epiphany, although one that seems bent on spoiling the processes that produced it. What may have begun as an age of the womb appears to be culminating in a journey through the asshole, a possibility encoded in the encircled serpent at the outset. In this regard, a patient once dreamt of an encircled snake trying to disappear headfirst up its own anus.

The contagion of murder and addiction in the consciousness of our times may well reflect the breakdown of the protective circle as a container for life. Addiction dissolves and murder explodes the circle, the noose. One hopes the path is being cleared for fresh visions, but such optimism is unwarranted until the devil's new face is seen clearly. This will be attempted in the final section.

Anality, Addiction, Murder

The life-styles of addicts and killers tend to be heavily tinged with excretory values: One slang term for heroin is *shit*. The subject injects shit and has shit ecstasies. The languages of murder and addiction share many common terms; for example; one is *blown away* or *wasted*. Although oral and phallic references play important roles, fascination with the Big Bang largely gains its power though symbolic association with anal explosiveness. The drugged subject does not exhibit the baby's or the lover's hungry oral–genital activity. He or she often sits alone passively waiting for the next rush, a spreading internal mushroom, his or her head a sort of bottom on top.

The addict hopes to clean out and finally be rid of what is clogging his or her soul of the inner filth and poison, but he or she does this by taking in more of the same, by transforming himself or herself into an eternal toilet. Over and over again the addict is *wasted, cleaned* or *wiped out, blown away*. She or he is endlessly in need of shit–mind orgasms: orgasms that can never be quite maintained; that she or he drops down under, more or less below, perhaps just missing; that often are in danger of inertly dying out. The right feeling is *almost* always there, at the brink. It finally comes, and the subject shits herself or himself out through it again, flying, coasting, climbing, falling.

One drug-addicted patient, at a particular turning point in her therapy, dreamt that she returned to her childhood home and found her mother's room filled with devil snakes. One offered her dope. The patient coolly thought that if she became drugged they surely would get her. On the other hand, if she were drugged she might not care. She screamed and woke in terror, more resolved than ever to break through the osmotic and poisonous atmosphere she lived in.

Her scream was one of terror but also outrage, filled with a baby's explosive force that broke the spell. In this case the devil worked through promises of parasitic stupor. He counted on the subject's vegetative need of the perverse ecstasies of psychic collapse. It was a need with early roots. This patient had experienced night terrors since early childhood but had not screamed even in her dreams. She handled her dread by becoming as still as possible, hoping the danger would pass over her if she stopped breathing. For her, an all-out nightmare was a real achievement. A moment's spontaneous explosiveness made the menace of her condition more dystonic.

In a somewhat related fashion, killers are often victims in their dreams. In one instance, a woman prisoner who showed no remorse over killing a friend's daughter was menaced in repetitive dreams by a man with a snake's head that was covered with snakes. As time went on this woman's therapist, who later discussed the case with me, appeared in the patient's dream as a possible helper.

The therapist naturally saw her own appearance in the patient's dream as a sign of progress. The tough, disdainful behavior of the patient continued as usual, however. She bitterly maintained that she would have "gotten off" if she had money or position, and the therapist inwardly agreed. The prisoner had had a hellish life and was hardened. The well-meaning therapist felt it was important to give this woman a taste of goodness, which surely would win out in time. She felt these nightmares tried to communicate unconscious guilt the patient could not openly acknowledge and was disappointed when no tangible change in the patient resulted and their relationship deteriorated. The therapist became inwardly remote and the patient even cooler. The therapist ceased to appear in the patient's nightmare.

I recommended to the therapist-supervisee that, the next time the patient reported her nightmare, she should say, "Your nightmare is the smartest thing about you. Without it you'd be in no pain at all." This particular suggestion was meant less for the patient than for the therapist. The patient was light years away from guilt, yet the therapist needed to whitewash this fact. The most pain the prisoner allowed herself was in nightmares, where the devil she played during the day menaced her. She was caught in a primitive fear-hate drama. She felt justified in attacking others because she basically felt under attack. In her dream she was the innocent victim, and the evil snake-man among other things carried her split-off omniscience-omnipotence, a potentially explosive force controlled by a mixture of calculation and indifference. Rather than stir up this explosiveness, the therapist bit on her own frustration and helplessness and played for time, vaguely hoping the counteromnipotence of goodness would see her through. The Medusa motif in the prisoner's dream had not escaped another student who heard this case; he remarked that perhaps therapist and patient alike were throwing snakes at each other. The reorientation this view provided helped the therapist to face the real suffering her struggle with the patient must cause her, so that she could be less afraid of facing the suffering the therapy must induce in the patient as well.

In another case, a battered wife escaped sentence for murdering her husband and entered into another relationship that seemed destined for murder. Again she was abused and resented it, but helplessly went along. Her new husband slept with a gun under his pillow, and the patient lay awake nights fearing for her life. She confessed thoughts of killing him with it when she was at last driven far enough. The therapist began to suspect that, in part, therapy was being used as a cover. The dismal picture the patient painted evoked exasperation and sympathy even for murder. Her accounts of her husband's stupidity and violence were enraging. The therapist eventually recoiled at beginning to believe, with the patient, that murder was the only plausible solution and sought supervisory help.

When in supervision this therapist began to study the merger induced by the patient, the therapy almost broke up. The patient became more disorganized and tended to miss sessions. I suggested that at their next appointment the therapist tell the patient her husband was dying to be murdered by her. This remark interested the patient. I then suggested that this woman be told that she was even more her husband's slave than she knew, that in fact he was exercising mind control in inducing her need to kill him. The idea of being directed by a demonic intelligence appealed to as well as annoyed her. She had been fascinated by the Charles Manson case and now revealed her secret longing to be "one of his girls." In a further series of fantasies, however, she pictured Manson as her dog, vicious to others but adoring with her. She saw her husband, too, as a big lapdog who could not live without her. The control aspect suddenly seemed less important than the sticky feeling between them. The idea of violence now arose to break through her stickiness. Her wish to murder now felt like a healthy urge to break through the morass of addictive clinging. It provided her with a breath of fresh air until the swamp reclaimed her. Her sense of inner justification tyrannically drove her.

In this case a second murder was actually averted by systematic pinpointing of the collusive omniscience that glued two bully-victims together. The patient felt justified for choosing the wrong man, since the choice gave her an opportunity to gratify her demonic killer self with impunity. The scenario to be played out involved a bad-child self (the husband) who at last compels a beating (murder) given by a righteous parent self (the patient) in the form of a well-calculated but real baby fit. The grown-up baby-bully creates the conditions for his undoing, while his obliging baby–parent partner marvels at her amazing power and in relieved, self-startled fear seeks a new day.

A close connection between murder and merger appears to have existed from time immemorial. The founding (and oldest) religion may well have been a religion of murder in which a mystical tie between hunter and prey played the leading role. Murder, like addiction, points to an elemental linking capacity, a complex interweaving of subject and object reduced and debased. Often enough the victim is a proxy for the killer's once wretchedly vulnerable baby self. The act of killing wipes out or voids an externalized sign of the killer's own potential subjugation. Here murder is a grotesque declaration of dependency: the victim signals the condition of traumatic servitude as such. The killer takes pride in not being cowed by what is clinging in human nature. Nevertheless, victimhood remains a magnetizing fact, even if momentarily obscured by the killer's fraudulent superiority maintained by brute acts of power.

In biblical psychology, primal murder grows out of invidious comparisons. Indeed, envy played a major role in the Fall. Murder cancels covetous differences and inequalities. The killer heightens and affirms his or her uniqueness in the face of all, but at the expense of obliterating if not controlling life, of leveling otherness. For moments at least, the subject feels on top of everything, with nothing truly unknown. Murder simplifies. The manifest corpse prematurely ends uncertainty; if only death would not slip away so quickly. For the moment time stands still. Even fear heightens a killer's grip on survival and adds point, if not direction, to the heightened vigilance. Nevertheless, the very areas of numbness necessary to make this operation work tend in the end to blind the killer to the true meaning of his or her situation, at times with dire consequences.

Whereas the murderer exterminates her or his helplessness through the victim, the drug addict mimics the primal rape of her or his passivity within her or his own person. He or she tries to achieve a hallucinatory supremacy over sensed helplessness. The need to cling may go deeper than hate, although he or she feels very alone in the clinging. Addiction draws upon and perverts an elemental area of adhesiveness in the human self. The subject's addiction to his or her own clinging (to drugs) masks an irresolution in the face of dependency: the addict can bring herself or himself neither to cultivate nor to annihilate what is innately most sensitive. His or her stupors are also epiphanies, a way to milk and glorify dependency without genuinely evolving with or through it. The addict preserves a sector of ideal experience that he or she values above all humanity, and so remains tender yet fanatically inhuman. Heightened awareness is a way of vanishing, of dulling oneself by leaving pain behind. If performing an act of murder, he (she) is not really there in the killing; someone on "automatic pilot" is. As killer he or she is a shadow subject, thinking only of slipping away to drug land, where victims continually reproduce themselves until they finally leave themselves behind.

Addiction does not really cancel dependency as murder seeks to do. The addict's parasitic world is a kind of perverted apotheosis of dependency, a grim and narrowly shifting galaxy of interlocking fecal devil gods from pushers to police. "C'lom Fliday" (Burroughs 1959) epitomizes the addict's date with absence. Clinging comes to take on meaning for its own sake (abjectness is a basic value), whereas in murder it becomes an object of hate as a means of establishing the self's power.

Addiction and murder cannot rigorously be tied to a wish for suicide, although there may be such a relationship. In suicide the subject is pulled apart by contrary desires to be wholly separate *and* wholly fused, but gives up on both. The subject vengefully repudiates the tension he or she foresees or inertly collapses. In both addiction and murder the subject's interest in both separateness and union still sustains the person. The best killers are experts in manipulating the isolated egoistic needs and the merger needs of others. Addicts tend to content themselves with making a fetish of solitude, a seemingly impenetrable solitude punctuated by the most bizarre stimulus blitzkreigs. Here extreme states are not integrated but nonetheless offer a remarkable sense of achieving the impossible, a state in which suicide becomes superfluous. A murderer is more apt than an addict to commit suicide because the murderer's trade is bodies to begin with: she or he values materialistic signs of affection or power. The addict is more apt to aim after an inner experience rather than material good as such. He or she is happy enough when material reality does not interfere. The murderer's body is more important than is the addict's, and so would be more subject to wrath if it finally failed.

Of course the addict (like the murderer) may miscalculate in his or her omniscience and self-destruct. Miscalculation from a position of omniscience: it is an image that haunts our age on a grand scale.

HISTORICAL OVERVIEW: THE AGE OF THE BABY

Violence appears always to have been a basic part of human life, sacred and secular. The earliest and most enduring religion appears to be a religion of the hunt. Magical ties were cultivated between hunter and prey. The kind of "sensing" that connects subject and target must have played a prominent role in stalking. The luminous testimony of paleolithic cave drawings bears witness to a mysticism of the hunt antedating by far the more settled mandala orientation to come (Campbell 1969).

As mentioned previously, the Age of the Circle developed with the increasing importance of the farm, barnyard, and hieratic city-state. It began about 14,000 years ago, which from then to the present amounts to roughly 0.008 percent of humanity's time on earth. The neolithic town's form was mandalic, with walled periphery and center tower. The macrocosms and microcosms, the perfect heaven and humanity's life on earth, were believed to be governed by arithmetic and, finally, geometric principles. The crowded eidetic images of the cave gave way to the geometric articulation of forms, space, and music.

With the increased division of labor among social groupings, the mandala emerged as an organizing image for maintenance of self-cohesion in the face of the tensions of a more differentiated social (and self) structure involved (Campbell 1969). With the rise of priestly castes the cult of the sacred victim continued with the sacrifice of scapegoats, of which Christ, the victim to end the victimhood of all humanity, is a most recent epiphany. There is reason to think the idea of demons prospered in settled communities.

A multitude of demons seem to have preceded the more unified notion of *the* devil, a fairly late consolidation of evil intentionality. It is not clear that the devil conceptualized by moderns can be simply derived from earlier demons, although, once conceived, the monolithic image draws to itself and reorganizes many diverse aspects of potentially malevolent consciousness. The idea of the devil also makes use of meanings drawn from activities (the military, juridical, or natural sense of *adversary* and *hindrance*) that in themselves were not always explicitly linked with demons (Kluger 1967).

Once present, the devil is an irritant. He will not let human beings rest easily in their hierarchies. Like desire and conscience, he creates havoc, overturns, goads, pricks, tempts, and torments. With him is associated the experience of hell itself, of pure spiritual madness. As time goes on, as though to discredit him, his trademark becomes increasingly excremental in humanity's wish that he be easily eliminated. He turns the tables, however, and makes the most of the powers of corruption, to settle in humanity's "anal mind," where he may be found today, fecalizing existence.

Tausk's "influencing machine" (1919) offers a vivid summary of basic mental and physical self-structures involved in a deteriorated materialism. In this paranoid fantasy, the psychotic patient feels that her or his mind is being taken over and her or his behavior influenced by a distant machine. Tausk understood this delusion as a projective expression of a mechanized body self. For Tausk the machine is a symbolic petrifaction of the sexually alive body, an attempt to freeze or deanimate the threat of feeling, of life itself.

Tausk's understanding of the transmitting machine as an effigy of the live body (the body rendered anesthetic via projective identification) incompletely captures the demonized dualism implicit in this delusion. The penetrability of the subject by an alien mind is also at stake: thought itself is taken as an invasive, alien power emanating from a foreign, controlling mind. The body is put out of play, and a megalomanic mental power holds sway. Space and physical boundaries become meaningless. Thoughts can be anywhere and everywhere, anytime and all the time. The patient's greatest fears seem to be focused not merely on a now reduced and mechanized body (the latter is almost comforting), but on the electrifyingly impalpable threat of invisible mental power as such. In structural terms, a devitalized or mechanized body self and perverse schizoid mental self form parts of a complex dissociative system that is compulsively lived out in a ruthless proliferation of ways.

The tormenting self-hate that is rigidly structured by the influencing machine is given raw and naked form in Lautréamont's *Maldoror* (1868), signaling the explosions that were to wrack the modern age. Lautréamont's art reads like the debris of an ongoing catastrophe. His writing itself becomes a catastrophic act, a scream beyond all apparent content. His work places all structures in jeopardy. His intent seemed to be to use what structures his makeup forced on him to blow up the category of structure itself. Maldoror is nothing less than a psychic nuclear explosion, the effects of which we are still feeling today.

The dominant attitude and feeling in *Maldoror* is searing contempt and uncompromising self-hatred, the tormenting self-hatred that has increasingly pervaded modern humanity. Maldoror, the evil one, stalks his victim, Mervyn, a dreamy adolescent who is the son of a retired English captain and feels himself to be an imprisoned member of a typical literal-minded, complacent family, a ward of the materialistic age. Through the machinations of his hunt, Maldoror objectifies the perverse will at the core of a blindly destructive materialism (the voice of the influencing machine). The bizarre psychic transformations expressed scene after scene are testimony to the "omnipresence of the grotesque" (Nelson 1970) soon to stain our age. In current psychoanalytic language, Maldoror is an embodiment of Bion's-K, an annihilating intentionality aimed at the felt truth about oneself, a cynical and diabolic consciousness set against the genuine possibility of experiencing saving meaning.

The language and style of Lautréamont's *Maldoror* combine the bitterness and intensity that mark so many phenomena of our day. Its images compose a veritable catalogue of soul murder with the warped accuracy of schizophrenia. To a significant extent, however, its wastelands, carcasses, marauders, and crippled victims of all sorts gravitate around an underlying image of the baby: mangled, ruthless, tender. A new awareness of babyhood grew in the Western world, the more so as it spoke of its own detumescence.

To be sure, the divine child had long been part of religious history, but not before these past 2,000 years did the idea of God born as a human baby so possess the imagination of a high civilization. With the rise of the bourgeoisie the divine child was secularized. A new sense of what family life might be formalized the idea that children were full-fledged human beings in their own right, a realization that was to seize the human spirit in startling ways. The romantics both idealized and demonized infantile experience, degenerating it at times to rank sentimentality and gothic horror. Above all they associated baby life with creativity. It was finally through Sigmund Freud that this interest organized itself into a passionate, abiding quest for knowledge.

The infantile psyche was now seen as important enough to become an object of systematic research and reflection. As mentioned earlier, for the first time in human history grown people could spend the better part of their creative lives thinking about babies. Baby mind was thematized as crucial for understanding the roots and possibility of personal identity. For Freud "His Majesty the baby" and "His Majesty the ego" became virtually synonymous.

This notion is two-directional. If babies could be seen as full-fledged persons, adults could be seen as big babies. At bottom the human race must have always known this. Now this truth crystallized with a vengeance. From this viewpoint medieval kings could seem like babies on the potty. Egoistic strivings in general were now viewed (in part) as infantile. The shift from Hobbes to Freud involved the baby as major signifier for what were once viewed as merely animal strivings (the human being as brute). *Maldoror* expressed the ghastly outcry of mangled baby hopes. It was perhaps above all something childlike in Mervyn that most attracted Maldoror. (Did Maldoror somehow hope to be repaired by the child he spoiled?) The "bourgeois interior" (Lukacs 1970) was not all negative. Its "coziness" was, whatever else, also meant to support personal tenderness, and no amount of debunking could still Maldoror's parasitic, envious shock that a child's heart (which Nietzsche linked with faith) might possibly exist.

The centrality of the human child as a psychic organizing image has long-range consequences for the way human beings must come to feel about themselves. Perhaps it carries experiential possibilities for at last breaking through the tyranny of the circle (together with its partner, the cross) and the beast. Freud's view of the body ego (his baby mind) has many similarities to the animal image that dominated humanity's view of its impulse life since antiquity. Baby consciousness is not simply animal consciousness. For example, the advent of the human smile in response to a face (or face representation) by roughly two months of age heralds an awareness of self and other, the universe "I'ing" itself (Eigen 1980a,b, 1981a,b, Elkin 1972, Spitz 1965). This radiantly expressive and coherent smile at the heart of human consciousness remains the felt criterion for the rightness or wrongness of future emotional experiences. Over and over, like Job, it comes through the struggles self-feeling must suffer.

This nuclear joy kernel, I believe, is inexhaustible, but so, it seems, are suffering, terror, and rage. Human consciousness amplifies and transforms desire through boundless echoes. As life feeds on life, human imagination, in turn, feeds endlessly on its own products. A hairbreadth separates breathtaking beauty from ineradicable horror. Only human consciousness, from infancy to death, is capable of magnifying hunger by megalomania, the price of self-feeling. Today this giant baby requires more and more magnification of self and life in order for anything to be seen or felt at all; His Majesty the ego in a nursery world is ever ballooning.

A baby God. Does the Old Testament God look like a father to us now? Doesn't he seem more a giant baby? His demands, fits, ruthless and loving ways: how much of our God-image now seems like a baby in disguise? What about that perennial troublemaker, the devil? Everyday language and notions glibly link him with the baby, that innocent, cute, clever little devil; that greedily possessive and ravenous spoiler too smart (and dumb) for his or her own good. In a certain key this awareness provides a waking nightmare. The clean ruthlessness of baby appetite, deformed by a sense of injury and wisened by calculation, now has in its hands the toys of modern technology. If God once revealed himself as a baby, it did not take the devil long to join him.

Freud (1957) saw this when, in 1914, he traced the displacement of ideal feelings from our own self to parents and on to other objects throughout a lifetime. The implication is that the baby ego magnifies itself and that self-worship lurks behind all future idolatry. The baby ego as a magnifying machine may or may not be a statement of possible fact, but it is an important vision: big balloon babies everywhere. In 1917, Freud (1955) explicitly equated primordial baby mind with Schopenhauer's *will,* thus underlining the intensity of this self's basic striving.

It is a boomerang striving. The driving force of childhood is to become big and to be one's own boss, like grown-ups are, only to discover the truth about adult life and to wish to be small again (Freud 1959). To be small, however, may be to be very big indeed—sometimes. In an earlier paper (Eigen 1979d) I argued that a baby may think she or he can do many things that in fact she or he cannot; for example, a baby very early may think he or she can talk and be surprised to find he or she cannot talk. It may be something of a blow to realize that long and difficult learning is necessary in every area of life. It takes time to discover that one must be where one's body is or to realize the significance of size differences in the dramas of personal power. Even so, one may follow one's heart's whim as though one's body were a feather and will struggle to push past and through its awkwardness into the clearing. A baby may feel like a bull in a china shop, not simply because of actual destructive wishes but also in light of the damage (to oneself and outside objects) the discordance between one's will and one's abilities inevitably causes.

The shock of adult life is that in some ways one grows smaller than one was as a baby. At one time feelings of expansiveness helped one's body grow bigger. One *lived* a boundless consciousness, for good and ill. If we make use of Freud's thinking on narcissism, we may suppose that some of the bigness the infant ascribes to the merely physical giants around him or her was once also his or her own soul-feeling. It is a feeling of bigness that never leaves one, but also may be displaced into one's own future (ambition) or into fantasies of success for one's progeny. In terms of the incessant magnifications and diminutions one's self-feeling undergoes, one is happy when one feels just the right size (which may vary). Adults often feel too big *and* too small and must keep negotiating with these shifting, contrary pulls.

On a recent panel I spoke about our Age of the Big Baby. A colleague spontaneously responded with an apotheosis of the "ego's executive function" as the nub of what separates the baby from the grown-up. Was he content to picture a human being as a sort of demonic baby with a steering wheel tacked on, a potential explosive trying desperately to learn how to push and pull the right levers to avoid going off, a kind of computer working out a calculus of advantages? I really do not think so. Yet the formal view he developed did not leave much room for pondering how the *intrinsic quality* of a subject's experiencing could be engaged. I was left picturing an ego sector (selecting, inhibiting, evaluating) as a sort of bureaucrat or engineer or traffic manager in diapers, bemused and benumbed at finding himself or herself in such a position of power, wondering what to do next, and finding something. I turned my baby-oriented eye toward my colleague and saw a two- or three-year-old insisting, "I'm a big boy. I'm not a baby." I suppose to him I must have seemed like King Kong tearing at the bars of his playpen.

On my way to this very panel, I heard the radio broadcast news of savage marauders invading the subway while other lone hunters killed two old women. Adolescent hoods took on names of warriors while their immediate betters scrawled graffiti — cave drawings — on walls and benches and roads and subways. By and large these drawings are antimandalic. To be sure, the tight leer of the Aryan cross emerges like a sick sun, but only from time to time. It comes and goes through a vast tangle of scribblings that are closer to the waves and pulse of primordial perception, cartoon-style. The warrior of Castaneda (1972, Nelson 1976), too, breaks through geometric barriers to another kind of space, but he hopes also to discover the kind of consciousness that can work with it.

The circle, the sitting Buddha, and Christ on the cross: these are images of the dynamics of immobility, echoes in the prayer by a modern poet, "Teach us to be still." He might have said, "Teach us to move truly." The recent movement therapies will not likely swamp the couch, but do aim at finding a place for body wisdom. They may constitute, too, attempts to find exercises to exorcise the introjected demonic models of contemporary culture. To a certain extent they find a respected place for a culture of baby (and hunter) movements: the unforeseen, erratic, rapidly shifting, immediately sensing. Our most profound organizing images have been oriented toward stillness and have, by and large, left movement to its own devices, or worse, tried to channel it through models (e.g., the Nazi goosestep, typical of the narrowing aspect of mandala organization) that must finally be deforming.

It was roughly some 2,600 years ago that the idea of an immortal consciousness distinct from the animal body began to grow up in virtually all parts of the then civilized world. It was an idea linked with the experience of geometric thinking, wherein perfect, changeless, nonmaterial, necessary principles could be conceived (cf. Chapter 1). Humanity's body sense has suffered under the impact of thousands of years of geometric ideals (which governed forms of political power as well). In our times more than ever, the *human* body is in jeopardy. In the end this body paid the price for the admired Greek harmony of body and mind, a harmony whereby the body was molded to resemble a pure form but an ideal no animate body could live up to. It was only a matter of time before the logic of its limitations would catch up with it. The human is so devaluated today that the body is often treated as a fecalized machine or mechanized shit. Human beings deeply need an awareness of the dignity of movement in its own right. This applies in an important sense to mental movement as well.

After some 7,000 years of high civilization, a set of tracks leads back to the baby. Through Saint Matthew an image of becoming like a child in order to find heaven (he might also have said hell) became a steadfast part of Western consciousness. With the rise of the bourgeoisie, the cult of the child was secularized and correlated with a new sense of self-feeling. It is no accident that such words as *self-love, self-esteem,* and *self-confidence* arose in their modern sense in the same era that came to see adults reaching out to children — as never before — for their own personal deepening (indeed, salvation). Child and self: in modern consciousness these two realities are profoundly linked. Whatever we now find wrong or limited in Freud's picture of human beings, his was the decisive voice in bringing into relief this rising sense of a ubiquitous, timeless child in the dramas of time.

Today the Freudian baby is only one of a growing number of models of what early mind is like. Images of baby life proliferate. To one acquainted with these explorations and controversies, it sometimes seems as if the medieval disputes concerning the nature of God and spiritual life have turned into attempts to reconstitute the earliest paradigm of self and other. Indeed (and this might have horrified Freud), a bridge between the secular and the divine is being made by a growing number of workers (Eigen 1979c, 1980a, 1981a,b, 1982, Elkin 1972, Loewald 1980) by means of visions of the baby's possible experience. This is a new, breathtaking frontier of the human imagination (which, incidentally, reflectively reworks the age-old folklore belief in the baby's contact with the divine and demonic, albeit in ways scarcely conceivable before the present).

Perhaps one of the most astonishing results of the growing mythology of infantile experience is the apparent success many therapists now have in treating mental conditions that once seemed virtually intractable, a success made possible precisely by engaging aspects of the patient as if they were parts of an infant self (Balint 1968, Bion 1977, Ferenczi 1955, Milner 1969, Searles 1965). I use the term *myth* in a constructive sense, as an organizing dynamism capable of giving life meaning. The cases reported here were approached as if the therapist were in fact working with an infant soul. Immediately felt reverberations, such as those that often characterize mother–baby experience, were imaginatively reworked into therapeutic interventions. The key meditation by the therapist at every juncture was: "What kind of baby is here now? What is the baby doing now, and now, and now?" The therapist always asked: "What image or reconstruction of the baby fits this moment most effectively? What kind of baby must be envisioned so that the complex feelings and behavior now arising can be most usefully understood?" This sort of thinking constituted the inner methodology that made therapeutic contact work, often with personality areas and patients who at earlier times might have been thought unreachable (Eigen 1977, Fries, Nelson, and Woolf 1980, McDougall 1978).

Nevertheless, the investigations described earlier (pp. 6–20; 26–32) did stress certain patterns that recur when working with aspects of the baby self. These include body-ego tendencies toward fusion and explosiveness coupled with mental-ego tendencies toward omniscience, isolation, or more bridled forms of megalomania masked in the will to mastery and lived out in what might appear to be more or less successful adaptations. The so-called realistic ego often turns out to be quite psychopathic and tainted and tends to circumvent or ignore intimations that the psychic integrity of the whole self is being compromised. (Reasons are always found to justify this, given the facts of life.)

The baby self that emerges often appears to be in part poisoned and debased or inertly engaged: a sick and undeveloped baby. To a frightening extent this feeling is expressed through an unconscious identification of self and world with fecal values. An anal model of mind in general is perversely adopted, with no way of securely integrating the positive and enriching aspects of anality. (Freud, using the language of the body, dramatically spotlighted this predicament for Western culture, namely, the great war between anus and vagina and between anus and penis, and the great problem of establishing a psychosocial primacy of the penis–vagina combination, symbol of fecundity.)

The preceding discussion also stressed the snake as a key organizing image for complex mental structures that gravitate toward anal transpositions (and have done so ever since the birth of the mandala person, from the Neolithic on!). The containing aspect of the snake has become more suffocating with time, whereas its self-assertive aspect, increasingly cut loose from any mitigating context, seems bent on tyrannical acquisitiveness and murderous fraud. Today the snake is bursting its own bounds even as it strives to manipulate them. The demonized ego qualities that reflect these menacing acrobatics are rampant.

Systematic corruption begins very early in life, and repair to merely "executive" functions may do little to alter more profoundly misshapen areas of self-feeling (cf. Chapter 3). The individual may sense demonic operations that induce or take advantage of areas of psychic collapse but be unable to withstand or even pay attention to them for long. He or she may need training in learning to recognize and absorb the shock of these transactions and to own a participatory role in their shifts of meaning.

As therapy progresses, many patients describe images of a baby self ever coming into being. The therapist experiences living in an atmosphere of creative activity wherein he or she witnesses and aids in the incessant reconstitution of the sense of self and other. In my view it is this generative awareness that authenticates the feeling of wholeness and must certainly be regarded as the most creative encounter of humankind. The image of a baby self helps guide our attention to a dimension of experiencing that potentially undercuts and transcends one's demons, one's everyday pathology. In imaginative vision, at least, one can experience oneself as starting afresh over and over again.

The relationship between self and history is necessarily "circular" or interwoven. Historical processes are manifest only through the consciousness of individuals. There is no history outside the self-feeling of persons, no history without self, no self without history. Demonized ego structures found in individuals reflect the texture of the times (at least of some cultural subsystem) and make their own, however circumscribed, historical input.

REFERENCES

Balint, M. (1968). *The Basic Fault.* London: Tavistock.

Bion, W. R. (1977). *Seven Servants.* New York: Jason Aronson.

Burroughs, W. (1959). *Naked Lunch.* New York: Grove.

Campbell, J. (1969). *The Flight of the Wild Gander.* New York: Viking.

Castaneda, C. (1972). *Journey to Ixtlan.* New York: Simon & Schuster.

Chasseguet-Smirgel, J. (1974). Perversion, idealization and sublimation. *International Journal of Psycho-Analysis* 55:349–357.

Ehrenzweig, A. (1967). *The Hidden Order of Art.* Los Angeles: University of California Press.

Eigen, M. (1974). On pre-oedipal castration anxiety. *International Review of Psycho-Analysis* 1:489–498.

———— (1975–1976). The differentiation of an androgynous imago. *Psychoanalytic Review* 62:601–613.

———— (1977). On working with "unwanted" patients. *International Journal of Psycho-Analysis* 58:109–121.

———— (1979a). Female sexual responsiveness and the therapist's feelings. *Psychoanalytic Review* 66:3–8.

———— (1979b). Common failings in analysis and therapy. *Psychotherapy: Theory, Research and Practice* 16:246–251.

———— (1979c). Ideal images, creativity and the Freudian drama. *Psychocultural Review* 3:289–298.

———— (1979d). On the defensive use of mastery. *American Journal of Psychoanalysis* 39:279–282.

———— (1980a). Instinctual fantasy and ideal images. *Contemporary Psychoanalysis* 16:119–137.

———— (1980b). Expression and meaning: a case study. In *Expressive Therapy,* ed. A. Robbins, pp. 291–312. New York: Human Sciences.

———— (1981a). On the significance of the face. *Psychoanalytic Review* 67:427–441.

———— (1981b). The area of faith in Winnicott, Lacan and Bion. *International Journal of Psycho-Analysis* 62:413–433.

———— (1982). Creativity, instinctual fantasy and ideal images. *Psychoanalytic Review* 69:317–339.

Elkin, H. (1972). On selfhood and the development of ego structures in infancy. *Psychoanalytic Review* 59:389–416.

Ferenczi, S. (1955). *Final Contributions*. London: Hogarth Press.

Freud, S. (1955). A difficulty in the path of psycho-analysis. *Standard Edition* 17:135–144, 1917.

——— (1957). On narcissism: an introduction. *Standard Edition* 14:73–113, 1914.

——— (1959). Creative writers and day-dreaming. *Standard Edition* 9:142–156, 1908.

Fries, M. E., Nelson, M. C., and Woolf, P. J. (1980). Developmental and etiological factors in the treatment of character disorders with archaic ego function. *Psychoanalytic Review* 67:337–352.

Khan, M. (1979). *Alienation in Perversions*. New York: International Universities Press.

Kluger, R. S. (1967). *Satan in the Old Testament*. Evanston, IL: Northwestern University Press.

Lautréamont, le Comte de [Isadore Ducasse]. (1978). *Maldoror*. New York: Penguin, 1868.

Loewald, H. (1980). *Papers in Psychoanalysis*. New Haven, CT: Yale University Press.

Lukacs, J. (1970). *The Passing of the Modern Age*. New York: Harper & Row.

McDougall, J. (1978). Primitive communication and the use of countertransference. *Contemporary Psychoanalysis* 14:173–209.

Meltzer, D. (1973). *Sexual States of Mind*. Perthshire, Scotland: Clunie.

Milner, M. (1969). *The Hands of the Living God*. New York: International Universities Press.

Nelson, B. (1970). The omnipresence of the grotesque. *Psychoanalytic Review* 57:506–518.

Nelson, M. C. (1976). Paths of power: Psychoanalysis and sorcery. *Psychoanalytic Review* 63:333–360.

Searles, H. (1965). *Collected Papers on Schizophrenia and Related Subjects*. New York: International Universities Press.

Segal, H. (1978). On symbolism. *International Journal of Psycho-Analysis* 59:315–319.

Spitz, R. (1965). *The First Year of Life: A Psychoanalytic Study of Normal and Deviant Object Relations*. New York: International Universities Press.

Tausk, V. (1919). On the origin of the "influencing machine." *Psychoanalytic Quarterly* 2:519–556.

Weil, E. (1958). The origin and vicissitudes of the self-image. *Psychoanalysis* 1:3–19.

17

Between Catastrophe and Faith

Perhaps the title should be *Toward Bion's Starting Points*. He tries to start over and over again in his work, as if he were always working toward and from a fresh beginning. The tracks he leaves behind vanish in a number of places, a network of starting points. It would take more than a short essay to locate them, place them in relationship to one another, and set them in motion. The present paper is an initial foray or probe yet aims at the heart of the matter. As Bion repeatedly reminds us, we may expect to find invariant structures in any subject. One way or another a constant thread runs through Bion's journey toward the beginning. I will try to pinpoint something of the essential quality, tone, and structure which characterize Bion's account of the birth of psychic life.

In order to read Bion fairly, one must read him closely and, in part, on his own terms. He is one of the most precise, if elusive, of psychoanalytic writers. He struggles to say exactly what he means, to see what he says, and say what he sees. At the same time the very saying and seeing are parts of an ongoing process in which psychic life strives to (re)create itself. However, part of Bion's elusiveness is not simply due to the incessant movement of the experiences (the experiencing capacity) he struggles with, but his success in often saying something one scarcely believes he is saying. One's difficulty as a reader is, finally, not Bion's abstruseness, but his nakedness. One does not want to hear or bear or believe in Bion's message.

In the present study I will confine myself to a close reading of Chapter 9 from *Elements of Psycho-Analysis* (1963), complemented with a discussion of the central thrust of *Attention and Interpretation* (1970). I have chosen these texts because through them we can get down to the most basic terms of Bion's discourse: the movement between catastrophe and faith. Other areas of his writings could have been chosen and traced to a similar place. However, my selections are more than arbitrary inasmuch as they bring out fundamentals of Bion's thought pattern with special clarity.

Bion vs. Klein

The "*vs.*" in this section title must be qualified. Bion's work could not be what it is if it did not grow out of and make use of Melanie Klein's. To an important extent, it is a reflection on Klein's and makes use of many Kleinian conceptual tools. Bion himself tells us this repeatedly. Nevertheless, he also takes pains to tell us that his work is not simply Kleinian. He reaches for areas the Kleinian framework forecloses. He asks questions Klein didn't and pulls on loose threads in Kleinian thinking. He makes use of Kleinian language in new ways.

Bion begins Chapter 9 from *Elements of Psycho-Analysis* (1963) by subtly differentiating his own concerns from Klein's or, rather, by showing the need to get underneath Kleinian thinking. Klein associates the birth of symbolic thinking with the depressive position. The depressive position requires the capacity to use the other as a container in positive ways. For example, in the depressive position the subject can introject the object's ability to contain and process projections and so tolerate ambivalence. Through introjection of the container or containing function ('breast') one moves from a primacy of the paranoid schizoid (Ps) to a primacy of the depressive (D) position.

In a broad sense, Ps breaks up and D tolerates wholes. The tolerance of a whole object within already is tinged with ethical value: one affirms love while knowing hate. From the position of this tolerance further operation of Ps can have creative value. For example, one tears apart or discriminates and builds anew. The Ps moment plays a role in keeping one's relationship to the whole object fresh. However, it is fair to say that Kleinians have been less interested in investigating the positive role of Ps than in discussing what is necessary to get past Ps to D. This is perhaps true of all positions that emphasize the structuring role of internalization processes at the expense of other capacities.

Bion asks the more basic question of how the containing whole object is reached or constituted in the first place. In many patients it is precisely the ability to discover and use the object as container which is problematic. Klein's account takes too much for granted. A good deal of thinking must go on prior to the constitution of the container which finally makes the latter possible. Bion develops the issues at stake in four interrelated moves.

1. Bion sees the interaction between Ps and D as thoroughgoing. Ps and D mutually constitute and depend on one another, so much so that Bion represents their relationship with a double arrow between them (Ps ↔ D). The copresence of Ps and D in psychic acts was already noted by Klein, although she too quickly placed a higher value on D (e.g., as the ground of a proper ethics, the need to make reparation, etc.). Bion makes D as dependent on Ps as Ps is on D. He keeps open, for the moment, the question of value. He seems to feel that the Kleinian association of Ps with bad and D with good prematurely stunts a full investigation of all that Ps may have to offer.

To be sure, Klein also points out the positive function of splitting processes

(Ps) as an early and necessary maturational step and notes their continued value as a part of psychic life in general. But Bion is more emphatic. For him the double function, Ps ↔ D, is at the center of a theory of mind. It represents the elemental and ubiquitous presence of the mind's ability to divide-and-unite. As such it has a certain priority over Klein's stress on the need for development to move toward D (to achieve or "make" the depressive position). For Bion the breaking-up of D has as much primal value as its creation. As we will see, Bion does not want to get stuck in D. He does not want to be blocked by an internal object, good, bad, or both, whole or part.

2. Bion differentiates Ps ↔ D from the container-contained function. Ps ↔ D expresses a capacity for thinking independent of and prior to the emergence of the container-contained relationship. The latter is dependent on the former. For example, he writes,

> The bringing together of elements that have apparently no connection in fact or in logic in such a way that their connection is displayed and an unsuspected coherence revealed, as in the example from Poincaré, is characteristic of Ps ↔ D. [1963, p. 37]

> it seems as if Ps ↔ D is as much the begetter of thoughts as ♀ ♂ [container-contained]. [1963, p. 37]

> before ♀ ♂ can operate, ♀ [container] has to be found and the discovery of ♀ depends on the operation of Ps ↔ D. [1963, p. 39]

There are indications that Bion would like to remain indecisive as to whether Ps ↔ D begets or derives from ♀ ♂. At one point he writes that the attempt to assign priority "distracts from the main problem" (1963, p. 39). Nevertheless, as we will see, the thrust of his thought opts for a primacy of Ps ↔ D. In his attempts to envision the most elemental levels of experiencing he strips away the notion of container-contained, as if the latter interferes with the personality's nakedness to itself. Bion tries to tap into a dimension in which it is an innate part of the self's rhythm to fall apart and come together. For this to happen, it is unnecessary to hold on to anything or to make anything part of oneself. The tendency of the self to seek a container often forecloses the incessant fall apart–come together rhythm. This may happen insofar as one tries to hold on to the container rather than be true to more basic movements.

3. If the emergence of the containing function depends on Ps ↔ D, the latter, in turn, may depend on still earlier mental acts. Bion notes that the earliest development of thinking through Ps ↔ D which he could observe depended on the production of signs. He continues,

> That is to say the individual had to bring together elements to form signs and then bring signs together before he could think. [1963, pp. 37–38]

Bion feels it is imperative to try to take a closer look at the elements which one brings together to form the first signs of thinking. The distinction between signs and symbols is made by many anthropologists, students of language, and analytic philosophers. In Bion's vision these signs are made up of and point to elemental components or psychic materials which have raw affective qualities. The earliest language is a kind of emotional sign language. According to Bion, the emotional states pointed to are catastrophic.

4. Bion calls the elements or raw material of psychic life *beta elements*. He describes this starting point as,

> a mixed state in which the patient is persecuted by feelings of depression and depressed by feelings of persecution. These feelings are indistinguishable from bodily sensations and what might, in the light of later capacity for discrimination, be described as things-in-themselves. In short β-elements are objects compounded of things-in-themselves, feelings of depression-persecution and guilt and therefore aspects of personality linked by a sense of catastrophe. . . . [1963, pp. 39–40]

The first thinking is affective thinking and the first signs are signs of catastrophe. Bion here tries to glimpse the "undifferentiated" realm which antedates the division and mutual constitution of Ps ↔ D. More generally, his work is a warning against the promiscuous use of symbolism in psychoanalysis and other disciplines. What passes for symbol may be an elemental sign of distress and horror. The psychotic patient signals rather than symbolizes his ongoing sense of catastrophe. The materials he uses may resemble symbols but they are used to point to an unnameable psychic reality. Similarly, the borderline patient must often be taught to link words with feelings. He often lacks the verbal labels for elementary emotional states and thrashes wildly about or sinks in kaleidoscopic confusion. This basic creation of link between word and affect is not so much the use of words as symbols, as signals for imminent psychic events. The catastrophic nature of its own life is the first and most basic task the psyche must take up. A toehold is achieved in catastrophic oblivion and the oblivion of catastrophe by the growth of elemental signals for one's predicament.

Doodling in Sound

Bion's picture of primitive beta elements is a kind of "Big Bang" image of the starting point of psychic reality (also see 1970, pp. 12–15). In part, he imagines the origin of affective thinking as a catastrophic explosion and uses psychosis (and, we will see, religion) as an example to aid exploration. His assumption is that psychosis reflects, albeit perversely, the catastrophic foundations of human existence. It is difficult to know whether, at any moment, the psychotic patient is signaling the birth or loss of his psychic universe, whether he is trying to stay out of or discover existence. In psychosis beta elements are often debased (and debasing) end products of a disintegrated or never-achieved capacity to think, rather than pristine initiators of a growth process. Sometimes they are both. Bion gives an example in which this ambiguity is developed.

The psychotic patient he has in mind utters what appear to be meaningless patterns of sound (1963, pp. 37–9). The subject believes he can see these patterns as or in the objects in the room. That is, Bion's patient is convinced that his sounds are connected to or even create the objects he sees ("In the beginning was the sound"). As Bion puts it, this person utters actual objects, not simply phrases. On the one hand the chaos of his utterances reflects a de- or un-forming and utterly obliterating catastrophic state approaching an entropy of sense. However, this patient also has the possibility of learning about himself by observing the objects he speaks. He has the possibility of meaning something by noting the nothing he tries to create.

We cannot tell from the data how Bion's patient got to the point of making meaningless patterns of sound. Is the person's apparent incoherence an attempt to reduce meaning to zero in order to maintain an invulnerable position? Or is it an attempt to return from zero and participate in an alternate reality? If the former, does the patient null meaning by hostile attacks on linking or are his noises residues of a massive dismantling process in which mind and self fall away? If the latter, does catastrophe as link also dissolve into nothingness?

If the patient is trying to seal himself off or maintain a nonposition in the null dimension, he is doomed to partial failure. Bion attributes at least a minimum of meaning to the patient's incoherent utterances. He likens his client's gestures to "doodling in sound." Bion writes,

> In his case writing preceded not talking only but thinking. His actual speech was incomprehensible if I tried to unravel it by applying my knowledge of ordinary words and grammar. It became more meaningful if I thought of it as doodling in sound, rather like tuneless and aimless whistling; it could not be described as speech, poetic speech, or music. Just as aimless whistling fails to be music because it does not obey any rule or discipline of musical composition, just as doodling fails to be drawing because it does not conform to the discipline of artistic creation, so his speech for lack of obedience to the usages of coherent speech did not qualify as verbal communication. The words employed fall into an undisciplined pattern of sound. [1963, p. 38]

Bion attributes to the patient's incoherence the coherence of doodling. We do not know whether the patient really was doodling in sound or whether this is solely Bion's invention. It is likely Bion did not know. His own sensitivity produces an image which has ordering value for him. We can guess that this thought made the patient's wayward meanderings bearable for the therapist. Seeing the patient as doodling in sound enables the therapist to remain empathic, yet maintain distance and even humor. Supported by such a thought the therapist may not only survive the session, but find himself quietly enlivened and perhaps of use.

Who orders whom? In this instance Bion not only perceived the spewing of incoherent beta elements but could not avoid acting as a rudimentary maker of sense. It is Bion's psyche which develops the patient's invisible writing (Bion calls the birth of thinking a kind of writing, here a signature of chaos), but it is the patient's impact which stimulates him. The patient is seen to utter objects in the room with the possibility of finding or disorganizing the shape or shapelessness of his existence through these objects. The therapist's inspiration acts as a lens which discloses or invents the patient's un- or misborn world. The patient's incoherence expresses the zero state he attempts to achieve and at the same time is more than zero.

We can imagine how frustrating such a thought must be to the patient bent on sealing himself off from meaning. Where he would finally achieve a universe of absolute meaninglessness (painlessness), he is thwarted by the therapist's pigheaded stumbling on to sense. By entering the consulting room he has tacitly consented to the intermixture and play of psyches. His space is not his own. He is prey to the other's visions and impulses. We would like to know whether the patient is bothered or relieved by Bion's conclusion. Is he reassured by the therapist's interest that follows upon the latter's surprising and pleasing idea? Does he increase his efforts to jam meaning-producing gestures? Does he try to step up from or burrow more deeply into zero?

Bion relates the patient's movement within, toward, or out of the null dimension to a failure or lack. In the last quotation above he stresses the patient's lack of discipline, his inability or refusal to conform to the rules of discourse and discovery. Again, we cannot tell from this sketchy example what this lack owes to destructive hate and what to a sense of deficiency. This very inability suggests how profoundly linked these two elements often are.

The Catastrophic Moment

It is difficult to trace where the break with oblivion comes for Bion. He describes the first elements of mental life as both mindless and hallucinatory. As quoted earlier, beta elements loom as "objects compounded of things-in-themselves, feelings of depression–persecution and guilt and therefore aspects of personality linked by a sense of catastrophe." The first thoughts are nonthoughts, raw materials which must be reworked before they can become part of a thinking process. They grip the subject with catastrophic intensity. One might depict them as raw affective states which fuse image–sensation–perception. The personality lacks any frame of reference for them so that they spread through the infantile cosmos with infinite horror, a kind of electrocution from no tangible source.

It is the psyche's basic job to transmute these initial catastrophic globs of experience into psychically soluble events. Bion calls the capacity to do this alpha function. The great creation–destruction myths, so basic a part of religious and psychotic imagery, express this transformational work. They are signals for the sense of catastrophe (and wonder, curiosity, etc.) which are part of the advent and evolution of the self. Beta elements are gestated by alpha function into an alive thinking process (dream work, mythic systems, signs into symbols, reflection on signs and symbols, etc.). Bion uses terms like beta and alpha elements and alpha function, in part, as reminders that our picture of the birth of our psychic universe is still open. They are thorns or stimuli which keep us revisualizing our beginnings. Bion once called them "nests" where some unknown bird of meaning may alight.

In psychosis the transmuting of beta elements into food for thought runs amok and the process may even be thrown into reverse gear. The personality may collapse to the point where raw beta elements run wild. The latter now assume the more malignant status of failed thoughts rather than merely preborn ones. However, even as the psyche seeks to undo itself and approximate an absolute entropy of meaning, the very meaninglessness of its productions also functions as signs of meaninglessness.

For example, the incoherence (something observable) of Bion's patient who doodles in sound, functions as a sign of incoherence (something unseen). The objects he utters and sees represent something unseeable. An unseeable object may be the absent mother but may also be something unnameable. For the psychotic person visible objects are part and signals of an ongoing catastrophe. The catastrophe itself is invisible and intangible. Tangible events are its more or less momentary compressions. The unnameable catastrophe may be conceived of in various ways but remains nameless. It may be dread of somethingness-nothingness, creation–destruction, oblivion–aliveness, or a cipher beyond these terms.

It is uncertain from Bion's account exactly what relationship beta elements have with thinking. How do they link up with thinking? Isn't this linking up a form of thinking? Or perhaps beta elements somehow act as stimulus releasers for the thinking capacity? What kind of mental acts give rise to beta elements in the first place? Bion characterizes the latter as raw material, primal thoughts, nonthoughts, mindless hallucinatory globs. Is there a thinking which subtends thinking or primary process of primary process *ad infinitum*? Or can one break off this redundancy, say, after the third cycle (on the model of consciousness of consciousness of consciousness)? Are we creating subhorizon after subhorizon or discovering how we are made? Isn't such creation/discovery, after all, an essential characteristic of our make-up? And so on.

Whether or not the problems in Bion's thought are insuperable, it is important to bring out the governing vision. The self is born, evolves, and dissolves with a sense of catastrophe. Catastrophe may not be the only ingredient but it is an invariant one. Bion's account of human psychic life begins with catastrophic beta elements, whether pristine prethoughts requiring a birth process or the perverse dendritis of psychic collapse.

At the minimum, thoughts are persecutory and depressing because they must be tolerated. One must suffer the buildup of tension for thoughts to become part of a genuine thinking process. One must work them over and be worked on by them without knowing where this encounter may lead. Yet primordial terror is something more than the tension between the requirements of emotional truth and survival or the break of thinking from oblivion. Something more pervasive and ineffable is at work. For Bion there is something terrifying in the very birth of the self and the latter's inextricable tie to the oblivion that is part of it and that it is part of.

Bion writes that the sense of catastrophe *links* aspects of personality. It is the cement that holds personality together, a primordial forming principle, the sea or atmosphere we live in. In psychosis personality itself is an ongoing catastrophe. But Bion's vision goes beyond the conventionally pathological. The sense of catastrophe already seems to have had a history when the infant first screams and perhaps is older than life itself. Emotional life bears the imprint of the combustible/conservative universe in which it grows. Given the nature of the universe we are part of, it seems inevitable that cataclysm is a formative pole of our beings.

Whether or not Bion is right to view the sense of catastrophe as our point of origin, it is a basic fact of our emotional lives and in psychosis, often all. Bion tracks a free floating sense of catastrophe which is a fundamental term of our existence. It functions as an invariant which can be filled in with a range of more specific contents (dread of birth, death, change, boundlessness, sameness, the predator, castration, disease, burning, drowning, suffocating, falling, etc.). One strains to see its face clearly in what can be seen but it grips one blindly from behind the scenes.

If beta elements are worked over into something which is psychically soluble, it would seem that the results still retain traces of their catastrophic origins. The whole personality is linked by the horrific materials of its beginning through all their transmutations. However, the self is not simply one with its sense of catastrophe. Even the incoherent utterances (at once catastrophic and warding off catastrophe) of Bion's patient involved something more than catastrophe. Bion begins his description by calling his patient's jumble of noise and blankness a kind of writing. And writing always involves some modicum of differentiation and deferral. As the self goes under it broadcasts signals of dissolution in progress. It can do so only from some remaining quality of difference which it cannot shake off. In the end a difference remains between oneself and zero and however minuscule, it is infinite.

Is a distance element inherent in the sense of catastrophe to begin with? Is catastrophe experienced as catastrophe precisely because of this distance element? In Bion's terms, without a sense of catastrophe, there would be no self and without a self no sense of catastrophe. For Bion this includes those individuals for whom the self and sense of catastrophe seems to have vanished or never properly appeared. The investigation of a total nulling of or failing to achieve a self, studies the catastrophic annihilation of or failure to experience catastrophe. As Bion (1970) puts it in one example, the failure of the sense of catastrophe to function as a link between aspects of personality is analogous to how the infant's scream fails to achieve communication. Although early expressive signals (e.g., screaming) are part of the catastrophic reality they point to, they also carry an implicit distance element which can evolve (e.g., scream as evacuation, projection, communication). Bion's work is filled with many microanalyses of how this evolution is prevented or goes awry.

It must be emphasized that the distance element which seems both threatened and inherent in the sense of catastrophe is not simply our observing capacity. More is involved than the capacity to know. In psychoanalysis, at the levels at stake, knowledge can be part of the disease. A capacity as deep or deeper than the sense of catastrophe must be called forth if healing or profound maturation is to occur. Bion's solution is a radical one. He fights fire with fire by moving the grounds of discourse between catastrophe and faith.

Faith in O

For Bion faith (F) is the proper primordial and developed response to catastrophe. As his writings developed he relied less and less on knowledge (K) as the path toward Truth and groped for a way of expressing a more fundamental vision. His dictum that the psychoanalytic attitude requires one to abstain from expectations, memory, desire, and understanding leaves one nothing to hold onto. It leaves one simply open in faith. For Bion (1970) faith becomes *the* essential quality of the psychoanalytic attitude, at once a method and saving moment (Eigen 1981).

Bion (1970) associates the struggle to know (K) with possessiveness (Keats's "irritable reaching after facts and reasons"), sensuousness, and the container-contained relationship. Strictly speaking, the data of psychoanalysis are non-sensuous and ineffable. Faith is the medium of access to psychoanalytic data. It undercuts and transcends our controlling needs and enables us to experience the impact of emotional reality in a way that allows the latter genuinely to evolve.

Bion uses the sign, O, to stand for the emotional reality of moment or, in general, ultimate reality as such. In itself it is unknowable but the analyst opens himself in the faith that he will meet it. He aims at the emotional truth of a session. The impact the patient has is translated into guesses or convictions about what is truly happening. The situation is both Kantian and mystical. The analyst aims at ultimate reality but must work with hypotheses. Yet the personality change which occurs is one of being, not simply knowing. The subject becomes more at-one with himself and his capacity to experience. A paradoxical result is that faith enhances rather than mutes precision. One's contact with subtle nuances of experience deepens as one develops an appreciative sensibility for what remains out of reach. The very taste of experience gains new meaning. The subject learns the gesture of repeatedly starting from scratch, of living in a wall-less moment and sensing his walls in a way that makes a difference.

F in O approaches an attitude of pure receptiveness. It is an alert readiness, an alive waiting. Bion describes how uncomfortable one may be in this open state. One must tolerate fragmentation, whirls of bits and pieces of meaning and meaninglessness, chaotic blankness, dry periods, and psychic dust storms. Yet Bion also suggests such states can be trancelike and akin to hallucinosis. He writes,

> Receptiveness achieved by denudation of memory and desire (which is essential to the operation of "acts of faith") is essential to the operation of psycho-analysis and other scientific proceedings. It is essential for experiencing hallucination or the state of hallucinosis.

> This state I do not regard as an exaggeration of a pathological or even natural condition: I consider it rather to be a state always present, but overlaid by other phenomena, which screen it. If these other elements can be moderated or suspended hallucinosis becomes demonstrable: its full depth and richness are accessible only to acts of faith. Elements of hallucinosis of which it is possible to be sensible are the grosser manifestations and are of secondary importance; to appreciate hallucination the analyst must participate in the state of hallucinosis. [1970, pp. 35–36]

Apparently the momentary vagueness or clarity of F in O is incidental to the basic attitude of readiness without hooks or supports. It is not that knowing and memory are lost. Our psychic life could not exist without them. Rather, Bion attempts to situate our capacities in a broader context. A primacy of faith enables us to know and remember less dissociatively, as part of a profound growth process. The intimations that arise through F in O may lead to or, as Bion puts it, "intersect" with K and through such intersections our knowing self may glimpse surprising horizons. Our personality deepens when we are led by F in O.

One surprising dimension which becomes visible in the kind of suspension of mind Bion advocates is the hallucinatory mode of being. The psychoanalyst is able to make productive contact with the domain the psychotic person vanishes, freezes, or drowns in. Hallucinosis is employed as an empathic method, a method of discovery, whereas the psychotic is lost or sealed off in it. One might call the psychoanalytic attitude a scientific use of faith, and vice versa. Through F in O one is able to allow experience in hallucinosis to evolve. In this instance one grows through hallucinosis. Insofar as the psychotic individual forecloses faith, he gets caught in his hallucinations. It may turn out that even in psychosis, hallucination has some relationship to faith, inasmuch as both hallucinosis and faith have been caught in a warping process. The psychotic patient who, in time, develops a taste for the psychoanalytic attitude may begin to put the capacities he has stumbled upon to better use.

In general, Bion depicts F in O as a gateway to hallucinosis. He describes the latter as an unnatural but ubiquitous mode of being which can be tapped by adherence to the psychoanalytic attitude. Much of our everyday behavior is governed by hallucinosis without knowing it. It is more natural to be related to objects in sensuous terms and avoid the uncanny intuition of alternate psychic realities. The psychoanalytic attitude itself is unnatural. Its temporary suspension of attachment to the operation of everyday capacities goes against the usual pull of psychic gravity. Its emphasis on "free floating attention" (the bracketing of memory, desire, understanding, etc.) allows one to follow psychic gradients which are missed or tend not to appear while in an everyday attitude.

The dimension of hallucinosis which presents itself through F in O brings us back to beta elements, our starting point. Beta elements appear in hallucinosis. They are the essential content of hallucinations. F in O opens us up to the ground of our being, our point of origin, the pristine catastrophe of psychic birth. If we approach this dimension through psychosis rather than F in O, we fall upon the perverse catastrophe in which birth is incessantly undone. If a growing individual learns to attend to what menaces him he may be rewarded by the rich elaboration of a perceptual–conceptual network in which the meaning of things evolves. However, where the psyche works in reverse, beta elements portend not new beginnings but the end of the psychic universe. The rebirth archetype degenerates into demonized repetitiousness and finally vanishes in a mindless sea of catastrophe. The psychoanalytic attitude, too, involves a certain mindlessness, a letting-go of attachment to mind, a clearing oneself out. Hallucinosis vanishes and returns through the open attitude of the mindless moment. Through specific hallucinations bits and pieces of an unknowable catastrophic psychic reality are brought into focus. In time the analyst creates/ discovers interventions which make sense of them. If his sense is deeply rooted in the non-sense (F) beyond knowing (K), his work may have a resonance that makes a difference.

Faith and the Precocious Container

Bion depicts beta elements as dispersed. They are catastrophic hallucinatory bits and pieces which seem to function chaotically, that is, without reference to one another. In optimal growth processes this dispersed state culminates in the temporary emergence of genuine coherence. Unintegration moves toward integration, Ps toward D. A selected fact spontaneously throws the disarray into a useable order. In time the operation of Ps breaks up or refines the results. A spontaneous oscillation between Ps and D is part of the basic rhythm of mental processes. This rhythm can be interfered with by trying to force the outcome. One may lack the patience or ability to tolerate living with Ps long or well enough for a productive D distribution to take shape. Similarly, one may try to hold on to a D result past its time. Bion associates the premature rush toward or holding on to D (moving ahead or behind of oneself) with poor or mis-use of the containing function. He writes,

> The β-elements are dispersed; this dispersal should be terminated by Ps ↔ D and
> a selected fact unless the patient seeks a container, ♀ , that compels cohesion of the
> β-elements to form the contained, ♂ .

The dispersed β-elements, insofar as they seek the ♀, may be regarded as an abortive prototype of a container, a container loosely structured like the reticulum of Dr. Jaques. They may equally be regarded as the abortive prototype of the contained, a loosely structured ♂ before compression to enter ♀. [1963, p. 40]

Bion has ventured a unique blend of the language of problem solving, religion, and psychoanalysis, not to mention philosophy and mathematics. In one way or another the study of creative processes has noted a period of study, immersion in the requirements of a situation, a period of unknowing, learning, gestation, and often an impasse point. Bion quotes Poincaré, but similar descriptions are found in Freud, Kohler, and the story of Buddha's enlightenment. Bion's method finds a parallel in "the dark night of the senses." The content he explores is the descent into hell. He takes the term "function" from mathematics and his raw material of psychic life, beta elements, have structural parallels with (and differences from) Kant's sensory flux prior to temporal-spatial organization. All of these topics require study. What has Bion done with the cultural terms he inherited? Has he composed a sloppy hodgepodge? A further array of dispersed beta elements seeking form? Or has he been compelled by the requirements of the situation to initiate explorations at inter-disciplinary boundaries. He insists that he is developing a depth exploration of the psychoanalytic experience, especially psychoanalysis as it meets psychosis and as it meets itself. No discipline is born in isolation. All arise from the human subject and convey something about the latter's way of existing. It is not surprising that psychoanalysis meets its brothers and sisters as it discovers itself.

The dispersed beta elements face a dual danger. Insofar as the subject cannot sustain and work with their impact, they may be twisted into (out of) shape in order to fit a container or find no container at all. The former case may result in hatred of or addiction to containers and the latter more frenetic dispersal. Beta elements on the loose assume greedy containing properties and intensify splitting activities. The psychoanalyst is under pressure to find a way of containing such a state of affairs but his efforts often become part of the problem.

Whatever the problems inherent in Bion's formulations, it is clear that he tries to develop a basic vision, to allow an intuition to speak. His intuition has many facets and he attempts to develop it as finely as possible. We have only touched some of its aspects, enough as may be necessary to reach its center. Succinctly put, through F in O we tolerate the work of Ps ↔ D. The mindlessness of catastrophe is met by the mindlessness of faith.

Many questions remain. Where does F in O come from? Is it the result of Ps ↔ D? Obviously, then, Ps ↔ D would not require F in O if it gives rise to it. Is it a counterpole to Ps ↔ D from as deep or deeper a place? Do Ps ↔ D and F in O make one another possible, at least in benign rather than malignant processes? How? In psychoanalysis Ps ↔ D is met by and most fully constituted through the psychoanalytic attitude, F in O. Does F in O function like an infinite container? Is it the only container which cannot be blown apart or misshapen by the pull toward catastrophe? Is it the privileged medium of access and necessary condition for Ps ↔ D to use projection properly, to generate or link up with a container that truly meets its needs? Does the need for a container vanish as F in O approaches, in the words of the Zen master, our "original face"? We do not know whether such questions are answerable or where investigations of them might lead.

A Note on Starting Points

However conceptualized, catastrophe and faith are fundamental terms of experience. They are the rock-bottom givens of Bion's psychoanalytic journey. Which has the first word? Which the last? Or are they inextricably linked at every turn? According to Bion's vision, the free play of Ps ↔ D through F in O would be the way we would function if we did not interfere with ourselves. It is the way our basic nature works. Yet it is also natural to get in our own way and a most difficult (unnatural) achievement to be ourselves.

Catastrophe–faith is a double term of our experience and our approach to experience. A traditional view is that catastrophe takes its subjective meaning from well-being, as evil does from good. In Winnicott's (1965, 1971) work, for example, primal catastrophe is the failure of the infant's continuity of being to be supported or established. It may take the form of unthinkable anxieties or primitive agonies such as going to pieces, falling forever, lack of relationship to body, and loss of orientation. In structural terms, discontinuity gains its meaning from continuity.

The infant maintains its continuity in the face of or through disruptions up to a point. But a breaking point can be reached and the sense of continuity lost. In normal circumstances the mother nurses the baby back into existence to the point where discontinuity can once more be tolerated and used for growth purposes. Over and over the baby dies out and is reborn. Faith is nourished by this repeated resurrection. It has roots in an underlying sense of continuity which is reestablished in new ways. Our first symbolizing activity expresses our sense of ongoing being.

Bion's Ps ↔ D also expresses a kind of dying or going to pieces and coming back as an invariant of psychic processes. His account and Winnicott's (and Freud's) have many similar ingredients. However, his emphasis is different. For Bion fragmentation and division is as much a part of our starting point as union and continuity. Our sense of continuity depends on division and vice versa. A double arrow between Ps and D is primary. We owe more to Ps than we might like to think. For Bion, in contrast with Winnicott, we are first concerned to signal a catastrophic emotional reality. We need to build up an emotional sign language for our sense of catastrophe as a step toward thinking about ourselves.

The sense of catastrophe may be part of a feedback system which mirrors how poor a start the self is getting or how skewed a direction its development is taking. It may be a warning with vectorial properties which urge the personality to reset itself. Often the personality fails to right itself and the sense of catastrophe loses its value as signal and becomes one's entire reality. In time the subject adapts to it and the sense of catastrophe grows dull and blank. One loses one's sensitivity to catastrophe and no longer experiences the increasing horrors which unfold. It may be possible for a culture to do this on a grand scale. We lose our sensitivity to our most pressing dangers, much as the toad boils to death without noticing as the heat in its water gradually increases.

Bion has many descriptions of how an originating sense of catastrophe goes awry. The psychotic individual often falls upon the raw catastrophe of our psychic origins only to turn it into a permanent anesthetic. He learns to administer doses of catastrophe as needed in order to blank out aspects of himself and external reality. In contrast, faith saves catastrophe and grants this term of our origin, growth, and end its due. It recognizes catastrophe as a basic condition of our being. To blunt our awareness of catastrophe is to lose or never gain our sensitivity to ourselves.

Bion notes that the human race is ill-equipped to tolerate its own experiential capacity. It naturally orients itself toward external objects and the tasks of survival. The grim paradox is that insofar as we cannot admit and work with the sense of catastrophe which constitutes psychic reality, we may heighten external catastrophes as a way of objectifying ourselves. We may finally know ourselves through the dramatizations which hurl us into oblivion. For Bion faith (F in O) is not an avoidance or opiate in this situation. It sustains our approach to and tolerance of ourselves.

Bion leaves open where faith comes from. It is not simply from containers because it ultimately explodes and transcends containers. It is characterized in his writings as a mature yet original tendency, something that appears (like catastrophe) when all else is stripped away. It is perhaps fitting that Bion does not attempt to track it down. It is the freeing capacity *par excellence*. It is our heritage and most profound destiny yet so easily troubled, lost, or warped.

In various contexts Bion speaks of faith as lie and a condition to undercut lying (e.g., 1970, p. 100). Faith of a sort plays a self-soothing role and is even capable of fostering denial of the most obvious facts of life. However, this is not what Bion means by F in O. The latter has a shattering impact on lies. In this context, faith presents itself as catastrophic to the various security systems we have erected over the abyss. It meets catastrophe with catastrophe. The history of faith is not only one of lying but of shattering and gathering together, the spontaneous rhythm of Ps ↔ D.

If there is an ethics here, Ps plays as large a role in it as D. The sword and fire clear the way for new beginnings. It is not simply the primacy of D (the Kleinian ideal) but the Ps ↔ D unit which is the ground of value. However, it is F in O, the groundless arrow from beyond and toward the heart's center, which keeps Ps ↔ D honest and prevents its perversion by madness. Bion sets out to trace the link between catastrophe–faith. The biography of this link tells the story of how we rise or fall.

REFERENCES

Bion, W. R. (1963). *Elements of Psycho-Analysis.* London: Heinemann.

———— (1970). *Attention and Interpretation.* London: Tavistock.

Eigen, M. (1981). The area of faith in Winnicott, Lacan and Bion. *International Journal of Psycho-Analysis* 62:413–433.

Winnicott, D. W. (1965). *The Maturational Processes and the Facilitating Environment.* New York: International Universities Press.

———— (1971). *Playing and Reality.* New York: Basic Books.

18

Omnipotence

In working with deep levels of character resistances, much of the patient's communications are often attempts to support defensive patterns which offer at least some illusion of partial mastery over areas of sensed helplessness. Even obsessive clinging to pain and manifest inability are often attempts to mask and encapsulate a dreaded loss of control. In dreams the ego frequently appears to be in control of feelings it fears are uncontrollable. Of course, these controlling gestures may slip or otherwise fail, with a resulting sense of terrifying helplessness. Both attempts at mastery and their breakdown quickly spiral or are governed by a pull toward omnipotent–impotent extremes. Unconscious operations move toward extremes or, better, maximal states (Matte Blanco 1975). Defensive operations often bear an infinite exponent. It is, in part, the imaginative leaps of the therapist that enable the patient to gradually bear experiencing difficult areas muted by cycles of pseudomastery and the latter's collapse (Eigen 1979b, 1980a,b, 1981, 1982, 1983, 1984).

In the work with the dreams reported below, special attention is given to aspects of omnipotence and attempts to overcome it. The subject frequently traps himself by trying to solve his problems with various omnipotence–impotence stratagems, often subtly so. Creative struggle is necessary on the part of both dream teller and listener to stay open to fresh perspectives. The dreams reported below were given by experienced patients and/or practitioners. After sketching the play of tendencies related to omnipotence or impotence in these scenes, a more general, although still informal, discussion follows.

What Is and Isn't There: A Missing Function

Fran, an experienced therapist and patient, reported the following dream in my dream seminar:

> Fran's daughter and son appear [actually she only has a daughter]. There is some confusion as to which is which sex. A deformed or retarded boy appears. He is

damaged, monstrous. He needs help. A good willed, motherly woman tells Fran
that the boy needs love. This woman seems to be Fran's social worker, as if Fran
were on welfare [she is a successful therapist]. Fran's ex-husband is in the
background. Fran feels she loves or can love the boy.

Fran's reactions to the dream were mixed. She felt pleased that she had the
love which could help the boy. She also liked the good woman who wanted to
help. These were positive elements which made her feel good about herself. She
recognized that sexual confusion was expressed in early images as the dream
began to take form, but did not know what to make of it. The deformed boy
frightened her. He seemed alien. She tended to gloss over him when she
discussed the dream, as though she wished to distance herself from him, in spite
of her expression of love. She expressed anger at her ex-husband for "not really
being there," which she felt was the main reason her marriage did not work. Her
husband often withdrew from emotional situations. Fran expressed some
resignation. She accepted the fact she must help the deformed boy alone, relying
only on the love she had in her and the encouragement of the good woman.

Fran let us know that she had recently ended her analysis (bio-energetic)
which she felt was very successful. She voiced much improved feelings about
herself. She said she was attending the class because of her wish to learn more
about dreams. Her analysis had not used dreams much and she was interested in
them. She appeared to be a caring person who expressed herself openly and
fully. However, her face seemed to be characterized by a certain vagueness, a
muted atmosphere of confusion. When I questioned her about this she said she
did feel fuzzy, often mentally numbed-out in some way, a sensation she usually
tried to hide. It was a felt deficit which bothered her and was another reason, at
the advice of a friend, she came to class.

The sexual confusion as the dream was forming could be worked on from a
number of perspectives. I simply called attention to it but it was not the center
of my gestalt at this time. The overall impetus of the dream led to the emergence
of the deformed boy and the help drama related to him. Deformity is a common
theme in deep analysis and often refers to some aspect of the damaged self (Weil
1958). Getting in touch with such shadow aspects of the self can play a positive
role in one's transformation (Zimmer 1948). Fran felt mother love was enough
to help this neglected male element in her personality. She is told so by an inside
good mother (the social worker). Here, however, the dream's expressed view is
too limited. *The mother realm over-estimates its power,* a sort of *benevolent maternal
omnipotence.* However, it is not likely that maternal omnipotence, however loving
and benevolent, is enough to cure mental confusion. In order for confusion to be
set right, *comprehension* linked with good will also is necessary. The dream gives
an incomplete picture or, rather, is a temptation to support a certain one-
sidedness in Fran: her belief, for good and ill, in *the omnipotence of good mothering.*

However, the dream also shows what is needed by what is weak or missing.
There is something wrong with the males in the dream: withdrawn ex-husband

and deformed boy. There are no good males in this dream world. Only female figures are well developed. Male elements in Fran's personality are weak or damaged, which she, in part, associated with her mental confusion. Through her therapy she built up a good inside mother and feels good in her body. However, her ability to understand herself remained relatively underdeveloped. Fran spoke of a mental inability which frustrated her even though she now felt generally good about herself as a person. Fran felt thwarted in her hope to understand herself and others with the kind of complexity and nuances which would do her sense of human subjectivity more justice. Her inside good mother was too global, not mentally precise enough. In terms of her dream language (which here seems to conform to cultural stereotypes), her inside damaged boy needs good fathering as well as mothering, and for this further evolution is necessary (Eigen 1980a, 1982).

The week prior to presenting this dream Fran discussed a patient who suffered from deep mental confusion which the patient tried to encapsulate and hide. Her patient's dream also involved confusion, a damaged male, and a strong female. Fran felt blocked in face of her patient's resistance after initial progress. As she discussed her own dream she began to feel more ready to face her patient's problems. She remarked, "Perhaps my patient and I can cure each other." It is quite possible that the patient's block played a role in provoking Fran's dream. The patient's inhibition mirrored an area which hampered both of them. In this case the patient was providing her a service. Fran now felt it was up to her to dig more deeply into what was missing before the patient could find the courage to do so also.

Tricking Mother

Kevin, a therapist in my dream seminar, reported the following dream:

> Kevin was in a grade school class in which the students were not listening to the woman teacher. The problem was partly her fault. She did not really know how to communicate. Kevin tried to help the situation by calling attention to the communication problem in such a way that she might become more responsive without realizing she had been criticized. He felt proud of this accomplishment, pleased by his ability to trick her into being more communicative. For some moments it seemed to work and the class went well. However, in the end, when he wanted to have a meaningful interchange with her, she was psychologically not available. He felt alone and withdrew.

Kevin began the discussion of his dream by expressing satisfaction that he had momentarily been able to make communication between class and teacher better. He felt he meant well and was pleased he could bring things together. He tended to distance the ending, that he ultimately failed, and expressed bewilderment at the final result, not quite believing it. Classmates related the dream to Kevin's attempts to make the bad mother or therapist or teacher good. Initial emphasis was placed on his wish for the other to be there. Kevin saw this from a position of innocence. He was the good one. The other needed correction. It was especially a point for him that he kept making this effort.

In fact Kevin had a soft and breast-like bearing, yet not without nobility. One classmate saw him as a knight. In response he admitted that above all he did not want to lose his sense of purity. He felt in contact with a radiant, innocent self and did not want it marred or compromised. Another classmate saw him as playing the *omniscient* child, one who *knew better than mother* and wished to maintain a controlling position. He seemed baffled by this comment and maintained his innocence. He simply wanted to help mother (or us) and make things good.

Some of us (including myself) respected the innocent baby aura Kevin wished to preserve. The *innocent baby soul* certainly plays a basic role in my life and work (Eigen 1979a, 1982, 1983). My own stance is not merely or primarily one of suspicion. Still, in the dream Kevin does try to trick mother into being as he wishes. He avoided direct confrontation and exercised covert control. In this regard he did feel "baby knows best." If he were only clever enough he might entirely be able to turn the withholding mother (or therapist or teacher: the Other for self-object) into an obliging puppet, or, more kindly, one who fills his needs (or wishes).

In real life he was a beautiful soul. His innocence charmed others enough of the time to get along. However, the dream clearly indicated that in the end this is no real solution. One cannot really go through life controlling others. Even if successful, one would not believe oneself truly likeable for one's own sake or, finally, cure one's sense of isolation. Covertly he would remain a trickster forever.

With further discussion Kevin began to feel how his sense of goodness (whatever its genuine core) kept him above or at a distance from the others he wished to help (all of us, including his patients). In the dream he felt he could take the law in his own hands for the other's (and ultimately his own) good. This suggested a lack of respect, much as his own autonomy had been clearly violated by seductive tricks and withdrawals. Above all, the dream suggested he had fallen without knowing it. By implication it calls for a refocusing of vision of what makes one human. In spite of his therapy work, it had not yet *emotionally* occurred to Kevin that contact with the good can include, support, and work with contact with the bad, without being spoiled. Fully *human* development requires the conflicts and paradoxes of our nature. Perhaps through it all a virgin does truly thread her way, growing rich in experience (Eigen 1975). And perhaps in this context seduction and withdrawal are two terms of the drama that unfolds as one moves along.

The Puppet Show

Taken together, Fran and Kevin presented aspects of baby–mother omnipotence. In Fran's world the advent of maternal benevolent omnipotence was both an achievement and a trap. It enabled the release of good feelings but, in important ways, left or kept her blind. On the other hand, Kevin played the charming baby who believed he "knew" how to make mother act as he wished. In his baby omniscience he also paradoxically, played the omnipotent good mother with others. Such baby–mama role reversals are common and play themselves out in any number of ways.

In another instance, Vera, an experienced therapist, presented a related dream of one of her patients. In this dream her patient, Lois, came to watch her stage a puppet show. First Vera did some cartwheels. Then she displayed a number of beautiful puppets with wonderful costumes. When Vera went backstage to get ready for the show itself, Lois flew (literally, off the ground) downstairs and out of the building holding hands with an old friend. Lois did not wait for the puppet show.

Lois woke up feeling good and presented this dream to Vera as an achievement. Both Lois and Vera agreed the dream suggested that Lois felt less isolated. Instead of being stuck and having only therapy in her life, she could enjoy going off with a friend. The woman in the dream actually was an old friend, the only person Lois had been close with. Their relationship had tapered off as Lois continued therapy. Lois was prone to suicidal isolation. Vera also felt "funny" that Lois flew away, since flying was an obvious reference to Lois's trying to stay above her problems. However, Vera did not emphasize this perception because she felt relieved that Lois felt less isolated and suicidal for the moment. In this instance, wishful thinking on the therapist's part led her to side with a manic defense. However, she felt nagging misgivings.

Through supervisory discussion Vera was more able to acknowledge her muted sense that the dream outlined growth problems in therapy. With support she could let the dream picture speak more clearly. Lois, fearful of becoming Vera's puppet, left with her old friend before the show could begin. She retreated into the safety of an old tie rather than meet the dangers therapy presented. Vera, fearful of losing or damaging the patient, tried to keep Lois by entertaining her. In some way Lois was able to make Vera do cartwheels for her and/or was perceiving aspects of Vera's controlling needs. Lois's attempt at control was greatly endangered by the temptation to become Vera's beautiful puppet. In the end flight seemed safer. The current bind or resistance node facing the therapy couple appeared to hinge on a drama involving who would have omnipotence and how: Each was involved in making a puppet of the other. Lois retreated to manic withdrawal rather than succumb and give Vera omnipotence.

The Killer Snake Man

Killers are often victims in their dreams. In one instance a woman, who showed no remorse over killing a friend's daughter, was repeatedly menaced in her dreams by a man with a snake's head which itself was covered with snakes. As time went on this woman's therapist, who later discussed the case with me, appeared in this dream as a possible helper.

The therapist naturally saw her appearance in the patient's dream as a sign of progress. However, the everyday tough, disdainful behavior of the patient continued as usual (the case was treated in prison). The woman righteously insisted she would have gotten off if she had money or position, and the therapist inwardly agreed. The prisoner had had a hellish life and hardened. The well-meaning therapist felt it important to give this woman a taste of goodness, sure that the latter would win out in time. She felt these nightmares tried to communicate unconscious guilt that the patient could not openly acknowledge. However, she finally was disappointed when no tangible change in the patient resulted and their relationship deteriorated. The therapist became inwardly remote and the patient even cooler. The therapist ceased to appear in the patient's nightmare.

I offered that the next time the patient brings in her nightmare to say, "Your nightmare is the smartest thing about you — without it you'd be in no pain at all." This particular suggestion was meant less for the patient than for the therapist. The patient was light years away from guilt, yet the therapist needed to whitewash this. The most pain the patient allowed herself was in nightmares, when the devil she played during the day menaced her. She was caught in a primitive fear–hate drama. She felt right in attacking others because she basically felt under attack. In her dream she was the innocent victim, and the evil snake man, among other things, carried her split-off omniscience–omnipotence, a potentially explosive force for the moment controlled by a mixture of calculation and indifference.

Rather than stir this explosiveness up, the therapist bit on her own frustration and helplessness and played for time, vaguely hoping the counter-omnipotence of goodness would see her through. Another student who heard this case remarked that perhaps therapist and patient were throwing snakes at each other. The reorientation this view provided helped the therapist to face the real suffering her struggle with the patient must cause her, so that she could be less afraid of working with the suffering she must induce in the patient as well.

The Detour

Laura had nearly thirty years of analysis and therapy of various sorts. She was trapped in a destructive process and was expert at killing off any pieces of goodness in herself she could find. At times it seemed that whatever goodness she managed to keep alive was in order to have something to feed the pleasure of killing it. The following dream indicated a breakdown in this negative omnipotence, wherein a genuine moment of health emerged.

> Laura was in a cab. The male driver chewed on a root. The road to her house was being torn up, preliminary to reconstruction. An indirect route to her place had to

be taken. This included a street she ordinarily would not have gone on. It was a nice block, lined with green lawns, rich plants, and beautiful trees. One tree was especially fine. It reminded her of another she had seen in my lobby. She had one like it in her apartment, but felt mine was nicer.

Laura in fact did try to tear this dream down in every way she could think of. But it had the structural strength to sustain her attacks. She was forced to tolerate a break in the negative screen she hid behind. There was very little in this rare dream that she could make come out to her detriment. She had to tolerate the difficult fact that something positive was happening. In this case the dream was bigger than her hate.

The overall structure of the dream was new: a detour. Construction was going on. A new route had to be taken in the meantime. The very structure of this dream expresses a growth in symbolization. Apparently while hostile omnipotence is mainly at work, detour experiencing is impossible. Hostile omnipotence is one track. In Laura's case, it was a continuous, self-protective series of complaints and accusations. It would not let the original wound or demand go. Her hostile omnipotence was like a hammer riveted to a single target, or a prison made from one bar that was everywhere: no other conclusions except those based on hate/self-hate were possible. Such rigid thought processes function as a kind of encapsulating armor which fills gaps before she could truly experience and integrate them. Detour thinking, by contrast, requires tolerating gaps, movement, and space.

Her idealization of my tree at the expense of her own was to be expected. She also tried to see something wrong with the man chewing a root. She could accuse herself or me of castrating wishes. This may be so, but it is also possible that the root meant something basic was at work, linked with the fact that a new route was needed and here envisioned as possible. This dream, with my support, was able to act as a viable reference point for something outside Laura's closed system, a beginning container for the inconsolable attacker.

In fact Laura had been a chronic and compulsive head-banger through much of her life. It was as if, in part, she was trying to break through a sense of suffocation, a nooselike sense of constriction. This symptom strikingly diminished in the months after this dream. The sense of greater mental space represented in the dream seemed to spread throughout her body. Within months, too, Laura was able to enjoy a Caribbean vacation. The one-track world of rigid omnipotence could now enter another level of struggle with a world beyond it.

DISCUSSION

In the dreams discussed a central drama unfolded along the omnipotence–impotence dimension. Omnipotent hero or villain roles were diversely distributed among the various dream personae. The ego aims at maintaining some sense of mastery, directly or by stealth, in face of areas of sensed resourcelessness. At times one's sense of omnipotence is projected on to figures experienced as alien, while one acts out impotence (e.g., the snake man dream). If the defensive use of mastery fails, one has recourse to a mask of innocence which, finally, may give way to sheer terror. In the case of Laura's dream, what began as a scene of helplessness in face of change (which would usually prompt omnipotent operations), surprisingly resulted in a relatively healthy solution. In this case a detour situation (which stands for symbolization) replaces omnipotence.

The core imagery of Freud's greatest case histories gravitate around the omnipotence–impotence dimension. The dynamics of each case revolve around an image of being overwhelmed, flooded, invaded. In the Wolf Man the drama rushes toward a dream which Freud translated into Father overpowering Mother from the rear. In the Rat Man the core fantasy fear involved rats burrowing into the patient's anus. Schreber's feared and courted longing was to be possessed by his doctor god and, finally, by God himself. All, explicitly or by innuendo, involved rape by sodomy and war between passive–active, male–female tendencies.

Sodomic rape, as a paradigmatic image combining power and helplessness, may be viewed on many levels. In the present context it involves an experience of being taken over or managed by a greater power, by something uncontrollable (which one tries to control). One can envision as a kind of prototype the very early danger of being flooded by sensations of various sorts, possibly even in the womb, a "stimulus rape." The embryo-infant-child soon learns to dampen and filter stimulus input to a manageable level. However, stimulus and sensation may speed up or shut off in a variety of conditions. Certain phases of schizophrenia and artistic creation may involve massive stimulus streaming. It is as if protective barriers have been somewhat lifted and the individual feels inundated by wave after wave of intense experience. Some individuals may try to protect themselves from their own sensitivity by turning off their attentional capacity. From early on our mental equipment gives rise to images, thoughts, and feelings it cannot handle well. We scare ourselves with the imaginings we produce but cannot adequately process. Our mental creations are often ahead of our ability to assimilate them in meaningful and useful ways. In this sense we are at the mercy of the very psychophysical processes which constitute and sustain us. We are in a position of experiencing omnipotence and impotence at the same time: omnipotent creators, impotent receivers. These two positions intermingle in complex ways, and may be structured, for example, in sexual, social, or religious terms.

The omnipotence–impotence ambiguity is given decisive form in object relations. One may give omnipotence to the bad object one seeks to escape or outwit. Or, again, impotence and omnipotence may be variously divided and assigned to a combination of figures which form shifting facets of the dream mirror. A benign self-feeling seeks to maintain itself in the face of fluctuating dangers and obstacles. If it fails one may locate the personality's sense of power in some opposing image, where it may be gathered up, condensed, and frequently demonized.

In its pure form the ego's relation to power carries a hidden God-image, an idolatry. In Freud's psychology the God-image was associated with Father. In Jung's the God-image was fused with Mother and Self. In most Eastern religions the God-sense is identified with Self. Since All is Self essentially, there is no radical otherness. In Western religion God presents himself as a wholly Other with whom the Self mysteriously exists in communion, a dual unity—united yet distinct.

Recent work on psychosis, borderline states, and narcissistic disorders generally (disorders of the self) indicates that a proper location of the shifting God-image is of central importance. For example, Kohut's (1971) clinical descriptions chart oscillations between what may be termed "I am God" (grandiose self) and "You are God" (idealized other). Divine and demonic images often reflect inflated or deflated attitudes or states of being. The God-image is always active in psychic life.

The question of who or what carries the God function for the subject and how one's ultimate sense of power is distributed at a given time is critical for understanding the nature of the subject's distress and the direction of his or her movement. In work at the deepest levels of character it is necessary to search out and clarify the subject's relation to the power source. The subject tries to maintain and give away power in complex ways. As therapist one helps the subject search out new relations to felt sources of power and moments of surrender, incessantly unmasking and moving beyond subtle forms of megalomania and abasement. Dreams, in part, reflect ways felt power and powerlessness are distributed. As one's waking and sleeping life grow more connected, dreams can increasingly be relied on to suggest new ways to experience omnipotence and its correlates. Ideally, as time goes on, positive aspects of omnipotence interact with humility and fuel creative activity.

REFERENCES

Eigen, M. (1975). Psychopathy and individuation. *Psychotherapy: Theory, Research and Practice* 12:280–294.

_____ (1979a). Ideal images, creativity and the Freudian drama. *Psychocultural Review* 3:287–298.

_____ (1979b). On the defensive use of mastery. *American Journal of Psychoanalysis* 39:279–282.

_____ (1980a). Ideal images and instinctual fantasy. *Contemporary Psychoanalysis* 16:119–137.

_____ (1980b). On the significance of the face. *Psychoanalytic Review* 70:427–441.

_____ (1981). The area of faith in Winnicott, Lacan and Bion. *International Journal of Psycho-Analysis* 10:415–428.

_____ (1982). Creativity, instinctual fantasy and ideal images. *Psychoanalytic Review* 69:317–339.

_____ (1983). Dual union or undifferentiation? A critique of Marion Milner's sense of psychic creativeness. *International Journal of Psycho-Analysis* 10:415–428.

_____ (1984). On demonized aspects of the self. In *Evil: Self and Culture,* ed. M. C. Nelson and M. Eigen, pp. 91–123. New York: Human Sciences.

Kohut, H. (1971). *The Analysis of the Self.* New York: International Universities Press.

Matte Blanco, I. (1975). *The Unconscious as Infinite Sets.* London: Duckworth.

Weil, E. (1958). The origin and vicissitudes of the self-image. *Psychoanalysis* 1:3–19.

Zimmer, H. (1948). *The King and the Corpse.* Princeton, NJ: Pantheon Books.

19

Mindlessness-Selflessness

Although selflessness and mindlessness cannot be equated, there is much to be gained by studying one in relation to the other. Insanity is often described as "losing one's mind." As is often the case, the vernacular touches a profound, if one-sided, truth. The capacity to blank oneself out and inwardly vanish is a form of self-protection widespread in human life. It may be that the capacity to blunt pain and anesthetize oneself is a general characteristic of living beings. In human existence this elemental capacity is raised to a new power. It can vary from a momentary going blank to a vast nulling of the self.

A patient, Leila, speaks about her "oblivion machine." She vanishes in the face of life's difficulties. She is "not there" when she most wishes and needs to be there. It can happen in the seemingly most simple situations. She arrives at my office and the door is locked. Usually it is open. Should she ring or wait? She cannot decide. She goes back and forth until her mind starts spinning. She blanks out. After a time I go out to see what has happened to her. She is pale and in a cold sweat, dumbly tense and fit to be tied. She cannot make a sound. She cannot find herself at all. Later she said she wanted to cry when she saw me but was paralyzed. She saw me from under water or inside her "bell jar." My absence opened up an endless hole in her being through which she disappeared.

This particular episode was mild and easily gotten through. She began to find her voice after we were alone again. She had been startled to find a locked door. The startle reaction quickly turned to feeling stunned and she felt herself start to go under. She remembers a whirl of thoughts and feelings. Her need for me is so immense. How dare I not be there? Fury at her need and at me. Horror at her demand. Fear of fury and fury at fear. Weakness. Drowning. Partially vanishing forever, partially transfixed and staring blankly at and out of her vanishing.

The unexpected paralyzes her. Surprise, loss of control, and cataclysm go together, as they do for brain-damaged persons (she often refers to herself as brain-damaged, although she is not). Here the loss is associated with me. Any

237

kind of social exclusion (whether an attack, slight, or being ignored) provokes an unbearable sense of isolation, a numbing pain that ends with a dying-out of her self. My absence is a sign of her deficiency and makes her more deficient and vacant. In the present instance she is able to say that her not ringing the bell is already a kind of choice, an expression of her not being there. She wanted me to find her on my doorstep. Simply, she wanted me to find her. But by the time I did she forgot she wanted this. It was remembered only through a stifled urge to cry. Upon my arrival she wants me to see her paralyzed and to feel it my fault. In general, I ought to feel it my fault for the way she is or isn't. Yet such blaming is already an ascent from oblivion, the beginning of a return, the mark of my presence recalling her to herself. The moment before there had been nothing.

This relatively simple example mixes up a number of states and levels of being. For example, she and/or I speak of startle, fear-fury, blaming (hostile self-pity with an attribution of causation), loss, deficiency, isolation, weeping, cataclysm, spinning, paralysis, mesmerization, numbing, fading, blanking, dying, oblivion, and nothingness. These states vary in degree and quality of awareness of self and other and in the way mental and physical aspects of the self are organized. They form a complex and dynamic network of mindfulness and mindlessness.

In a sense, Freud's work can be read as a meditation on mind's encounter with its own apparent mindlessness, a "mindful mindlessness." His concepts of repression, dissociation, and decathexis deal with gaps, splits, or ruptures in mental functioning. He shows active dynamisms at work in mind loss. He studies how the mind slips away from itself yet continues to express its most basic concerns indirectly through all one is and does.

Perhaps the most formidable of all defenses that Freud describes is decathexis, a withdrawal of energy from or loss of interest in others. In his earlier writings Freud noted that a loss of interest in others is "balanced" by a correlative inflation of one's own ego: megalomania. Later he added that decathexis can go further and deplete the ego as well. One can withdraw from oneself. He depicts stages of withdrawal. Rather than simply return to an earlier narcissism as protection against life's difficulties, one may seek to cancel oneself altogether by approximating a return to an inorganic state, an absolute insensibility. Rather than an exaggerated or inflated I, all life-feeling and I-feeling are lost.

Whatever the status of Freud's concept of psychic energy, decathexis, death drive, and his mythic–mechanistic metapsychology, the psychological realities he points to are crucial. He attempts to deal with a tendency to numb or deaden oneself by postulating an urge to return to a zero point. In effect, the subject commits a kind of psychological suicide by emptying or denuding experience, by becoming as if inanimate. Absolute decathexis is absolute painlessness. This is more than a return to the womb and primary narcissism. It is an undoing of all psychic aliveness and all that might keep one in existence.

It may not be possible to achieve an absolute zero point of psychic activity and still be alive. But various mental states approximate such a hypothetical position. An extreme example is the "blank psychosis." Here the subject's psychic life seems to be radically impoverished. One has very little ability to tolerate neurotic fantasy, perverse illusion, or psychotic hallucination. One gives the appearance of operating by massive denial. Nothing bothers or grips one or has any real meaning. One imperturbably goes along with the day-to-day routine.

I met one such man, call him Lenny, after his release from a mental hospital. Once every so many years his implacability breaks down and he threatens to become violent. His violence seems to occur without any accompanying mental content, although immediately preceding the hospitalization after which I saw him, his attacks had been directed against the milkman and his mother. No experience of fear or rage is reported. However, his fits follow a breakdown of his usual behavioral routine. He starts to mumble to himself. He and those around him say they do not know what he says. His life is a mystery to everyone in it but he does not think there is anything unusual about it.

When I saw him he looked like a vacuous Buddha. He was chronically overweight yet his appearance was not unpleasant. He was cherub-like. His fat seemed a comfortable cushion, a cozy life-jacket. If I let myself go I could feel a warm and quiet ecstasy while staring at his face. It was a stillborn ecstasy because I have no evidence that he ever felt it. He tended to sit without initiating conversation and to reply monosyllabically or with simple sentences if I asked questions. Within this framework I could detect subtle variations in quality of mood and attitude. At times his expression and tone were slightly disdainful and he shrugged me off as if I should know better. At other times he was complacent and tolerant of my presence. If I tried to stir him up he looked at me with a benign, quizzical, and unblinking gaze, as if waiting for my madness to run its course. He remained more or less unruffled throughout the year (it felt like five) I knew him.

Nearly twenty years later, what is most memorable is his mysterious maternal warmth. Anything can be read into his Mona Lisa-Cheshire Cat grin. He was like an old lady who knows everything and sits and rocks as life goes by. Often I felt nothing at all was going on inside his mind. The little he said showed me he was not retarded. He seemed just as happy when I spoke or didn't speak or whether we saw or didn't see each other. At the outset he came because his father brought him. About a year or so later he dropped away. Was he back in enough of a routine for his father to stop worrying? Was he on the way to another spell in the hospital? He was unshakably friendly with me to the end.

In Lenny's case it mattered little if I interpreted elements in his milkman–mother duo or trio. In a sense his whole existence was womb-like. He exuded an aura of prescience with which he appeared to be out of contact. His eyes might sparkle but, like the stars, were mute. Perhaps this reflected some kind of identification with the breast mother or mother's reverie, a cushion or omniscient no-nothing mother. His appearance was breast-like. Perhaps from time to time his suppressed active body-ego broke through with baby fits? No hint of a spontaneously active baby appeared throughout the time I knew him. One of my fantasies was that I might be of use to him if we were in a hospital together when he was violent, if his violence were not whisked away too quickly by modern miracle drugs. In the time I knew him he did not need medication because his whole state of being seemed to work like a massive dose of tranquilizers. Perhaps from time to time his self-administered well-being wore off and unconscious rage built up. Perhaps, in the long run, there were cycles of inhibition–disinhibition, denial and irruption. Was this rhythm (if it was a rhythm) governed chemically, psychodynamically, environmentally, all or any of these?

Does it make much sense to call Lenny's problem lack of integration or is it closer to the mark to say that not enough of his personality came into existence in the first place? What came through most of all was that Lenny in some important sense was not there. From time to time Lenny's blankness broke into bits of quasi-hallucinatory violence. His absent self possibly became present in a fragmentary way as the milkman–mother called some stillborn or blunted desire into being. Flickers of life rose and fell out of and back to a baseline numbness. He had fallen out of play and out of reach. He vanished in the cherubic glow he floated on. The most striking impression about his mysterious maternal warmth was its blankness. It was as impersonal as Mother Nature and as silent, yet lacked the fecundity and variety of the living Mother. It was steadfast and unreasoning. He had no thought about himself he wished to articulate. In his absence psychic growth passed him by.

If Freud studied gaps and distortions in mental functioning, it can also be said that his work was a sustained exploration of ways the psyche substitutes pleasure for pain. He early characterized the infant's first attempts at thinking as an hallucinatory substitution of a pleasurable for painful situation: the baby hallucinates satisfaction at the breast for the absent mother. Similarly, Freud depicted the motor of dream work as wounded desire seeking fulfillment. When Freud says that a dream attempts to fulfill the ego's wish to preserve sleep, he is saying that the psyche is trying to achieve a painless state. To an extent, the dream is a kind of psychic womb or pearl created around an irritant. It dissolves pain by representing it.

Whatever the correctness of Freud's specifics, he draws attention to a fundamental tendency in human life to imagine pleasure where there is pain. Freud's concern is more radical than hedonistic utilitarian philosophy that seeks a balance of pleasure over pain in practical affairs. Freud says we imagine ourselves satisfied when we are not and we do this at the most fundamental levels of our being.

Lenny's blankness seemed to be a kind of mindless well-being akin to a blank quasi-hallucinatory state. Leila's oblivion was more obviously related to the pain of desire. Her life was more explicitly nightmarish, alive with terror. Together they illustrate difficulties Freud perceived in his formulations. Many dreams represent psychic pain in an attempt to master, not simply to obliterate it. Moreover, two main polar routes to obliteration often are at work: imaginary wish-fulfillment (Freud's pleasure principle) and voiding (Freud's death wish). If I may translate Freud's insight into phenomenological language more congenial to me, we run away from pain by *blissing* or *blanking out*. At the same time, we use the fullness–emptiness polarity as a source of inspiration and support to face what must be faced and to live what must be lived.

In critical moments we are caught between hallucination, zero, and a tormenting reality. In optimal circumstances we use our tendency to anesthetize ourselves as a resting place and launching station for further encounter with our lacks and distortions. However, our spontaneous use of psychic anesthesia can gain the upper hand. The natural "dosing mechanism" runs amok or is unable to be balanced by other tendencies. We may fall so far in the null dimension that a hallucinated state of fulfillment is more than we can bear. Once habituated to catastrophic nothingness, pleasure itself becomes painful. In this black hole hallucinated satisfaction becomes a risk, not simply a flight. If desire and fulfillment fuse in hallucinations, at least the latter bear witness that desire is still alive. Wounded wishes find a home in hallucination. But desire is lost in the null dimension where there is no home and nothing to have a home for.

Whereas Saint Paul knew that human nature was given to sin, Freud knew it was immersed in madness. The capacity to be out of contact is more ubiquitous than commonly imagined. The ability to be in touch richly and accurately with ourselves and others is a precious capacity and one not to be taken for granted. Freud may not solve the problems his work raises. But his preoccupation with the inherent link between madness and the lie we live stands as a bulwark and warning against the dangers of a silently megalomanic self-righteousness. We have been warned about human vanity, hubris, and pride throughout the ages. The depth psychologies round out this warning with special urgency inasmuch as life on earth is now in jeopardy in a most horrific and literal way. We actually possess the weaponry with which to dramatize our attraction to the null dimension, an enaction that will at once fulfill and explode our fantasy of painlessness.

Today our inherent capacity for pleasure and good feelings is systematically exploited in the commercial and political arenas. This was always so. But the current economic manipulation of incredibly effective public media, particularly television, can arouse and structure our wish to feel good to an extent scarcely conceivable in earlier ages.

The recent (1984) United States presidential election campaign provides ample demonstration of the power exerted by the illusion of good feelings vis-à-vis the claim of painful realities. One candidate focused on painful realities while the other dismissed him as a harbinger of gloom and doom. The implicit winning message seemed to be that accuracy of perception and thoughtfulness breed pessimism. To think problems through is too troublesome. Better to enjoy the positive side of life and count our blessings than take too close a look.

It is probably no accident that the winner was also characterized as mindless, inattentive to details, and blank, a professor of wishful rather than informed optimism. This candidate did not once expose himself to hard, extended questioning in a public situation. He was characterized as walled off, possessing an immunity shield, a "Dr. Feelgood." He seemed to want to give the impression of well-being, strength, and concern without pain. In such an instance it would seem that pleasantness and emptiness converge. Such playing with the null point is alarming and would be even more so if not for the consideration that those in power possess some kind of sanity to so manipulate our wish for happiness.

To be sure, the failure to achieve enough good feeling to support healthy mental functioning is as real a danger as the exploitation of good feeling in collective brainwashing maneuvers. To a certain extent, the motherly voice of the President or the TV announcer helps soothe the terrors that threaten to break through one's imperturbable good sense. Nevertheless, there is always a price to pay. The rash of recent youthful suicides, bombings of abortion clinics, violence against synagogues and private property of Jews and blacks, and the like, are symptoms of an illness, a madness that threatens the social body as a whole. The attempted induction of mass scale "good feelings" and the potential for violence seem to go together. They are elements of a broader structure handed down through the ages and which we are only beginning to understand.

There is a mixture of cynicism and naiveté in madness which hideously mocks the innocence and sophistication of health. The joy that arises and persists in the developed personality takes account of and absorbs human suffering. It is tempered by an ironic awareness of evil. It is instinctively cognizant of the play of reversals and so wary of polarizations in daily life. It is no less pristine for being chastened. It is enriched through experience and attentiveness to details in ways that make a difference. In the mature personality irony and faith balance each other. Vision and the requirements of situations struggle to meet.

Meeting is not free of difficulty and lack of fit. On the contrary, we often are born and reborn through each other precisely because of our difficulties. We come through our own and each other's blocks. We get through to ourselves and to each other over and over. We collide head-on, we wait it out, we try out possibilities, we give up, we try again. Visionary hope will not settle for less than breaking through cynicism and despair. At the same time our cynicism tells us that distance is important. We cannot trifle with the gaps between and within us. We learn to live in the movement between face and facelessness, at the point where union and difference cocreate one another.

20

Omniscience

Omniscience is not once mentioned in the index of Winnicott's major works; it is not a term he uses. Yet we will see that his thinking is concerned with omniscience by implication and in basic ways. His clinical writings would not be what they are if they were not preoccupied with the underlying problem of omniscience. Omnipotence is explicitly at the center of his concerns; omniscience works more invisibly.

Feeling Unreal and Benign Omnipotence

It can properly be argued that Winnicott directs his major efforts to problems revolving around the phenomenon of depersonalization. The agonizing sense of not feeling real to oneself is at the heart of his work. Whether and how one comes to feel real is his central clinical concern.

In developmental terms, this involves more than depersonalization. Strictly speaking, the latter refers to a sense of one's own reality undone. Winnicott focuses our attention on what factors enable the self to feel real in the first place and, conversely, what prompts failure of true self-feeling.

The connection between omnipotence and feeling real is not our focus here but we must say enough about it to provide a background for our study of omniscience. Winnicott associates a kind of benign and creative omnipotence with what he calls the infant's "vital spark," "continuity," "going on being," "psychosomatic unity," and "True Self." This undefensive omnipotence gains its meaning from an interactive milieu. The quality of interweaving of baby with mother provides a place for the baby's genuine expressiveness, or mars it. Does the infant create or discover the objects that enter his experiential field? The mother does not ask the baby this question but participates in a context in which creation and discovery are one. The intunement of baby's and mother's activity supports his sense of aliveness. Winnicott (1960) writes, "The good enough mother meets the omnipotence of the infant and to some extent makes sense of it. She does this repeatedly. A True Self begins to have life through the strength given to the infant's weak ego by the mother's implementations of the infant's omnipotent expressions" (p. 145). "At this early stage the facilitating environment is giving the infant the *experience of omnipotence*; by this I mean more than magical control, I mean the creative aspect of experience" (Winnicott 1963, p. 180).

At this point the infant's feeling real evolves through the support his omnipotence gains. It is tempting to say, through the support his *activity* gains. However, in another context Winnicott places the sense of passive being before active doing (Winnicott 1971a). Is the early omnipotence he refers to active, passive, or both? Questions such as these run through Winnicott's work. Partly to solve this ambiguity he notes that infantile experience is essentially paradoxical, at least when viewed from an adult perspective, and perhaps from the infant's own perspective as well. Human experience is marked by paradox from its inception. We move back and forth between blending capacities.

A host of interrelated tensions characterize Winnicott's work. He does not leave Freud's conflict theory behind but transposes aspects of it to a peculiar Winnicottian key. There may be an interactive basis of omnipotence but what does the baby know about "dependency"? How is the latter negotiated? What happens when the milieu does not fit in with the baby's wishes or needs? What happens if it fits too well? The sense of aliveness requires an adequate fit and nonfit in order to prosper (Winnicott 1963). Timing and quality are crucial.

Winnicott came to see the infant's fury at failures of omnipotence as implicated in the creation of the sense of otherness. In his paper "The Use of an Object and Relating Through Identifications," this failure, fury, and sense of otherness are interconnected (Winnicott 1969). He takes up and reworks Freud's suggestion that hate is the first reaction to externality. For Winnicott there is a sense in which rage helps to create the sense of the otherness of others or, rather, a new and fresh sense of self and other. Winnicott tries to envision how the fit and nonfit between self and other enhances aliveness or leads to the dying-out of self (a phenomenological restatement of Freud's death wish, particularly decathexis of the self).

Perhaps the most basic and guiding paradox of Winnicott's thought is that there is something sacred about human autonomy which interdependence must protect and mediate. The infant's sense of ongoing being requires a mediating milieu to survive or thrive—yet there is something irreducibly private about it. Long before the infant becomes a "unit self" in the ordinary sense, a self vis-à-vis others, the infant's experiencing is his own experiencing. What kind of self–other is there prior to clear spatial-temporal representational mapping? How to talk about this union yet distinction is a fundamental issue which Winnicott takes up again and again. It is as if he is never satisfied with what he can say about it. Perhaps in his "Use of an Object" paper he came as close as he could. The author believes it to be Winnicott's climactic paper and that all else in Winnicott must be reread in light of it.

Object Usage and the Problem of Knowing

The individual becomes able to use objects for growth purposes after discovering that the other survives one's destructive attacks and fantasy control attempts. A kind of psychic explosion takes place in which one lets go as fully as possible. In the other's survival, otherness is born (or reborn) and the self quickens. One feels a fresh sense of aliveness in a joyous shock of difference. Spontaneity *is* possible. We survive ourselves. We come through. We become more real together. Our very sense of what real means keeps shifting.

The author has written in detail elsewhere on Winnicott's "object usage" idea (Eigen 1981a). Here the emphasis is on the hidden omniscience which is transcended in the birth of otherness. Winnicott emphasized going beyond omnipotent control. By the latter he means, in important part, projective–introjective fantasy — a psychic web-spinning. He pictures the patient caught in a kind of fantasy structure. In extreme cases the individual can spend the better part of his life trapped in fantasy (recall Winnicott's distinction between the unlived life of fantasying and the lived life of dreaming (Winnicott 1971b). It is as if a projection–introjection machine takes over and works in an automatic, dissociated way. No room for real otherness is left and so no room for real self is either. At first the self may enjoy the cocoon existence it hits upon but eventually it becomes more and more entombed. In this context a welling-up of destructive feeling may try to burst the bubble. In destructive outbursts the subject tries to break his "bell jar" and let fresh air in.

Insofar as the bell jar is or involves encapsulation in projective–introjective fantasy webs, omniscient as well as omnipotent control must be a core component. What is let in by destructiveness which clears the air is precisely new ways of experiencing and knowing self and other. The individual scarcely realizes he is inured in omniscience. He may feel intensely ignorant and inferior. Yet a certain obliviousness pervades his existence. The details in his experience which might make a difference are glossed over. Experience is not static but the fantasy-trapped individual may act as if it were. It is as if he knows ahead of time what is and is not possible. He knows what fate has allotted. All existence is evaluated in terms of his projective–introjective frame of reference. In effect, he lives from a standpoint of omniscience without knowing it.

It is difficult to overestimate the role unconscious omniscience plays in deadening the capacity to experience. If one knows what is going to happen ahead of time, one does not have to experience it. Paradoxically, omniscience combined with omnipotence can play a role in the hallucinatory heightening of experience; for example, the power of the magician, the one who knows, mind over matter. In such instances it is the gnostic element which lends omnipotence its force. Without guiding omniscience, omnipotence would be dumb.

Our sense of knowing has a way of spreading through our mental field and acting like an anesthetic. What we know may lead to or block the new; it may heighten or dull experience. However, our sense of knowing as such is an implicit part of all or much of our experience. It is not too difficult for the sense of knowing itself to become a refuge (or torment) whether one knows or not. In this context knowing as a general capacity is abstracted from its specific contents. It becomes its own content. The philosopher may turn this mental gesture into a creative act and investigate the knowing of knowing. But in psychopathology an empty knowing or omniscience can substitute for the struggle to know. A purpose of Winnicott's account of object usage is to try to speak about experiencing which surprises us, which we cannot steal by omniscience, in which difference is really news (Bateson 1979).

Omniscience and Formlessness: Winnicott's Clinical Attitude and Unintegration

The individual who feels unreal to himself must be helped to learn how to play. This is no easy matter. Play can be very serious. It is hard work to let go what one is used to, even if it is killing one, and still harder to let something new happen. Religious writings which stress how difficult it is to let in or bear saving grace come to mind (Eigen 1985). The very term, *grace*, suggests an approach to life, a taste, or tone, which seems closed insofar as we are lost in unreality.

In order for playing to occur Winnicott tries to create a setting in which the individual can relax (often "relax" into a deeper intensity), psychically doodle, let happen what will. This is not to imply that playing is simply nonpurposive. Freud's description of the fort-da game alerts us to what pain the child seeks to triumph over in play. Yet a nonpurposive moment is necessary before the form one works on becomes clear. The child is intensely alive in real play and this is just what the patient Winnicott is concerned with fails to achieve. As Winnicott writes:

> It is in playing and only in playing that the individual child or adult is able to be creative and to use the whole personality, and it is only in being creative that the individual discovers the self. [1971c, p. 54]

> The person we are trying to help needs a new experience in a specialized setting. The experience is one of a nonpurposive state, as one might say a sort of ticking over of the unintegrated personality. I referred to this as formlessness in the case description. [1971c, p. 55]

Winnicott stresses the need for the analyst to be there in a receptive way. He must lend to the patient an alive and perceptive presence, an atmosphere implicitly rich with psychic nutrients. He, too, must be able to play, to allow spontaneous oscillations between form and formlessness. So often it is the analyst's attitude or mood which determines whether or not a drop into formlessness is possible. Above all Winnicott stresses the analyst must not be too "smart"—he must not be omniscient.

Winnicott writes, "I think I interpret mainly to let the patient know the limits of my understanding" (1969, pp. 86–87). He speaks so that the patient will know he is not omniscient, so that the patient experiences lack of omniscience as possible. Of course, this does not mean that Winnicott feigns stupidity. Playing dumb is the other side of omniscience. Obviously Winnicott is not stupid. His best interpretations are often inspired (and even, he later says, perhaps a bit mad). They preserve and further the link between experiencing and knowing (not omniscience). The method of unknowing he recommends works at or beyond the edge and limits of knowing and is not simply the mute collapse of the will to know.

One can distinguish several sorts of "unknowing" in Winnicott's work and life generally. There is the unknowing of simple ignorance. One does not know many things. This, of course, does not mean one knows nothing at all. But however well educated, there are always gaps. There is everyday as well as cultural ignorance. Winnicott may know something about creating a milieu in which unknowing is possible but not do so well repairing an airplane or a heart. From infancy on our life is shot through with matrices of knowing and blank spots. Knowing and not knowing are so finely interwoven that together they constitute an essential characteristic of our capacity to experience. We may focus on what we know or do not know or various combinations; or we may focus on our knowing–unknowing capacity. At certain moments we may choose to emphasize the gaps, the blank spots, and unknowing may seem mysterious. It becomes a method or approach that opens up new possibilities or turns into a valued state for its own sake. One lives in and through unknowing and the unknowable. At this point simple, everyday ignorance gives way to the numinous. There is a danger that in certain instances the mystique of unknowing and omniscience fuse. The freedom of embodied ignorance and acknowledgment of genuine limits opens up into the unknowing which is one with the formless infinite.

In Winnicott's work unknowing and unintegration go together. What is crucial is that the analyst does not pretend to know the patient more than he really does. This gives the patient (and analyst) space. The patient, too, is relieved of having to know more than he does. This helps him let go of the myths he has spun around himself and become "unintegrated." For Winnicott disintegration means one would hold onto something if one could, but a process one cannot control is spinning one out of existence. The ways one has tried to hold oneself together have not worked and the mess one is takes over.

Unintegration, by contrast, is a purer state. The subject dips into creative formlessness. He lives between the lines of his built-up personality. He gets to where he was before defensive encapsulation took over. It is implicit in Winnicott's vision that we sense our baby soul as it was before it was marred, that intimations of a pristine thread continue throughout our lifetime, that we never quite lose contact with something that we sense is our most precious us.

Unintegration refers to the chaos of experiencing before it congeals into psychic formations which can be used defensively. It refers to a time or dimension of experiencing prior to the ability to split off and oppose aspects of the self to one another (particularly mind–body, thinking–feeling). It remains a state between organizations one can repair to, a kind of rest in which one forgets who one thinks one is, perhaps a moment's absent-minded immersion in nothing in particular. It is a letting go and clearing out. It is a relief to be rid of oneself and feel the deeper order opened by unintegrated chaos. In it one senses a groping toward an original face.

This does not mean that one's original face is always pretty or that there is total lack of friction. In unintegrated moments one may experience a profound well-being one scarcely imagined possible. But holocaustal rages also rise and fall as the emotional weather changes. Or one may be gripped by terror beyond words (the baby terror Rilke depicts before mother "organizes" or gives an "identity" to the nameless abyss). In unintegration one is not frozen into any one position. It refers to a time in infancy before one can adequately process or make sense out of so much that one is experiencing. One cannot yet split oneself off from experiencing or what one undergoes.

The important point is that in a state of unintegration anything can happen. One does not know or think one knows what will happen next. One is not closed or split off from oneself. To be sure, the infant shuts off. It can fall into a stupor or avert attention, but usually it returns. The storm or irritant passes; it starts from scratch, all new. There may be extreme instances in which it must deaden itself most of the time, but this is not the normal case. It is more usual for human beings to both shut *and* split off from themselves a bit later, when they develop the mental resources to do so (Eigen 1980, Elkin 1972).

A mild example of the tension between omnisciences of analyst and patient can be found in Guntrip's account of his analysis with Winnicott (Eigen 1981b, Guntrip 1975). Guntrip and Winnicott agree that Guntrip needs to (re)experience unintegration. Guntrip keeps himself in existence through activity. He cannot really rest unless he is ill. Through Winnicott, Guntrip gets a taste of a mothering milieu which allows unintegration and respects just being. Simple being had been impossible in Guntrip's infancy and early childhood because his mother had been too vacant and empty or intrusive. Either his passivity was violated, his mother a hate-inspiring psychic rapist — or he was threatened with a fall into emptiness and nonbeing. Guntrip argued that the latter was the more profound menace and that any hate he might experience was a defense against it.

Winnicott felt uncomfortable about doing away with aggression too quickly and continued to agitate for some further acknowledgment of rage from Guntrip. At this point Guntrip felt he "knew better" than Winnicott. He felt Winnicott was not Winnicottian enough. Winnicott sensed it is part of a baby's spontaneous responsiveness to rage at absence before dying out. He affirmed this baby rage, so much so that in his "The Use of an Object" paper he made it responsible for creating the sense of otherness. He gave spontaneous baby destructiveness a positive valuation Guntrip did not. Guntrip felt a baby would not be angry if mother were perfectly present. His theoretical position kept him sealed off from a certain range of infantile spontaneity. He went too far toward an idealized possibility in reaction against Freudian drive theory. Of course, he "knew better" than Freud.

Winnicott was modest about what he felt he saw. He and Guntrip never came to blows. The friction was subtle and perhaps played down. One might view it as a necessary difference of sensibility and vision. But one also can sense the hidden play of omniscience, particularly in Guntrip's use of knowledge as a defense as well as a probe. Winnicott seemed to be more aware of his own use of knowledge as a defense and hoped to avoid this kind of smartness. He must have been aware how ubiquitous omniscience is, since he tried to work from a position of ignorance and repeatedly called attention to ways in which thinking one knows cuts one off from unintegration. We can only guess what Winnicott's personal struggle with omniscience must have been.

From a position of unintegration it might not have been necessary for Guntrip to call emptiness his most basic psychic fact. Emptiness is known, in part, with reference to a plenitude which one may be furious at losing (one could argue that *plenitude–emptiness* are co-constitutive or interlacing terms of human experience [Eigen 1983]). In unintegration a variety of feelings might have freely appeared and transformed themselves without need of precocious closure of the rivalry between them. Emptiness, too, may be one with creative formlessness, a pregnant rather than an inert void, a perennial starting point, a nakedness. It is a tribute to Guntrip that he held fast to his sick point, that he could not compromise with the emptiness which deadened him. To the end he had one eye on his pathology. But a hidden omniscience in the use of his therapeutic vision marred his part-triumph and reconciliation (Eigen 1981b).

Omniscience and Omnipotence

Omniscience refers to limitless mental power and omnipotence to limitless physical power. Colloquial speech distinguishes between the know-it-all and the bully, brains and brawn. Many fables suggest the self must face dual tendencies in extreme forms expressed by figures such as the magus–magician and stupid, fearsome monsters. The Old Testament God condenses omniscience and omnipotence in ways which at times make Him seem like a big baby. In human terms, omniscience and omnipotence can be seen, in part, as two aspects of infantile narcissism. In psychoanalytic terms they tend to correspond to mental and physical self-functions (Eigen 1984, 1986).

Few psychoanalytic writers have systematically tried to distinguish omniscience from omnipotence; those who have done so include Bion (1977), Elkin (1972), and Meltzer (1973). Lacan (1978) offers scathing analyses of omniscience in the psychoanalytic situation as well as in infantile development. He tries to fathom the role of the analyst as "one who is supposed to know." He undresses patient and analyst alike in their collusion with this attribution. In Winnicott, we have seen, the concept of omniscience is silent but pervasive. He formally speaks of omnipotence but much that he says has omniscience in mind.

Dramas revolving around omniscience play an important role as therapy unfolds. Patients often expect the therapist to possess more (or less) knowledge about the patient and therapy than the therapist actually does. A therapist may be revered for possessing godlike qualities or despised for not being godlike enough. In the latter instance the patient may assume that the analyst ought to know more. A collusive situation can develop in which the therapist feels guilty at not being better, gets angry at the patient's demands, affects superior knowledge, or plays dumb. The patient's tacit overvaluation of knowledge may go undetected, be catered to, or provoke retaliation. Therapists who begin therapy by inviting patients to join in the search for understanding set the stage for a resistance which later will come home to roost: "I know all this but how does it help? I'm just the same."

The pressure to know sometimes stimulates but often blocks the therapist's openness to the impact of psychic reality. New therapists are especially vulnerable to self-reproaches engendered by an appeal to their omniscience. Older therapists sometimes harden in their masks.

How do we choose what we say in therapy from the myriad of possibilities which at all times confront us? When shall we speak, when stay silent? Bion (1970) depicts this situation as a geometric solid with an infinite number of surfaces. Each analyst chooses or stumbles upon what he must say from alternative sets of interpretations which approach infinity. If he does his job right his remarks grow from contact with the deeper logic of his patient's (and his own) life. But each authentic therapist enters this psychohistorical field from a slightly different angle. Paths may converge and/or go to very different places. The patient's destiny is, to a point, dependent on the analyst's quality of vision and being, and vice versa.

Since selection (what to attend to, when, what to say or do, how, and so on) is always necessary, the patient knows that whatever the analyst does or doesn't do reflects his personal bias. All hinges on how this belief is related to by patient and analyst alike. Either party can abuse his just claim to know more (or less) than the other about what is happening between them. The patient can see through his analyst's pretensions to be an analyst and so discount his truth as well. Similarly, an analyst can be misled (usually through his own narcissism) by his patient's pretensions or refusal of patienthood: omniscience opposes omniscience. The question of resistance here hinges on whose omniscience is superior, who is the greater know-it-all. The analyst who falls through this trapdoor can spin interminably in ambiguity, yet to compromise the infinity used as a weapon would also be an error. The ability to undercut an analysis because of its uncertainty thrives only with a demand for omniscience as its background. The omniscient one invites others to join in some variation of the omniscience game. The analyst cannot solve or get out of this situation simply by pretending not to be omniscient. We must enter and wrestle with the capacities and tensions which constitute us. Bion's description of the psychoanalytic attitude in terms of the abnegation of desire, memory, and understanding is one way of approaching the unknowing which undercuts and opens the field of omniscience.

We turn now to clinical examples which move in and out of this psychic field. Will the author speak from the viewpoint of the omniscient analyst? Creativity moves through the gaps in our sense of omniscience. How can we escape the oddities of a discourse in which one says one knows or doesn't know about one's omniscience? We cannot escape such Möbius strips of the mind. They are our partners and we must see where we go together.

An Omniscient Therapist

We will explore the dreams of two patients who were working with the same therapist, Dr. Omnis, the author's supervisee. The approach is sketchy, and perhaps arbitrary, but it is expedient in bringing out various facets of omniscience, which is our focus here. The reader can assume that what is presented involves shreds of a work torn out of context.

Dr. Omnis felt his main problems as a therapist were fear of loss and seductiveness. He was a handsome man who triggered intense erotic transferences which bound his patients to him. At the time the author supervised him he was recovering from a divorce and the ensuing difficulties of making contact with himself and others. He oscillated between isolation and overactivity. Nevertheless, he showed a calm front to patients and could tolerate profound areas of depression. It almost seemed as if he courted his patients' despair. However, he short-circuited anger by acting as an advice-giving friend at crucial moments. The dependency he elicited worried him, yet made him feel superior. He often acted as if he knew best.

Dr. Omnis saw himself more as a humanistic than an analytic therapist. He thought it useful to share aspects of his feelings, which he hoped would help take the sting out of his patients' sense of isolation. Yet he did this from a somewhat cut-off, superior position. Patients were invited to open up and share experiences (which happened at times and was beneficial), but tended to bounce off his pose. To an extent, his wish for intimacy remained a wish. Patients loved him for it only to find their depressive isolation intensified by his own evasive despair and inaccessibility. Since he kept up a well-meaning front, his patients took the onus of their despair on themselves.

The supervisor's approach was to help Dr. Omnis clarify what it was like for him to be with his patients. He easily related his patients' strong erotic transferences to his own needs, and could soon try to take his fear of loss as a signal that he was about to try to bind the patient to him. At times he felt his patients ought to leave him because of the way he used them. However, his behavior did not appreciably change. His patients' despair fascinated and froze him. He was drawn to it yet distanced himself. He felt panicky as his therapy work provoked one messy situation after another (this was so before consultation) and the more overwhelming it threatened to be, the cooler he became.

Since it was difficult to penetrate or really move this mess, the supervisor found himself starting to play with a dangling thread, his advice giving. This seemed to be something we could locate and begin to study more finely. Dr. Omnis found himself face to face with the paradox of giving advice when his life was a wreck. He acknowledged that when he advised his patients he felt a deeper calm, a superior well-being. He could sense how he might provoke additional misery in order to gain this momentary sense of mastery. As his patients lived out turmoil similar to his own, he could taste what it might feel like to be above the storm. Their dependency allowed his omniscience freer play than he could get away with in ordinary circumstances.

Dr. Omnis soon observed that a sense of "knowing better than" pervaded much of his life. It had been an element in the making and breaking of his marriage. Both he and his ex-wife had been attracted to the air of mental superiority each gave off. But the chronic contempt implicit in this attitude made living together impossible. Similarly, knowing better than his superiors had led to self-destructive difficulties in various job settings. In social life his all-knowing stance severely limited the kinds of people he could tolerate. An attitude which seemed to work with patients sabotaged his life as a whole. He previously had not considered his problems from this particular angle.

As time went on he permitted himself to confess his own underlying despair as a person and therapist. He had always felt inferior–superior, and at some point the idea of becoming a therapist seemed to offer a way out. It afforded him a prestigious base of operation. In his fantasy, at least, people looked up to him and social circles opened. But in a secret place he remained cynical and lost. He could get into his patients and manipulate that place through them. For a moment he could experience something intensely, if only by proxy, but in the end an iciness won out. He did not know what to do with what he stumbled upon. A cynical despair blocked the way. His fusional gestures humored his narcissism but left a bad taste. He stayed away from the hate and unreality he glimpsed.

In this context, the "dread of surrender to resourceless dependence in the analytic situation" Masud Khan (1972) writes about applies to therapists as well as patients. Dr. Omnis's dread of resourcelessness in the face of his own and his patients' situations contributed to premature verbalization from a position of "seeming to know." Unconscious (or conscious) omniscience spread through his life and prevented experiential sequences from unfolding. It may have provoked vicious scenarios but it kept more basic holes and knots intact.

As supervision unfolded, Dr. Omnis struggled with suspending the need to know (a need to be on top of) which so greatly saturated his psychic field.

Pretending to know ensured he could stay sealed off from himself. It was an inviolable position of safety. To venture forth would require him to be attentive to the impact of patients from moment to moment and keep open to what was evoked. His tentative forays in tolerating this kind of tension resulted in the dreams reported below.

The Owl and the Seal

The first dream is that of a patient we will call Mr. Lamen. He had long been in great pain and felt inwardly isolated. At the time in question he was a withdrawn man, 32 years old, who spent most of his free time at home watching TV. His social conscience nagged him and he tried to force himself to go out and be with people. But such efforts usually made him feel more unreal. He feared life was passing him by and he would enter old age alone. He felt intensely inferior and unworthy and was nagged by a sense that things were wrong and rarely righted themselves.

Mr. Lamen dreamed that somehow an owl was trapped. It was not clear how the owl had been trapped. Had an owl trap been set? Was the owl caught in a trap meant for another animal? The scene switched and a healthy seal appeared. The seal was in a body of water not in the woods. It was enjoying itself swimming around. Were there other seals? Would there be soon?

As we discussed the dream, Dr. Omnis remarked that the owl must be the "wise old owl," a creature awake in darkness. It represented his patient's and his own hidden omniscience. Both had been trapped by the latter and now were trapping it. They had some self-doubt and reservations about what they were doing. But trapping the owl allowed the seal to emerge.

The seal expressed playful social feeling. This contrasted with the secluded, serious owl. Such social feeling can easily be abused. Seals can be taught tricks and turned into performers. Such a danger may make the prescient, reclusive owl important for self-preservation. However, in the dream Mr. Lamen definitely got a good feeling from the seal. The seal gave him a lift. It represented a potentially wholesome tendency which had been thwarted. Together owl and seal represent mental and body self tendencies which had become distorted or been thwarted. The work Dr. Omnis and the supervisor were doing on his hidden omniscience enabled Mr. Lamen's tyrannical owl and playful seal to enter a dream scene and perhaps evolve.

Snake and Mouse

A second patient, Ms. Ferva, had many feelings in common with Mr. Lamen. She, too, had long been in pain and felt isolated. Similarly, she suffered from an intense sense of inferiority and unworthiness. She had periodic suicidal impulses and an awareness that something basic was wrong. However, she was more outgoing than Mr. Lamen. She could not stay alone. She felt best with others and often went to parties. She felt so much partying was forced, but nonetheless saw herself as a basically social person. She was generally a far more anxious person than Mr. Lamen. He was apparently more compressed, she more diffuse. Ms. Ferva was more able to feel excitement.

At about the same time Mr. Lamen reported the dream above, Ms. Ferva dreamed that a mouse was trapped (or somehow trapped itself) in such a way that it acted as a plug for the water in a pond. When the mouse would get stuck (or stick itself) in a certain hole, the water level rose, but if the mouse got out the water would disappear down the hole as if it were a drain. When the pond was filled, fearsome snakes swam in it. The snakes vanished without water. The sequence of mouse getting stuck and pond filling with water and snakes, followed by mouse freeing itself and water and snakes disappearing, occurred repeatedly. It was unclear whether the dream ended with the mouse victorious and free, or with snakes still threatening.

A dream like this can be worked with profitably in many ways. Given the patient's associations in the context of therapy, therapists will have preferred routes on the overall map and perhaps different maps as well. We stay here with our focus on omniscience.

Ms. Ferva and Dr. Omnis both felt, according to the latter, that the dream expressed something of Ms. Ferva's pulled-apart style. Both felt it good if the mouse won, bad when the snakes did. They saw the mouse as innocent and the snakes as evil. Dr. Omnis associated the snakes with destructiveness, including attacks upon needs and strivings. Ms. Ferva was caught between them but consciously identified more with the mouse. At some point she recalled being chased by snakes in the dream but this remained vague.

Both patient and therapist believed the dream expressed an inner drama, yet each tended to take sides prematurely. Their style of structuring the dream more or less fits Fairbairn's (1954) depiction of a struggle between libidinal and antilibidinal ego structures. Work on this broad existential plane was valuable, yet Dr. Omnis and Ms. Ferva felt there would be more if they could tap it. They were also aware of the dream's references to birth and sexuality but this was insufficient.

Since we were working with Dr. Omnis's omniscience, the supervisor suggested they tune into the mouse's fleeting sense of triumph. This led the therapy couple to an array of childhood stories in which the smaller, weaker, and smarter party turned the tables on the bigger, stronger, more stupid one. The physically tiny baby manipulates surrounding giants: mind over *mater*. The baby disarms the evil mother and seduces the good one. In truth, baby and mother disarm and seduce one another.

Were the snakes only evil and the mouse only good? Such a stereotypical viewpoint must be taken as a signal that experiencing is short-circuited. The mouse's sense of triumph is too easy. The hungry, tricky baby's victory over violent fears is fragile. In Western symbology snakes are tricky, too. However, in many myths a snake may symbolize the dangers of the unconscious in general (Eigen 1981c, 1984).

In the present dream snakes are associated with water and so are suggestive of the unconscious as such. In effect, by siding with the mouse the therapy couple tried to wish the unconscious away. The triumphant mouse made water and snakes appear or disappear, as if life's dangers and the unconscious itself were in its power. The smaller, survival-oriented ego (mouse) wishes to preempt the place of the larger, mysterious self (snakes in water: many = intensity), to the point of doing away with the latter entirely. We may be terrified of the depths of our nature, of what is uncontrollable in life, of death, the predator, and creativity. The mouse's gambit is to find a way of making what is ubiquitous disappear.

In part, the terrifying snakes in water symbolize the wisdom of the unconscious, an omniscience far greater than the mouse's cleverness. In actuality both forms of knowing are necessary and, in optimal circumstances, feed each other. Often they are in conflict and the subject is caught between two forms of omniscience, now allying with one, now the other. The dream's lack of decisiveness mirrors an ambiguity rooted in the polar tendencies of our nature.

Insofar as Dr. Omnis could open himself to the fuller play of possibilities, Ms. Ferva could more readily experience what was snake- and mouselike about herself along a number of dimensions. For example, she became a mouse to avoid her snake power, which nonetheless tormented her. Primal sources of creativity gave way to survival greed. The partial victory of her smaller ego endangered her psychological environment as a whole. In retaliation or as part of a dissociative process, the snakes doubtless did become evil. In reality both mouse and snakes likely possessed creative and destructive elements.

The relevance of the analysis of the above symbols in terms of our current crises of civilization is obvious. Today we are endangered on a grand scale by the possibility of miscalculation from omniscience. People in positions of power may think they know (or ought to know) more than they really do. The mouse may assume serpent powers and act for the psychosocial whole, only to be governed by a misguided sliver of omniscience. The owl and seal are tame by comparison. Wisdom as a cultural ideal seems an archaic relic at this point of time. By now the snake's poison has gone into its eyes as it is pressed into service of a calculus of minute advantages, which writhe at the edge of catastrophe. We rehearse with pockets of mayhem throughout the globe, barely paused on the brink.

Omniscience and Invisibility

Experiencing as such is intangible and ineffable. We cannot locate a thought as we do the brain. However much we can associate emotions and centers of consciousness with the body, or read a soul in a face or gesture, something invisible remains. This may be summarized in the adage that consciousness sees and hears but can't be seen or heard, at least not like spatially localizable events can. Winnicott has greatly amplified our sense of the invisibility and ineffability of experiencing by elaborating on the dimension of *between* (Winnicott 1971d).

The basic invisibility of experiencing contributes to a sense of boundlessness that tinges our existence. It can assume diverse valences and function for good or ill. Evil uses invisibility as a mask. It exploits the invisible quality of mental life. That is one reason evil can be naked in broad daylight and move as if unseen.

In omniscience the structure and resistance of physical reality give way. Omniscience tends to "externalize" the mind's immateriality so that the latter spreads through physical existence. Physical boundaries tend to be dematerialized by omniscience. This is so more radically than with delusive omnipotence, wherein the world retains a primacy of the physical. In omniscience physicality collapses in the face of mental power. Winnicott describes a beneficent "between," but the latter can be demonized as well (Eigen 1984).

Tausk's (1933) "influencing machine" is illustrative. In this paranoid delusion the psychotic patient feels that his mind is being taken over and influenced by a distant machine. Tausk understood this as a projective expression of a mechanized body self. For Tausk the machine is a symbolic petrification of the sexually alive body, an attempt to freeze or de-animate the threat of feeling, of life itself.

From the perspective of omniscience, the permeability and penetrability of the subject by an alien mind is at stake. The "between" is petrified, dissolved, and/or demonized. Thought is taken as an invasive, alien power emanating from a foreign, controlling mind. The body is put out of play and a megalomanic, immaterial dimension of mental power holds away. Space and physical boundaries become meaningless. Thoughts can instantaneously be everywhere and anywhere. The patient's greatest fears seem to focus not merely on a reduced and mechanized body (the latter is almost comforting), but on the electrifyingly impalpable threat of invisible mental power as such. A devitalized or mechanized body self and a perverse mental self form parts of a dissociative system lived out in a ruthless proliferation of ways. In the example of the "influencing machine," the body self is not strong or alive enough to withstand the onslaught of a demonized mind. It should be clear that what is being described is part of the structure of our time. Fusional answers intensify the predicament.

In human life the problem of boundaries is (and remains) problematic in a far more momentous way than with animal territoriality. The boundlessness involved in our invisible sense of self infinitely magnifies the material stakes. Omniscience is rooted in an invisible sense of boundlessness and draws on the intangible to befuddle embodied souls. This is not to say that omniscience is unconcerned with physical existence. On the contrary, it seeks to master and triumph over it, to wrest its secret. However, its transcendence easily becomes perverse. It loses respect for competing powers. Omniscience manipulates omnipotence. Omnipotence becomes an arm of omniscience. Tyrant enslaves tyrant.

Our journey in the sense of the infinite is, ironically, limited not by realistic finitude (which is its raw material), but by our discovery of alternate infinities, infinite pretensions. After a first exaltation, we gasp in horror to glimpse how thoroughly enmeshed we are or can be in a sense of omniscience gone wrong. It is not something that can simply be rooted out of our nature, any more than breathing can. We must learn how to breathe with it, how to follow its transpositions, how to interact with it in saving ways. We cannot be too careful in our explorations of the capacities which constitute us. Our gropings continuously change our psychophysical environment in unanticipated ways.

REFERENCES

Bateson, G. (1979). *Mind and Nature: A Necessary Unity.* New York: E. P. Dutton.

Bion, W. (1970). *Attention and Interpretation.* London: Tavistock.

———— (1977). *Seven Servants.* New York: Jason Aronson.

Eigen, M. (1980). On the significance of the face. *Psychoanalytic Review* 67:427–441.

———— (1981a). The area of faith in Winnicott, Lacan and Bion. *International Journal of Psycho-Analysis* 62:413–433.

———— (1981b). Guntrip's analysis with Winnicott. *Contemporary Psychoanalysis* 17:103–117.

———— (1981c). Comments on snake symbolism and mind-body relations. *American Journal of Psychoanalysis* 41:73–79.

———— (1983). Dual union or undifferentiation? A critique of Marion Milner's sense of psychic creativeness. *International Review of Psycho-Analysis* 10:415–428.

———— (1984). On demonized aspects of the self. In *Evil: Self and Culture,* ed. M. C. Nelson and M. Eigen, pp. 91–123. New York: Human Sciences.

———— (1985). The sword of grace: Flannery O'Connor, D. W. Winnicott and W. R. Bion. *Psychoanalytic Review* 72:335–346.

———— (1986). *The Psychotic Core.* Northvale, NJ: Jason Aronson.

Elkin, H. (1972). On selfhood and the development of ego structures in infancy. *Psychoanalytic Review* 59:389–416.

Fairbairn, W. R. (1954). *An Object Relations Theory of Personality.* New York: Basic Books.

Guntrip, H. (1975). My experience of analysis with Fairbairn and Winnicott. *International Review of Psycho-Analysis* 2:145–156.

Khan, M. M. R. (1972). Dread of surrender to resourceless dependence in the analytic situation. In *The Privacy of the Self,* pp. 270–279. New York: International Universities Press, 1974.

Lacan, J. (1978). *The Four Fundamental Concepts of Psycho-Analysis.* New York: Norton.

Meltzer, D. (1973). *Sexual States of Mind.* Strath Tay, Scotland: Clunie.

Tausk, V. (1933). On the origin of the influencing machine in schizophrenia. *Psychoanalytic Quarterly* 2:519–556.

Winnicott, D. W. (1960). Ego distortion in terms of true and false self. In *The Maturationial Processes and the Facilitating Environment,* pp. 140–152. New York: International Universities Press, 1965.

———— (1963). Communicating and not communicating leading to a study of certain opposites. In *The Maturational Processes and the Facilitating Environment,* pp. 179–192. New York: International Universities Press, 1965.

———— (1969). The use of an object and relating through identifications. In *Playing and Reality,* pp. 86–94. New York: Basic Books, 1971.

———— (1971a). Interrelating apart from instinctual drive and in terms of cross-identifications. In *Playing and Reality.* pp. 119–137. New York: Basic Books.

———— (1971b). Dreaming, fantasying, and living. In *Playing and Reality.* pp. 26–37. New York: Basic Books.

———— (1971c). Playing: creative activity and the search for the self. In *Playing and Reality.* pp. 53–64. New York: Basic Books.

———— (1971d). *Playing and Reality.* New York: Basic Books.

Afterword

THE PRIMITIVE BACKGROUND OF EXPERIENCE

I lived more than eighteen years before discovering psychoanalysis. There was *no* psychoanalytic consciousness in my hometown, Passaic, New Jersey. Passaic, as I knew it, was an immigrant town — Jews, Poles, Italians, Irish — filled with hard, gritty life, people struggling to make a living. Pain was taken for granted — and psychoanalysis is a psychology of pain.

I mention this because I spent much of my adult life immersed in psychoanalytic processes, and one of my learnings is the importance of linking up with one's pre-analytic and extra-analytic selves. In Passaic I learned the value of immersion in everyday experience. This meant immersion in painful as well as pleasurable realities, painful–pleasurable struggles with peers, parents, and society.

Sometimes, unexpectedly, spontaneous moments of absolute joy emerged from immersion in mixed realities. One such moment was seeing the stars when I was a little over 2, a moment that never left me. The shock of awe-filled joy was definitive. Another was the way I felt after kissing a girl I loved when I was 16 or 17. I danced and sang all the way home — all stars. This kind of joy is an elemental given, reducible to nothing. If anything other than itself at all, it is a song of God.

In college I met Socrates and discovered a whole new world of heavenly bodies, the Idea of the Good, incorruptible Truth at the center of a moral/intellectual/spiritual universe. I could scarcely believe such Beauty existed. Contact with Socrates made integrity palpable.

It seemed fitting that within a few months of this meeting, I had sexual intercourse for the first time, as if confirming, celebrating, and extending my soul's opening. Such different worlds of experience converged at the heart's center! Socratic and erotic ecstasies are not identical. They feed, tug, fight, and

259

play with each other, currents of a broader sea of experience. In time I would learn how far apart and close together they can be.

In my second year of college my roommate began therapy and told me a dream with his analyst's interpretation. Again bells rang. I fell in love with dreams and read Fromm, Jung, and Freud. When I graduated college I decided to enter analysis with the man whose interpretation lit me up. For me he was a kind of living Socrates. I followed the lines of my maximum enlightenment experience, as close to Truth as I could get. I scarcely realized what sort of serpent I was grabbing hold of.

Psychoanalysis fit a line of experience that blew a hole in my Passaic self. Near the end of high school I chanced upon e. e. cummings and in an instant the prison of language melted. Plasticity of words let self breathe easier. Self, like meaning or sound or color, could melt, spread, and re-form. In my first year of college I discovered James Joyce and linked the breakthrough of language with a quest for origins and identity. The "who am I" marvel of subjectivity never could be exhausted.

In psychoanalysis my love for dreams and the stream of consciousness had room to play. However, psychoanalytic work was never simply or mainly academic. My sexual opening-up brought new forms of suffering, the difficulties of almost adult relationships. By the end of college so much adult life seemed phony. What seemed most real at the time was simply living and analytic work. Everything that was wrong with me poured out and eventually lodged in transferences. Analytic work became a matter of life and death, a way of working with the pain of existence. I was choosing my life's work without knowing it.

Before going on to a discussion of analytic themes, I need to mention several other elemental areas of experience. First, religion. Like many children (and adults), I sometimes talked to God. I prayed for what I wanted and to avoid catastrophe, and could not avoid noticing the lack of one-to-one link-up of prayer and outcome. Yet in time prayer opened realms of experiencing I could hardly anticipate. I was able to reach places through prayer that I could not get to by analysis, although each made better use of the other possible. This sort of enrichment by diverse realms of experiencing shifts one's sense of what it means to be alive.

I know that religious feeling is associated with infantile helplessness, dependency, and the wish for protection, but cannot leave it at that. I remember an old man who visited our home once or twice a year—Rabbi Kellner. I did not understand that he came for a contribution, but I remember the light that came from his face. It took many years for me to begin to grasp that the stirring I felt in his presence was a sense of holiness. I am thankful this sense survives my life, uplifts me as an analytic person, and ignites sessions. It might easily have died in suffering and sophistication.

Finally, sports and music. I was never much of an athlete, but after the age of 6 I played ball long and hard. The loneliness and isolation of my first five years remains a persistent part of me. I longed for friends. When I was 5 my parents moved to a neighborhood where there were plenty of kids my age and we played all the time. Sports gave me a chance to use my body with all my might and I loved the exertion. Something of Winnicott's "use of object" experience gets lived out in sports. In adulthood this current was amplified through body therapies, yoga, breathing meditation, and spontaneous movement improvisation, although sports of my childhood returned through playing with my children. One might say there are sport elements to therapy, especially use of body sensing, but also issues of pace, timing, sequence, endurance, and agility.

Music has always been part of my life. My mother played piano and my father violin and I started piano when I was 5 or 6. A couple of years later I could not believe my ears when I heard a beggar play Jewish songs on a clarinet. I felt I must play clarinet and took lessons. My clarinet teacher would play a little song at the end of each lesson, and the sound tickled me. I laughed and laughed. He would say he could not play if I laughed, but I could not help myself. Later I added saxophone and started a band. We actually were paid for playing and got good at it. I played jobs through high school and college, and occasionally played at nightclubs when I was well into analysis.

The following dream ended my playing for many years. I walked into Birdland and sat down to dinner with Charlie Parker, Dizzy Gillespie, Miles Davis, and Bud Powell—jazz greats. I noticed they were eating Jello and I wanted steak. My analyst said that jazz was not nourishing enough for me (a dessert rather than main dish) and was a manic defense. His remark seared me. I wanted substance and my devotion to analysis intensified. Such experiences taught me how devastating analysis can be, helpful some ways, harmful others, like many things that touch one deeply. It is commonplace to observe that we are wounded by what helps us.

Eventually my playing returned, although never again professionally. I can't imagine a day without music. I no longer play hour after hour, as I did when I was young. But what listening and playing I do are part of the day's riches. Vivaldi is at the center of my life, but so is music sung at temple services. My love of jazz improvisation informs my analytic work. A lot of analytic work involves singing blues and shouting praise.

ANALYTIC THEMES: SELF-OTHER AND MIND-BODY

From the outset it seemed clear that I could never be a strictly orthodox analyst, whatever that may mean. I loved Freud and Jung, body therapies, phenomenological and existential philosophers, Gestalt psychology, Melanie Klein, D. W. Winnicott, and the British Independents, R. D. Laing and Harold Searles, and later, Kohut, Lacan, and Bion. I chose Henry Elkin as my major analyst. He has written a small but beautiful body of work, a true affirmation of the human spirit (Elkin 1958, 1972).

I stayed with Elkin nine years, until he left the city upon the breakup of his marriage. My analysis did not end well and I eventually went to a child analyst, Dorothy Bloch, who taught me much and genuinely helped me. I also found a later experience with Michael Kriegsfeld, a Gestalt therapist, very useful. My supervisors and control analysts (Richard Mulliken, John Beletsis, Jeanette Levitt, John Brinley) were important at the time, but in the long run my work as a patient is what made me an analyst.

My growth as a mental health worker was long and unrushed. In my twenties I worked with autistic and schizophrenic children at schools and treatment centers. In my thirties I saw a wide range of patients for long-term work at New Hope Guild, an excellent psychiatric clinic in Brooklyn. In my forties and fifties my emphasis has been on private practice, but I feel grateful for the long period of seasoning and grounding in fundamentals clinic work provided. When I see young people propelled before they are ready into the rigors of office work, I realize what a gift I was given.

In my late thirties I found myself trying to give voice to aspects of my analytic work and wrote from inner pressure. Talking over cases at meetings with colleagues and supervisors was not enough. The voice that comes out in writing speaks from the depths of one's aloneness to the aloneness of others. Psychoanalysis is a writing cure, not only a talking cure. Writing helps organize experience of sessions, but also helps discover and create this experience.

At first my writing fastened on at least three main areas: (1) "ideal" experiencing, (2) issues of psychosexual identity, and (3) the interactive field, especially use of countertransference. My papers were not primarily theoretical, but attempts to let clinical experiencing speak. They all have been concerned with dramas of self.

My work with addictive personalities (or addictive aspects of persons) brought home the importance of what might be called "pure self-feelings" for many patients. In "Abstinence and the Schizoid Ego" (1973) an individual withdrew from world and body to a dense, contracted I-feeling. One might view this as defensive regression, fear of fusion or aggression, or perhaps terror of social or corporeal invasion. But for the patient it made a positive contribution to his sense of self and resulted in expanded living.

In the nearly twenty years since I wrote this paper I have had occasion to observe many shifts of mystical awareness, embracing I-feeling, You-feeling, and varieties of Winnicott's "between" (allied with Martin Buber's "between"). Self is resonant and cannot be reduced to categories like "I" or "You" or "Between," but employs these and other categories of experiencing.

For practical purposes I posited a *distinction–union structure* that characterizes the self at all of its developmental levels. To realize that no experience is without distinction and union elements, whether muted or obviously compelling, enables a more wholesome outcome to processes involving deep regression. I do not know how to theorize about this but I feel it is more than a matter of "representations" of self and other. We are predisposed to organize experience in self–other terms, with softer and/or harder boundaries. This seems to be built into the system, a matter of hardware. We are the sort of beings for whom the sense of self–other makes a difference.

All manner of combinations, conjunctions, separations, dissociations, unintegrations–integrations, meldings (fusions) of the self–other sense occur. Either self or other or both may be muted or highlighted. The pure "I-am-I" distillation achieved by the alcoholic man described above (1973) took the holding of the therapy situation for granted. I was a background being, a silence in his depths, a sign of safety and possibility. There is no question here of an isolated ego, a stimulus-free state, a sealed monad. The healing contraction to a nearly pure slide of I-feeling occurred within a broader field that was assumed and used as a matter of course. The sliver of I-feeling at stake was not merely static and uniform. Its density pulsated with inner and outer horizons. It stood out vis-à-vis the Other's implicit presence.

The line between self–other might have an arrow on each end (self ↔ other) to indicate permeability, interweaving, and even interchangeability at times. But arrows are also weapons and pointers, indicating opposition or place. I do not think a decision can be made about which state is more primary than others. Life is porous. So much that is not alive seems porous too: even a stone can be stained. Rigid boundaries like bones are made of processes similar to those that govern circulation of liquids or patterned whirls of solar bodies. Firmness and plasticity are aspects of systems. It is unlikely that patternings of self–other experiencing will be simpler than physical functions.

It also seemed useful to think of relations between body self and mental self in terms of the distinction–union structure. Experiencing may veer toward one or the other pole, but is made up of both. Like self and other, body and mental self may meld, dissociate, interweave, and form all sorts of relationships. The major theories concerning mind–body relations (interactionism, parallelism, isomorphism, epiphenomalism) find counterparts in actual clinical phenomena. Plasticity of diverse terms of experience characterize mental–physical self and self–other.

To unite and distinguish are basic operations that permeate and govern experiencing. I mean something more than superficial cognition or rationalistic thinking. Division–connection are seamless parts of our perceptual field. In early infancy and throughout our lives, they characterize our affective field as well, although in a muted, implicit way. Metaphorical, analogical, relational experiencing–thinking grow out of an elemental distinction–union matrix.

STARTING POINTS

Since there is no self without other (or vice versa) in living experience, it seems senseless to disconnect them at the self's starting point, whatever that may be.

For several years my discussion of starting points emphasized certain experiences of the face, such as the following:

> I see you but not just you. I am experiencing a more real, perfect version of you, a glowing-light you, inexpressibly radiant and fluid. I can go in and through you yet feel more myself than ever. It is as if I entered and passed through a highly charged yet resistanceless medium and feel newly conscious and restored. [1980, p. 439]

The above passage condenses my concerns with special clarity. Boundaries are simultaneously upheld, intensified, and relinquished. Materiality and immateriality blend and enrich each other. So-called real and ideal dimensions touch each other in ways that open horizons.

In psychoanalysis the infant's experience of face tends to be reduced to experience of breast. This is an amazing simplification of an essential ambiguity constitutive of human experience: the tension and interplay between vision and touch. The face-breast association may be basic, genuine and powerful, but face goes beyond breast, and provides a context or frame for the latter. One ought not lose the unique contribution and enrichment provided by different sensory domains.

The tendency to reduce visual to tactile experience is still rampant in psychoanalysis, and in some of the best workers. I recently found this reduction to be part of serious misinterpretations of Bion's work. Bion has been very careful to leave questions about the primary data of psychic life open. His writings are complex and suggestive. Yet as fine a worker as Boyer (1990) can write, "Origins for him [Bion] . . . meant early sense data as relived in the analytic situation, a position consistent with Freud's . . . idea that the ego is ultimately derived from bodily sensations, chiefly those arising from the surface of the body" (p. 6).

Such a "sensationistic" reduction of Bion's O (origins, zero, ultimate reality, the unknowable x or emotional truth of a session) is untenable and misleading. Bion's writings slide between domains (immateriality, materiality, mix-ups of materiality–immateriality) that contribute to whatever the originary data of psychic life may be. It would be unfair to slice off one aspect of Bion's work and call it his starting point (Eigen 1985). Double arrows between dimensions and functions are his hallmark, and they indicate reversibility, oscillation, and co-origination.

Tustin (1972, 1981) is perhaps the master psychoanalytic painter of tactile roots of self. She sensitizes us to the role tactile hallucinations play in filling in the black hole of separation from maternal contact. Her emphasis on the critical importance of sensations in generating and maintaining self-feelings helps offset too great an emphasis on visual dominance. However, she underplays the visual and loses its unique contributions.

For example, the autistic child's fascination with shiny objects is not reducible to his need to control the breast-nipple in order to offset premature tearing/separation. Shininess also refers to eyes, where personality shines and one experiences spontaneous animation with distance-yet-contact, subject-to-subject contact. The dilemma may be more complex than understanding the importance of sensation as bridge or filler or primary builder of self. The vision–tactile tension is at stake. Each modality contributes to and assimilates aspects of the other.

Somatic sensations may exacerbate or soothe the sense of catastrophe. Body sensations can be used to blot out visual torment, just as holding on to moments of visual stability can relieve body fragmentation. Each modality contributes in essential ways to constitution and growth of self, although self may drown in body sensations and rigidify via visual stability. More depth psychological writing is needed on the interplay of vision and touch.

The term *sensation* is highly packed and needs investigation. For example, Bion (1965) contrasts Freud's "consciousness as a sense-organ of psychic quality" with thoughts or affects that are treated as material objects or sense-perceptions (p. 107). Neither usage is identical with what usually is meant by the five senses. Nor is any of these identical with William Blake's sense of perception as infinite, or the sensory fields of Merleau-Ponty's body subject.

The term *sense* slips across many domains. One can suffer painful loss of I-sensation, or excruciating loss of sense of self or sense of reality, or sense of God, or sense of meaningfulness. At times it feels good to slip away from sense, to drop the burden of meaning, to feel senseless and free, although the sense of infiniteness may creep up on one and be uplifting or overwhelming.

For Bion the infinite precedes the finite. Infiniteness circulates throughout the personality like libido. One could say that for Bion libido represents privileged ways that infiniteness works, ways that formlessness incarnates. Destructiveness is infinite too. Bion describes a force that continues after it destroys existence, time, and space—a madness that undoes personality without reservation.

Faith mingles with catastrophe, a mix of infinites. One infinity limits another. Catastrophic dread may be part of processes that destroy personality, but it also can help keep personality honest. Faith can elevate or sweeten existence, but may suffocate curiosity. How a capacity contributes to or impedes growth is an open matter. There is no substitute for fresh exercise of one's equipment in the moment at hand.

The self moving between spacelessness and space is transitional. What a beautiful thing it is to help a person open and work with his capacity to vanish–return, empty–fill, fall apart–come together. One comes through catastrophe after catastrophe. Perhaps it is the quality of *coming through* that therapy most helps (see Eigen 1992).

One returns to starting points in order to reset oneself. It is not possible to grow another personality from scratch. One is stuck with oneself. Yet one *can* dip into the storehouse of possibilities, shift attitudes, and rework one's sense of what it means to be an experiencing subject.

Therapy is many things. In spite of protests to the contrary, it *does* provide corrective parenting and reeducation of emotional life. It is no contradiction to say that it also is libidinally charged. At moments it soothes and relieves elemental pain or sets inspiring challenges. It can be pedestrian and boring. Growth occurs through piecemeal, repetitive therapeutic struggle, a rhythm of going over and over things and letting go going-over. Yet a moment's glimpse of a lifelong pattern, a new experiencing of it, can set into motion a change, a lightening and deepening of relating to self and others that runs down one's backbone to the very toes of being.

One senses work going on in the basement, a placeless place where elements of personality mix and re-form, and one enters into a new sort of partnership with unconscious processes. Meaning grows from bottom up, not only top down. Where top or bottom begins or ends nobody knows.

From the depths of one's being it is as easy to get to God as libido. For Freud libido seeks an ideal imago, in traditional terms, ultimately God. The unconscious does not do away with God so much as provide a privileged point of contact with the unknowable. After good sexual intercourse one may feel closer to God, and after opening up to God sexual intercourse may shine more brightly. One ought not prejudge what direction intersection with the unknown may take.

One of the great contributions of modern cultural history is to question the basis of traditional hierarchies, perhaps the very meaning of hierarchy (top-bottom). In psychic reality double arrows are placed between traditional oppositions. What a relief to be able to flow back and forth between antagonistic currents and not pit one against the other. One takes and learns from each. Each contributes to growth of self. Without polarities life would be poorer, but we do not have to be trapped by polarities. Our model now is paradoxical–dialectical––dialogical (conflict is a branch). This leads to explorations of processes that may blow the lid off traditional categories, or open these boxes to see what is there, including ways they interweave and enhance each other. I think we have very exciting journeys ahead if we do not kill each other off with polemics and prejudice.

ORIGINARY INFINITENESS AND TOUCH-VISION

The baby spends time staring or gazing. At times his stare seems stuporous, or he may watch things that attract attention. But there is also quiet staring into space cushioned by a background of well-being. Perhaps he is enjoying the pleasure of gazing for its own sake and the luxury of doing nothing. Perhaps he is luxuriating in visual boundlessness, supported by "yummy" body sensations.

At such moments he does not appear to be scattered or at loose ends, nor intensely organized. Words like "fused" or "separate" do not seem relevant. The "just so" of Buddhism comes to mind.

I would like to suggest that this experience is made possible by a seamless doubleness, body sensing, and visual openness. The mute surround of bodily well-being is not identical with the visual field. Since there is no clear-cut image of one's bounded body, the somatic sensational field has its own sort of infiniteness. Yet it also has containing properties. The body is a kind of infinite hug. We are endlessly caressed (and/or assaulted) by body sensations. Visual experience opens other encompassing infinities, spreads of color, light, movement of shapes, horizons, and frames. Sight and sound move beyond body sensations, although each contributes to the other. This "beyond" is built into or encoded in the self and has its own developmental journey.

I am not suggesting that there is a clear delineation of the spatial properties of things at the beginning. But I suspect a pleasurable sense of closer–farther does not require clear spatial mapping. One does not think closer–farther, but enjoys the implicit contrast-and-commingling of somatic and visual fields. The most seamless intunement draws on more than one root or current.

IDEAL BEING

Freud suggests one becomes addicted not simply to pleasure (or pain) but ideal pleasure (or pain). I wonder how widely understood this point of Freud's is. For Freud hallucination is an early mode of cognition tied to wish fulfillment, substituting pleasure for pain. The infant cathects a memory of prior satisfaction in an unsatisfactory present moment. It seems to be taken for granted that this memory of satisfaction constitutes a hallucinatory moment of ideal or perfect satisfaction. Whether the past satisfaction was truly perfect, or triggered a sense of perfection, or whether the sense of perfection exploited an actual moment of relative satisfaction is unclear. We do not know the origins of the link between actual and ideal satisfaction.

Perhaps we can say that a memory of ideal satisfaction is some sort of act of imagination. This ideal antedates superego ideals. It is built into the fabric of human pleasure, including use of elemental sensations. Addiction to sensations means addiction to an imaginary ideal state.

Freud's pleasure-ego or ideal ego extends this line of thinking to the ego itself. The ego is addicted to itself as its own ideal. It tries to maintain itself as an ideal state that seeks ideal states. Breaking into this scenario is the ubiquitous threat of pain and insufficiency. The pearl around the irritant is on the verge of exploding.

In one way or another the importance of ideal states permeates Freud's work. He emphasizes their defensive use. His writings on the ego's use of idealization to cover hostility and express sexual love are masterful and ring true. His analyses are lacerating and he is right to think of psychoanalysis as wounding the Western ego (although it does not create the wound so much as grow out of it).

Yet Freud smuggled ideal states and images into his descriptions of pleasure and pain. In pointing to undersides of ideal realities, he takes the latter for granted. He offers no adequate account of this momentous capacity in its own right. He peers into ideal realities and sees the work of instincts, as if wrestling with God to expose his backside. But why we should be creatures who hunger for ideal satisfaction, not mere satisfaction, remains a mystery. Why this surplus or excess or extravagance — why such intimacy between instinct and imagination and ideal being? Far from solving anything, Freud's exposure makes us wonder more.

TIMELESS TIME AND A BREATH OF OTHERNESS

It is not enough to say that in early infancy a time sense has not developed and so sensations seem endless. The endless duration of sensations or feelings may imply a sort of time that has not yet become firmly attached to a sense of materiality. The eternality or going-on-forever of states of being suggests a lack of temporal perspective or time/space mapping. To say that time precedes space means that timeless time precedes awareness of the materiality of spatial objects.

At times boundlessness may seem objectless. But I do not see why one must think this is always or even primarily so. As the self arises sensations are linked to affects and images, and tied to subject-to-subject, moment-to-moment dramas. Body-to-body contact is often self-to-self contact (or breaking of contact), since the materiality of objects may not be an issue. One may feel permeated, or encompassed, or uplifted, by winds of Otherness, without a comprehending frame of reference. This does not at all deny how physical self-to-self contact gets.

So much of Melanie Klein's sensory universe is animated, but the animation gets wedded to material objects too quickly. God (or devil) is prematurely reduced to breast or mother. In Klein's work the possibility of an immaterial encompassing/permeating Other loses out to more specific materialistic fantasies. The analyst succumbs to the pull of common sense and premature dominance of materialistic space.

The ineffable self–other matrix of earlier, immaterial space is multivalanced and multifaceted like self–other dramas throughout life will be (Elkin 1972). The primordial boundless surround contributes to the biography of the sense of infiniteness, which underlies, cushions, and informs the emergence of time-space coordinates. Convergent–divergent realms of experiencing enrich living, but the subject may never quite feel they fit together.

OMNIPOTENCE, OMNISCIENCE, MINDLESSNESS

Most psychoanalysts do not systematically distinguish omnipotence from omniscience. They usually write about defensive aspects of omnipotence. Winnicott and Kohut point out ways that the baby's sense of omnipotence can contribute to healthy narcissism, a sense of aliveness, and a feeling that life is worth living. Omnipotence can fuel growth of self, not merely compensate for deficiency.

Western religions attribute omnipotence to God. The ego's omnipotence is disease, folly, madness. Human beings must grow in humility and respect for limitations. God is the great frame of reference in which ego must find its place. Today frames of reference for understanding ego include libidinal, social, and genetic factors.

My case histories give detailed portrayals of defensive–undefensive ways that omnipotence–omniscience contribute to personal blocks and growth of self. Sometimes I am asked, "Why bring in omnipotence-omniscience? Isn't this preoccupation some kind of aberration of psychoanalysis? We can talk about development without such notions."

Perhaps we *can* talk about development without such notions but I am not sure the gain offsets the loss in doing so. Omnipotence-omniscience points to a boundlessness that grips experiencing. A free-floating infiniteness can characterize id- or ego- or superego-dominated moments. Omnipotence can become a wish or compensatory fantasy (allied with powerlessness), but it grows around a spontaneous, elemental kernel of might that comes and goes. Moments of might and helplessness oscillate and intermingle in primitive experience and are magnified by free-floating infiniteness. One does not simply throw off underlying limitlessness by achieving cognitive boundaries.

It is useful to distinguish omnipotence from omniscience. Omnipotence is more associated with body self, omniscience with mental self. I have tried to point out ways each may contribute to growth of self, but when they lock into destructive modes, omniscience can wreak even more havoc than omnipotence. This is important to bring out because a global approach to omnipotence can miss the particular horrors of destructive omniscience, which come closer to nameless dread.

Omnipotence and omniscience apply to different areas of boundlessness. Omnipotence refers to might in physical terms, thus is open to eventual discomfirmation. A king can be dethroned. A champion who feels invincible can be knocked out. However, a know-it-all can always marshal evidence in alternative ways and evade the punch of truth. This asymmetry is represented in popular art by portrayals of the omniscient (malevolent or benevolent) seer controlling physical bullies.

The sense of omnipotence is rooted in surges of body sensations which make one feel high and mighty. The elemental ebb and flow of seas of sensations tends to get lost with emphasis on muscular control. Sensations of omnipotence fuse with control over muscles and muscular control of objects. Omnipotence contributes to the good feeling that accompanies the ability to do things. Soon enough omnipotence spreads to include dramas of material power and control of every sort.

Omniscience is more connected with vision, inner and outer. It contributes to omnipotence the special pride of mind over matter. However, it is at its poisonous or healing best in its privileged province of mind over mind. Mind sees through mind and the dread of malevolent use of this kind of knowing outstrips the fear of mere physical power. Winnicott warned against invasion of the sacred core of personality by therapeutic omniscience.

Loss of mind to another's mind is one sort of mindlessness. In this case there is a double arrow between omniscience ↔ mindlessness. Omniscience feeds on omniscience and mindless slavery is a result. International disasters can be fueled by omniscience ↔ mindlessness. Gaps in knowledge are filled in by what one thinks or imagines one knows. Bits of knowledge about x plug uncertainties about y, at times resulting in lethal mix-ups of what one knows and does not know. A mindless force clothed in knowing (or pretending to know) may prefer destruction to a buildup of realistic complexities.

One may blank or bliss out in order to avoid unpleasant realities. In ordinary living this kind of mindlessness acts as a natural anesthesia. It provides momentary vacations from self, time off, a bit of space. Relentless conflict or trauma or pain can precipitate a mindless spin, so that one loses the ability to move between time-off and time-on. One may avoid or rush into growth, so that steps are bypassed or never reached. In such instances mindlessness masks a chronic rigidity aimed at getting rid of difficulties having a psyche brings. In extreme cases one may have to make psychic life disappear in order to get rid of its horrors. All too often one sees cases in which the psyche did not have a chance to develop because of the immaturity or violence of atmospheric factors, including elements of systems (societal, familial) that ought to have provided support.

Bion and Winnicott heightened my awareness of problems involved in constituting a psyche in unfavorable conditions. Psychic growth is difficult enough in favorable conditions. To have or not to have a psyche goes with to be or not to be a person. There is much pressure not to hear oneself (or selves) and, on the basis of insufficient evidence, to decide who one is and is not, or not decide at all. There is not much patience with regard to one's own complexity, or with the complexity of psychic factors generally. Fear of being Hamlet results in not being Hamlet enough.

DISORDERED FOUNDATIONS

Today Hamlets are still being produced, but headlines are obsessed with impulse disorders (impulse was less a stranger to Hamlet than reflective thought is to current impulse addiction). In some ways *impulse disorder* is an accurate term, especially if it implies not only a breakdown of impulse control, but a disordering of impulses themselves.

Freud may be right to point to the timeless ubiquity of the id, yet I think it is misleading to say that drives remain unaltered as the eternal base of personality. The drives themselves can be driven crazy by what happens in life. The very foundation of personality can be more or less disordered depending on a variety of factors.

In Freudian terms, the id can be sick too, not just ego or superego. If I were a Jungian, I would say that archetypes can be ill too, not just as a result of conscious restriction. The Freudian id is a sort of sun in the basement of personality, but it can turn into a black sun or black hole that swallows life-feeling rather than gives rise to it. Or it can be a poisonous sun satisfied only by horrific visions and monstrous actions. This kind of id could only love an ego venomous or mangled enough to fit it.

Freud relates drives to energy, but also to a style of thinking — primary process thinking — in which plasticity reigns. Anything can be anything else, the law of contradiction does not hold, opposites stand for each other, meld, break apart and displace each other, come together again, jump tracks, get stuck in ruts, melt, reappear somewhere else. Meaning is used to discharge energy. Yet real work is being done. For one thing, as Bion points out, raw globs of catastrophic affect are being broken up, cooled, turned this way and that, given moments of form, shaped into streams of dream images as parts of elemental narratives, distilled through dreams and myths into springboards for further experiencing and thinking and the making of histories.

Yet something can go wrong with the elemental processing of catastrophic affects. Primary process does not take place in a vacuum; it is part of the fabric of life. It has warps, gaps, twists, and does its work more or less well. If things are horrible or skewed enough (chemically-environmentally-subjectively), it becomes misshapen and misshapes the future that depends on it.

Primary process can get stuck, or remain embryonic, or fail to evolve or become adequately constituted in the first place. A supervisee's patient dreamt of lying on death or perhaps lying on a dead body, although the sense was on death itself. My supervisee felt that his patient's unconscious must be speaking a truth about her life, its deadness, and hoped this communication proved valuable. He was surprised that neither the dream nor his interpretations meant much to her. He could take whatever tack he liked (dead objects or parents or siblings, dead self, dead analyst) but it was useless. He resonated to an image and tried to communicate meaning to a person in whom a life of meaning was stillborn or missed or deleted or otherwise circumscribed.

I felt my supervisee was probably right to think that the dream was an existential communication about the patient's life or state of self. But I suspected it also *was* that life, no mere portrayal. It was itself an example of the lack of support she received from primary processing. In a sense her dream was insignificant: it did not point anywhere, except perhaps to chronic failure to achieve alive functioning. Primary process was spinning its wheels, exhibiting profiles of its deficit or malformation. The job in such a case is long-term building-up of the patient's psyche, so that primary process can function and play a role as background support of personality.

A FEW ODDS AND ENDS

It is good to have a section in which to speak more or less haphazardly, make apologies, and say a few more of the things on one's mind. So this potpourri:

Touch-Vision and Obvious Omissions

I emphasized body sensations and the visual field in the constitution of the self. What about smell and hearing? Sound encompasses and spreads through one in uplifting-terrifying ways. Human beings have long connected life with music. We know how sensitive babies can be to tone and how important auditory hallucinations can be in "ordering" psychosis. We follow our noses to find the main lines of destiny. What about other interoceptive and exteroceptive sensory cues, and various sorts of proprioceptive and kinesthetic sensations that contribute to our sense of rhythm and "ownness"?

Bion noted the emphasis on digestive and reproductive images in psychoanalysis and wondered what might be revealed if things also were explored via respiratory or circulatory models. Our thinking tends to be quite biased and needs to keep turning things around.

Touch and vision represent a minimal doubleness, although things are more complex and interesting. I think one can observe the birth of humor in some sort of minimal doubleness like this. Moving between touch-see touches a funny bone. Babies smile and even laugh going back and forth between sucking, touching, and looking. It is as if the baby gets a kick out of adding or subtracting vision to/from feeling and vice versa, as if saying, "Wow! So this is what the thing I've been feeling looks like. So this is what the thing I've been seeing feels like!"

The Psychoanalytic Mystic

In one of my meetings with Bion he began talking about the Kabbalah, apparently out of the blue. We quickly reassured each other that neither of us was a Kabbalah scholar. Then he went on to say how important it was for him personally and as a way of approaching psychoanalytic work.

My meetings with Bion marked a turning point. This great psychoanalytic mystic gave me practical advice and encouragement. He told me to get married and stop psychoanalysis. He said marriage was just finding a partner in life, someone to speak truth to, someone to mitigate the severity to oneself. What an unforeseeable concatenation of events led to my marriage and family within a few years of this meeting—and how I wish this had happened so much earlier!

Yet even as a child I knew I would bloom late and not come near my prime before my mid-fifties.

I now see that we had spoken about Plato, whom we both loved, before Bion mentioned the Kabbalah. The Plato–Kant line in Bion's work is obvious, but how his use of Plato–Kant is partly structured by Kabbalah has not received attention. I did not know what use to make of this information at the time, and was a bit baffled as to why he brought it up. He unconsciously anticipated my development by about ten years.

Ten years later, in 1987, my father died and I began to immerse myself in my Jewish roots. With help I found the sons of Rabbi Kellner from my childhood, now old men themselves. They were pious Chasidim living in Brooklyn, a few minutes from my home. I studied with them and discovered a mystical tradition in Judaism unsurpassed in power, beauty, and sweetness. Throughout much of my adult life I used aspects of Oriental and Roman Catholic teachings to organize my mystical propensities. Now I rediscovered the treasure buried in my own hearth.

The paradoxical-dialectical-dialogical way of listening–speaking that marks clinical practice mitigated against religious orthodoxy, but my encounter with Judaism made me a better and richer person. The flow between Divinity and libido is so much freer now.

The kabbalistic aspect of Bion's thought would make a worthwhile study. But it must be realized that Bion used shells of many kinds as models for experiencing. He moved between invariant structures and the fire no structure can contain.

I believe that workers like Milner, Winnicott, and Bion pave the way for a more undogmatic psychoanalysis. There are so many branches and subbranches of every field now. Creativity thrives at the boundaries between fields. There are so many ways to go and room for so many different kinds of contributions. I propose that psychoanalysis will thrive not only in interaction with aspects of physics, mathematics, art, history, and the social sciences, but with authentic mystical experience as well.

If time and circumstances permit, I hope to do more writing on the psychoanalytic mystic. Psychoanalytic mystics can be very practical and down to earth, like Bion and Milner. Among other things, I would like to relate the *Ein Sof* (Infinite of infinites) of Kabbalah, to Bion's O and his preoccupation with formlessness ↔ structure in the analytic session.

Note that neither Bion nor Winnicott relies on terms like *oceanic* or *undifferentiation* to describe primordial experience or openness to O in the here and now. In *The Psychotic Core,* as well as in papers in this book, I argued that oceanic and undifferentiation have retarded and skewed psychoanalytic dialogue with mystical experience.

My view (with Buber, Elkin) is that the soul's union with God is better described as communion (co-union), preserving the paradoxical distinction–

union element. The Kabbalah safeguards this moment by developing a complex mediating system for the flow of originary infiniteness, a sort of jolt spreading from head to toe (the Kabbalah is fairly unique in including the feet: the Jew stands up at the height of prayer). A serious limitation of kabbalistic structure is that it is too hierarchical, vertical, top–bottom, up–down oriented. Perhaps one can keep shifting it ninety degrees around the heart–gut centers to get the full benefit.

Bion's grid is also hierarchical and he is painfully aware of its limitations. However, his concrete description of processes goes beyond inevitable linguistic hierarchies, and touches the wavy-curvy-curly flow of things. It is, partly, the distortions hierarchical thinking engenders that lead him to keep repairing to the idea of formlessness, as Winnicott and Milner did. Hierarchies keep emerging, as they did when Freud let himself drift with the unconscious. However, Bion, Winnicott, and Milner tend to emphasize the moment beneath hierarchies.

Milner says that this moment is (or can be) orgastic-ecstatic. I do not know of any recent analyst who so emphasizes the importance of fullness or plenitude in growth processes. For her the ego's symbolic capacity tries to give expression to its most precious experience, its sense of creativeness, which is inherently orgastic-ecstatic. As I have noted in my papers and books, Milner includes disillusionment, pain, not having the object, and so on, as a necessary part of growth and symbolizing also. But she seems to be less apologetic about affirming that life is orgastic–ecstatic, and that ecstasy drives creativeness (or vice versa). And, of course, life is lonely and filled with suffering.

Recently I heard a speaker point to Van Gogh's "Starry Night" and emphasize Van Gogh's sadness, loneliness, alienation, his exclusion from the city below, his having to make do with closeness to the starry sky (instead of people). "Yes," I thought. "But what ecstasy there is in the heart of darkness. What radiant darkness in Van Gogh's heart." After reading Milner one senses that analysts may not properly credit ecstasy in depths of torment. It tends to be dismissed as epiphenomenal, another symptom. A symptom of the human heart perhaps, as well as a sick ego.

The ecstatic element of analytic sessions is rarely acknowledged, yet may be one of the most important background ingredients. Perhaps there is justified fear of abuse of this capacity. The emphasis on hard work, slow growth, struggle, and aloneness is very real, but may also be used as protection against ecstasy.

I suspect fear of ecstasy is often responsible for premature termination. Therapists have difficulty acknowledging how much gratification they receive from being with people who are in pain. A therapist who has difficulty being with people may feel guilty for using therapy as a refuge and react against his own pleasure. Therapists who have difficulty with ecstasy may begrudge secondary gains patients get from their symptoms. The therapist's sense of being victimized may accelerate astronomically upon sensing the patient's pool of ecstasy behind a particularly annoying trait. Part of the current emphasis on the negative countertransference (the therapist's exasperation) hides the therapist's confusion over muted ecstasy that clings to work that drives one crazy.

Premature termination is one way of controlling the breakthrough of ecstasy (as well as rage). At least it prevents mutual exploitation of therapist and patient. Boundless emotionality is a temptation to indulgence, abuse, and psychopathic calculation. Better to be free of each other and seek another partner, until the unbearable climactic moment arises or things fizzle out again. One can point to one's wounds and gain a new hearing.

To the Future

What a challenge therapy is! Often a therapist does not have equipment to support the sort of therapy a patient may need. What sort of therapy or equipment is needed may be unknown or inaccessible. The therapist may be tempted to give up too quickly (in some instances too quickly may be twenty years), rather than wait on the evolution of capacities that may make a difference. One cannot predict when or how one will find the spot or particular point of entry that will do the trick.

One can see evolution of capacity in the therapy field in general. Not many therapists would be stymied by a patient speaking of "soul murder" now. Most workers would feel existentially at home with a lot of Schreber's language. In time we may catch on to the language of other patients that now evades us. We will be better able to let our personalities spontaneously find the particular shade and blend of formlessness–form that the moment requires.

Now that I am in my mid-fifties and have spent the greater part of my life involved with therapy in one way or another, I can say that I have been helped by very different kinds of people in different ways — and have been more or less useful to many kinds of people in different ways. Different therapists work with different regions of being. This is a matter of sensibility, taste, tone, and atmosphere, as well as ideology.

There are very real differences between therapists along the adult–child continuum. Some therapists are more adult or childlike than others and there is something to be said for either side. A therapy can be boring when an adult gets together with an adult, or too wild when a child works with a child. But a grown-up therapist can be the wrong model for a patient destined to be more childlike his or her entire life, and an adult patient may find a childlike therapist incomprehensible. Of course, there are all sorts of adults and all sorts of children and all sorts of combinations are possible.

I would like to say a word for the more childlike therapist and patient. Some people never grow up and are not meant to, and some people suffer a Peter Pan deficiency. Neither being an adult nor a child is any reliable criterion of worth to self, others, or community. One can grow richer, deeper, fuller along one's own line. One can mature as a child. Growth is endless, miraculous, and one doesn't have to become a different sort of person to discover who one is. There are so many ways to light up the world.

I also would like to say something about therapist snobbery–slavery. In my position as Program Chair for the National Psychological Association for Psychoanalysis I have had the chance to experience, at close quarters, presentations by some of the best analysts in the field. Among the varied impressions that have grown is the way therapists make use of or defend against subtle self-righteous ↔ masochistic tendencies. I particularly want to emphasize the therapist's "snottiness" as a reaction against fear of slavishness.

In the preceding section I mentioned how fear of ecstasy can short-circuit therapy. This must be complemented by acknowledging how "shitty" therapy can be. The day-to-day work in the trenches involves difficulty after difficulty, often with slimy, messy, rigid stuff. It can be unnatural and inhuman and unhealthy to sit still hour after hour trying to be there. With certain patients more than others the therapist may feel pulled into the patient's force field, or repelled by the latter, or both. In my "unwanted patients" paper I tried to describe some of these states. By now there exists an enormous literature on the use of countertransference or induced feelings.

It can be irritating, enervating, even deadening and horrifying, to come against a hard wall of pain, misery, need, demand, torture, truth disguised as lies, and lies disguised as truth (or truth and lies well-nigh indistinguishable), psychophysical spiritual poisons mixed with the cry for help. So often a therapist is bothered by some particular trait or set of qualities or irksome, unchangeable x which refuses to go away. The therapist is both repelled and drawn in at the same time. Every hour he prepares to start over, to give the new moment a chance, only to find himself run into the ground again.

The well-meaning worker may find himself becoming a slave to therapy, taking it, being eaten up alive by the thing that does not change. I think there is a moment, a flash, a pop, as if one screams, "I can't take this anymore. And I won't. I don't have to." The therapist's rebellion can take many forms. It does not matter what trouble he causes the patient, as long as he gets some space and air and freedom and aliveness. The therapist's change is usually rationalized by some imaginary growth in the patient, or simply the "aha" of at last catching on to the patient. Then all the old pre-Freudian emphasis on "will," "morality," "choice," "malingering" comes out of the blue. One feels fleeced by the depth dimension and colludes with the patient in throwing it over.

The patient may be oddly relieved at being thrown out. He identifies with the illusion of the therapist's freedom of action: at least someone can do something in this situation, someone can still move. Identification with the therapist's snobbery lets the patient fly above the stuck point and imagine things can be different, although deep down he knows they can't and won't.

There is no answer to this situation, but I want to describe some things I sometimes go through. At such moments I fight to sit in prayerful openness. To reach prayer and stay there is a struggle, but I am driven to it, since all my analytic efforts are nought. Now in the eye of the hurricane diverse images, feelings, thoughts, come and go. If I am dead, that is all right: deadness has its uses too. There are many shades of deadness and noise, many mixtures of things and no-things. I glimpse shades of destructive processes, self-damage, loss of opportunities to grow, deaths within deaths, horrific misshapenness. Do I believe in miracles?

I have experienced many miracles of growth. Mangled areas of torment and stagnation have opened gardens of subjective delight. Out of Egypt, through the wilderness, to the Promised Land: repeatedly. How does this happen? What is *It* that does it? One can spend lifetimes etching ways this works. I am astonished by the variety of psychoanalytic poets who sing this song. How the psyche glistens and glows through their celebrations. Every one of them I have been able to dip into has added to my appreciation of the gift of self and the enchantment of therapeutic work.

How can one call the therapist's exasperation impatience when it may take years to reach the blowout-burnout point? Therapist outbursts *can* be helpful. Offhand remarks in a context of persistent struggle and hard work *do* change lives. Can one know ahead of time whether letting go of self will amount to worthless indulgence or stimulate aliveness? It is inhuman for the therapist always to be on good behavior. Therapist need and narcissism may ruin things at times, but it is hard to imagine real work without them.

Nevertheless, impasse points call for sacrifice. Winnicott and Bion may have seen as deeply into the nature of this sacrifice as any analytic writers I know. Traditionally, sacrifice calls for transformation of animal desires. Bion also stresses cognitive and empathic desires, including the need to help. If one stays with the sacrificial journey long enough, one may begin to *be* a therapist, rather than act the part. Once this level is touched, *being* with a patient for decades passes like a moment. Who can say when this person came back from the living dead, or became passionate about work, or discovered a mate, or unearthed the capacity for friendship (including friendship with self)? I am almost always surprised by what the patient tells me was most important in our work.

Snobbishness (fear of slavery) about pathology runs deep in our field. I fear there are still many therapists who take themselves so seriously that they fail to envision a time when they and their patients can laugh good-humoredly about the traits that drive each other crazy.

Existential writers link sacrifice with sacred with holy with making whole (Ghent 1990). I wonder if all therapists feel the sacred element of this work. I suspect many do, in one way or another. Bion explicitly thematizes the faith (F in O) underwriting psychoanalytic encounter. In this business we deal with broken lives and heartbreak, and we do so with our own broken hearts. Yet we discover, within our patients and ourselves, heart within heart within heart. An endless opening–closing with every beat. What a breathtaking experience to discover such richness at the null point, always more than we can take.

REFERENCES

Bion, W. R. (1965). *Transformations.* London: Heinemann.

Boyer, L. B. (1990). Introduction: psychoanalytic interventions in treating the regressed patient. In *Master Clinicians: On Treating the Regressed Patient,* ed. L. B. Boyer and P. Giovacchini, pp. 1–32. Northvale, NJ: Jason Aronson.

Eigen, M. (1973). Abstinence and the schizoid ego. *International Journal of Psycho-Analysis* 54:493–497.

———— (1980). On the significance of the face. *Psychoanalytic Review* 67:426–444.

———— (1985). Toward Bion's starting point: between catastrophe and faith. *International Journal of Psycho-Analysis* 66:321–330.

———— (1992). *Coming Through the Whirlwind.* Wilmette, IL: Chiron.

Elkin, H. (1958). On the origins of the self. *Psychoanalytic Review* 45:57–76.

———— (1972). On selfhood and the development of ego structures in infancy. *Psychoanalytic Review* 59:389–416.

Ghent, E. (1990). Masochism, submission, surrender. *Contemporary Psychoanalysis* 26:108–136.

Tustin, F. (1972). *Autism and Childhood Psychosis.* New York: Science House.

———— (1981). *Autistic States in Children.* London: Routledge & Kegan Paul.

Credits

Index